Rude Kids: The Unfeasible Story of *Viz*

RUDE KIDS:

The Unfeasible Story of *Viz*

CHRIS DONALD

HarperCollins*Entertainment*
An Imprint of HarperCollins*Publishers*

HarperCollins*Publishers*
77-85 Fulham Palace Road,
Hammersmith, London W6 8JB

www.harpercollins.co.uk

First published by HarperCollins*Publishers* 2004

1

A catalogue record of this book is
available from the British Library

ISBN 0 00 719096 4

Printed and bound in Great Britain by
Clays Ltd, St Ives plc

Contents

Dedicated to the memory
of my mum, Kay,
who would not have approved.

Also to my dad, Jimmy,
and my wife, Dolores.

Oh, and 'hi' to my kids.
Hi kids.

Introduction

Way back in 1992 *Viz* publisher John Brown suggested I write a blockbuster book telling the story of our magazine. And what a remarkable story it would be. In the space of a few years the tatty rag I'd started from my Newcastle bedroom, with a print run of 150, had grown to become the third best-selling magazine in Britain, with an astonishing circulation of 1.2 million, outselling *Woman's Own*, *Cosmopolitan* and *Hello!* Only the *Radio Times* and *TV Times* sold more copies. *Viz* was a publishing phenomenon, revolutionizing the magazine market and making household names of Biffa Bacon, Johnny Fartpants and Buster Gonad. Its social effects had been dramatic too, launching words like 'oo-er!' 'hatstand' and 'hairy pie' into the national vocabulary, and paving the way for the great 1990s chauvinism revival through politically incorrect stereotypes like Sid the Sexist and the Fat Slags. *Viz* had even pre-empted the chronic decline of TV broadcasting standards through the creation of Roger Mellie the Man on the Telly.

As the founder and editor of *Viz* I had enjoyed a remarkable, rags-to-riches, roller-coaster ride of against-all-odds achievement and outrageous controversy. I'd won publishing awards, offended gypsies, been invited to tea by Prince Charles, and been taken in for questioning by officers of New Scotland Yard's Anti-Terrorist Branch. Along the way I'd gained incredible insights into the world of light entertainment as I launched, almost single-handed, the hugely successful showbusiness careers of Harry Enfield and Caroline Aherne, to name but two. I'd caught my wife up to no good with Keith Richards in Peter Cook's attic, I'd wined and dined the delightful Catherine Zeta-Jones, and I'd seen John Leslie's cock in the showers at a celebrity football match. By any standards the book would have been a sensation – a bean-spilling, blockbusting, number-one best-seller.

But I turned to John and I said, 'No'. I didn't want to write a book at that stage. I didn't need money – I was already a millionaire. I drove a BMW, holidayed at Sandy Lane, and bought ridiculous children's bedroom furniture from Harrods. And I didn't want to write a book that would crassly hit the shelves while *Viz* was at the peak of its popularity. Unlike Geri Halliwell and England rugby skipper Martin Johnson, for example, I don't believe in the opportunist, cash-in autobiography. I prefer to see a fuller picture, a retrospective view. For me the most interesting part of Brian Clough's autobiography would not be the glory days, the championship victories and European Cup success. I'd want to read the bit where he ended up asleep in a neighbour's hedge, pissed as a fart. And if I was reading Rod Hull's autobiography I wouldn't want to hear him brag about knocking Michael Parkinson off his chair in the 1970s. I'd want to know what the fuck he thought he was doing up on that roof.

Unfortunately Rod Hull's book can never be published, but I'm hopeful this one will. Because now that *Viz* has reached its twenty-fifth anniversary, and Roger Mellie has had a few problems with his own TV aerial, this seemed like a perfect time to write it.

Chris Donald
January 2004

CHAPTER ONE

The Beginning of Things

We were not rude kids to begin with. When I was ten my family moved to a nice terraced house in Jesmond, a leafy suburb of Newcastle. At the bottom of our new garden was a quiet road where we could play football relatively undisturbed by passing cars, and just across the road was a railway line. On the first day in our new home I joined in a game of football with some of my new neighbours. We'd not been playing for very long when the game suddenly stopped and everyone leapt up onto the fence alongside the railway. Not wishing to be the odd one out I joined in. Suddenly there was a loud throbbing sound from behind the trees and bushes to our left where the railway emerged from a cutting, and a filthy diesel engine crawled slowly into view, a hazy plume of black fumes rising above it. The iron railings in my hands vibrated as the train struggled up the bank, and as it passed us everyone shouted out the number written on the side of the driver's cab. '8592!' they all said. Naturally I joined in. '8592,' I said, although I didn't know quite why. From that moment on I was a train-spotter.

Coincidentally this was 1970, the year that *The Railway Children* movie was released. But there was no old gentleman waving at us from the last carriage – ours was a filthy goods train heading for the Rowntree's sweet factory at Fawdon – and life for the railway children of Lily Crescent wasn't quite as exciting as it was in the movie. There were no landslides or disasters to be averted. Instead we passed the time putting coins on the track and watching them get squashed, or smoking cigarettes in an old platelayers' hut up the line. And rather than steal coal from the station yard and give it to my poverty-stricken mother, I stole Coke bottles from the back of the off-licence adjoining the railway and returned them the next day to collect a sixpence deposit.

The Bobbi figure of our gang was Justin, the eldest and by far the most sensible train-spotter in our street. Alas, he looked nothing like Jenny Agutter. He was snotty-nosed, bespectacled, and had rather greasy hair. Needless to say he wore an anorak, a blue one with toggles, hood and an array of commodious pockets. Justin liked all sorts of numbers, not just train numbers. When we played cricket in the street he kept score, worked out the batting averages, bowling figures and run rates. He administered our local Subbuteo football league, all three divisions of it. He also organized weekly visits to Newcastle Central station and Gateshead engine sheds, as well as outings to more exotic locations, like Cambois.

Train-spotters have always had a bad press and I don't want to add to that here. Most of the criticism is born of ignorance. Think of train-spotting like fishing. You sit and you wait, often for hours on end, for something to happen. Yes, it's boring, but as with fishing that's the whole point. When a train finally appears, one you haven't seen before, it's every bit as exciting and fulfilling as catching a fish, but with the obvious advantage that no fish are harmed in the process. It's a perfectly healthy and harmless pursuit.

Train-spotting also provided me with an escape from home life, which could be a little tiresome at times. My dad wasn't wrongly imprisoned for spying, but my mum had suffered an equally cruel injustice. In 1963 she was diagnosed with the incurable disease of the nervous system, multiple sclerosis. Her condition was gradually deteriorating and we'd moved to our new house by the railway in anticipation of her becoming totally wheelchair-bound. The plan was that Mum and Dad would live entirely on the ground floor, which left me and my two brothers with the upstairs to ourselves.

My big brother Steve was a bookworm, an eccentric, and led an isolated, antisocial life in his bedroom, building robots and reading vast quantities of science fiction books. Steve was a bit like a robot himself, entirely logical in his thinking, and with no apparent emotions other than anger. When I first watched *Star Trek* it was a revelation. 'That explains it,' I thought. 'My big brother is a Vulcan.' Steve had a logical, emotionless take on everything, and a total disregard for other people's feelings. He got into enormous rows with my dad over tiny little things, like milk jugs. Steve believed that at breakfast time the milk should be poured directly from the bottle onto the cereal. My mum and dad liked it to be served from a Cornishware jug. 'Clearly it is more efficient to pour the milk directly onto the cereal from the bottle thereby negating the need to use, and subsequently wash, a second vessel,' Steve would say, deliberately flaunting his intellect and vocabulary in order to bait my dad. Dad's argument would be less cogent but more forcefully put. 'Listen, you clever bugger, it's my bloody milk, it's my bloody jug, and it's my bloody house! So I'll do what the hell I like.' These pointless rows would kick off once or twice a day and would often spiral out of control. Sometimes crockery would be thrown and furniture broken, and Steve, who simply could not let it lie, would end up having to be physically restrained. He was like a Dalek spinning out of control. Meanwhile my dad was like a desperate Frankenstein, wondering what sort of monster he had created.

Dad often bluffed that he was going to call the police to 'sort Stephen out', and during one particularly violent argument he actually kept his promise. I'd gone outside to get away from it all and was playing football when a police car screeched to a halt outside our house and two burly police officers hurried up the path. 'Look! They're going to your house,' said Tinhead, Justin's excitable little brother. 'Oh, it's probably nothing,' I mumbled, and urged him to carry on with the game.

My younger brother Simon sat that particular argument out inside the airing cupboard and was able to give me a detailed report on the police raid later that day. Simon had no interest in train-spotting, or in picking pointless arguments with my dad. He was a big fan of *Dr Who* and American comics, and was also involved in a local theatre group. I got on reasonably well with both my brothers when we were alone together. We all shared a similar sense of humour; an ironic appreciation of Peter Glaze off *Crackerjack*, for example. I think that came from my dad's side. My dad Jimmy was always a joker and he constantly used humour to cope with Mum's illness. He introduced us to Laurel and Hardy and the Goons, and before we had our own telly he'd take us to a friend's house once a week to watch *The Morecambe and Wise Show*. Dad also found George Bailey very funny. Bailey was a local TV sports reporter who wore false teeth and Dad would fall about laughing as he read the football results. He was forever laughing at people. Jesmond was a trendy, middle-class suburb, full of CND-supporting, Citroën-2CV-driving families, and Dad took great delight in poking fun and laughing at our 'lefty' neighbours. He was always giving people funny names too. A long-haired art lecturer who lived along the street was 'Buffalo Bill'. Then there was 'Mrs Eating Rolands', one of our larger neighbours. And for some reason Dr Ian Paisley, the Northern Ireland Unionist politician, was always referred to as Ian 'Have a Banana' Paisley when he appeared on TV. Dad's parents were from Shieldfield, the neighbouring working-class suburb, and from what little I remember of them they had the same sense of humour. Nana Donald took to calling my uncle Jack 'Lord Shite' after he got himself a job as chauffeur for the Lord Mayor and started dressing in fancy suits.

From my mum's side all three brothers inherited an ability to draw. My mum Kay was an artist who had worked as a window dresser in Fenwick's department store during the 1950s. After giving up her job to start the family she set up her own business, Kaycrafts, making children's toys. But the MS stopped her from sewing and stitching so she had to give up the business. Instead she buried herself in voluntary work, becoming an active campaigner for disabled people's rights. As co-founder and secretary of the local branch of DIG, the Disablement Income Group, she fought long, hard and successfully to get state benefits paid to disabled people.

Home life settled down a little when Steve, or the 'Queer Fella' as my dad had taken to calling him, left home and went to art college in Bournemouth. At the time Steve was more renowned for his drawing ability than either me or Simon. He'd been given a set of Rotring pens one Christmas and specialized in drawing humorous, slightly smart-arsed cartoons. The only one I vaguely remember involved a Roman soldier, a man holding a gun and a punch-line featuring the word 'anachronism'. I didn't get it. Simon and I were more into sound comedy than drawing. Around 1975 Dad got us a music centre for Christmas and we recorded our own comedy radio versions of *Doctor Who*, *Grandstand* and *Farming Outlook*. We would have tried others but these were the only programmes we had the theme tunes for in our record collection. Dad didn't let any of us read comics. The *Beano* and the *Dandy* – along with ITV and any kind of sweets – were deemed to be 'rubbish'. As a treat Dad would take us to the local health food shop, to buy peanuts, and to the library where he encouraged us to borrow books. I loved books, me. I didn't read them, I just loved them. I judged books purely by their covers. I'd often take out *Heidi*, in German, because I liked the cover. The only books I actually read were Tintin books. The drawings were beautiful, colourful, detailed and yet so simple. Equally important, the covers had a uniformity in their design. On the back of the Tintin books there was a list of all the other books in the series, and that appealed to the train-spotter in me.

I liked things to be uniform, ordered, numbered and in series.

In November 1975 I launched volume one, issue one, of my very first magazine. It was called the *Lily Crescent Locomotive Times* and was targeted specifically at train-spotters living in Lily Crescent. I typed it – very hard – on my mum's typewriter using multiple layers of carbon paper to replicate it. Features included a list of engines recently spotted in our street (for three years I kept a log of every locomotive that went past), a report on a recent trip to Chesterfield and a column from my 'Heaton Carriage Sidings Correspondent', a friend called Jim Brownlow.

Jim Brownlow's family moved from Blackburn to Newcastle around 1973 and Jim was deposited into my class at Heaton Comprehensive School. On his first day I managed to strike up an awkward conversation with him about Preben Arentoft, a Danish footballer who had recently been transferred from Newcastle to Blackburn. We were both football fans and Jim and I quickly became friends. A few weeks later, when I felt I'd got to know him well enough, I let Jim in on my dark secret – that I was a train-spotter. Being a train-spotter wasn't something you talked about in a large, inner-city state comprehensive like Heaton. Jim came along on our train-spotting outings but he was never totally committed to the hobby. I think he was more interested in the social benefits of train-spotting. Yes. Train-spotting is a *very* sociable hobby. Sitting with a group of mates at the end of a railway platform for eight hours at a time – with no TV, no radio, no computers – does wonders for the art of conversation. Trains didn't really enter into it that much. We would just sit there, huddled together at the end of a platform, or on wasteland in Gateshead overlooking the engine sheds, philosophizing, making jokes and talking absolute nonsense.

Jim and I were a bit more socially aware than the other train-spotters around us. We spent as much time observing our neighbours as we did looking at the trains. Obese couples in their thirties or forties with massive lunch boxes would sit and train-spot together. There were veteran former steam-spotters in their fifties, their anoraks covered in dozens of train badges, every one worn with pride, like a medal. Then there were the next generation, high-tech train-spotters, platform yuppies who yelled numbers into Dictaphones instead of writing them down. Audio-enthusiasts with tape recorders who'd stand alongside the locomotives recording the sounds they made. And of course there were the dodgy-looking train-spotters whose attentions seemed to waver between the trains and the nearby gentlemen's lavatories. You had to watch out for those ones. All of them seemed oblivious to the reactions they got from the general public, blissfully unaware of the disdainful looks being aimed at them from inside passing trains. Jim and I had an overview of it all. When a crowded train went past we'd always hide our notebooks and sidle a discreet distance away from the hard-line anoraks.

At school Jim and I tended to be loners, slightly too weird to fit into the social mainstream. We hung around with other misfits too. One was Paul, a goose-stepping Hitler fan with a swoop of black hair and, for a very short time, a swastika painted on his school bag. Another was John, a child actor whose life had become a living hell since he'd appeared in a Sugar Puffs advert. And a third was a strange boy called Chris Scott-Dixon. Scottie was short, plump, freckled and wore Michael Caine glasses. On his first day at Heaton he was the only boy in a school of 1,400 who turned up wearing short trousers, and he staggered home that lunchtime his legs beetroot red from slapping. On the face of it he was the dullest, most grown-up and sensible child you could meet – like a little chartered accountant trapped inside a child's body. But beneath his dour façade he had a bizarre and often comic imagination. Jim, Scottie and myself once had a private competition to see who could write the highest number of deaths into their English essay homework. This ran for several weeks and reached its climax when we were set the innocuous title, 'A Visit to the Theatre', for our homework. In my story a bus full of theatregoers got stuck beneath electric wires on a level crossing. The occupants were all burnt alive and then a crowded passenger train slammed into the wreckage at high speed. With a body count of over 300 I thought I'd won at a canter, but I was wrong. Scottie had engineered a calamitous Ronan Point-style gas explosion into his essay. Careless theatre-goers had left the gas on in their high-rise apartment and in the resulting explosion an entire block of flats collapsed and over 600 people perished in the rubble. By now our English teacher, Mrs MacKenzie, had noticed the increasing death tolls in our work and rightly guessed that we were having a competition. One at a time she took us aside, complimented us on our imaginative work, but warned us that the examination boards would view anything more than one or two deaths per essay as excessive.

As well as sharing a rum sense of humour Jim and I also shared an ability to draw cartoons. Over the years I'd become the unofficial class cartoonist and often had unwanted commissions thrust upon me. The closest thing to a bully we had in our class was a big lad called Jeff, and Jeff was very proud of his Doctor Marten boots. Jeff's desk was right alongside mine and every morning he'd hitch up his trouser leg with theatrical style and proudly reveal a highly polished knee-length Doc Marten. Then he'd say, 'Draw me boot!' I'd routinely draw a flattering picture of his boot on a scrap of paper, hand it to him, and he would sit and titter at it for a moment or two before discarding it. One day Jeff told me to draw Mr Hesketh on the blackboard. Mr Hesketh was our French teacher, and very easy to draw. He had a flobby, jowlish, slightly over-inflated sort of head with a funny little wiggish haircut perched precariously on top of it, and an *extremely* big and pointy nose. It was most unfortunate that Mr Hesketh's career as a French teacher coincided with the advent of the Anglo-French supersonic aviation programme. The tip of Concorde Hesketh's conk was due to appear through the classroom door at any minute, followed not long afterwards by the rest of him, so I did a hurried sketch on the board. 'Divvn't forget his nurz hair,' said Jeff, casting a critical eye from behind me. Mr Hesketh had long, bushy, black hair billowing from his massive nostrils like inverted smoke clouds, and from my seat near the front of the class I would watch these hairs gradually turning grey due to the amount of chalk dust his frantic blackboard-wiping technique generated. I quickly added a big clump of nasal hair to my drawing then turned to go back to my desk, but my path was blocked by Jeff, smiling menacingly and brandishing a compass point in my direction. At that moment in walked Mr Hesketh, and there was I, chalk in hand, dithering about in front of my portrait. 'Mr Hesketh,' said Jeff with a glib smile. 'Donald's done a picktcha of ya.'

Jeff wasn't a real bully, he was a hilarious parody of one. A comic actor. He dressed like a bovver boy in his Crombie coat, sharply creased two-tone trousers and blood-red knee-length boots with bright yellow laces. But he wasn't violent. The closest to fighting Jeff ever got was tripping up first years at break time. There he was, all six foot of him, flicking his toes gracefully to unbalance these tiny little children who were running around his feet. It was cruel but it was hilarious because he did it with such style and panache. There were plenty of real bullies at Heaton, or 'hards' as they preferred to be known. Each had their own hardness rating. The system was a bit like conkers, but instead of smashing someone's conker to improve your own conker's rating, you had to 'kick someone's fucking heed in' in order to acquire their points. Hard kids would swagger around the school like gunfighters in a Spaghetti Western, constantly in search of a showdown. The toilet was their saloon where they all hung out, smoking tabs, gambling and discussing the latest hardness rankings. Between the ages of eleven and sixteen I developed phenomenal bladder control, but it wasn't always possible to avoid trouble. Sometimes if you strayed too far from your pack of friends you'd be picked off by a stray bully and a confrontation would ensue. One second-division hard case called Brian had a very original technique of picking a fight. He'd stand in front of you and block your path by doing an impression of Alvin Stardust singing 'My Coo-Ca-Choo'. This would involve twisting and turning his fist slowly, right under your nose, in an Alvin Stardust leather glove style, which was strangely hypnotic as his arm looked a bit like a snake slowly rising from a basket. Then at various points in the song – on the words 'Coo' and 'Choo' I seem to recall – he would punch you lightly on the chin, hoping you would retaliate. He tried it once on me after cornering me above the bicycle sheds, but after a few moments it must have dawned on him how ridiculous he looked, so he made some mumbled excuse and left.

A far more conventional way to start a fight was for a bully to say, 'Are you lookin' at me?' But this gradually became less effective as victims developed clever responses, like 'No'. You had to watch your eye-line very carefully if you were in the presence of potential aggressors. Any look adjudged to be 'funny' could be punishable by a severe kicking. You also had to make sure there was nothing *the matter* with you. 'What's the matter with you?' they'd ask aggressively. 'Nothing,' you'd assure them. Occasionally they'd up the ante by asking the rather ridiculous question, 'Are you calling me a puff?' despite the fact you hadn't said a word. 'No,' you'd say. This inane line of questioning would go on and on until your interrogator finally felt he'd received sufficient provocation to hit you, or got bored and let you off with a warning. Over the years the nature of bullying changed as the hard kids developed more sophisticated opening gambits. 'Do you fancy wor lass?' for example. This was check, in one move, as the answer 'Yes' would be clear justification to hit you, while the answer 'No' could be followed up with, 'Why not like? Is there something the matter with her?' Checkmate.

My dad worked as an oil salesman and brought home piles of Esso Blue calling cards and invoice pads which I'd turn over and use as drawing material. In the privacy of my bedroom I did a series of pictures featuring ugly monsters – globular piles of fat with tiny arms and big faces – being chopped up on bacon slicers and mutilated in similarly macabre ways. I amassed dozens of these drawings, called them my 'mut cartoons', and kept them neatly filed away in a drawer in my bedroom. I never showed them to anyone but Jim. 'What if somebody saw them?' he once asked. It was a worrying thought.

Jim studied art O-level at school but I dropped the subject as fast as I possibly could. The art teachers, who both had beards and suede shoes, would scribble a title for a painting on the blackboard and then fuck off out of the room. You wouldn't see them again until the end of the lesson. In their absence the art class would deteriorate into a massive paint fight and I'd usually spend the last ten minutes or so crouched under my desk sheltering from flying paint. The following week you'd turn up and the title for the painting would still be the same. The idle bastards hadn't even bothered to think up a new one. It was strange to think that at the same school twenty-five years earlier my mum had produced the most wonderful watercolours, but in her day Heaton had been a grammar school where teachers followed antiquated teaching practices, like wearing capes and mortar boards, caning pupils for misbehaviour, and remaining in the classroom during lessons. I used my other lessons for art practice, scribbling away in the back of my exercise books instead of paying attention to teachers. By 1976 my 'mut' drawings had evolved into something that I deemed suitable for a wider audience. Using my dad's invoice pads, ballpoint pens and coloured pencils, I put together a series of comic books which began circulating around the classroom at school. These starred my old friend Scottie as a dour and boring schoolboy who could transform himself into a caped superhero. Whenever his pals were being bullied the Fat Crusader would appear on the scene, rounding up the troublemakers, cutting them up on bacon slicers or sharpening their heads with giant pencil sharpeners. It was still a tad on the morbid side, but the Fat

Crusader books became very popular at school. Each little booklet would first circulate around my classroom and then around neighbouring classes. As soon as I finished one, people would start asking for another, and I got requests from people wanting to appear in the stories. I did thirteen Fat Crusader books in all, each one numbered of course, with titles like *The Fat Crusader Takes the Sunderland*, *The Teds Are in Town* and, as a Christmas Special, *The Fat Crusader versus the Staff Aggro*. That one got as far as the staffroom and was never seen again.

The Fat Crusader

While I was drawing the Fat Crusader Jim was leaving school, aged sixteen, and getting himself a 'scheme' job in an architect's drawing office. I stayed on into the sixth form studying Geography, Biology and Woodwork A-levels. The people around me wanted to be mountaineers, caterers, doctors, dentists, nurses and quantity surveyors, but I hadn't got a fucking clue what I wanted to do. At my first careers interview I said I wanted to be a train driver. The careers adviser didn't look too happy and came up with a story about needing three A-levels, including Maths and Physics, and a degree in Engineering, to drive trains. I'd seen plenty of train drivers in my time, and none of them looked like engineering graduates to me. After that I lowered my sights a little. In fact I lowered them about as far as they would go and said I wanted to be a geography teacher. The reasoning behind this hugely important career decision was quite simple. I like drawing maps. Unfortunately I'd never heard of cartography at the time, and neither had my careers adviser, so I was duly lined up to go to Aston or Loughborough University and do a degree in Geography. Fortunately my A-level results weren't good enough. I hadn't understood a single word in Biology from day one, and although Woodwork was my best subject I failed the exam on a technicality (using panel pins to hold a panel in place). So I left school in 1978, aged eighteen, with six O-levels, a Geography A-level and a perfectly good but technically incorrect panel desk.

Jim's work experience job had run out by now so we were both on the dole and spent the summer of 1978 hanging out, playing pool and drawing cartoons. By now I'd got a set of Rotring pens for Christmas and my drawing had been trans-formed. I undertook my first commercial venture, doing line drawings of local tourist attractions such as Bamburgh Castle and the Tyne Bridge, and selling framed prints to tourists. A sixth-form colleague called Baz was now working behind the bar in a city centre hotel and we'd developed a neat little scam. I drew the pictures and got them printed and framed, and Baz talked drunken Norwegians into buying them for £15 each as he plied them with alcohol. It all went well until Baz left the hotel and a drunken Scottish night porter fucked off with all my money.

Having left school I no longer had an audience for my car-toons, so in July 1978 I suggested Jim and I print a few cartoons in a magazine and sell it to people we knew in the pub. I say 'magazine'… The *Daily Pie* was actually a single sheet of paper, photocopied on one side only. The miniature cartoons included Tommy's Birthday, a five-frame strip in which a young boy tries to blow out the candles on his birthday cake, and his head falls off. There was a brief horoscope – Your Stars by Gypsy Bag – that read, 'Today you made a bad decision and bought something crappy.' And there was Jim's first ever Rude Kid cartoon, a single frame in which a beaming, wide-eyed mother drags a reluctant child by the hand. 'Come to the shops, dear,' she says. 'Fuck off!' says the child. Despite its flimsiness I managed to sell most of the *Daily Pie*s in our local pub, The Brandling, by offering substantial discounts on the strategically high cover price of 90p. I printed twenty copies, at a cost of £1.13, and I sold sixteen of them for a total of £1.43, giving me a profit of 30p. By this time I'd more or less kicked my train-spotting habit but I was still very much anally retentive, so I kept a detailed record of every *Daily Pie* sale. Its significance was then, and remains now, a mystery. But here it is anyway (with the amount paid in brackets): Nicholas Clark (10p), Simon Donald (10p), Phil Ramsey (10p), Peter Chamley (10p), Fenella Storm (10p), Vaughan Humble (10p), Jeremy McDermott (10p), John Reid (10p), Bobby van Emenis (4p), Janice Nicholson and Lyn Briton (10p), Christine Hopper (10p), Kerry Hastings (9p), Dave Hall (10p), Pam Lawrence (10p), Marcus Partington (10p), Claire Beesley and Janet Davison (still owe me 10p). The *Daily Pie* was well received, so the following month I printed a hurriedly produced follow-up, this time calling it *Arnold the Magazine*. Mercifully I didn't keep a detailed record of sales.

If nothing else, peddling these papers in the pub gave me an excuse to talk to girls like Claire Beesley. She was the sizzling school sex siren, and when Claire was in fourth year and I was in the lower sixth we exchanged notes through my brother Simon who acted as a messenger. Claire would write telling me what music she was listening to – Lou Reed's *Transformer* I seem to recall – and how hot and sticky she got when she thought about me. Everyday teenage stuff like that. We'd never actually spoken, Claire and I, but she occasionally smiled at me as we passed in the corridor. One day I plucked up the courage to call her only for the phone to be answered by Mark Barnes. It turned out that Barnes, leader of the local chapter of 50cc Hell's Angels, was her new boyfriend. I felt humiliated, but not nearly as humiliated as I was the following weekend when Barnes swaggered past me in the Brandling pub armed with a note I'd written to her weeks earlier and read it out loud to all his hair-dryer-riding motorcycle mates. Now at last I had a new opportunity to impress Claire and the other girls with my cartoons … although why girls should be impressed by cartoons about a young boy whose head falls off, and a drawing of a dog shitting on a dinner table, I hadn't really stopped to consider.

As the summer of 1978 drew to a close I started looking for a job. I had no career ambitions but fancied working for a year, then perhaps going to college. I applied for twenty-seven vacancies in all, but my solitary A-level meant I was 'over-qualified' for most of them. I went for one interview at a bus depot in Gateshead, hoping to get the job of clerk. An oily foreman in overalls interviewed me. 'You'd have to make the tea, you know,' he said, as if such a menial task was below someone with a Geography A-level. He was clearly looking for someone with fewer qualifications and bigger tits. But I persevered and thought I was still in with a chance until the final question, 'Why do you want to work in a bus depot?' I thought about it for a second. 'Because I like buses,' I said, with a hint of rising intonation. I didn't get the job.

By the time my interview for Clerical Officer in the DHSS came around I'd given a lot of thought to the 'Why do you want to …' question. It seemed to crop up at every interview. This time I was ready with an answer. 'And finally, why do you want to work in the civil service?' asked the chairman of the panel. 'I don't particularly,' I said. 'I'm just looking for a steady job that pays well in order to fund my hobby, which is railway modelling,' I told him, trying to look as nerdy as possible. It worked an absolute treat. All four members of the panel smiled simultaneously and I was told there and then that I'd got the job. You had to be pretty fucking thick not to get a job at the Ministry. Even Mark Barnes had got in the year before me. In those days the Ministry was a safety net for school leavers who couldn't get anything better. The Department of Health and Social Security Central Office Longbenton, to give it its official title, was a massive complex of huts and office blocks spread over several acres, housing upwards of 10,000 clerical staff. It had its own banks, post offices, at least five canteens, a hairdresser's, and running through the middle of it was the longest corridor in Europe. I spent the first few weeks in a classroom learning about the history of National Insurance, which I found quite interesting, then I was posted to Unit 4, Overseas Branch D1, Room A1301. This was a huge open-plan office, about the size of a five-a-side football pitch, where over 100 people sat stooped over desks, writing letters and filling in forms. My specific area of responsibility was dealing with people whose National Insurance numbers ended in 42 (C or D), 43 or 44.

I loved having my own desk, my own 'in' and 'out' trays and my own stationery items, but what I liked most was all the forms there were to fill in. In the DHSS you had to fill in a form before you could go to the loo, and if you were having a shit you'd have to send a requisition slip to Bumwipe Supplies Branch at least three days in advance. I liked filling in forms and I enjoyed the daily routine too, although it wasn't particularly healthy. Stodgy fried food was available in the canteens all day long, and there was a tea trolley serving hot drinks and Empire biscuits. These consisted of two big, sugary rounds of shortbread stuck together with jam, covered in icing and with half a cherry on the top. The tea trolley came every day, morning and afternoon, and with almost the same frequency someone in the office would have a heart attack and fall backwards off their chair. From our window we could see the main gate and the constant flow of ambulances going in and out, carting heart attack victims off to hospital. Life expectancy wasn't high in the Ministry, and neither were the levels of job satisfaction. You were in big trouble if you stopped to think about what you were actually doing. The majority of the work was putting right other people's mistakes. For example, an oil worker would write in from Saudi Arabia with an enquiry and some daft sod would send him a leaflet which clearly didn't provide the information he wanted. So he'd write back, repeating his query. This time he'd get a stock reply asking what his National Insurance number was. So he'd write back a third time telling us what his National Insurance number was. But in the meantime we'd have lost his file, so the person who received his third letter wouldn't have a clue why he was writing in and telling us what his National Insurance number was. So we'd write to him a third time, this time asking why he was sending us his National Insurance number. And so on. Mix-ups like this occurred every day, in their thousands, because all the filing systems were kept manually by people, the vast majority of whom didn't give a toss. So the whole place was in effect a self-perpetuating human error factory.

If you could take your mind off the work, and say no to an Empire biscuit, the Ministry was a great place to be. The social life was brilliant and there was a wonderful mix of characters, from Joe the Trotskyite union rep to John the racist nutcase who refused to urinate in pub toilets on the grounds that he'd paid good money for the drink and he'd be damned if he was going to piss it straight back into their toilets. One of my favourite characters was a bloke called Dave who sat at a desk behind me. Dave was the best swearer I have ever known. For some reason only working-class people can swear properly, and Dave was a master of the art. His swearing was never aggressive, it was always done for emphasis and comic effect, and when he swore I found it pant-pissingly funny. Every day I'd find myself scribbling down little things he'd said and expressions he'd used. I didn't know what I was going to do with them, I just felt an instinctive urge to record them for posterity.

I put my name down for the office football team, but unfortunately the manager was an early pioneer of the squad rotation system, and he tended to rotate me from one end of the substitutes' bench to the other. I couldn't get a game, so to pass the time I started writing reports on our matches which I then typed up at home and took in to work the following day. Like my *Fat Crusader* books these match reports caught on, circulating around the office and causing much sniggering and laughter. But the office audience contained a broader spectrum of public taste than I'd previously been used to, and it wasn't long before one miserable old bat took offence at some of the language. I'd faithfully quoted our captain telling our centre forward, 'You couldn't score in a brothel with a ten pound note tied round your chopper.' Pretty harmless, you'd think, but this was the civil service and a complaint was made to the Higher Executive Officer. Sending non-official circulars around the office was an offence in itself, but including the word 'chopper' was a definite breach of civil service protocol. I was summoned to HEO Frank Redd's office and was still cobbling together a garbled excuse involving helicopters as I opened the door. Fortunately he didn't give me a chance to use it. Mr Redd said my football reports showed imagination and initiative, but he felt my journalistic skills could be put to far better use. He wondered, in no uncertain terms, whether I'd like to apply for the voluntary, unpaid job of assistant editor at *The Bulletin*, the monthly magazine of the DHSS Central Office Sports and Social Club. The job had been vacant for some time, and he said he would use his considerable influence to make sure I got it. At last! I had my first break in journalism.

The next few months were a whirlwind of excitement as I dashed about the DHSS, notebook in hand, reporting on the thrilling activities of the Horticultural Club, the Carpet Bowls League, the Philatelic Society and the Wine Making Circle.

CHAPTER TWO

The Gosforth

From the age of sixteen or seventeen Jim and I began to rendezvous in pubs instead of railway stations. We were still loners to a large degree. We'd sit in the corners watching people and pass cynical remarks on their behaviour and appearance. The fact that good-looking girls were going out with other blokes and not us gave us a shared, nerdy sense of injustice. In terms of cultural identity Jim and I were hovering somewhere between being hippies and punks. We both had long hair and wore denims, and sometimes we'd go to the Mayfair Ballroom for the legendary Friday Rock Nights. But neither of us played air guitar. We were only there to gawp at the hippy chicks with their tight jeans, cheesecloth blouses and supposedly liberal attitudes towards sex.

In our schooldays Jim had displayed a fondness for Steve Hillage, which I could never quite understand, and he once went to Knebworth to see Rush. I was a bit of a Seekers fan myself. Them, the Beatles and Abba. But if anyone asked me I always said I liked Thin Lizzy. I tried to broaden my tastes but most contemporary music didn't grab me. A friend once suggested I try lying down on the floor, in the dark, and listening to a Pink Floyd album. I did, but it still sounded shit to me. Punk, when it came, was an absolute godsend. The fashion was a trifle severe, but I loved the spirit of it and particularly the fact that Radio 1's Mike Read didn't like it. Jim was more a connoisseur of music than I was. He introduced me to The Buzzcocks and The Stranglers and we started going to see New Wave bands. We were still dithering, going to see Judas Priest one week and The Jam the next, until one night our loyalties were put to the test. It was a Friday at the Mayfair and we'd gone to see a mod-revival package tour, Secret Affair and The Purple Hearts. A battle broke out between the Mayfair's native rock fans and the visiting mods and punks. As chairs started to rain down from the balcony Jim and I instinctively found ourselves running towards the mod end of the room for shelter. It was a defining moment.

The Two-Tone Ska revival was happening at the time and in Newcastle a new record label had been set up, clearly inspired by Coventry's porkpie hat-wearing fraternity. The name of the Newcastle outfit was Anti-Pop, and on Monday evenings they promoted bands at a pub called the Gosforth Hotel. Jim discovered the place and suggested I come along the following week. Jim's musical tastes were still a lot broader than mine so I didn't hold out much hope for the entertainment, but he'd also mentioned that there'd be girls from Gosforth High School there, and to a couple of likely lads from Heaton Comprehensive the prospect of a room full of high-class teenage totty from Gosforth High was a major attraction.

The Gosforth was a typical two-storey, brick-built Victorian pub, situated next to a busy road junction in a fairly well-to-do suburb. There was a traditional old codgers' bar downstairs plus a lounge, and upstairs there was a very small function room where the bands played. The function room was dark, with blacked-out windows, a corner bar that looked as if hadn't been used since the 1950s, a big round mirror on the wall above a fireplace, and beneath that the band's equipment taking up about half of the overall floor space. Most of the crowd who squeezed into the other half of the room – and some of the musicians – were under-age, so they'd sneak in the side door, dash upstairs and dart into the function room before the red-faced ogre of a landlord could catch them. He was an obnoxious, drunken git who didn't approve of loud music and alternative fashion, or under-age drinking on his premises. Every now and then he'd storm up the stairs in search of under-age drinkers, threatening to set his dogs loose in the function room if he found any kids inside.

ANTI-POP ENTERTAINMENTERAMA

Anti-Pop admission stamp

Admission to the function room was 50p, payable at the top of the stairs. As proof of payment you got your hand stamped 'anti-pop entertainmenterama'. Sitting on the door counting the money was a scruffy bloke who looked as if he'd just spent a night on a park bench, and then walked through a particularly severe sandstorm. His name was Andy Pop and he always looked like that due to a combination of Brillo pad hair and bad eczema. Andy was the business brains behind the Anti-Pop organization. Sitting alongside him was his partner, the creative guru, a tall, thin man called Arthur 2 Stroke. Arthur 2 Stroke's eponymous three-piece band were playing that night, and Jim had recommended them highly. 2 Stroke cut a bizarre figure on stage. He was an awkward, gangly sort of bloke, dressed in a dandy, second-hand, sixties' style. He wore a powder blue mod suit that was far too small for him and a comically extreme pair of winkle-picker boots, and he had an unmistakable Mr Spock haircut. He was a bit like a cross between Paul Weller and Jason King. He couldn't sing very well, or play the guitar, but he had a wonderful comic aura about him. Next to him was an upright, smiling, red-haired guitarist who went by the name of WM7, and in the background there was an almost unseen drummer whose name was Naughty Norman. Their manic set included a

Arthur 2 Stroke

half-decent cover of 'The Letter' and a plucky tribute to the well-known 1970s French TV marine biologist, 'The Wundersea World of Jacques Cousteau'. Also on the bill that night were the Noise Toys, a power-packed post-punk four-piece who bounced around in oversized baggy suits and raincoats, shaking the ceiling of the old codgers' bar below. Singer Martin Stevens was a timid, slightly built, shaven-headed bloke – a more energetic, better-looking, heterosexual version of Michael Stipe. In total contrast his sidekick, the trilby-hatted guitarist Rupert Oliver, was a bullish, ugly, bad-tempered prima donna, prone to lashing out at the audience with his microphone stand. The rhythm section were the industrious but less noteworthy Mike and Brian, and the highlights of their set were their own song 'Pocket Money' and memorable covers of 'Rescue Me' and 'King of the Road'. As well as the Noise Toys and Arthur 2 Stroke there'd be anything up to three or four other bands on the bill, and a lot of them would be playing their first ever gig. Anti-Pop's policy was to encourage kids to come along and have a go. You didn't need fancy equipment, or talent. Anyone could ring them up and book a support slot. This was the punk ethic being put into practice, and it attracted quite a few weirdos. But it was always entertaining, intimate and exciting – the very opposite of going to Knebworth to see Rush or lying on the floor and listening to Pink Floyd. At the Gosforth Hotel I felt like I'd found my spiritual home.

Another positive effect of punk was the emergence of fanzines, small DIY music magazines – usually the work of one obsessive individual – that were hawked at gigs or sold through independent record shops. My brother Steve had put me and Jim in touch with a new Newcastle fanzine that was looking for cartoonists. When we met the editors at the Market Tavern pub in town we were dismayed to find they were all hairies, and their new magazine – *Bad Breath* – was going to be a 'rock' fanzine. I drew a cartoon about a punk band called Angelo's Nonstarts for their first issue, but when I saw the finished magazine I wished I hadn't bothered. It was a feeble orange pamphlet with very little content, badly designed too, but the worst thing about it was the tone of the editorial. It took itself so fucking seriously. There was an article about Lou Reed, and an earnest review of a pub gig by The Weights. It was all such a load of wank. Jim and I had been toying with the idea of producing our own magazine, a proper one this time with more than one page, and *Bad Breath* was so bloody awful it inspired us. We wanted to produce a comic that was also a fanzine, and the only artists we wanted to write about were Arthur 2 Stroke and the Noise Toys. The Gosforth Hotel would also be the ideal outlet for selling this magazine – and it would give us an excuse to talk to Gosforth High School girls – so we decided to take our idea to Anti-Pop. Whether we were looking for advice and encourage-ment, or merely an excuse to visit their office, I can't quite recall.

The Anti-Pop office was in the Bigg Market, in a run-down

building full of small rooms with glass-panel doors – the kind of office suites where private detectives sit drinking whisky and waiting for their next mysterious client to walk through the door. Their room was up on the third floor, wedged between a hairdressing salon and a derelict former pools collecting agency. We knocked and nervously entered. The room was tiny, like a

Andy Pop

short corridor with the door at one end and a sash window at the other. Already it was full of people. There was a solitary desk, a chair, and a built-in cupboard running along one wall which was being used by half a dozen or so people as a communal seat. All of the Noise Toys seemed to be there, plus their slightly dim roadie Davey Fuckwit. Arthur 2 Stroke himself was perched on the windowsill, gazing at a shit-covered shoe lying on the ledge outside and repeating the word 'guano' to himself over and over again. It looked like a form of meditation. 'He's thinking of ideas,' someone explained. Jim and I were a little intimidated finding ourselves in the presence of so many pop idols, but we somehow managed to blurt a few words out about our proposed magazine and I held out a folder of our cartoons as a sort of peace offering. These were passed around the room and met with grins of approval. Turning to Andy Pop I asked if they would allow us to sell the magazine at their gigs in return for a free advertisement on the back cover. This was immediately agreed. Then came an unexpected bonus. Martin, the singer with the Noise Toys, said that he was a cartoonist and offered to contribute to the new magazine.

Our project had got the green light – the only problem now was that we didn't have a clue how to put a magazine together. Someone at Anti-Pop suggested approaching the Free Press for help. The Tyneside Free Press described themselves as a 'non-profit-making community print co-operative', whatever one of those was, and Jim and I went to see them at their print works in Charlotte Square. I explained to the man on the front desk that we wanted to produce a magazine but had no idea how to put it together, technically speaking. He was most helpful and began by explaining a few of the basics. For important technical reasons we couldn't have ten pages as I'd suggested, we'd have to have eight or twelve. And if we had twelve pages they would be printed in pairs, page 12 alongside page 1, and page 2 alongside page 11, etc. This was called page fall. I was fascinated. Then he talked about the artwork, explaining how the ink is always black and how greys are made out of lots of little black dots. Finally, he produced an estimate for printing 100 twelve-page magazines. This came to a staggering £38.88, in other words almost 40p per copy. He must have noticed my face drop and quickly pointed out that the more we printed, the cheaper it would become per copy. He mentioned that a T Rex fanzine they'd printed recently had sold out of 100 copies in a week and had since been back for a reprint. Encouraged by this I asked him to price for 150 copies, and this came to £42.35. It was four quid more, but it brought the cost of each comic down to 28p each. It still seemed a lot of money so I shopped around for some other prices. The Co-operative Printers in Rutherford Street quoted me £153, and Prontaprint on Collingwood Street said they'd do the job for £156. I decided to stick with the Free Press.

Jim and I had quite a collection of old cartoons in hand, but all of our work was small and I needed a lot more material to fill twelve pages. Martin's contribution was more of a collage than a cartoon, a three-dimensional conglomeration of paint, glue, print and paper featuring an angry metal bloke in a hat, called the Steel Skull. Jim wrote a tabloid-style exposé about the Anti-Pop movement, and I received another written contribution from a newspaper reporter in Kingston upon Thames called Tim Harrison. Shortly after leaving school I'd got bored and put a pen friend advert in *Private Eye*. The first person who replied was Tim Harrison, and I'd been corresponding with him ever since. But when Tim's contribution for my new magazine arrived – a girly piece of grown-up satire suggesting that Prince Charles was gay – it was totally out of keeping with everything else I'd gathered. I didn't want to hurt Tim Harrison's feelings – at least not until now – so I decided to use it anyway.

We still had to choose a name for the new magazine. At one point Jim's favoured title had been *Hip* because he liked the slogan, 'Get Hip!' Another proposal was *Lump It*, as in 'If you don't like it (and you won't like it) you can *Lump It*'. But in the end I went for the catchier and much more concise *The Bumper Monster Christmas Special*, which just seemed to roll off the tongue. *Viz* was an afterthought and sprang from an experiment I'd been doing with lino cuttings. My dad had some spare lino tiles left over after tiling our living room floor and I'd been carving bits of them with chisels, rolling them with ink and then pressing them onto paper in a vice. While playing around I came up with the word *VIZ*, which was easy to carve, consisting only of straight lines and no curved letters. That's what I always tell people anyway. Unfortunately the lino blocks, which I still have today, don't say *VIZ*, they say *Viz Comics*, with several curvy letters. So fuck knows where the name came from. I can't remember.

I assembled the artwork on a card table in my bedroom. It was a bit like doing a jigsaw, trying to slot everything together neatly. There were still a few gaps to fill, so I asked my brother Simon if he fancied doing a cartoon. Simon had recently formed his own noisy youth club band, Johnny Shiloe's Movement Machine, but he took time out from his budding acting and pop career to do a three-frame cartoon containing sex, cake and vomiting. It was a terrific combination. Eventually all the gaps were filled and on Wednesday 28 November 1979 I took a half-day off work to deliver the artwork to the Free Press. They said it would be ready on Friday the following week.

The original Viz *Comics lino print*

A bit like those twats out of Spandau Ballet, me and Jim made a big song and dance about *Viz* before the first issue had even been published. Pre-launch publicity included sticking posters up around Newcastle Polytechnic Students' Union and lino-printing *Viz Comics* logos onto a roll of typewriter address labels. These were stuck randomly on windows, contraceptive machines, lamp-posts and bus stops around the Gosforth Hotel and Newcastle Polytechnic areas, and we somehow managed to stick one high on the façade of the Listen Ear record shop on Ridley Place. That one was still visible from the top deck of the 33 bus for several years afterwards. Unlike those twats out of Spandau Ballet, we weren't students, and so we weren't allowed inside the Students' Union buildings. The Poly Students' Union entertainments officer was a horrible bloke called Paul something-or-other who wore fashionable knitwear and had blond, swept-back hair. We called him Mr Fucking McGregor because every time he caught us fly-posting he'd chase us out of the building muttering various garbled threats about putting us in a pie. But every time he chased us out we'd come back even more determined. Eventually the object of the exercise wasn't to promote the comic, it was purely to antagonize that daft bastard. This spell of aggravated promotional activity earned us a rather ironic reputation as an 'anti-student' magazine which lasted some time. Jim and I hated students. If townies like us wanted to get into either the University or the Polytechnic to see a band we had to stand at the door looking humble and beg passing students to sign us in. We were envious of their cushy, low-price accommodation, their cheap booze, cheap food, cheap and exclusive live entertainment, and the fact that they were surrounded by young women. It was the male students we hated, not the girls.

I took Friday 7 December off work and went with Jim to collect the finished comic from the Free Press. When we got there, the first thing that struck me was how small the box was. I was expecting a stack of cartons, not one flat box. But 150 very thin comics didn't take up much room. It was raining as we carried them the short distance from the Free Press to the Anti-Pop office. There was nobody there so we retired to a nearby café, Country Fare, where, over a cup of tea and some cheese scones, we sat and read our very own comic. The ink was blacker than black and the paper was creamy and smooth. It made the cartoons look different, more clean and deliberate, almost as if someone else had drawn them. The spines of the comics were neatly folded, and the staples were shiny and new. We sat and admired them for ages. For some reason I'd decided to give away a 'free ice cream' with every issue and this meant taking the comics home and spending the best part of the weekend lino printing pictures of ice creams and then stapling them onto the back pages. I'd taken a few advance orders from friends, and the first person to pay for a copy of *Viz* was a Gosforth High girl called Karen Seery. But it was on Monday 10 December at the Gosforth Hotel that *Viz* was officially launched.

Myself, Jim and Simon all went along, although Simon was

only fifteen and risked being fed to the landlord's dogs if he was caught on the premises. I decided to take thirty copies of the magazine as I couldn't imagine selling any more than that in one night. Early in the evening we positioned ourselves on the landing outside the function room door and started offering them to passers-by. None of us were natural salesmen and a typical pitch would be, 'Funny magazine. Very wacky. Twenty

Skinheed Poster

pence.' People weren't interested. 20p was a bit steep for a twelve-page black-and-white comic. The *Beano* was twice as thick, colour, and half the price in those days. There were no takers. One passing Gosforth High girl called Ruth snarled and called me a capitalist. That hurt. I'd paid the print bill out of my own pocket with no prospect of getting my money back. Even if

I sold out I was losing 8 pence on every copy. It was hardly capitalism at that stage, love. Things weren't looking too good until a little man with a gingerish beard and a scarf, more of a social worker than a student or punk, came skipping up the stairs. He looked a bit right-on, the kind of guy who'd give some kids doing their own thing a break. 'What's this?' he said with exaggerated enthusiasm. He had a quick look, smiled, bought one and disappeared into the function room. Not long afterwards people started coming out and buying copies. Once they'd seen someone else reading it and laughing, suddenly they all wanted one. It was the first sales phenomenon I'd ever witnessed, and it was a phenomenal one. Soon we were running out of comics and a friend called Paul, who had a car, offered Simon a lift back home to pick up some more copies.

As well as the Gosforth I also sold copies at a Dickies gig at the Mayfair later that week, and the following weekend at a Damned gig in Middlesbrough. There was only one shop that stocked the first comic, Listen Ear on the corner of Ridley Place and John Dobson Street in Newcastle. The little man behind the counter, who was short and far too old for his comical punk attire, seemed rather non-plussed at the idea of stocking yet another fanzine, but reluctantly agreed to take ten copies on sale or return. He placed them inside the glass counter and under the till, where nobody could see or reach them. 'If I leave them on the counter they'll be nicked,' he said. As well as hawking the comic around pubs and student discos in Newcastle I made a couple of futile efforts to reach a wider audience. In February 1980 I invested £3.25 in a classified ad in *Private Eye*:

Viz Comics. Very hilarious indeed.
20p plus SAE to 16 Lily Cres, Newcastle/Tyne.

At about the same time I wrote a hopelessly optimistic letter to a magazine distribution company called Surridge Dawson Ltd. and received my first rejection letter:

Dear Mr Donald
Thank you for your letter of 1st February in connection
with the distribution of your comics. Firstly, as you are
most probably aware, the comic market in the United
Kingdom is very competitive indeed, and would be
difficult to break into without reasonable financial
backing.

From our point of view as national distributors, we
would require a regular publishing date and also need to
be selling about 10,000 copies per issue to make it a viable
operation. To be quite frank, at present I do not think you
are in a position to consider distribution on a national
scale, but nevertheless we will give the matter further
thought on sight of a complete copy of your magazine.
Yours sincerely
T. H. Marshall
General Manager Publishing Department

I hadn't dared send them a complete copy, just a few selected
highlights, because I knew full well that if I'd sent the whole
comic it would have gone straight in the bin.

With the benefit of hindsight it was probably a wee bit early
to be thinking of a commercial deal, but I was getting some
grassroots distribution thanks to a few enthusiastic individuals
each taking a handful of copies here and there. A Newcastle
University student called Jane Hodgson took twenty copies to
sell to her mates and my pen friend Tim Harrison also took ten
copies. Then at the end of February I got my first big break.
Derek Gritten, a bookseller in Bournemouth, had spotted my ad
in *Private Eye* and wanted to see a sample of the comic. If he liked
it he said he would order twenty-five copies, my biggest order so
far! My £3.25 investment looked to be paying off, and I rushed
Mr Gritten a copy of the comic by return ... but he didn't reply.

Never mind. The first comic had been surprisingly well
received by the public and I knew that the next one could be

much better. By now a second issue was underway on the card table, but this time I was taking care to plan it better, make it look neater and more attractive. Jim had drawn a couple of new cartoons, Simon had done another cartoon with vomiting in it, and Martin Stevens had come up with a brilliant new character called Tubby Round. For music content I'd interviewed a fellow DHSS employee called Dave Maughan about his very serious prog rock band Low Profile – and then written an entirely different story in which they became a disco band. And Jim had written about a new Anti-Pop artist who was rapidly becoming a legend.

Anti-Pop's first record release, a double A-sided single by the Noise Toys and Arthur 2 Stroke ('Pocket Money'/'The Wundersea World of Jacques Cousteau') had been getting air play on John Peel's show, but a new Anti-Pop album called *Anna Ford's Bum* by Wavis O'Shave was causing a bigger stir both on radio and in the music press. Wavis O'Shave wasn't a comedian and he wasn't a singer. He definitely wasn't a musician either. He was a sort of cross between Howard Hughes, Tiny Tim and David Icke. He was never seen at the Gosforth Hotel and I'd only ever caught a glimpse of him once in the Anti-Pop office, when he didn't speak at all. To promote the album he only played one gig – at the Music Machine, Camden, in March 1980 – and he didn't even turn up for that. A heavily disguised Arthur 2 Stroke went on in his place. None of his fans knew what Wavis looked like, so there were no complaints. (Wavis would become better known in later years as The Hard, a bizarre character who made brief appearances on *The Tube*, hitting his hand with a hammer and saying 'I felt nowt'.)

Viz comic No. 2 went on sale in April 1980. This time I really pushed the boat out and printed 500, and gave away a free balloon with every copy ... stapled to the inside back cover. The print bill was £66.67, plus another £4.91 for balloons purchased from fancy goods specialists John B. Bowes Limited, late of Low Friar Street, just round the corner from the Free Press. In those days you never had to walk more than 100 yards to buy a bag of 500 balloons. *Viz* wasn't going down too well in Surrey. Having struggled to shift ten copies of issue 1 in Kingston-upon-Thames, Tim Harrison cut his order down to six. But sales were up elsewhere. The Listen Ear record shop took an astounding seventy-five copies, Jane Hodgson took thirty, and Jim's dad Jack Brownlow, a progressive school teacher and a thoroughly nice bloke, bought twenty-five. My dad didn't buy any though, largely because he didn't know *Viz* existed. By now he was out of work and spending all his time looking after my mum. Both of my parents were blissfully unaware of the comic's existence, and I wanted to keep it that way for as long as I could.

Issue 2 was clearly a big improvement on issue 1 so I sent an unsolicited copy to Derek Gritten, the bookseller in Bournemouth who'd gone very quiet since receiving issue 1. He wrote back confirming that he hadn't liked the first one, but the good news was that he did like issue 2 and he promptly ordered twenty-five copies. Despite this promising progress the vast majority of the 500 comics had to be sold in Newcastle by hand, and at nights I'd walk from pub to pub in Jesmond selling comics on my own. I didn't like going into pubs alone, and I hated cold selling. It was totally against my nature. But something drove me to do it. I did it obsessively, a bit like train-spotting, going from room to room asking every single person if they wanted to buy a comic. The aim wasn't to sell comics, it was simply to ask everyone. Once I'd asked everyone then I could go home happy, even if I'd sold none. On one of these fleeting runs, through the Cradlewell pub, I inadvertently offered a comic to the new Entertainments Officer from the Polytechnic; a big, bald bloke called Steve Cheney. 'So ...', he said, standing up and turning round to face me, 'this is the new anti-student magazine I've been hearing about, is it?' His predecessor, Mr Fucking McGregor, had obviously briefed him on our activities. 'It's not anti-student at all,' I told him with a convincing smile. It wasn't actually, only me and Jim were. 'Here, have a read and see for yourself.' I gave the big, baldy twat a free copy and he smiled, said thank you and sat down to read it while I made my escape.

I preferred selling comics when there were two of us. Jim didn't actually do much selling – he preferred drinking and watching the bands, and the women – but he provided physical and moral support. That could come in handy in the Students' Union bars where every cluster of students contained at least one gormless twat just waiting for an opportunity to show off to his mates. Occasionally things turned nasty, like the time I foolishly walked into the 'Agrics" bar at the University and some stumpy, little fat-necked student grabbed about a dozen comics out of my hand, tore them in half and threw them all up in the air above my head. Then he just glared at me as if to say, 'What are you going do about it?' I looked at him as if to say 'Erm… nothing, I suppose,' then sidled away like a coward.

I hadn't shown the comic to anybody at work. They were all regular, working-class sorts of people. They liked drinking in the Bigg Market and disco dancing, so I thought it might be a little left-of-field for their tastes. But gradually they began to find out about what I was doing and started asking for copies of the comic. When I eventually took some in, to my surprise and delight they all liked it too. All except the old ladies, that is. People laughed out loud, passed them around, and asked for copies of the next issue. This was a revelation to me. Ordinary people found it funny as well as rebellious youths and student types.

As well as crossing socio-economic divides, the geographical spread of sales was also expanding. So far *Viz* was strictly a Newcastle, Bournemouth and ever-so-slightly Kingston-upon-Thames publishing phenomenon. There was a conspicuous lack of outlets in the capital. Luckily Arthur 2 Stroke had a brother called Tim who lived in South London and Tim volunteered to do some footwork, taking the comic to Rough Trade records and Better Badges. Both shops agreed to stock it. I'd also placed two more ads in *Private Eye*, one in 'Articles for sale', advertising issue

2 for 32p including postage, and the other in the 'Wanted' column, offering £1000 for a copy of the first issue. Eager to spread the message I'd also sent copies of issues 1 and 2 to the local newspaper, and this resulted in our first ever press cutting. On 10 April 1980, beneath the headline, 'A comical look at Newcastle social problems', the *Newcastle Evening Chronicle* described *Viz* as 'a new comic which is not the usual light revelry, but more a social commentary'. According to their reporter *Viz* was 'taking a wry look at society in the form of cartoon strips', and he summed up by describing it as '*Sparky* for grown-ups'. It was all strangely flattering. They didn't mention the shit drawings, the foul language or the violent and unimaginative cartoon endings. This was my first ever dealing with the tabloid press, and I'd soon discover how flexible their approach to a subject could be.

Celebrated television producer Malcolm Gerrie, who would later launch *The Tube*, was in those days producing a dreadful 'yoof' show on Tyne-Tees TV called *Check It Out*. Getting on '*Checkidoot*', as it was known locally, was the height of ambition for many local bands who assumed that stardom would quickly follow. In reality it didn't work like that. If they'd looked at the statistics they'd have realized that an appearance on this cheesiest of yoof shows would virtually guarantee them obscurity for the rest of their careers. But *Check It Out* seemed like an ideal place to publicize *Viz*, so I bombarded Malcolm Gerrie with copies of the comic and accompanying begging letters. Eventually he invited Jim and myself to his office at the City Road TV studios. Gerrie was a surprisingly geeky-looking bloke with buck teeth, fancy geps, wild eyes, a pointy hooter and ridiculous corkscrew haircut. As if one such face wasn't bad enough, the wall behind him was plastered with photographs of himself grinning at the camera while clinging to the shoulders of various pop luminaries. Could this be Michael Winner's illegitimate son I wondered. Jim and I were disappointed by what Gerrie had to say. He explained that he liked the comic very much but he couldn't possibly consider it for his TV show because of the expletive nature of some of the contents.

By the summer of 1980 changes had taken place at Anti-Pop. Arthur 2 Stroke's three-piece band had evolved into the eight-piece Arthur 2 Stroke and the Chart Commandos. Around the same time the Noise Toys had folded and Martin Stevens had gone home to Coventry, promising to keep sending me cartoons. I felt like it was time for a change too. At one of the Noise Toys' final gigs I'd been chatting to a friend called Stephanie and she asked me how my job was going. I told her about all the money I was earning, the tea trolley and the Empire biscuits. 'You should get out of there,' she said, 'before you get addicted.' She meant to the money, not the biscuits. And she was right. I was getting too comfortable. My dad had told me that if I played my cards right the civil service would be a job for life, but that prospect appalled me. I still had no idea what I did want to do, but I decided to quit anyway and turn my back on the Empire biscuits and £170 cash every month. I handed in my notice and tempered the news by telling dad not to worry, I'd be going back to college soon. But my only real plan at the time was to sign on the dole and produce the next issue of *Viz*.

CHAPTER THREE

Ghost Town

In the summer of 1980 Newcastle's Quayside wasn't the glitzy playground for footballers and fat slags that it is today. On the corner of Quayside and Broad Chare there now stands an estate agent's office where river view apartmentettes are advertised for £250,000 and penthouse suites overlooking the Baltic Art Gallery and the landmark Egg-slicer Bridge sell for a million plus. On the same corner site twenty-four years ago Anti-Pop rented a derelict rehearsal room for £7 a week. Nobody wanted to live or work on the Quayside back then, largely because the river stank of shit. As you walked beneath the railway viaduct, along The Side and into what was once the thriving commercial heart of the city, it was like entering a ghost town. Beneath the north pier of the Tyne Bridge buildings stood empty, their stonework blackened with a century of soot. On the river front itself the Port Authority and a solitary advertising agency seemed to be the only buildings in use. The city's party epicentre was much further north, and at night you could walk from The Side to the Baltic Tavern in Broad Chare without passing a single under-dressed, drunken woman staggering about in high heels.

The Baltic was a rough-and-ready pub with a reputation for violence dating back to an unfortunate shotgun and testicles incident that had taken place a year or two earlier. But there was cheap rehearsal space in the run-down buildings that surrounded it and the Live Theatre group had established themselves just up the road, so the pub had a pretty bohemian clientele. It was still a sailors' pub too, with the odd naval vessel mooring nearby, and on Sundays it filled up with dodgy market

Pathetic Sharks

traders. The Baltic was decorated in a half-hearted nautical theme with fishing nets and orange buoys draped above the bar, and there were a couple of token lifebelts hanging on the wall next to the tab machine. But this was no theme pub. It was a good old-fashioned boozer. The jukebox featured an eclectic mix of disco, soul and early Adam Ant records, and the wall behind it was a sea of posters advertising gigs, plays and exhibitions. In front of the jukebox was a pool table, and it was here I whiled away most of my free time after packing in my job.

By now Jim Brownlow had got himself a girlfriend. Fenella was a petite and pretty brunette whom I'd known at school, but since we'd left school Jim had got to know her considerably better than me and they now shared a flat. Fenella was a revelation when it came to selling comics. She worked in a clothes boutique by day and by night she'd accompany us on our rounds of pubs and Students' Union bars. With her looks, patter and personality, Fenella could sell a dozen or more comics where I would have struggled to sell two or three, blokes literally queuing up to hand her their money. Armed with this new sales weapon, in July of 1980 I ordered an ambitious 1000 copies of the third issue. The bill came to £126.57. I hadn't minded losing money on the first two comics but now I was living on £14 a week state benefit and if *Viz* was going to continue it would have to start paying for itself. Editorially one of the highlights of the new comic was the début of the Pathetic Sharks. This was a fairly crude half-page strip which had started out as a *Jaws* spoof before I abandoned it halfway through. Shortly afterwards Jim had picked it up and added a speech balloon, something to the effect that my sharks looked crap. And thus the Pathetic Sharks were born.

During the summer of 1980 I got a message that Brian Sandells wanted to see me. Brian owned the near-legendary Kard Bar tat emporium in what was then the Handyside Arcade. This run-down Victorian shopping arcade stood in Percy Street, on the site of what is now 'Eldon Garden', a notably plant-free, glass and tiles shopping mall. Today the place buzzes with footballers' wives spending their husbands' cash on fancy knickers and designer jewellery, but in the early 1980s it was at the opposite end of the commercial property scale. In the sixties the Handyside had been home to the famous Club A-Go-Go where The Animals had been the resident band. Twenty years on the club was now a grotty carpet warehouse, better known for the historic hole in the ceiling where Jimi Hendrix had once carelessly thrust his guitar, than for its carpets. Most of the low-rent shops in the arcade below sold second-hand kaftans, incense or punk clobber. The Kard Bar was the biggest of these and sold every shade of shit imaginable, from pop posters to dope pipes, via Japanese death stars. The shop was compact and packed, a maze of shelves and racks displaying any manner of tasteless tat. Marilyn Monroe pillow cases, Steve McQueen cigarette lighters, Jim Morrison bath salts. You name it. Brian, the owner, was a smartly dressed, grey-haired man in his late forties who would have looked more at home working in an old-fashioned bank. Standing behind his unusually high counter he looked a bit like a glove puppet operator without a puppet. Brian told me he'd seen copies of *Viz* and been impressed. A lot of it was rubbish, he added quickly to counteract the praise, but he thought it was well produced. He ordered a modest ten copies of issue 3 to begin with, but paid me £1.50, cash up front, and immediately put them on sale right next to his till.

By now my nationwide distribution network included top retailers like the Moonraker science-fiction bookshop in Brighton and the Freewheel Community Bookshop in Norwich. I got in touch with these unlikely places by scouring the national Yellow Pages archive in the Central Library and sending off unsolicited samples by post. Meanwhile the south coast retirement resort of Bournemouth was becoming an unlikely sales hot spot thanks to the efforts of Derek Gritten. He had even approached the local branch of WHSmith with issue 2. They'd told him where to go, of course, but Derek was still confident enough to order a staggering eighty copies of No. 3. I had distribution north of the border too, a Stirling student called Bill Gordon having forked out £15 for 100 copies to sell among his friends. But selling 1000 copies was proving to be difficult, and after five months I still had a couple of hundred left and not enough money to pay the next print bill. Brian Sandells got me out of a scrape, buying the lot off me and paying cash up front.

Sales hadn't been helped by our second press review, this time in the local morning paper. I'd sent offbeat columnist Tony Jones at the *Newcastle Journal* copies of the first three comics and he invited myself and Jim in to meet him and to pose for our first ever press picture on the roof of the local newspaper offices. His review was a bit more objective than the *Evening Chronicle*'s. Under the headline 'Comic is a five letter word' he said that most of the magazine was 'cheap, nasty and misdirected'. But he wasn't entirely negative. His concluding words were, 'If they clean up their act, this enterprising duo could yet find *Viz* has a future.'

Despite struggling to shift issue 3, I printed another 1000 copies of issue 4 in October 1980. This comic featured the first ever letters page, a combination of genuine letters I'd received (such as the stock letter from the dole office that accompanied my weekly giro) and letters that I'd made up to mimic the vacuous style of the tabloid letters pages. As more and more of my time got taken up by selling – posting off parcels and chasing up payments – the interval between comics was increasing. The next comic didn't appear until March 1981, but No. 5 was worth waiting for as it marked a watershed. We had our first full-page cartoons, with Jim's brilliant Paul Whicker the Tall Vicar instantly becoming our most popular character to date. There was also Simon's SWANT, parodying the American TV series SWAT, and for my money a strip called Ciggies and Beer was Martin Stevens's best ever contribution. I'd also made my first crude attempt to mimic the teenage photo-romance stories I'd read in girls' comics like *Jackie*, taking the pictures at home on my dad's old camera and using our neighbours as actors. Issue 5 also included the first genuine commercial advert. Brian Sandells asked if he could advertise the Kard Bar and I agreed, on condition that the advert was in keeping with the editorial style of the magazine. This set a famous trend of amusing adverts that was to last for several years. I charged Brian £11 for his half-page advert, and he gave me £15. Brian could be very generous – a little too generous at times when it came to offering advice. On every visit to his shop I'd receive a lengthy lecture on business or graphic design and I'd be stuck there for up to an hour smiling and nodding my head. He was also a real stickler when it came to proofreading his adverts. He always insisted I got the spelling right, for example. He was a real nit-picker, Brian.

When issue 5 was printed the Free Press invited us to come in and do some 'self work' finishing which meant that they printed the pages and we put the comics together ourselves. This cut the production costs considerably and was also an important gesture of compliance with the Free Press's socialist principles. They were, after all, a bunch of commies, not a commercial printer, and for them the object of the exercise was to give us a share in the means of production. Jim, Simon and myself spent many a happy day at Charlotte Square collating, folding and then stapling comics together on a Dickensian saddle-stitching machine. Eventually they let us use the guillotine too, and finally the 'Hobson', a fully automated and highly temperamental page collating, folding and shredding machine.

The Free Press was a fascinating environment to work in, with a wonderful mix of characters present. For me that place encapsulated the comical conflict between trendy, right-on socialists and down-to-earth, working-class people that was central to some of my favourite cartoons at the time. Cartoons like Woolly Wilfy Wichardson who orders weal ale in a working-class boozer, and Community Shop where a bloke in a vest goes into a community wholefood collective and tries to buy twenty Embassy Regal. The Free Press was a co-operative where all the workers were equal, but there was an obvious divide between the middle-class political ideologists whose idea it had been to set it up, and the working-class printers who'd been drafted in to work there. Printers like Jimmy, a fat Geordie bloke from Scotswood. He may not have had the intellect of colleagues like Howard, the idealistic hippy, and Andy, the hardcore socialist Scouser, but Jimmy could debunk the lot of them with his blunt wit and choice turn of phrase.

Despite having been fobbed off by Malcolm Gerrie I kept on bombarding *Check It Out* with copies of *Viz* and eventually a researcher called Alfie Fox got in touch and invited myself and Simon to a meeting. It turned out Fox was new to the show and didn't realize *Viz* was off limits. But our meeting wasn't a complete waste of time. Alfie Fox took us to the canteen at Tyne-Tees

Television for a chat, but I spent the entire meeting listening to someone talking on an adjoining table. A local TV newsreader and continuity announcer by the name of Rod Griffiths was holding court with a group of colleagues, and he was swearing like a trooper. It was astounding to hear such a familiar voice coming out with such unfamiliar language, and I was mesmerized. When we left the meeting we were no closer to getting *Viz* on TV, but the seeds for a new cartoon character had just been sown.

Bizarrely, after trying for over a year to get *Viz* onto a shoddy local yoof programme, a slot on national TV fell into our lap. In June 1981 a hand-written note addressed to 'Anyone from *Viz* Comics' was left at the Kard Bar. It came from Jane Oliver and Gavin Dutton, producers of a BBC2 yoof show called *Something Else*. They were planning to make an alternative programme about Newcastle and were in town looking for suitably disaffected young people to take part. *Something Else* was a product of the BBC's Community Programme Unit, and the idea of the show was to give 'the kids' access to television.

When we met the two producers they explained that we, the kids, were going to make the programme, not them, the boring grown-ups. They were just going to help us a little. They hand-picked a panel of five appropriately discontented youths from the area, all of whom had got 'something to say'. As well as myself, representing the comic, there were four others. A motorcyclist called Mick wanted to draw attention to the plight of motorcyclists who are occasionally barred from pubs just because they wear leather clothing. Mick was a fireman, and it occurred to him that if the pubs from which he was barred caught fire, it would be *him* the landlord would turn to to put the fire out. The irony and injustice of this situation clearly rankled with Mick, and the idea of filming people riding around on bikes clearly appealed to producer Gavin Dutton, who was himself a bit of a biker. Then there was Mark, a chubby, monotone mod who wanted to moan about local bands not getting a 'fair deal' from London record companies. There was also Tracey, an actress who I suspected was on the other bus, and had some sort of gripe about the stereotyping of women. And there was Stephen, a long-haired hippy who didn't like being stereotyped as a long-haired hippy just because he was a long-haired hippy. This was going to be some show.

As with all yoof shows there were a couple of live music slots in the programme to try and entice people to watch it, and because it was our programme the producers said it was up to us to choose the bands. I realized this was a golden opportunity for Arthur 2 Stroke and The Chart Commandos so I got to work lobbying the other panel members. The Chart Commandos were just about the biggest band in Newcastle at the time and their recent single, a dub version of the theme from *Hawaii Five-0*, had recently stormed in at number 175 in the charts. After a lot of arm-twisting all five of us eventually agreed that Arthur 2 Stroke and the Chart Commandos, and notorious South Shields punk outfit the Angelic Upstarts, would provide the music for our show. With this settled I ran all the way from the BBC studios in Newbridge Street to the Anti-Pop rehearsal room on the Quayside to break the good news.

The next day producer Gavin Dutton rang me. He said he'd been thinking. Because the North-East had such a reputation for heavy metal music, would it not be a good idea to have a heavy metal band on the programme? 'Not all Geordies are air guitarists,' I told him. 'You'd just be reinforcing another stereotype. Can't we just stick with the bands we chose?' No, we couldn't. It turned out that Dutton, himself a bit of a heavy metal fan, had already twisted the arms of the other panel members and the decision had been made to replace Arthur 2 Stroke with a bunch of tight-trousered, cock-thrusting *Charlie's Angels* lookalikes, the Tygers of Pan fucking Tang.

My next contribution to the programme was to draw cartoons of a few other North-East stereotypes, such as a man with a flat cap and whippet and a woman chained to the kitchen sink.

These were to be included in the show in the hope that the use of such stereotypes on national television would in some way help put a stop to the use of such stereotypes in the media. I seem to recall that was one of the producers' ideas too. Jim, Simon and I were also going to be interviewed about *Viz* by another member of the panel. On the day of our interview the film crew were scheduled to arrive at my house at 2.00 p.m. We'd never been on telly before so the three of us decided to pop out to a local pub beforehand in order to calm our nerves. By the time the TV crew arrived we were fucking rat-arsed, Simon especially so, and for some reason we'd dressed up in a selection of silly wigs and false moustaches. Mark, the monotone mod interviewer, read out his questions with some difficulty, and a total lack of enthusiasm, while we gave a giggling performance of Ozzy Osbourne-esque incoherence. When filming was complete all three of us were invited down to London to make a trailer for the show. As a special treat they let us write out the programme credits by hand, in white paint on a very long roll of blue paper. It took us most of the night to do it, and we later learned this had saved them £125 in production costs. The tight bastards didn't give us a penny. But the benefits of our TV exposure were apparent even before the programme had been finished. In July 1981 I got a letter from TV presenter Tony Bilbow saying he'd seen a copy of *Viz* at the Community Programme Unit offices and wanted to subscribe to future issues. He generously enclosed £10 and in doing so became our first ever celebrity reader. '*Something Else* Newcastle' was broadcast on BBC2 at 6.55 p.m. on Friday 25 September 1981. In those days there were only three TV channels, and being on telly was a real event. Everyone either saw us or heard about it, and the programme resulted in a massive upsurge of interest in the magazine, from my parents in particular.

' Up till this point they'd been unaware that *Viz* existed, but keeping it a secret had been getting harder by the day. I knew full well that a BBC film crew arriving at the door might need some form of explanation, but before I'd had a chance to say anything my dad had invited them into the living room for a cup of tea and casually enquired about what they were filming upstairs. The cat was finally out of the bag and a few days later my mum broached the subject of this 'comic' on one of my brief visits to the kitchen. 'Can I see one of these *comics* of yours?' she asked. 'Yes, of course,' I said. 'Actually … I've not got any at the moment. They're all sold out. But I'll get one for you as soon as I can.' I kept stalling her for days and then weeks, but the pressure to produce a comic became unbearable once the *Something Else* programme had been broadcast. To make matters worse my streetwise Auntie Thea had heard about *Viz* by now and had started mentioning it to Mum. Ashamed to show her the real thing I took an old back issue and used Tippex to obscure every swear word in the comic. I seem to recall making twenty-seven alterations before I had the nerve to show it to her. I went into the living room, handed it over unceremoniously then darted back upstairs before she'd found her reading glasses.

Despite our big break on TV I didn't see *Viz* as anything other than a slightly shameful hobby. In the year since I'd left the Ministry I'd been supplementing my dole money by dabbling in design work. I'd started off doing a few posters for Anti-Pop, but one job led to another and before long I was producing designs for all sorts of people. I was totally untrained but I particularly enjoyed the design side of the comic and I'd managed to glean the basics of typography by hanging around the Free Press's design studio and looking over people's shoulders. I enjoyed the whole creative process of graphic design – from ripping off someone else's idea, all the way through to cobbling together some makeshift artwork and forging a union stamp on the back. This seemed to be the direction my career was heading in so I decided it was time I went to college and trained to become a proper, professional graphic designer. One that charges £30 an hour instead of just a couple of quid.

No art qualifications were necessary to enrol on the Art Foundation course at Bath Lane College in Newcastle. I found this a little bit disturbing but as I didn't have a single art qualification myself I couldn't really grumble. The one-year course was designed to give would-be art students a basic grounding in graphics, ceramics, sculpture, fine art, fashion and eccentric behaviour. For my interview I packed together a few of my early works: a pencil portrait of my late grandfather on my mum's side, a caricature of Jimmy Hill and my line drawings of castles tailored towards the drunken Norwegian market. I'd been warned by my brother Steve, an art college veteran, that conventional pictures with discernible subject matter – like castles and grandparents – were frowned upon in the academic art world. And a couple of years earlier a friend of Steve's, an artist called John Boyd, had warned me specifically about drawings of Jimmy Hill. 'It might look like Jimmy Hill,' he said, 'but is there a market for that type of thing?' John Boyd's paintings would later sell for tens of thousands of pounds, and sure enough none of them would be of Jimmy Hill. But I left Jimmy in. The only concession I made was to leave my watercolours of diesel trains in the drawer at home. I also decided not to include any copies of *Viz* in case the bad language counted against me.

The interviewer, who wore suede shoes, whipped through my portfolio like a customs officer searching for duty-free cigarettes. He didn't seem interested in anything he found, tugging the corner of each drawing then quickly pushing it back into place. Jimmy Hill got nothing more than a cursory glance, as did Granddad and Bamburgh Castle. He seemed so unenthusiastic about my work it came as quite a surprise when he told me I'd been accepted.

The moment I arrived at art college I knew I'd made a mistake. In my first week one of the lecturers, a man called Charlie, was suspended for dancing naked around his studio and trying to stab female pupils in the bottom with a compass point. I sensed I wasn't going to fit in. I was old, twenty-one by now, and the rest of the students were young, kids of eighteen who all dreamed of being either Vivienne Westwood or David Hockney when they grew up. As the course progressed their dress sense became more extravagant and their hair dye more colourful. Free at last from the social restrictions of their comprehensives and surrounded by like-minded, creative spirits, one by one they were coming out of the closet and declaring themselves Marc Almond fans. All I wanted was for some fucker to teach me how to draw hands properly and explain typography and print, but I'd arrived at art college thirty years too late for that. We rotated subjects every couple of weeks. All I learnt from my brief spell in Graphics was not to call the lecturer 'Sir'. Everyone laughed when I did that. The correct form of address was 'Les'. The Photography module was probably the most useful. They didn't teach you anything about composition or lighting or how to take a decent picture, but they couldn't avoid showing you how to develop and print a film. What I dreaded most was my two weeks in Fashion and I got through it by keeping my head down and making a 15-inch-high, soft-toy version of a Pathetic Shark. The worst experience turned out to be Fine Art. That did my fucking head in.

At Heaton school my Woodwork teacher, Mr Venmore, spent his spare time working in a small room at the top of the class making himself a beautiful solid ash dining table and a set of matching chairs. At art college the Fine Art lecturer, Brian Ord, spent his spare time in an almost identical room at the top of the class, sawing up tables and chairs and sticking them back together in ridiculous, silly shapes. This was sculpture, apparently.

Over a year the Foundation course sorted the wheat from the chaff. By the end of it the wankers had become hardened art students, destined to have failed pop careers and eventually work in advertising, while dismayed and disillusioned individuals like myself, who were happy with their natural hair colour and preferred Gloria Jones's version of 'Tainted Love', found ourselves back at square one. My parting advice from the senior graphics lecturer, Dave, was that I should get away from this dirty old town, quit Newcastle and head for the bright lights and the big opportunities. He said I should go to Exeter. Apparently Exeter University had an illustration course where I could hone my cartooning talents and qualify to become a greetings card illustrator. If there was one thing I hated it was 'humorous' greetings cards. If anyone ever sent me one it went straight in the fucking bin. So I ignored Dave's advice and decided that my next career move would be to sign on the dole again.

Billy Britain

Throughout my spell at college I'd continued to publish *Viz*, but my graphic design work had really started to take off. I'd had one major job to do, designing a clothing catalogue, and this meant working late at night, often all night, trying to cram in other jobs for my regular customers too, then going to college the next day feeling like shit. One morning I actually went to bed for ten minutes thinking it would make me feel a bit brighter when I got up, but it didn't. *Viz* No. 6 came out just before I started college, in July 1981, and featured my new creation, Roger Mellie the Man on the Telly. I based his director Tom, the straight man, on my recollection of *Something Else* producer Gavin Dutton. But a far more popular character launched in the same issue was Billy Britain, a patriotic, right-wing racist who had the catchphrase,

'What a glorious nation'. The sort of person I'd imagine subscribes to *This England* magazine. Initially Billy Britain was a much bigger hit with readers than Roger Mellie, but a fatal design flaw would limit his long-term potential. His face was too complicated. I just got lucky the first time I drew it, in the title frame, but subsequent attempts to reproduce the same face weren't so good. I could only draw him from one angle and with one facial expression, which drastically limited the scope for character development. Roger Mellie, on the other hand, and Norman the Doorman who also made his debut in issue No. 6, were much better thought out. Their simple designs took into account the fact that I was, at very best, a rather mediocre cartoonist. Norman the Doorman was based on the gorillas whose job it was to uphold the ridiculous dress codes imposed by licensees in Newcastle city centre. No white socks, for example. It was also one of those strips where the name came first. You'd think of a name and it sounded so good you simply had to follow it through and come up with a cartoon to match.

When issue No. 7 appeared in December 1981 it featured the first appearance of Biffa Bacon. Biffa's name, kneecaps and elbows were undeniably inspired by the *Dandy*'s Bully Beef, but his character and relationship with his parents, Mutha and Fatha Bacon, were inspired by an incident I witnessed on a Metro train in Newcastle. Two young kids, aged seven or eight, had started squabbling in the aisle of a crowded train and were pushing and shoving each other. Their respective fathers were sitting on opposite sides of the carriage and you'd have expected them to intervene. But instead of reining his son in and telling him to behave, the heavily tattooed father sitting closest to me leaned forward and whispered in his son's ear, 'Go on, son, I'm right behind you.' From that sprang the simple idea of a bully whose father eggs him on rather than spanking him with a slipper. In fact his parents are more violent than he is. Issue 7 also featured a significant strip by Simon called the Lager Lads. This was inspired by a series of what seemed to us unlikely TV commercials for McEwan's lager in which three young lads went into pubs – laughing, smiling and drinking McEwan's lager – and never once got pissed or glassed anyone. The Lager Lads was the forerunner of Sid the Sexist.

Biffa, Mutha and Fatha Bacon

With a TV appearance in the pipeline I'd boldly ordered 2000 copies of No. 6, double the previous print run, at a unit cost of just over 11p, and I stuck with 2000 for issue No. 7. By 1981 the comic was reaching cult status among the student population of Newcastle, and sales in city centre shops were taking off. Brian at the Kard Bar was ordering an initial 500 copies of each issue, on condition that he had the comic at least a week before any other shops. By now I'd talked Virgin Records into stocking *Viz*, and HMV followed suit not long afterwards. Volume (formerly Listen Ear), Virgin and HMV were now all ordering fifty copies on an almost weekly basis. On the one hand this meant I could now retire from hawking the comic around the pubs, but it also posed one or two logistical problems. I couldn't drive and I had no car, so all the deliveries had to be done on foot and by bus. On at least one occasion Simon and I pressed two of my granny's 'Mrs Brady' style shopping trolleys into service to deliver comics to town on the 33 bus.

Getting HMV on Northumberland Street to stock *Viz* was a huge boost. The manager, Keith Armstrong, approached me in

Big Vern

the pub and asked how it was that his shop was the only record shop in town that didn't sell *Viz*. Frankly I'd never asked because I didn't think there was a cat in hell's chance of a mainstream music store like HMV touching it. Keith immediately started stocking it, right alongside his tills for maximum exposure. This put *Viz* under the noses of ordinary people who went to HMV to buy their Rod Stewart and Phil Collins records, and almost inevitably *Viz* wasn't to every Phil Collins fan's taste. One miserable old cow – probably the same woman who reported me to the boss at the DHSS – complained to the HMV head office about the contents of the comic and *Viz* was immediately banned from the shop. But that didn't stop Keith from selling it. He simply ignored the ban, kept on stocking it by the till, and told his staff to whip the comics out of sight if they saw anyone from head office entering the store.

The HMV shop had also joined the growing list of advertisers in the magazine. Keeping the adverts funny depended entirely on the cooperation and understanding of the client. Some people just couldn't get their head round self-parody. Sometimes if a client turned down what I thought was a really funny advert, I'd put the ad in anyway and simply not charge them. But Keith was game for anything and as a result HMV's ads tended to be among the funnier ones.

Issue 8 came out in May 1982 with a print run of 3000, and as sales rose so the new characters kept on coming. This one saw the birth of two familiar faces, Big Vern and Mr Logic. Big Vern was my tribute to *The Sweeney*. Like most of my cartoons it was intended as a one-off, a manic précis of the entire 1970s Euston Films genre, all compressed into a silly half-page throwaway strip. A straight man, Ernie, and a funny man, Vern. The same

Mr Logic

thin joke – that Vern is paranoid about the police – is repeated a few times, and at the end Big Vern kills himself. That was it. Artistically speaking there was nowhere else for Big Vern to go, besides which, from a continuity point of view, he'd already blown his brains out. But people liked it, so Big Vern was duly resurrected and the fact that he always killed himself at the end of the strip became part of the joke.

Mr Logic was different. He was based very much on real life. The product of a rare collaboration between myself and Simon, Mr Logic – an extreme social misfit – was unashamedly based on our big brother Steve and his hilarious Mr Spock behaviour. It wasn't until years later we discovered the real name for it was Asperger's Syndrome.

CHAPTER FOUR

Celibacy and Drugs and Rock'n'Roll

One underlying reason for *Viz's* growing success was probably the fact that I wasn't getting my end away. I had none of the distractions of a serious relationship, or indeed any relationship at all. I was a bit of a detached, emotionally independent sort of teenager myself. I'd only had one real girlfriend who I'd ditched when she declared herself a *Saturday Night Fever* fan in 1977. She was the type of girl who expected you to open doors, brush your hair and take regular baths, and I found all that a bit restrictive.

With a CV that featured train-spotting and a record collection that featured the Seekers, my prospects with the girls had never been good. And from a practical point of view living at home had also become a handicap. By now my bedroom, overlooking the railway in Lily Crescent, had almost totally metamorphosed into a design studio. It was a big room, about 20 feet wide by 14 deep, but I'd managed to fill almost every square inch of it with furniture. I had my drawing board, shelves cluttered with ink, pens and drawing materials, a wardrobe full of back issues, my record collection and hi-fi system crammed into a corner, a filthy old settee, the card table for a drawing board, a plan chest, a wooden writing desk, a small set of drawers for my clothes, and finally, amidst all this mess, a very untidy single bed. To add to the romantic atmosphere there was always a whiff of Cow Gum in the air, and what little carpet remained visible wasn't, due to the amount of litter on the floor. The walls were painted in dismal two-tone green bands – based on the British Railways class 47 diesel locomotive livery of the early 1960s – and there was a large paint stain on one of the curtains where I'd managed to knock a two-and-a-half litre tin of paint off a stepladder. The place hadn't been properly cleaned or dusted since 1970. It was just about functional as a workspace, but far from the ideal bachelor pad.

I led a solitary existence at home, rarely exchanging more than few pleasantries with Mum and Dad. My social life centred entirely around the pub, and even there I preferred playing pool to talking. I could get on the pool table at 6.30 p.m. and still be winning by closing time. That, and two pints of Whitbread Trophy Bitter, made for the perfect night out. Then, in 1982, my late-running sexual awakening finally arrived.

Karen

Karen was an eighteen-year-old history student at Newcastle University. Andy Pop had told me that a group of girls were interested in starting an Arthur 2 Stroke and the Chart Commandos Fan Club and asked if I'd liaise with them. The girls in question all lived together in an attic flat not far from me. It was at the top of a huge, double-fronted Victorian house belonging to the University, and as I clumped up the communal stairwell I realized that all four levels of the house were completely full of teenage girls. I felt a bit uncomfortable. I found my way up to the top-floor flat and was introduced to three of the occupants. Then the fourth appeared from her bedroom. Her hair was dark and so were her eyes. She seemed quiet and shy but when she smiled her timid little smile, her teeth lit the room and her sparkling eyes gave off the same sexual charge as 10,000 Kylie Minogue's arses. I was smitten.

That night I tossed – in a purely restless sense – and turned, endlessly thinking about her. Over the next few weeks I made silly excuses to visit the flat but never summoned up the courage to ask her out. I knew I had to so I hit on an idea. Near the Free Press in the centre of town was a little-known medieval monastery called Blackfriars which contained a little-known craft centre and even littler-known restaurant. The perfect way to proposition her would be to ring her and hit her with the killer line, 'Do you fancy going out to a monastery for a cup of tea?' There was no way I could have simply asked her out for a drink.

I waited till the coast was clear so I could use the telephone without Mum and Dad overhearing the conversation. Eventually my chance came and I nervously dialled her number. There was a communal phone on a lower landing of the house and my heart pounded as the girl who answered it clattered away up the stairs to find her. When I heard Karen's voice on the end of the line I babbled my cheesy line out breathlessly and then continued wittering nervously until I eventually ran out of breath. Then there was a short silence after which she said, 'Yeah ... okay.' She'd actually said 'Yes'! I was in a state of shock and jubilation. We had a date, although I don't remember much about it. We met at lunchtime, in between her lectures, but I think she declined the offer of food. I might have had a cheese scone, but I couldn't say for sure. We drank tea and talked for a while. At one point I think she mentioned that her mum worked for the Halifax Building Society ... or maybe it was the Woolwich. When I'd finished my cheese scone we walked back up towards the University and I vividly remember a group of workmen wolf-whistling at her as we passed St Andrew's church. Karen had a short skirt on at the time, and very nice legs. Unfortunately our relationship budded for some considerable time without blossoming. Then one day we met up in town and she seemed excited. She had some great news. 'I've got a boyfriend,' she told me. I was over the fucking moon.

She said his name was Graham and he was studying Naval Architecture, whatever the fuck that was. She'd danced with him at the Student Union disco that weekend and then kissed him goodnight. He made his way home to Fenham, in the west end of town, and she'd gone home to Jesmond, which is just north of the city centre. 'And do you know what he did?' she asked me. I was all ears. 'He couldn't stop thinking about me, so he walked all the way from Fenham to Jesmond in the middle of the night just to see me again,' she said with genuine, bubbly excitement. 'Isn't that romantic!' Romantic? Fucking hell. I'd have walked to the end of the Earth just to see her smile, and this randy student git walks two fucking miles and gets a shag. There's no bloody justice.

I eventually got over Karen and we remained 'good friends' for some time after that. In fact she appeared in the photo-story 'Prisoner of Love' in *Viz* issue 8 where she spent the entire story locked in the lavatory. Our good friendship was so strong Karen knitted me a bright red jumper as a birthday present, with the word '*VIZ*' on the front in great big letters. I couldn't possibly have worn it but it was a lovely gesture. Mind you, I'd have still preferred a shag.

I hadn't been entirely celibate all this time. There had been a drunken one-night stand with a platonic, pool-playing friend whose fondness for Stella Artois had possibly affected her judgement on the night in question. She'd invited me back to her flat for the night and mercifully I can remember very little of the event, other than her using the phrase, 'Hey, what's the hurry?' rather often.

In the summer of 1982 I had a fling with a girl called Sally. I'd known Sally since our schooldays and I'd always fancied her, as had every other boy in the school, and most of the male teachers (I remember one teacher in particular loosening his collar, wiping his brow and mouthing the word 'Phewf!' after she'd walked past the classroom window). But Sally was unobtainable, way out of my league. She was the stuff of legend. She spent the night in hotel bedrooms with bass players from top punk/mod revivalist three-piece bands (two words, both one syllable), not nerds like me. So imagine my surprise when Sally rang me up one day completely out of the blue and asked whether I fancied meeting up for a drink

Sally was small and stunning with reddish brown hair, and eyes that had always reminded me of Angharad Rees out of *Poldark*. She was also extremely intelligent, and fluent in Russian which she'd been studying at University for the last three years. We went out a few times to pubs and to the local art house cinema to see *Macbeth*, but nothing remotely sexual happened in the back row. In fact I fell asleep halfway through the film, which was in Russian, and I missed the last two hours. I guessed she just wanted me for my intellect. Then one evening I walked her to the bus stop and instead of saying goodnight as she usually did, she kissed me … and we boarded the bus together. I boarded that bus – a Leyland Atlantean, I seem to recall – a boy. But when the sun rose the next morning, I was a man.

I was also struggling to get my trousers on in a hurry. Like me, Sally was living with her parents at the time and had been a little tipsy when she invited me back. When we woke up she was a different person. 'Quick, get out before my dad finds you!' she whispered loudly. I could hear that her father was already well advanced with his morning ablutions in the bathroom next door so I unscrambled my clothes and threw them on as fast as I could, then tiptoed down the stairs and dashed out the front door, fastening buttons as I went. Once I got round the corner and out of sight I slowed down to a cocky stroll and started to smile. Not only had I shagged the best-looking girl in our school, but I'd also gained valuable anecdotal material by having to flee from her father in Robin Askwith style. What a result.

My sexual dalliance with Sally may have put a spring in my step but, together with my burgeoning design workload, it seriously affected production of the magazine. Our summer romance ended in the autumn, rather appropriately, and had it lasted any longer there may never have been an issue No. 9. The new comic finally emerged in November 1982 and new cartoons included the debuts of two Tyneside-based characters, Simon's Sid the Sexist and my own Brown Bottle. The Brown Bottle was a variation on the traditional superhero theme whereby Barry Brown, a quiet newspaper reporter, transformed himself into an incoherent, foul-mouthed, alcoholic tramp whenever he drank a bottle of Newcastle Brown Ale. That character was partly inspired by Davey Bruce, the drummer with the Chart Commandos. Davey was a Geordie ex-council workman, not the college type like most of the musicians I knew. He was the only person in the Baltic who drank 'Dog', as Newcastle Brown is known locally. It took more than one bottle for Davey to make his transformation, but once it happened, by hell, what a transformation it was. The inspiration for Simon's Sid the Sexist was another friend of ours, Graham Lines. In fairness to Graham he was nothing like Sid, but he provided the spark for the idea with his hilarious sexual bravado and endless chat-up lines, none of which he ever appeared to use on girls. Graham was always inviting you out 'on the tap', to 'pull a bit of blart' and to 'get a bit lash on'. If you took him up on the offer you invariably ended up having a few quiet beers, sausage and chips from the Barbecue Express, and then it would be back to his flat to get stoned and watch Laurel and Hardy videos into the early hours of the morning. No girls were ever involved.

Getting stoned was something I rarely got the opportunity to do following an unfortunate experience in the Anti-Pop office. I'd been up all night working on a poster for Andy Pop and hadn't had a thing to eat by the time I arrived at the office. The

The Brown Bottle

minute I walked in the door someone offered me a joint. I took a quick drag, just to be polite, and the next thing I knew my head was spinning, there was a noise in my ears like the start of the music at the cliff-hanging end of a *Dr Who* episode, and all the voices in the room were suddenly distant echoes. I blacked out and smacked my head on a bench as I went down. When I came to I was lying on the floor with someone frantically loosening my collar. 'I think he's dead,' said one voice. 'Quick, call an ambulance,' said another. 'Nah, don't be silly. He'll be fine,' said Andy. My dramatic collapse became the stuff of legend, and from that point onwards whenever there were drugs about people made a point of not offering them to me, so drugs played no part whatsoever in my creative processes. People often asked whether cartoons were drug inspired, but I didn't even use alcohol for inspiration. Occasionally I might scribble down an idea while I was drunk, but you could bet your arse once I was sober that a good ninety per cent of what I'd written would be absolute shit.

I never tried any hard drugs. Apart from dope the only thing I was ever offered was a little blue tablet which someone once suggested I take to help me stay up all night and finish their poster by the following morning. I believe Andy referred to it as an 'upper'. The very sight of this tablet scared me stiff and I imagined swallowing it and being found dead in my swimming pool the next day, even though I didn't have one. I wasn't brave enough to say 'No', so instead I accepted the tablet and then threw it away.

Drugs may have been off the menu but rock 'n' roll was still an important ingredient in the comic. Another highlight of issue No. 9 was a Dexy's Midnight Runners exclusive. Kevin Rowland and Dexy's were due to open a wine bar in Newcastle and I'd been recruited to orchestrate the event. I sub-contracted my brother Steve to make a wax champagne bottle for use in the ceremony. Following spells at art college and film school Steve was now hoping to get into the special effects industry. On the day of the grand opening a large crowd was in attendance. Posing at the door of the wine bar, Kevin Rowland said a few words then turned and smashed the bottle of champagne over the head of drummer Seb Shelton. The crowd gasped before realizing the bottle was made of wax. I'd explained the stunt to Shelton in some detail, but being a drummer he hadn't fully understood and didn't seem to have any idea what was happening. I used a photo of the incident in *Viz* but made up my own story to go with it. Dexy's were famously teetotal under Rowland's strict fitness regime, so our scoop was that he'd caught his drummer drinking a glass of wine and reacted by smashing him over the head with the bottle.

Anti-Pop were now promoting touring bands in Newcastle in

an attempt to subsidize the activities of their only remaining act, Arthur 2 Stroke and the Chart Commandos. As a result I got unrestricted press access to various popular artists of the day. One of my first interviewees was Clare Grogan out of Altered Images, whom Simon and I visited backstage at a club called Tiffanys. For me 'interviewing' someone simply meant getting some sort of evidence that we'd spoken to them, usually a photograph, then I'd go away and make the words up later. I wasn't at all comfortable asking questions, but as you were entering the dressing room on the pretext of being a journalist saying something was pretty much unavoidable. Our pop coverage was supposed to be ironic, which is easy to do in print, but trying to be ironic in the flesh is a lot harder, especially if you're talking to Clare Grogan and you fancy the wee Scottish minx something rotten. We asked her: What's your favourite colour? Your star sign? Your favourite cheese? That sort of thing. Clare cottoned on immediately and answered every question with a smile, but the band's lanky guitarist wasn't getting the joke. He was expecting an earnest interview with a hip fanzine and got more annoyed with each question. 'What sort of a stupid question is that?' he snarled when we asked about the band's favourite biscuits. We persisted, and so did he. Eventually it got a bit embarrassing so I took my obligatory photograph, then we made our excuses and left.

Another act Andy brought to Newcastle was a group of comedians called the Comic Strip. I'd never heard of them until I saw Andy putting up a poster in the Baltic one lunchtime around 1981. 'They're fucking brilliant,' he assured me. He'd assured me A Flock of Seagulls would be fucking brilliant too, so that meant nowt. But the Comic Strip sounded promising so Jim, Simon and myself went along to see them, and thank God we did. Never in my life have I laughed so much and I doubt I'll ever get close to it again. I was rocking in my seat, aching in the ribs and on the verge of wetting myself. Jesmond was full of social workers in Citroën 2CVs yet I'd never heard anyone (with the possible exception of my dad) make jokes about them. Alexei Sayle and 20th Century Coyote (Rik Mayall and Ade Edmondson) were the highlights. I didn't know people could be so relentlessly, pant-pissingly funny. After the show we hung around the stage door and I pressed a copy of two *Viz* back issues into what looked like the hand of Jennifer Saunders. It was a very chaotic doorway.

Joe Robertson-Crusoe, from Viz *issue 65, 1994*

By now the idealistic Anti-Pop organization that had been such an inspiration for me and Jim was effectively no more. They'd lost a lot of steam with the departure of the Noise Toys, and now the label's last remnants, Arthur 2 Stroke and the Chart Commandos, were also heading for obscurity. They were brilliant live and won support slots with touring acts like Ian Dury and the Blockheads and The Q Tips, but it was impossible to keep an eight-piece band on the road playing pubs and college gigs. Eventually they pawned their ambition on the local working men's club circuit, and never got it back.

Changes were ringing down on the Quayside too. A man called Joe Robertson was in the process of transforming Newcastle nightlife with the introduction of wine bars such as

Legends. Robertson had once been a swinging sixties' DJ at the Club A-Go-Go. Now he was a successful businessman who, despite dressing like a *Miami Vice* drugs baron, was receiving plaudits from the police for 'cleaning up' the city centre. Heavy drinking and violence in and around the Bigg Market had been a huge problem in the 1970s, but now pubs and bars were going out of fashion and were being replaced by Robertson's pseudo-sophisticated drinkeries. He'd buy a run-down pub, like the Midland Hotel for example, refit it with lots of fancy chrome and expensive lighting, and change the name to anything ending with an 's'. Berlins in this case. The bar would then reopen, and hundreds of young people dressed in skimpy frocks and no white socks would queue to get in and pay through the nose for fancy cocktails and bottled lagers. Robertson was shrewd, if not a slightly cheesy dresser. His genius was realizing that Geordies loved to flaunt their money. If there was a lass watching, then a bloke would much rather pay £2 for a bottle of lager than £1.20. So Joe provided £2 bottles of lager, and even costlier cocktails for the ladies. The punters lapped it up, Robertson became a millionaire and developed an accent to match the superficial refinement of his 'hay clarse' drinking establishments. Newcastle's transformation into a party city had begun. By 1982 the first signs of the Quayside redevelopment were beginning to show, and it was announced that the Baltic was closing down for redevelopment. On the final night we all got pissed and drank Mackeson stout, because everything else had run out. It was the end of an era.

CHAPTER FIVE

Lunch in the Penthouse Suite

Viz's reputation continued to spread, largely through word of mouth but also through the music press. We'd had entirely positive reviews in *Zig Zag*, *Sounds* and the *NME*, not to mention a two-page spread in the *Loughborough Student*. *Jamming*, a short-lived music magazine of the day, described the comic as 'a fantastically irreverent load of shit'. In the twenty-two years since then I don't think anyone has described it more succinctly than that.

Fanzines also provided an important method of spreading the word. By 1982 my untidy bedroom was linked to a dozen or so other untidy bedrooms across the land via a national network of fanzine editors. Many of them would ask if they could reproduce *Viz* cartoons in their own magazines and I'd always agree on condition that they gave the comic a plug. One such editor – a teenager in Leeds called James Brown – used a couple of *Viz* cartoons without permission in his magazine, *Attack On Bzag*. I granted him retrospective permission and in return he agreed to distribute *Viz* for me in Leeds. The editor of *Real Shocks* fanzine in Kent, a bloke called Roger Radio, also produced a comic called *Cosmic Cuts*. That was about the closest thing to *Viz* anyone else seemed to be doing, and Roger soon became a regular contributor to *Viz*, specializing in lazily drawn, poor-quality, one-frame jokes. Pilot: 'Enemy plane at one o'clock!' Gunner: 'That's good. We've got half an hour to spare then,' for example.

By now the appearance of a new issue was so rare the event would be celebrated with a party. These '*Viz* Receptions' began with an afternoon soirée at a hotel in Jesmond to celebrate the launch of No. 5. By the time issue 10 was published in May 1983 the venue had switched to Dingwalls, a nightclub in Waterloo Street where I'd previously had the pleasure of watching exotic dancers from Nottingham perform during a Friday lunchtime outing from the DHSS. I'd been having trouble shifting issue 9, and with 10 being a summer issue – the students were away on holiday – only 2,500 were printed. The most notable cartoon début was perhaps Billy the Fish, albeit on a rather small scale. His first strip took up only two lines at the foot of the second last

Billy the Fish

page. I loved football adventure strips like *Roy of the Rovers*, particularly the disparity in time that always seemed to exist between the players on the field and the spectators off it. Time seemed to freeze as a shot was taken and members of the crowd would carry out lengthy conversations in the time between the ball being kicked and arriving at the goal line. The name Billy the Fish came first, a take on the *Dandy*'s Barry the Cat. It then occurred to me that if somebody was born half-man, half-fish, they would most likely be able to swim through the air and would therefore make a very good goalkeeper. There was a bit of a football theme to issue 10. Chris Waddle, a gangling youngster who had just broken into the Newcastle team, was a big fan of

Wavis O'Shave as The Hard

Arthur 2 Stroke and the Chart Commandos, and in order to promote their final record, a live LP, Waddle agreed to meet the band for a photo session at a pub in Gateshead. A few other players, including Terry McDermott, also turned up. I was the official photographer and took a couple of extra pictures, later making up my own story about Arthur 2 Stroke winning a music industry award after a penalty shoot-out.

On the back cover there was a poster of former Anti-Pop artiste Wavis O'Shave posing as The Hard, his *Tube* TV character. To get the photo Simon and I visited Wavis's house in South Shields where he lived with his mother. This was the first time I'd met him and he turned out to be a highly intelligent and articulate individual. Then he started telling us about the trouble he was having with the Greek god Pan, who had recently trotted into his living room (Pan was half-man, half-goat) through the wall next to the bay window. As Wavis explained this to us his mother came into the room with a tray of tea and biscuits. 'Mutha. Tell them aboot Pan, how he come through that waaaall,' he said. 'Yes, that's right, he did,' said his mother, who then gave us her own description of the event, followed by the question, 'Do either of you take sugar?'

Following *Anna Ford's Bum*, Wavis recorded a second album under the name *Foffo Spearjig* and a single from that was released on Eccentric Records, 'Tie Your Laces Tight', with the brilliant B-side 'You Won't Catch Me on the 503'. I spent weeks designing a cover for the album, which would have been called *Texican Raveloni*, had it ever been released. The last time I saw Wavis was in the mid-nineties. I was sitting watching TV and suddenly there he was on *Stars In Their Eyes*, calling himself Callum Jensen and doing a terrific impression of Steve Harley. Unfortunately Mario Lanza won it.

The cost of printing 2,500 copies of issue 10 was £393, or around 16p each. I could sell these to shops for around 20p, making a theoretical profit of about 4p on a cover price of 30p, but it wasn't a very healthy profit margin. Despite the fact I'd never taken a penny out of the proceeds, or paid any of the cartoonists, the comic was barely breaking even. In the autumn of 1983 my mentor, Brian from the Kard Bar, told me it was essential that I get a new issue out in time for Christmas. Realistically there was no way I could do it. I had my hands full with design work and at the rate new cartoons were being drawn a single issue was now taking six months to assemble. So Brian suggested reprinting some early back issues to satisfy growing demand and hit the Christmas market. I hastily threw together a 'best of' compilation of the first four issues and called it No. 10½. In order to beef it up a little, Brian had another idea. Why didn't we give away a free pop poster with it? He had rooms full of unsold posters dating back to the early 1970s if I was interested. Brian led me through the confusing warren of dark, dusty storerooms behind and above his shop like the Phantom of the Opera leading a captive performer to his lair. We eventually arrived in a small room full of unsold Osmond posters, crates of David Cassidy key rings and sacks of Bay City Roller scarves. Fashions were short lived in the pop world and Brian had clearly had his fingers burnt on more than one occasion. He pointed out a stack of boxes which he said were T-shirts for the hugely popular *ET* movie. Anticipating the huge demand he'd ordered them all well in advance, before the film had been released in the UK. Unfortunately he ordered all of them in medium and large sizes, not realizing *ET* was going to be a strictly under-twelves phenomenon. In another corner of the room were parcels of wall posters, some of them still unopened, featuring David Cassidy, the Bay City Rollers and the Osmonds. 'Unfortunately most of them are too big to fit inside the comic,' said Brian, 'unless you folded them somehow.' 'That's not a problem,' I said. 'We can chop them into quarters.' Quarter of a picture of the Bay City Rollers would be much funnier than the whole thing, I reckoned. So we carted the posters off to the Free Press, guillotined them, and inserted the severed remains of the seventies' pop icons into the middle of the comics.

By 1983 I was working virtually full-time as a graphic designer. I wasn't earning enough to make a living, but I was earning more than enough to get done for social security fraud. I wanted to go legitimate but couldn't see how I was going to do it. Then a customer of mine, Walter, mentioned the Enterprise Allowance Scheme. Apparently the Government paid budding entrepreneurs £40 a week, for a year, to get them off the dole and into business. Walter managed a band called The Hostages and was trying to get them signed up to the scheme as well. I looked into it and discovered that I wouldn't qualify for two reasons. Firstly, your business had to be brand new, not an existing enterprise. Secondly, your business couldn't involve anything immoral or controversial. But what the fuck. I decided to apply anyway.

At the interview I told them I was starting up a brand new graphic design business. They didn't seem in the least bit interested. In fact they didn't even ask to see the documents they'd told me to bring along, one of which was a bank statement proving that I had £1000 capital to start my business with. This was the money that had gradually been accumulating from comic sales over the years, which came to around £960, topped up with a few quid from my Post Office Savings Account. I was in and out the door in a matter of seconds. They simply rubber-stamped my application, wished me good luck and called in the next budding entrepreneur. The Enterprise Allowance Scheme was often ridiculed for being a political scam to cut the dole figures, and I suppose it was. But it did actually work, albeit on the 'throw enough shit at a wall' principle. Fortunately I was one of the shits that stuck.

So I finally signed off the dole and became self-employed in November 1983. Two months earlier I'd written to another BBC yoof programme in response to an ad I'd seen on TV. The producers of a show called *Sparks* said they wanted to hear from any 'bright young sparks' who were involved in setting up their own small enterprises. *Viz* seemed like an ideal candidate for the show and a couple of weeks later a producer called Tony Matthews came up to Newcastle and met myself, Jim and Simon. He liked what he saw and the following week he wrote offering us a slot on the show. Tony said he was keen to bring some of the characters to life on TV, either by animation or using actors. He was also keen for us to have a big input into the programme. We weren't supposed to be making the programme this time, but what Tony did was effectively give us a free hand to make our own TV commercial. Under the directorship of a girl called Alex Laird, who I think had a slightly bent nose, our little film was shot on location in Newcastle in late 1983. Jim, Simon and I were filmed drawing cartoons, talking about the characters and working at the Free Press. Simon's acting talents came to the fore as he posed as Charlie Pontoon, our right-wing newspaper columnist, and the BBC even allowed us to hire a proper actor to play Roger Mellie. We picked a bloke called Charles Pemberton out of an actors' sample book and the BBC Costume Department knocked up a black-and-white stripy jacket for him to wear. *Sparks* was a BBC Education programme, so our film had to be educational in some way, so I wrote a set of accompanying notes giving advice to any viewers who wanted to set up their own magazine.

Sparks was broadcast on 3 April 1984 at 7.05 p.m. on BBC2, and our little piece came across very well. Great credit must go to Tony Matthews and Alex Laird for capturing the spirit of the comic so well on the TV screen. Not everyone approved of the programme though. The following written complaint was received by the BBC the day after *Sparks* was broadcast.

Tonbridge,
Kent
3rd April 1984

Sirs

BBC2 programme at 7.05pm today (*Sparks*) I switched on to BBC2 just after 7 p.m. this evening to be greeted with absolute filth. What made me livid was that I could well have had my two grandchildren with me and they could easily have been tuned-in to that farrago of gutter language, etc. That apart, I myself have no wish whatsoever to see or hear such muck, and for the life of me cannot understand what sort of people now run the BBC. I noted who directed and produced this programme and that three females were also concerned with it as Production Assistants or similar. What delightful people they must all be …

Neither I, nor my wife, nor many of our friends, have any wish to see the sort of filth that *Sparks* was full of, and it's high time your organization cleansed itself of them. No wonder our times are what they are; you bear a heavy burden of guilt, but I suppose it doesn't really bother you.

R. H. Underwood

The programme made a more positive impression elsewhere, and while the BBC were fielding complaints I was taking a call from Bob Paynter of IPC Magazines. IPC were Britain's biggest and best-known magazine publisher. Paynter said he'd watched the *Sparks* programme the night before and was intrigued. He wondered if he might see some samples of our magazine. I posted off copies of issues 9 and 10 and was on tenterhooks for the next few days wondering what his reactions would be. Eventually he rang back. How did the three of us fancy coming down to London to have lunch with his board of directors?

Paynter sent me a cheque for £276. At first I thought he wanted me to buy a car and drive down, but when I rang him he explained that this money was to cover the cost of three first-class rail fares. 'There's plenty more where that came from,' he said in all seriousness. When the cheque arrived I sat and admired it for some time, then I used it to buy three saver return tickets. We pocketed the change, which came to about £60 each – the first money any of us had ever made out of *Viz*. We went down to London on 26 April 1984. At the time the *Sun* was serializing the kiss-and-tell memoirs of snooker player Tony 'the Lancashire hot-pot' Knowles. Jim, Simon and I rarely wrote anything together but I vividly recall writing a spoof of that on the train journey down. When we got to London we caught a tube to somewhere near the river and then walked the rest of the way, across a bridge, with me plotting our route on an *A to Z*. You couldn't miss King's Reach Tower. It was, and hopefully still is, a massive building dominating the south side of the Thames. This was the prestigious headquarters of the International Publishing Corporation. We announced our arrival at reception and a few moments later Bob Paynter came down to greet us. His overall attire – his smart green blazer in particular – made him look as if he'd just broken off from an important lawn bowls match to meet us. Paynter was in his fifties, with a greying, bouffant hairdo, and he bore an uncanny resemblance to Danny La Rue. He ushered us into a lift and told us we were going up to the Penthouse Suite to meet 'the board'.

When the doors opened we stepped cautiously out into a vast dining suite where a host of men in suits were mingling and sipping drinks. It was like walking into a dinner party. We all looked a right state in our jeans, trainers and T-shirts. A particularly well-dressed man came towards me smiling and I went to shake his hand. He was the waiter. I ordered a glass of orange. Then I was introduced to our host, John Sanders, the Managing Director of IPC's Youth Group. Sanders was a funny-looking bloke, a cross between Walter Matthau and Wilfrid Brambell, with what appeared to be a very expensive old lady's wig and a facial expression that made him look like he was permanently tasting soy sauce for the very first time.

The view from the top of King's Reach Tower was pretty impressive, due largely to the height of the building and the size of the windows. Sanders took me to one side and pointed out a selection of tiny little buildings below – London Weekend Television, the National Theatre, Waterloo Station and, finally, the headquarters of the International Monetary Fund. 'Do you know much about the IMF?' he asked with the enthusiasm of a man who clearly did and wanted desperately to tell someone about it. A few moments later I was saved from our one-way conversation about international monetary policy by a call to the dinner table. The table itself must have been at least six feet wide and three times as long. On one side, with our backs to the window, sat the three of us. Lined up all the way along the other side were 'the board', about eight of them in all. At this point Sanders, who sat in the centre facing me, formally introduced his colleagues. I can't remember any of their names but for each one he gave a boastful, and to me entirely baffling, summary of their CV, punctuated by poignant pauses during which he smiled and we were clearly supposed to look impressed.

For lunch we had shepherd's pie and a barrage of questions. Sanders was feeling us out, gauging our responses to various probes. 'I don't like the name *Viz*,' he said at one point, wiping mince from the side of his mouth with a serviette. He may only have been in his fifties, but he ate like a ninety-four-year-old. I didn't rise to the bait. After the main course Sanders got down to business. IPC were interested in the idea of a comedy magazine for students – a younger version of *Private Eye*, as he described it. They hadn't got very far with the idea themselves and when they saw *Viz* on the telly they wondered whether we might be the people to produce it for them. They were proposing a fortnightly publication date and a twenty-four-page magazine, produced by us from a studio in Newcastle. But first of all they wanted to put us to the test. Sanders offered to pay £1,500 for a dummy issue that would have to be ready by 31 May. We agreed. Once they saw the dummy they would then decide whether or not to proceed with the plan.

After the meeting Bob Paynter gave us a brief tour of the *Buster* comic studio where we marvelled at some of the artwork. We asked whether it was true that they regularly reused old artwork and simply updated the wording. Our evidence for this was that we often spotted ancient vehicles in *Buster* cartoons – vintage lorries, cars and motorbikes. Bob told us they didn't, all their cartoons were new, and the antique vehicles were the work of an eighty-year-old comic artist who still worked for them and didn't get out the house very much these days. After our tour we headed out into the fresh air and back across the river. It was all a bit much to take in and we wandered across Waterloo Bridge, through Trafalgar Square and along the Mall in virtual silence before stopping for a rest in St James's Park. I sensed a tiny bit of tension in the air and eventually Jim broke a longish silence with a question. 'What are we going to do with the £1,500?' Simon seconded it. I remember being furious and trying not to show it. There was me thinking, 'How the fuck am I going to produce a twenty-four-page magazine in just one month when it currently takes six months to produce a single issue of *Viz*?', and all they were thinking about was divvying up the money. I said I would use the £1,500 to finance production

Jim Brownlow

of the dummy, paying for materials, proper typesetting and darkroom work. Then whatever was left over we could split equally between the three of us. I could quite reasonably have demanded more as I'd be the one putting the dummy together and providing most of the cartoons, but a three-way split kept everyone happy. And, besides, I didn't give a shit about the money. It was the daunting prospect of the dummy proving successful that was worrying me. Doing one comic by 31 May was going to require a miracle. Repeating the trick every fortnight from then on would be absolutely impossible.

I didn't much trust IPC, so when I got home I wrote to John Sanders asking him to confirm his offer in writing. Then I wrote again asking specifically about the copyright situation. I wanted his assurance that £1,500 was only paying for an option to buy this comic, and if they turned it down they'd have no rights to keep or use any of the material. The dummy I put together was a hotchpotch of the best of *Viz* to date, including a lot of material from issue 11 which had just gone to press. I redesigned old news features, had them properly typeset (in the comic I just typed the text columns on a typewriter) and obtained proper photographs to go with them from IPC's photo library. I put in what I thought were the best of our cartoons, like Mr Logic, Big Vern and Paul Whicker, and I redrew the first episode of Billy the Fish and stretched it out to cover two pages instead of two lines. I realized I would have to spread material pretty bloody thin if *Viz* was ever going to be a fortnightly. At our meeting John Sanders had hinted that the political content would need to be increased so I made up a new story about a lorry driver who'd lost a consignment of cruise missiles as a token gesture not quite in that direction. I also commissioned a strip from Mick Kidd of Biff, later of *Guardian* fame, who had been a *Viz* distributor, as opposed to contributor, in London at the time.

After sending the dummy off on time I was expecting a prompt, definitive response from IPC, but weeks passed and I heard nothing. We got our money, but no news. Then Bob Paynter rang up and asked for some additional material. He was making a few slight changes and wondered if he could have something a wee bit more political perhaps. Then in late July I got a shock when he sent me a copy of what he called 'the actual dummy'. This was what he proposed to put before the board of directors. I was flabbergasted. The comic had been so much altered it was barely recognizable as our work. They'd truncated most of our cartoons, altered titles, changed punchlines and replaced entire chunks of the magazine with crap they'd written themselves. Some of the alterations were ridiculous. They'd changed the name *Viz Comic* to *Viz Funnies*. A cartoon called Frank the Princess had been altered to make the subject, Frank, gay. With a few subtle changes they'd turned it from a surreal fairy story into homophobic garbage. Sid the Sexist's name had been changed to Sid the Smooth-talker. And in Mr Logic the word 'penis' had been replaced by 'donger'. For fuck's sake! They'd missed the entire point. Mr Logic wouldn't say donger. He would say *penis*.

I wrote to John Sanders and highlighted thirty or so similar instances of them ruining jokes. I also pointed out that their treatment had robbed the magazine of an important but difficult to define quality, the fact that the joke was *on us*. In our hopeless prizes, botched competitions, rubbish letters and pitiful news features, *Viz* was taking the piss out of itself more than other people. In their treatment of the dummy IPC had done away with this entirely.

For the next few months we continued to send additional material to London for a new and definitive version of the dummy, but I was getting more and more frustrated at their inability to know a good thing when they saw it and their insistence on tinkering about with everything. It gradually dawned on me that I could never work with these people. While a final decision was being awaited I had to go to London again. The Hostages, the band that my mate Walter had got onto the Enterprise Allowance Scheme, had just been signed up by EMI. They'd been underpaying me for posters for ages and now they wanted to make it up by asking me to design the sleeve for their first hit single. Walter took me to EMI's head offices in Manchester Square to be given a design brief by the executive in charge. His brief was very simple – I wasn't doing the sleeve. Instead he wanted me to fuck off, and some mate of his with an airbrush would be doing the sleeve instead. It wasn't the most positive outcome I'd ever had from a meeting, but my visit to Manchester Square did prove useful for another reason. On our way into the EMI offices we witnessed a remarkable scene as the band Tight Fit tried unsuccessfully to gain admission at the front door. They'd had a couple of hits a few years earlier, but apparently their credit was no longer good. There they were, dressed in exotic black leather outfits, screaming at the doorman. 'Don't you know who we are? We're Tight Fit!' But he wouldn't let them in. I was able to use this story as an amusing music industry anecdote for several years to come ... until the day I met Pete Waterman. But more of that later.

By October 1984 I still hadn't been given a decision by IPC so I wrote to John Sanders with an ultimatum. They could either accept the dummy or give us our artwork back. On 22 November he replied:

Dear Chris

I am sorry I have not been in touch. This is not waywardness; I have been giving a great deal of thought to *Viz* and discussing it here with many people.

Very sadly, and somewhat against my own judgement, I have to tell you that we cannot publish *Viz*. It is thought that when it is toned-down sufficiently to satisfy IPC, what's left would not be successful enough for the kind of profit-making that we need. This is because we are a big company in the mass circulation market and, put basically, *Viz* is not sufficiently mass circulation.

I still think it has possibilities and I hope you make a go of it yourselves. I believe it has great potential and you should not regard this letter as the end of the road. Bob Paynter feels he has called upon your services to a greater degree than the value of the cheque we have already sent you, and he will therefore be sending you an additional cheque for £500.

I am sorry about this decision, and I wish you lots of luck in the future.

Kind regards

John R. Sanders
Managing Director
IPC Youth Group

In one sense he was perfectly right. When *Viz* was toned down to suit suit Sanders's superiors on the IPC board it wasn't funny. But in another sense he was spectacularly wrong. *Viz* could be mass circulation. It was just a question of finding a publisher with the bottle to take it on.

CHAPTER SIX

Four-Letter Comic on Public Cash

After the IPC rejection Bob Paynter called me up to say goodbye and good luck. 'I hear Virgin are in the market for a comedy magazine,' he said. 'Why not send a copy to Richard Branson?' After the trials and disappointments of the last six months I wasn't in any hurry to contact another publisher. In any case, my first year of self-employment was now up and I was doing very nicely on my own. My accountant announced that I'd made a net profit of £4,448 for the year ending 31 November 1984. He didn't seem impressed at all but I was positively delighted.

Issue 12 finally emerged just in time for Christmas 1984. Inside was a new strip called Johnny Fartpants that had originally been intended for IPC. There was also a début for Felix and his Amazing Underpants, and another newcomer called Victor and his Boa Constrictor. This brand-new cartoon was the work of a brand-new contributor, Graham Dury.

Graham hailed from Nottingham but was working as a postgraduate botanical research scientist at Leicester University. As far as I could gather his work involved messing about with the genetics of potted plants to make them look more attractive on shop shelves. He'd found out about *Viz* via his girlfriend Karen, a student at Newcastle Polytechnic. As well as a scientist meddling with things I didn't understand, Graham was a keen cartoonist, and he rang me, offering to come up to Newcastle and show me some of his drawings. Terrified at the prospect of having to pass judgement on someone else's work I made sure Simon was in the bedroom to give me moral support when Graham called. Graham arrived wearing a South American poncho, a large sombrero hat and cowboy boots. His clothes, together with waist-length brown hair and an overly generous moustache, made him look a bit like a young Gerry Garcia. The portfolio he brought with him displayed his considerable talents as a cartoonist – and also a fondness for drawing cowboy boots – but contained no cartoon strips. Just doodles. We suggested he go away and try drawing some finished strips and as he left we gave him one valuable piece of advice. If at all possible the names of the cartoon characters should rhyme. We were both impressed with Graham. Not by his drawings, or his Mexican attire, but by his personality. He seemed a really nice bloke and we'd got on with him easily. A short while later, sticking rigidly to our advice, Graham came up with Victor and his Boa Constrictor. I was a little concerned about the size of Victor's nose and the appearance of cowboy boots in the strip, but I used it anyway. But as I was gaining one contributor I was gradually losing another. By now I was seeing very little of Jim. He was moving in different social circles and had started working for a friend as a builder. His contributions had always been a bit sporadic but now the supply had virtually dried up. Issue 12 was the first comic not to feature any of Jim's material.

The print run was now up to 5000 and sales in Newcastle were going berserk thanks partly to a useful piece of publicity in the local press. I'd recently designed a poster for a Red Cross charity event and mentioned to the customer, a John Dougray, that I'd been on the Enterprise Allowance Scheme. 'Really? How's business?' he asked enthusiastically. It turned out Mr Dougray worked for the Central Office of Information, the

Government's PR agency, and his eyes lit up when he heard that my business was still solvent at the end of the year. He asked if I'd mind doing a few press interviews to give the scheme a bit of positive publicity. 'We're always on the lookout for success stories,' he said. Alas, this wasn't going to be quite the success story he'd envisaged. I agreed to the interviews and all the local papers sent reporters round to talk to me. It wasn't long till one of the hacks got a whiff of a bigger bone than the one he'd been thrown. He twigged that I'd been publishing *Viz*, a scandalous magazine, while on the Government scheme. The following day the *Newcastle Evening Chronicle* exposed this shocking state of affairs under the banner headline 'FOUR-LETTER COMIC ON PUBLIC CASH'. The story snowballed from there, with an avalanche of press enquiries the following day and stories on the local TV news. All this bad publicity did me no harm whatsoever. In fact I received orders for 960 comics the day after the story broke. Unfortunately the outcome wasn't so cheery for Mr Dougray. Not only did the COI end up with egg on their faces, but his Red Cross fund-raising event was cancelled due to a lack of ticket sales.

By now the distribution side of the magazine was becoming too much for me to handle on my own. The Kard Bar were ordering 1000 copies of every issue, and selling them. Virgin Records sold over 1000 copies of issue 11. HMV were selling over 500 copies, and a tiny little comic collectors' shop in Newcastle called Timeslip was selling 200. Pubs where I knew the landlords had started stocking it too: the Trent House, the Strawberry, the Egypt Cottage and the Barley Mow. Simon occasionally helped out with deliveries but he'd moved out of Lily Crescent by now and wasn't around most of the time. Around Christmas 1985 I went into Virgin Records in Eldon Square to collect money from comic sales, and left with a bag containing £400 in cash. I remember thinking to myself, if one Virgin shop can sell this many comics, imagine what it would be like if every Virgin shop stocked it! There must be thirty or forty

of them around the country. So on 7 January 1985 I took Bob
Paynter's advice and wrote a letter to Richard Branson.

I knew that Branson must get shedloads of letters every day,
each one of them trying to flog him some half-baked business
idea or another. I'd be lucky if he got to the end of my first
paragraph without throwing it in the bin. So I gave the letter my
very best shot, and started by getting the date wrong:

4th January 1984

Dear Mr Branson

I am 24 and I make a living publishing a magazine called
Viz. The magazine has been around since 1979 and the
circulation is at present 7,100 copies. Most copies sell in
Newcastle as I have not been able to devote much time
to getting distribution elsewhere. However several
hundred copies go to London, Edinburgh and other cities
where the comic is becoming popular, slowly but surely.
Part of the reason I am writing to you is that Virgin
Records store in Eldon Square, Newcastle, regularly sells
over 1000 copies of each issue at a rate of over 30 copies
per day.

Viz has received very good reviews in the national
music press and elsewhere (see enclosed cuttings) and we
have featured on national TV programmes twice. 'We'
being myself, my brother Simon, a contributor and helper,
and a handful of other contributors.

As a result of one of our TV appearances we were
contacted by IPC magazines, the international publishing
company of some repute. They displayed an interest in
publishing *Viz* fortnightly and were confident, as we were,
that we could achieve a mass circulation. We spent several
months producing prototypes and dummy magazines for
them. They eventually concluded that our original
dummy, a slight variation on our existing product, was
funny enough, but they dare not publish it. They also

found that, once toned down, it was no longer as funny. So in December they finally decided not to publish *Viz*. IPC have for some time been aiming to fill a perceived gap in the market by publishing a humour magazine for 16 year olds and upwards. While dealing with them I was shown their efforts to date. I am confident that, with their reluctance to publish anything they consider slightly risqué, they will never be able to win that market. However I am now more confident than ever that *Viz* could, in some form, be a success nationally.

To date every issue has sold out completely, and the circulation has increased with every issue. However, there is a limit to how far we can take it ourselves. Your reputation as an imaginative businessperson goes before you, and I hope you don't mind me writing this letter, if only to let you know *Viz* exists. Someone close to IPC suggested that you may be considering the idea of publishing a national magazine with the same audience as ours. If this is the case, and you think we may be of any help to you, we would be only too willing to discuss the matter, at a length of your choice.

If the subject of *Viz* inspires you in any way we would be glad to hear from you. I am convinced that the comic has a great deal of potential. I hope I haven't wasted too much of your time with this unsolicited blast on our own trumpet, and I trust that the enclosed copies of our magazine may be of interest.

All the best

Chris Donald

I needn't have worried how Branson would react. He never even saw the letter or the comics that I'd enclosed. The package was redirected to Virgin Books, the publishing arm of Branson's empire, where it landed on the desk of a man called John Brown.

As their name suggested, Virgin Books were in the business of publishing books, not magazines. Shitty books to be precise. They specialized in mass-market paperbacks about pop stars, books by chubby, camp TV astrologers and stocking-filler comedy books like *How to Be a Complete Bastard*. An awful lot of shit must have rained down on John Brown's desk too, so grabbing his attention wasn't going to be much easier.

As fate would have it John Brown had been ill on 20 May 1984. Instead of going to work as usual, he'd stayed at home and watched TV. At 1.25 p.m. on BBC2 he had stumbled upon a repeat of our *Sparks* programme. Like Bob Paynter at IPC, John Brown had been impressed by what he saw and had made a mental note to investigate further. Unlike Bob Paynter at IPC, by the following day John had forgotten the name of the magazine and so he never got round to doing anything about it. But he remembered the name, and the TV programme, when my letter came to the top of his in-tray.

John rang me straight away and arranged to come and see me. He said he'd be flying up on Wednesday 30 January and I should expect him at about 1.00 p.m. At about 1.00 p.m. I got a phone call from his secretary in London saying John would be slightly late. Being a southern media type he'd assumed that Teesside airport must be somewhere near Newcastle, as both were in 'the North', so he'd got off his plane, hopped into a taxi and asked to be taken to Lily Crescent, Newcastle. The taxi driver had to explain that Newcastle was forty miles away and took John to Middlesbrough railway station for an onward train to Newcastle, followed by another taxi ride to our door.

I watched with interest as John Brown got out of his taxi and strolled up the path. He looked nothing like the people we'd met at IPC. He was youngish, with a slightly flouncy haircut, and dressed in toff/casual, with jeans, expensive-looking brown leather shoes and a slightly crumpled Black Watch tartan jacket. He was carrying a very trendy-looking aluminium briefcase. Simon and I took John to lunch at Willow Teas, a small café nearby, where he launched into a barrage of questions. Often surprisingly forward and impertinent with his enquiries, he'd ask you one thing and as you started to reply he'd interrupt you by asking something else. It was relentless. I later learned that this was a tactic he regularly employed to prevent *you* from asking *him* anything. Another thing I noticed at our first meeting was that John tends to spit when he's eating and I made a mental note that day never to sit directly in front of him in a restaurant again.

After lunch we went back to the bedroom where John bombarded me with more questions about the magazine. Not about the contents, which he clearly liked, but about the business side. How much did it cost to print? How many pages? How much did it sell for? What was the wholesale price? What were the production costs of each issue? He seemed surprised by my answer to this last question. I said the production costs were nothing. It was true. I'd never balanced any production costs against sales. And none of the contributors had ever been paid a penny. If they had been the comic wouldn't have been viable. John seemed particularly excited by the fact that everything had been done on a shoestring. He kept on asking more questions, and with each answer I gave he began tapping away on a tiny Virgin-branded pocket calculator. Eventually he left, saying he'd have to discuss *Viz* with his co-director, and he'd be back in touch as soon as possible. He left his little calculator behind.

While I was waiting to hear back from John Brown I got a phone call from Mark Radcliffe, a young producer at BBC Radio 1. *Viz*'s reputation had by now permeated the walls of Broadcasting House and he wondered if we were available to be interviewed on their *Saturday Live* programme on 26 January. Jim, Simon and myself travelled down by train and on arrival at Broadcasting House found ourselves sitting in the company of Robert Plant. Plant got up at one point and asked directions to the lavatory. 'Off to drop a *Big Log* are you, Robert?' shouted Simon, a trifle too loud. After our interview we got a train

straight back to Newcastle and I was in the pub playing pool by
8.30 p.m.

The Trent House was now my regular, and it was here late in
1984 that I met an Irish girl called Dolores. We were introduced
by an old friend of mine from the Baltic days, an actress, artist
and sometime singer called Soo Sidall. Dolores had recently
come over from Ireland to work as a nanny and she'd met Soo,

Dolores

a single parent, at a local playgroup. Soo took Dolores under her
wing and offered to show her around the town and introduce
her to a few friends. She didn't specifically offer to find her a
husband, but in the event she did.

My opening line to Dolores was, 'I bet you were born in the
same street as Alex Higgins.' I reckoned their accents were
exactly the same. 'Alex Higgins is from *Northern* Ireland,' she
said. 'I'm from Galway, in the Republic.' I was only 150 miles
out. I met Dolores again at a New Year's Eve house party at the
end of 1984. She was sitting on the stairs dressed in a flouncy,
1950s party dress, her eyes sparkling like Christmas tree lights.
She seemed to be the only person in the house who'd made an
effort to dress up for the occasion. We sat and talked all night.
After that she started coming to the Trent House and often ended
up having to watch me play pool all evening. She must have had

some riveting nights. Then at Easter 1985 Dolores and match-maker Soo persuaded me to take a week off work and we booked a small holiday cottage in a village called Allendale in south Northumberland. I had a lot of work to finish first so I arrived a couple of days late, and Soo had to leave early for some reason. That left me and Dolores alone together in a cosy country cottage. On that, our first night together, I cooked a romantic meal of Bird's Eye chicken pie and Smash mashed potato. And then, after a couple of bottles of wine and a compre-hensive crawl around the village's five pubs, we staggered up the stairs to bed. I staggered up the stairs of that cottage a boy, but when I awoke with a headache the next morning, I was a man. Again.

My other new relationship, with John Brown from Virgin Books, was looking equally promising. He eventually got back to me on the evening of 18 February with the good news that Virgin wanted to publish *Viz*. John outlined his proposed deal over the phone. I would put the comic together as usual and deliver the artwork to the printer. Virgin would handle all the printing, sales and distribution, and pay a royalty for every comic sold. I scribbled down the bones of the offer and sat up for most of that night trying to work out whether or not it would be viable. At the time *Viz* was selling over 5000 copies. If all went well perhaps we could sell 40,000 eventually, 1000 for every Virgin store. Then just for a laugh I did another calculation based on the *NME*'s sales figure of around 100,000. That was the dream scenario.

I told John to make the contract out in mine and Simon's names jointly, and when it arrived in the post we both took it to a solicitor to get his comments. Richard Hart-Jackson had been recommended to me because he specialized in publishing. Music publishing as it happened, not comics, but it seemed close enough. In the event his advice proved invaluable. One crucial suggestion he made was that royalties should be paid on every comic that Virgin *printed*, not every comic they sold. This 'mechanical' royalty was much easier to account for, and of course it meant that we'd get more money. But the single most important piece of advice he gave me was this: 'If you sign this contract you and the publisher are entering a three-legged race,' he said. 'You cannot afford to fall out.' Negotiations with Virgin dragged on for a little while. One problem was the frequency. They wanted *Viz* to be monthly, and I didn't think I could achieve that. Certainly not to begin with. We eventually agreed on bi-monthly, once every two months, with the aim of increasing this to monthly as soon as possible. Before signing the contract I asked John if we could come down and take a look around the Virgin Books offices.

Virgin's squat, bunker-like single-storey building at Portobello Dock, alongside the Paddington branch of the Grand Union Canal, was in complete contrast to IPC's sky-scraping headquarters overlooking the Thames. It felt as if we were going to meet a lock-keeper, not a publisher, as Simon and I negotiated the tricky path to the front door. John was in a meeting so we waited patiently outside his office. When the door opened John briefly introduced us to his previous visitor, Tony Parsons, who was just leaving. Then John showed us around and introduced us to Bev, his secretary, and Mike, his young production manager. We looked around the studio where all Virgin's books were produced and I couldn't help noticing how tidy it was. There didn't seem to be a scrap of litter anywhere. It was as if these people never did any work.

We signed the contract in July 1985 and it was agreed that the first Virgin comic, issue 13, would be published in August. To meet the deadlines I knew I'd have to be a full-time magazine editor from now on, so I had the pleasant task of going round all my graphic design customers and telling them to stick their last-minute, penny-pinching jobs up their arses. During negotiations with Virgin I'd published one last comic myself, to plug the gap between issue 12 in November 1984 and 13 in August 1985. This was issue 12a, another compilation featuring edited highlights of issues 5 and 6. In order to save time I gave the job to a commercial printer, Wards of Gateshead. Sadly the Free Press had printed their last comic.

Virgin's attempts to find a new printer suffered an early setback. One large company in Birmingham flatly refused to handle it, describing the contents as immoral. If and when they did find a printer Virgin were planning to distribute the comic through the Virgin Records chain, and to the news trade via an independent distributor called Charles Harness. Getting a magazine published by Virgin into Virgin Records shops wasn't going to be too difficult, but getting a new title onto the news stands would be more of a challenge. Charlie Harness was just the man for the job, having played a pivotal role in the success of *Private Eye*. Harness had been working as a newspaper delivery van driver in the early 1960s when he'd volunteered to deliver bundles of the early *Private Eye* to shops around London. Now Charlie was about to repeat the trick with *Viz*. Not wishing to

Eric Daft

alienate the smaller shops and pubs that I'd been supplying over the years I asked John if I could continue distributing *Viz* in Newcastle, and he agreed.

Working arrangements in my bedroom underwent a few changes. Simon had recently decided to follow in my footsteps, and my mum's, by applying to join the Enterprise Allowance

Scheme as a toy-maker. Toy sales appeared to be a little sluggish so I suggested he run the distribution business in Newcastle while I continued to edit and design the magazine. Simon was ideally qualified to handle the distribution, because he had a car. I knew I could rely on Simon for perhaps two or three cartoons per issue but I was going to need a lot more contributors to fill thirty-two pages every eight weeks. Graham Dury looked a good prospect, and I enlisted the help of Mick Kidd who promised me one page of Biff cartoons per issue. Then I rather hopefully returned to the classified section of *Private Eye* with the following ad:

BUM RATES paid by big magazine for funny cartoons, etc. Cartoonists, writers contact Dept P, 16 Lily Crescent, Newcastle, NE2 2SP for details.

I hoped this would appeal to someone on the right wavelength, and sure enough it did. I got one reply, from a fine art student at Aberystwyth University. His name was Simon Thorp and he wrote, extremely politely, asking for more details. I sent him a copy of issue 12 and by return he sent me a wonderfully stupid one-line cartoon called Eric Daft which went straight into the first Virgin comic. The cover of issue 13 announced 'New Improved *Viz*, with added Toilet Humour', and alongside Eric Daft it contained the début of Simon's Bottom Inspectors and a photo-story entitled 'Too Young to Love'. This was about a young couple who defied their parents by running away to London. In the capital their dreams were shattered when they became exposed to the sordid world of sex and drugs. But the story had a happy ending when the young lovers became disillusioned and returned home to their loving parents. The principal 'joke' was that the couple in the story were aged three and four.

By now we were using a professional snapper, a friend called Colin Davison, and I'd carefully scripted and storyboarded the whole thing. The young couple were played by toddlers called Ian and Amber. For my money it was the best photo-story we ever did, but an opportunist reporter from the *Sunday Mirror* took exception to it. In one frame, during their nightmare in London a stranger with an ice cream tray – played by Andy Pop – approached the children. 'Hi kids. I'm pushing drugs. Wanna buy a bottle of heroin?' he asks. This was intended to parody the media's ignorance of drugs and drug culture, and in the context of the story it was totally innocuous. But taken entirely out of context it could of course be perceived as a sick joke in which young children were being offered drugs, and Lew Baxter of the *Sunday Mirror* wasn't going to miss an opportunity like that. On 15 September, as a part of their ongoing 'Drugwatch' campaign, Baxter's story appeared condemning the comic. 'HEROIN COMIC BAN', in 72 point type, was their initial comment, with the choice subheading, 'We get "idiotic" mag pulled off the shelves'.

Being pulled off by the *Sunday Mirror* was not a pleasant experience. 'Millionaire Richard Branson's Virgin Record company has called off plans to sell a comic treating heroin-pushing as a joke,' wrote Baxter. 'Copies were withdrawn from stores throughout Britain after the *Sunday Mirror* told the company about the furious reaction by drugs experts and police anti-heroin squads.' Mr Baxter had of course provoked these furious reactions himself by ringing the police and drugs experts and quoting them excerpts from our story. All in a day's work for a tabloid journalist. Superintendent Peter Deary of the Merseyside Drugs Squad was only too happy to give him a quote, although I doubt very much whether he ever saw the comic. 'I am amazed at the irresponsible and idiotic attitude of the publishers,' said he righteously. In a panic I rang John Brown to see if it was true. Apparently it was. Virgin had reacted swiftly to quell the potential bad publicity and copies of the comic had been withdrawn from their stores. Not the best of starts for our relationship with the company.

Significantly that newspaper story did not mention the fact

that 'millionaire Richard Branson' was in fact *publishing* the comic, as opposed to simply selling it in his stores. Mr Baxter could have had a field day if he'd bothered to do some research. John and I had decided to keep Virgin's involvement low-key and not mention their name anywhere in the magazine. But despite this secretive approach inevitable allegations that *Viz* had 'sold out' began to emerge. Mark E. Smith out of The Fall was first to pipe up. '*Viz* – haven't they sold out to Virgin?' he asked during a music paper interview.

Apart from the first issue being withdrawn from sale, the transition to Virgin was going smoothly. For the time being I continued to sell the advertising, so despite the magazine being on sale in shops all over Britain the adverts were all for small businesses in Newcastle, such as the Mandala wholefood shop on Manor House Road, Jesmond, which continued to offer its organic goat's milk to a slightly bemused nationwide audience.

In October 1985 Mark Ellen, the music broadcaster and journalist who looks a little bit like Paul McCartney, came up to Newcastle to see us. Over a pub lunch he told myself and Simon that EMAP, publishers of *Smash Hits* and *Q*, were thinking of producing a comedy magazine. Would we be interested? 'You're too late,' we told him. 'We've already signed to Virgin.'

Bloody typical, I thought to myself. You wait five years for a publisher to come along, then all of a sudden three of them come at once.

CHAPTER SEVEN

Onward Virgin Soldiers

I'd never really considered moving out of the family home in Lily Crescent. The bedroom was my cosy little womb and I didn't want to leave it. And since my brothers had both left I felt a slight obligation to stay. Mum's health continued to deteriorate and health visitors came in on a daily basis to help my dad look after her. Not that I ever did anything to help. Perhaps I was just a tight bastard and didn't want to have to pay for a place of my own. But a change in Dolores's circumstances – she had been offered a better-paid, 9-to-5 nanny job without accommodation – prompted me to make the big break. When we eventually found a small flat to rent nearby I dreaded telling Dad that I was deserting. Then I came up with a compromise. I'd live in the flat but I'd continue to work in the bedroom. That way I'd still be around every day, and I could continue to pay rent for what would now be a studio. I could also get rid of the bed and make room for a few more items of office furniture.

At first producing a thirty-two-page comic every two months didn't seem too difficult. The first one wasn't anyway, because we had eight months to do it. After that it got a lot harder. John Brown suggested we work with an issue in hand, which meant having each issue finished two months in advance of the actual deadline. I told him I'd work on it, but for the next fifteen years I would be scraping material together at the very last minute and only just meeting – and in some cases missing – deadlines with never so much as a single page to spare.

Our new cartoonist Graham Dury had been sticking very closely to his brief and for each issue he was coming up with a character whose name rhymed. Tristram Banks and his Jocular Pranks, Dr Theodore Gray and his Fantastic Growth Spray, Albert Gordon the Traffic Warden, and so on. Graham tended to deliver his cartoons by hand during weekend visits to his girlfriend, and Dolores and I quickly became good friends of Graham and Karen's. Graham was quiet but extremely good company, especially when he'd had a couple of drinks. He could make me laugh uncontrollably and once did so in a crowded pub, causing me to bellow a mouthful of beer all over Karen at point-blank range. Meanwhile Aberystwyth fine art student Simon Thorp was proving to be something of a mystery. He was

Graham Dury

clearly an exceptionally talented illustrator, and with each strip he sent the drawings became more intricate and heavily inked. His earliest characters included Doctor Bolus – a mad scientist; Norbert Colon – a tight-fisted old miser; and Cockney Ken, a chirpy East Ender who was an early incarnation of Cockney Wanker. These meticulously drawn strips, etched onto the paper with scrawny nibs in excruciatingly fine detail, would arrive by post in stout cardboard tubes and were accompanied by very brief but polite little missives. For some reason I imagined Simon Thorp looking a bit like Richard Attenborough in the movie *10 Rillington Place*. I didn't for one minute think he was killing women, but I could definitely imagine him in a tank-top, buttoned-up shirt and small, round glasses.

Cockney Ken

Down in London John Brown didn't seem to be spending a great deal of time on *Viz*. His calls always came at the end of the working day and I began to get the impression that the comic was more of a pet project for him than a commercial venture for Virgin. One of the main reasons I'd been impressed with John initially was his promise to leave the editorial well alone. But as soon as he'd read issue 13 he was straight on the phone offering advice. 'I think perhaps there are too many *bottoms*,' he said, as if bottoms were something he didn't particularly like talking about. I didn't know what he meant. Apart from the Bottom Inspectors, Billy Bottom and his Zany Toilet Pranks, and of course Johnny Fartpants, and perhaps the free pair of paper underpants, and a couple of references to arses in a strip called Mr Rudewords, there were virtually no bottoms whatsoever in issue 13. After a couple of issues John expressed the opinion that my cover designs all looked a bit too similar. In response to this I decided to make issue 17, the April 1986 edition, look totally different... by coating it in crispy batter. There were no illustrations and very little text. Instead there was just a sort of golden, crispy batter coating effect, and a small label featuring the name, a bar code and 'best before' date. The resulting magazine was virtually unrecognizable and only the most determined or perceptive readers were able to spot it on the shelves. Consequently sales of that issue were disastrously low, and John kept his ideas to himself for a while after that.

In a bid to sell some advertising space to Coca-Cola or Calvin Klein instead of Ozzie's Tattoo Parlour on Byker Bridge, John appointed an ad sales agency in London. The first thing they did was ask for a *Viz* 'reader profile'. I found this infuriating. It was bloody obvious to me, and anyone with any common sense, what sort of people bought *Viz*. But the agency needed a 'socio-economic breakdown' to show to potential clients. Oh dear me, I thought. We were now entering the world of advertising.

I fucking hate advertising. In 1985 I'd had my first close encounter with an ad agency. To cut a long story as short as possible, during the mid-1980s Scottish & Newcastle breweries found that they had an over-capacity to produce beer, which was going out of fashion, and an under-capacity for making the more popular fizzy lager. Their solution was to launch a new, weak-as-piss beer called 'Newcastle Bright' which they hoped to fob off on lager drinkers by inventing a new verb and describing the beer as a 'lagered ale'. Initially they only put this dubious new drink on sale in Newcastle – it was a trial launch – and they hired the services of a top London advertising agency to try and get the city's discerning lager drinkers to swallow it.

The first mistake they made was choosing the name Newcastle Bright. If it had been me I'd have gone for something that didn't rhyme quite so comfortably with *shite*. The agency involved, Grierson Cockman Craig & Druiff, then had the wonderful idea of making the product attractive to young people by publishing a magazine to accompany its launch. *The Pack* was a one-off, pocket-sized music, fashion and humour magazine given away free to anyone brave enough to try the new 'lagered ale'. The agency hired ex-NME editor Neil Spencer to put it together and Neil asked me if I'd contribute some *Viz*-style cartoons. Neil explained in a worldly-wise sort of way that he was only doing this for the money, and if I was prepared to similarly compromise my artistic principles they'd pay me £400. I immediately accepted, instead of asking for £500 which was probably what he expected me to do. *The Pack* was launched in October 1985 and was totally hip and trendy. It contained an interview with Alexei Sayle, features on Kitchenware (a new record label recently co-founded by former HMV manager Keith Armstrong), silly clothes and some half-hearted, *Viz*-like cartoons that I'd drawn in a hurry. Whether they managed to give the magazines away I don't know, but they certainly had trouble getting shot of the beer. It became a standing joke in the Trent House. Nobody would buy the stuff and every couple of days the price was dropped until eventually a sign appeared on the pump saying 'Newcastle Shite – FREE'. 'Not even the tramps'll drink it,' said Tom the barman, shaking his head. Newcastle Bright was poured into the sewers by the kegful, and never seen again.

Ever since Brian Sandells set the ball rolling, *Viz* had developed a reputation for amusing adverts. Some people preferred the adverts to the cartoons. In the past I'd dealt with all the advertisers personally and designed every advertisement myself. But now an outside sales agency would be dealing with a booking agent who would be working for an advertising agency who would be dealing with the client, or perhaps the client's marketing department. Nowhere in this chain was there going to be anyone with an ounce of common sense, so in April 1986 I obeyed orders and carried out a readership survey in the magazine, asking all the usual questions about income, occupation, etc., and with a few jokes thrown in to try and disguise the crass, commercial object of the exercise. Based on a total of 404 replies the results suggested that 91% of our readers were male. The other 9% were female. 46% had jobs, 40% were students and 14% were unemployed. Their favourite colour was blue and their earnings, not entirely surprisingly, ranged from less than £30 a week to more than £250. 78% bought the comic in a shop, 22% subscribed. The modal age of the *Viz* reader was twenty, the mean twenty-three. 41% were aged between seventeen and twenty-one, 40% were aged twenty-two to twenty-six, and 17% were twenty-seven or over. Only 2% admitted to being under sixteen. Geographically 8% lived in Scotland, 26% in the North-East, 8% in the North-West, 7% in Yorkshire, 25% in the South-East, 8% on the South Coast, 5% in the Midlands, 3% in Anglia, 8% in the South-West and only 1% in Wales. I also took the opportunity to ask people what their favourite *Viz* features were. Johnny Fartpants topped the poll, followed closely by the letters page and then Billy the Fish. Despite not having appeared for a couple of years Jim Brownlow's Paul Whicker the Tall Vicar had already attained legendary status and came fourth. As for the least popular feature, 29% liked the comic so much they abstained from voting, but among the people who did Billy the Fish was the least appreciated. I guess this proved that some people like football and other people don't.

A few months into our contract with Virgin I asked John Brown how sales were going and was slightly disappointed with the reply. He said they'd only been printing around 10,000 copies, which wasn't nearly enough to trigger any royalties. As agreed, Virgin were paying us an advance of £1,500 per issue but the cost of producing each comic, including paying the contributors, was running at around £900. I was only offering £35 per page for cartoons but there were also the costs of typesetting, photography, graphic materials and darkroom work. Then there were the overheads. By now I'd had a phone line installed in my bedroom and there was also rent to pay. (Heating wasn't a problem because my dad never turned it on upstairs.)

By the time I'd paid Simon £45 and myself £75 per week I was struggling to break even. On issue 20 the net profit was down to £2.20 and I asked John if there was any chance of Virgin bumping up the advance. His reply was an unequivocal 'No'. At that point he claimed Virgin were actually losing money on the comic and there'd be no extra cash unless sales picked up considerably.

One of my biggest costs was phototypesetting – getting all the words for news stories and letters set into neat columns with straight edges, like what there are in this book. It was time-consuming too. I had to type everything on a manual typewriter then mark it up with lots of funny Latin words and squiggles that I'd picked up at the Free Press. Simon would then deliver these pages to Alphaset, a room full of ladies overseen by an upright, Joyce Grenfell-ish figure called Gladys. Everything I'd written was then retyped by ladies into an enormous machine and a short while later the printed columns of type would pop out the other end. This was then delivered back to me and I would check it for mistakes and the corrections would then be returned to Gladys whose ladies would put them right and print the whole thing out again. It would have been much quicker if they'd simply not made any mistakes in the first place, but they insisted on making at least a couple every time. I think it was something to do with union rules. Once the corrected version came back to me I'd cut out the columns of text with scissors and stick them down onto a page using the noxious mixture of rubber and petrol known in the design industry as Cow Gum. Basically Cow Gum was a translucent treacle which, as it dried, turned into snot, binding paper surfaces together. Its fumes were overpowering, and quite invigorating too. An added complication to this laborious process was the fact that I didn't dare send Gladys any text containing rude words. If, for example, a story included the word 'fuck' I would type it as 'buck', then I'd tag a word onto the end of the paragraph, like 'fudge'. When I got the typesetting back I'd carefully cut the letters 'fu' out from the 'fudge' and glue them down on top of the 'bu' in 'buck', to make 'fuck'. It was a laborious process but well worth it as we couldn't possibly have risked offending Gladys or any of the ladies who worked for her.

I was still desperate to find new cartoonists to help fill the pages. We got a lot of stuff sent in by would-be contributors but most of it was hopelessly crude and vulgar. Every now and then there was the odd piece that showed promise, and I would use it. In June 1986 I tried out no fewer than eleven new contributors in the same issue, No. 18. One of them was a bloke called Arthur Matthews who'd sent in a couple of items from Ireland. These included an instructive article about how to play golf in the event of a nuclear war. I paid him £40. Young Arthur Matthews invested that money wisely. He bought himself a rusty old typewriter and, ten years later, his investment paid off when he co-wrote the brilliant *Father Ted* television series. Strange to think that if I hadn't spotted Arthur's great comic potential all those years ago and sent him that very generous fee, *Father Ted* would perhaps, quite possibly, never have been written.

The same issue also marked the first appearance of *Viz* merchandise. This was the beginning of a trickle that would eventually turn into a torrent of tu'penny ha'penny tat. Two T-shirts were what started it all – one a picture of Johnny Fartpants with the caption 'pump power', and the other an advert for the Gnatwest Bank:

> Left school?
> No job?
> No money?
>
> Then fuck off.
>
> Gnatwest. The frank bank.

This mail order business was initially carried out from my former bedroom in Newcastle. Virgin had no intention of doing any elbow work in London so Dolores undertook the task, using my former wardrobe in the corner as a makeshift stock room. As orders increased she'd make frequent visits to the local sub-post office carrying bundles of parcels ready for despatch. One day she came back incensed after being accused by the sub-postmistress of buying too many stamps. 'I need the stamps for my regular customers,' the old cow behind the counter had told her. Regular fucking customers!? I'd been posting bundles of comics at that post office for the last six years. For five years before that I'd worked there as a paperboy. I'd had a Post Office Savings Account there since 1974, and I'd also gone there to cash every single giro I'd ever received. But that didn't make us 'regular customers'. To be a 'regular' customer you had to be a dotty old pensioner with a shopping trolley and a silly hat, and instead of troubling the postmistress to supply you with stamps you had to jibber on at her about the fucking weather for ten minutes in a painfully slow build-up to eventually locating your pension book and claiming your money. It was while gritting my teeth in the queue at the Holly Avenue West sub-Post Office that the cartoon character Mrs Brady Old Lady gradually evolved.

Since dumping us, IPC's Youth Group had concentrated their efforts on another project, called *Oink. Oink* was basically a pork-based, pun-filled product, a bawdy version of a traditional kids' comic aimed at the largely theoretical group of kids who were too old for the *Beano* and not old enough for *Viz*. It was being produced by a cell of cartoonists similar to ourselves, operating in Manchester. These included Mark Rodgers, Pat Gallagher and Tony Husband. A fourth member of their team was an unlikely cartoonist in the form of ex-Fall musician Marc Riley. He would later become an equally unlikely Radio 1 DJ. *Oink* was launched in May 1986 and Bob Paynter invited me to the launch party at a small hotel in a well-heeled suburb of Manchester. Myself, Dolores, our photographer friend Colin and his then girlfriend Christine travelled down to the party where I was surprised to meet up with former Leeds fanzine editor James Brown who was by now writing for the *NME*.

Due to a certain amount of provincial rivalry, and perhaps the fact that IPC had passed *Viz* over, I felt a strong sense of competition with our *Oink* counterparts. As the night wore on and the free drinks flowed, this rivalry began to manifest itself in the form of comic-style mischief. There was something 'soft' about *Oink* having a 'posh' party. They'd even invited their mums. Tony Husband and his wife Carol had organized the bash, and Tony's proud mother had made a special cake to celebrate her son's big day. Towards the end of the night, while speeches were being made in an adjoining area, it occurred to us how funny it would be if we kidnapped the cake. It was looking rather vulnerable as it sat unattended on a table at the top of the room. A few staff and a handful of guests were milling around in the vicinity and I was still working on a kidnap plan when James Brown and Dolores suddenly sprang into action. In the blink of an eye, and with breathtaking aplomb, James strolled forward and cast a small tablecloth over it, like a matador flicking his cape across a bull's horns. Then he lifted it and whisked it sideways in a short rugby pass to Dolores who caught it and glided quickly out of the room with the tidy bundle tucked beneath her arm. It was all over in seconds and nobody saw a thing.

We left the party as discreetly as we could and collected the cake from its temporary hiding place in the hotel garden. Then we carried it to a neighbouring hotel where four of us were staying. It was there, in a dingy basement bedroom, that our initially good-humoured kidnapping plan went tragically awry. It was late, we'd had a lot to drink, and we were all hungry. There was no room service in this small, family-run hotel ... but there was a big, scrumptious cake sitting on the floor in front of us. First a tentative nibble, then a mouthful. Eventually all five of us were digging into it a fistful at a time, and before we knew it almost a quarter of the cake was either eaten or dispersed around the floor in crumb form. In the morning we did our best to clean up the incriminating evidence, bundled the remaining cake into the boot of the car and headed for home. I was still planning to pass the theft off as a joke so when we arrived back in Newcastle I posed for a picture, dressed in a combat jacket and stocking over my face, pointing a gun at the crumbling remains of the cake. I was going to print this in *Viz* along with a light-hearted ransom demand to our *Oink* rivals. But the next day Tony Husband rang. He told me their party had been ruined and his mother had been left in tears by the mysterious theft of their prized cake. The Bunter-esque comic irony of it all had passed completely over his head. Tony didn't go so far as to accuse us of the theft, but from his tone of voice it was clear that he knew it was us. Racked with guilt, I decided the only thing to do was to get rid of the cake. Over the next few days Dolores and I scoffed the lot, stopping occasionally to rub our tummies and go 'Arf! Arf! That's what I call a feast!' In a way the cake incident illustrated perfectly *Oink*'s shortcomings. How could anyone who claimed to know anything about the great traditions of British comic humour place a big, yummy cake on a table, turn their backs and not expect it to disappear? Hardly surprisingly, it was only a couple of years before IPC sent *Oink* off to slaughter.

As our sales grew, demand for earlier, out-of-print issues did too, and in September 1986 John suggested a *Viz* Christmas annual containing highlights of all twelve pre-Virgin issues. As this was going to be a hardback book we decided to call it *The Big Hard One*, giving us scope for a host of slogans crammed with sexual innuendo, such as 'Slip a *Big Hard One* inside her stocking this Christmas'. In December 1986, to promote the book, John had me and Simon whisked off on a whirlwind publicity tour by a company called Beer Davies. They were basically pluggers and their job was to whisk clients around the country promoting their books or products. Beer Davies were a close-knit company which had evolved out of a Birmingham rock band called Dansette Damage, though one of the founders, Eugen Beer (pronounced *Eujane* as in 'me Tarzan'), seemed to have come from somewhere slightly more refined. Our first-ever publicity tour involved doing dozens of interviews with local and national press, radio and TV, often as many as twenty in a single day. Being out on the road was manic, driving at high speed from one city to the next, in and out of radio stations and newspaper offices, then on to the next town to do it all again an hour or so later.

The hardest part of a plugger's job is persuading DJs or newspaper reporters that their client is worth talking to. In our case it wasn't too difficult. *Viz* was a cult phenomenon at the time, especially among media types, and people were quite keen to talk to us – providing we didn't say anything rude on the radio. But other clients could be a lot harder to sell. As we were being whisked around our driver was constantly on his mobile trying to schedule interviews for other guests and I got a wonderful insight into how the business worked. During one tour, I forget when exactly, Eddie our Beer Davies driver was trying to book interviews for the Chairman of Cadbury-Schweppes, whose name escapes me. But he was finding it tough going. Everyone he rang kept asking him the same question. 'What can we talk to him about?' Eddie had a stock reply which he delivered in his thick Brummie accent. 'Worrabout the proyce of soft drinks in pubs? That's a very controversial topic at the moment, actually.' People weren't keen, but Eddie had another card up his sleeve, and this was an ace. If they weren't taking the bait he'd merely mention the fact that the following week he had bubbly Sue Pollard from TV's *Hi-De-Hi* out on the road. Naturally *everyone* wanted to interview her, and Eddie was only too happy to accommodate them … once they'd agreed to talk to the Chairman of Cadbury-Schweppes.

Little did we know, while we were out selling our book Richard Branson was in the process of selling Virgin Books. The company was set to merge with another, much larger publisher called WHAllen. John Brown told me about the deal and said he'd been offered a job as a director at the new company. But he wasn't going. The reason he gave me was that they'd offered him an office with a fire escape blocking the window, but that wasn't the entire story. John saw this as an ideal opportunity to fulfil a major ambition and set up his own publishing company.

John Brown wasn't like us. His dad, or *father* as he would say, was Sir John Brown, former Chairman of Oxford University Press, and his mam was called Lady Virginia. John was educated at Westminster public school – although by his own admission he was thick – and had done a variety of jobs before getting into publishing. These had included a spell in New York working as a chauffeur for clients such as Diana Ross and the Village People, not to mention a bevy of high-class prostitutes. John's first publishing job was with Pete Townsend's Eel Pie company, from where he moved to Virgin. He seemed to be doing all right for himself considering his lack of qualifications, but when your dad has been the Chairman of Oxford University Press, your becoming a Director of Virgin Books is no big deal. It's a bit like a plumber's son getting a job as a lavatory cleaner.

John was ambitious, but for the time being his fairly modest plan was to set up a small company to publish *Viz* and one other magazine, *Hot Air*, the in-flight freebie given away on Richard Branson's aeroplanes. He'd already got the go-ahead from Virgin, now he just had to talk me and Simon into signing our contract over to him. I had instinctive reservations. Virgin was a household name and Richard Branson was a role model for entrepreneurs the world over. I'd never met the smug, grinning twat, but I felt secure in the warmth of his corporate bosom. John Brown on the other hand was a young upstart who talked too loud, spat when he ate, and had big feet. If his new business failed we'd be fucked. But in reality there was no decision to make. It was John who had signed *Viz*, not Virgin. And most important of all, John *got the joke*. This was by no means a unique gift – most of our readers tended to get the joke too – but among magazine publishers John Brown seemed to be a rare and valuable find. So we signed on the dotted line and in March 1987, after just seventeen months on the Virgin ticket, *Viz* became a John Brown Publishing magazine.

CHAPTER EIGHT

The Fizzing of the Blue Touch Paper

John's voice seemed to have changed dramatically the first time he called me from his new office. He'd rented a single room in the Canalot Studios on Kensal Road, West London. It was a big room, with stark white walls, a high ceiling, a polished wooden floor and no furniture at all. The echo was unbelievable. He had a desk, but nothing else. I wasn't sure if this was a design thing or a lack of money to buy furniture with thing, but John had a phone on his desk and as long as John had a phone he was always quite happy.

While John was settling into his new office, Dolores and I were making ourselves comfortable in our new flat. So was our landlady. A wrinkly old Mary Whitehouse lookalike with a Ronseal dark oak satin finish tan, Mrs Collins owned and let out several flats in the area but seemed to have a basic problem grasping the concept of a tenancy. As far as she was concerned they were her flats so there was nothing to stop her popping in any time it suited her. One day we came home and found her sitting comfortably in our living room drinking a cup of tea which she'd just helped herself to from the kitchen. 'Oh, never mind me,' she said, ushering us in and offering us a seat. We chased her away noisily and from that point onwards the dotty old hag seemed to have it in for us. Not long after that she announced that we were getting a new carpet. Her fat handyman came in one day while we were eating, bent down, exposing a particularly unappetising bum crack, and rolled up our perfectly good old carpet and carefully carried it out to his van. Then he dragged in the replacement which looked like it had come direct from a skip. Judging by the pattern on this 'new' carpet it had first been bought, fairly cheaply I'd imagine, some time in the early 1970s. Fortunately for us several years of accumulated dirt had dulled the gaudy colours down considerably. Unfortunately in one corner there was a huge, black oil stain which repeated itself across the room, gradually diminishing as it did so. Someone had obviously emptied oil into the skip while the carpet was still rolled up. A couple of days later our sitting room chairs were replaced. Out went the comfortable settees and in came a black two-seater office reception seat with a broken tubular steel frame, and an over-designed white leatherette revolving chair which would have been perfect for Warren Beatty's hair salon in the movie *Shampoo*, but was starting to look a little dated by the mid-1980s. Increasingly I got the impression that our flat was being downgraded.

My mum and dad had no obvious objections to Dolores and me living in sin, but to her Irish Catholic parents it was a major issue. Dolores had confessed to her mother about our living arrangements, and she had graciously accepted the situation. But Dolores didn't dare tell her dad. She told me that he was an alcoholic ex-soldier who was currently in a psychiatric hospital drying out. I wasn't in any great hurry to meet him. Then one day Dolores got a call from her mother. Her dad had returned unexpectedly from hospital and found a letter in which Dolores had mentioned our premarital cohabitation. He'd flown into a rage and headed straight for the ferry terminal, threatening to kill me. She just thought we ought to know. Dolores didn't seem too concerned. She doubted he'd get any further than the nearest pub.

111

A few days later we came back to our flat late one evening and found the front door locked from the inside. 'I bet we've been burgled,' I said to Dolores. I ran round the back of the house just in time to see three young men dressed in casual sports attire disappearing into the darkness at the top of the lane. They'd left the back door swinging open so I ran through the house and opened the front door to let Dolores in. Standing next to her in the darkness was a shady-looking figure in a dark overcoat. My head was in a spin. We'd just been burgled and I was panicking about the damage they might have done upstairs and all the stuff that would be missing. Who the hell was this? 'This is my dad, Charlie,' said Dolores. He'd picked a bad time to call, but then again if he was going to kill me no time was going to be ideal. Fortunately he didn't. He stayed at a nearby B&B for a few days, met my parents, and then went home again to Ireland. Dolores's mother also came and paid us a visit. I was on my best behaviour of course, and Dolores had very wisely decided not to tell her about the comic until after she'd met me. I think I made a reasonable impression, but when she found out what I did for a living it was a big disappointment. 'He's a nice boy,' she told her daughter. 'It's just a pity he couldn't put his talent to better use, drawing birthday cards or something.'

Although I hate to have to say it, having John Brown at the helm seemed to have an immediate effect on comic sales. In April 1987 he printed 29,000 copies of his first issue. By the end of the year the print run was over 60,000. The April 1987 issue, John's first, is a particular favourite of mine because it marked the pinnacle of my artistic achievement. Not a very high pinnacle, I should add, but a pinnacle none the less. For me drawing cartoons was always a frustrating battle against my inability to match Hergé's Tintin books. When I eventually realized how much research and preparation had gone into every single frame of his work, I gave up. I was too lazy to be a good cartoonist, so I resigned myself to working within my very limited means. Proper cartoonists use brushes and ink nibs to draw flowing, natural lines; and they vary the thicknesses of those lines to give the impression of shape, texture and movement. Trying to obtain the same effects with my Rotring pen – a technical drawing tool designed to give a constant line thickness – was like trying to score a David Beckham-style swerving free kick wearing a pair of mountaineering boots. I tried using ink nibs from time to time but there was only one occasion, in issue 23, when I was happy with the result. The cartoon was called 'Raymond Porter and his Bucket of Water' and, unfortunately, the plot wasn't up to the same standard as the nib work. The

Raymond Porter and his Bucket of Water

same comic featured one of my all-time favourite cartoons. 'Scooter-Dolphin Boy' was the story of young Danny Dixon, owner of an incredible pedal scooter, who had befriended a highly intelligent dolphin while on holiday in Cornwall. Danny scooted everywhere, dragging his dolphin pal behind him in a large bath full of water. Together Danny and his amazing dolphin rounded up rogues in a typically plucky, comic strip kind of way, with Danny doing all the work and the dolphin just lying in the bath going, 'Eeeeek!' from time to time. Also in that comic were two cartoons by a brand new *Viz* cartoonist. Davey Jones was a student of philosophy at Manchester Polytechnic, and it showed. His first two submissions were called 'Vlad the

Impaler and His Cat Samson' and 'Waggy Tail – the Dog Who Loves a Good Shit'.

In Newcastle a new nightclub had recently opened called the Jewish Mother, run by a couple of lovable second-hand car dealers called the Gosney brothers. They'd hit upon the splendid idea of disregarding the licensing laws and opening a nightclub with only a restaurant drinks licence. As you entered you were charged £1.50 for a burger and chips which you seldom actually saw. Thereafter you could stand at the bar and buy as many drinks as you wanted to accompany your 'meal'. During its inevitably brief existence the Jewish Mother was a fantastic venue. There was live music, a great crowd, an illicit atmosphere, exciting brawls on the door (the Gosney brothers did their own bouncing) and, if you wanted, you could even sit down and order a nice meal at very reasonable prices. The place was eventually closed down after a works outing from the Market Street police station booked in for a meal and weren't happy with their burgers and chips. Not long after that the empty building mysteriously burnt down.

In August 1987 I booked the Jewish Mother for a party to celebrate our 'Silver Anniversary' 25th issue, and what a night it was. Legendary local pop underachievers The Young Bucks topped the bill, but the highlight of the night was a performance by a promising new band called Tony O'Diamond and Top Group Fantastic. I'd turned pop mogul for the occasion, recruiting the band especially for the show. Tony O'Diamond was the artist formerly known as Arthur 2 Stroke, 'Top Group' was the default prefix given to bands on the billing at working men's clubs, and Fantastic was what they were. I paid for a theatrical costumier to dress them up in black nylon catsuits with bell-bottom flares and white plastic chain belts. The stage was dressed with tasteless tinsel and the word FANTASTIC hung in huge, spangly polystyrene letters above their heads. Their set consisted of cheesy 1970s covers and classics, punctuated by the explosion of stage pyrotechnics. They went down a bloody storm. Tony

Wadsworth, who later rose to great heights as Chairman and Chief Executive Officer of EMI, was in the room at the time, playing guitar in the Young Bucks. Tony was the man who would later make Robbie Williams 'rich beyond his wildest dreams' with an £80 million recording contract. If only he'd had his business hat on that evening he could have signed Tony O'Diamond instead.

I'd made a point of inviting all the *Viz* contributors to the party. It was strange meeting some of them face to face for the first time. A cartoonist called Nicholas Schwab introduced himself. To my horror he was stocky, with a shaven head and a very thick neck. I was struggling to find anything to talk to him about when Simon leaned across and helpfully whispered in my ear that Schwab looked just like a Sontaran, the Humpty Dumpty-esque *Doctor Who* monsters. He did as well. Early on in

Simon Thorp (Thorpy)

our conversation Schwab boastfully mentioned that he was a black belt in karate. I never used another one of his cartoons after that. The mysterious Simon Thorp was coming too, so I had my eyes peeled for any shifty-looking Richard Attenborough lookalikes coming through the door. In the event he turned out to be a thin, black-haired, pale-skinned young man wearing a casual/smart fawn jacket, matching corduroy trousers and a clean white shirt. He'd obviously made an ill-judged attempt to look smart for the occasion. In his hand he had a large black holdall, and after a brief formal introduction he handed me the bag. 'Can you put that somewhere safe?' he said. 'It's got my dialysis machine in it.' Of course! I thought. He's got some serious kidney disease that prevents him from going out and leading a normal life. He's a recluse, and that's why he's able to spend hours labouring over his intricate drawings. It all made perfect sense. I carefully handed the heavy bag over to Dolores who put it behind the bar and warned the staff about its contents. Then I spent the rest of the evening going around the room spreading the news about Simon Thorp's medical condition. It wasn't until several months later that I realized his dialysis machine comment had been an exceedingly dry throwaway joke and there was in fact nothing wrong with him at all.

Thorpy was a prolific cartoonist and had an insatiable appetite for money. He'd recently left university, returned to his family home in Pontefract, and set himself up as a freelance illustrator (on the Enterprise Allowance Scheme, of course). He was eager to earn as many £35s as possible and contributed four pages to issue 25. These included the first appearance of a brilliant character whose name – Finbarr Saunders and his Double Entendres – would soon become legend, along with phrases like 'Fnarr! Fnarr!' 'K-yuk! K-yuk!' and, 'Oo-er!'

John Brown shrewdly gave away 6,500 copies of issue 25 free with *Media Week* magazine to help spread the word. Then, in what seemed like another good idea at the time, he agreed to a similar giveaway with another magazine. In October 1987 10,000 specially produced 'free sample' copies of *Viz* were given away to readers of *Your Sinclair*. Unfortunately no one had taken into account the likely ages of the recipients, and the free comic provoked a storm of complaints from the parents of young, pioneer computer buffs. The *Your Sinclair* issue became a rare collector's item, as did the first *Viz* record, released at about the same time.

'Bags of Fun with Buster' was recorded by Johnny Japes and his Jesticles, a previously unknown band made up of Andy Partridge (out of XTC), John Otway, Neville Farmer and Dave Gregory. They sent me the song – about a new *Viz* character called Buster Gonad and his Unfeasibly Large Testicles – on the off chance we might want to do something with it. John Brown and I decided to release it as a single on our own Fulchester Records label. (Fulchester was of course the fictional home town of Billy the Fish – our equivalent to Roy Race's Melchester – and before that it had been the fictional setting for a 1970s daytime TV drama called *Crown Court*.) We didn't anticipate a hit record – only 1000 copies were pressed – and we didn't get one. John Otway later told me that the original plan was to record a song about Scooter-Dolphin Boy but they'd had to scrap that idea when Danny Dixon and his highly intelligent dolphin failed to reappear in the comic. Buster Gonad on the other hand had rapidly become a regular and was the latest creation of Graham Dury who had by now gained enough confidence to venture away from characters whose names rhymed. Either that or he couldn't think of anything that rhymed with *gonad*.

John Brown wanted to follow up our *Big Hard One* with a new annual featuring all-new material, but there was no way we could fill an entire book with new cartoons so in 1987 he reluctantly settled for another compilation of reprints. He was glad he did. Reprinting a hastily assembled selection of old cartoons was a lucrative money-for-old-rope trick and one that we would repeat annually for years to come. The second annual was given the working title of *The Naughty Bits* but evolved into *The Big Hard Number Two* by the time it went to press. To promote it we did a book signing at the Forbidden Planet bookshop in London, and cartoonists Graham and Thorpy joined up with me and Simon for the occasion. Two rather friendly-looking girls were hanging around at the end and after chatting for a while they asked, with a smile, whether we had anywhere to stay for the night. We could all stop at their flat if we liked. We exchanged nervous glances then sidled out of their earshot for a team talk. 'Count me out,' said Graham immediately. Thorpy frowned and shook his head. Simon raised his eyebrows in a non-committal sort of way, so it fell to me to cast the deciding vote. 'It's okay, we're staying with friends,' I told them, and they left looking rather forlorn. This was the first experience of comic groupies we had encountered. If I'd known it would also be the last I'd have probably voted 'yes'.

Viz's popularity was spreading like wildfire, and the night before our book signing Simon and I had appeared on national TV. We'd met a young researcher called Jonathan Ross in February of the previous year when he'd invited us down to London to talk about a project he was planning. Ross greeted us at his cramped, untidy office perched in an attic high above Soho. A dashing, debonair and highly self-confident young man, he was the sort of bloke I'd normally take an instant dislike to. But his designer wide-boy appearance was more than made up for by the quick wit that was evident the moment he opened his mouth. And he opened his mouth rather a lot. Ross explained in machine-gun Cockney that he was a fan of *Viz* and wondered if we might like to get involved as writers for a TV project he was working on. He then showed us a pilot episode of a chat show called *The Last Resort*, featuring scary has-been TV chef Fanny Craddock as the star guest, and chaotic inserts from an inept roving reporter called Marco – a kind of Italian Manuel meets Dr Scrote. On the strength of this tape Ross was confident he could get a series of *The Last Resort* commissioned by Channel 4. I didn't think so. We left nodding politely and saying we'd think about it, but we didn't bother getting back in touch. In my view Jonathan Ross's *The Last Resort* was clearly a dead duck.

Twenty-two months later Simon and I were all set to make a hat-eating appearance as guests on Channel 4's incredibly popular new chat show, Jonathan Ross's *Last Resort*. This was our first experience of live TV, and we were shitting bricks. We weren't the only ones. Steve Naïve, leader of the show's house band and a veteran of live television broadcasting, was making alarmingly frequent visits to the lavatory outside our dressing room door. During the rehearsals Dolores sat dewy-eyed in the empty studio and watched Mick Hucknall sing 'Every Time We Say Goodbye', unaccompanied, not once but three times. Every time he was note perfect. Later we saw Hucknall sitting alone in the green room. Offstage he looked quiet, shy and vulnerable – like an injured songbird cowering in the corner of a garden. Dolores was a huge fan of his but she didn't have the nerve to go over and say hello. She's regretted it ever since. Personally I'm glad she didn't. If the randy little ferret's subsequent CV is anything to go by, he'd have been down her knickers in a flash.

As well as making appearances on cult TV chat shows, *Viz* was now becoming a common sight in universities, offices and classrooms all over Britain. Simon's girlfriend at the time, a primary school teacher, had already had to confiscate a copy from one of her young pupils. John Brown had recorded an incredible 300% upturn in sales during his first year in charge, but this had only been the fizzing of the blue touch paper. As 1988 dawned John had barely had a chance to retreat to a safe distance when the rocket suddenly ignited. When the year began the comic was selling around 60,000 copies. Twelve months later it would be selling half a million.

Proper royalties started coming through from the moment John took over. A trickle at first, but eventually enough to make producing the comic a profitable business. But distributing comics to shops and pubs around Newcastle was becoming less economic. I didn't want to dump on all the pubs and shops who'd helped get *Viz* off the ground, so I asked Andy Pop, formerly the business brain behind Anti-Pop, if he would take the job of distributing comics off our hands. Never one to look a gift horse in the mouth, Andy jumped at the chance and scurried off to set up his own distribution company, taking with him the many bundles of comics and piles of T-shirts that had been cluttering up the bedroom. This freed up a considerable amount of space and for a while I thought about buying some new office furniture to fill it. Then I had a better idea. Why not get a person instead? I knew Graham Dury was growing disillusioned with his job engineering housewife-friendly cacti at Leicester University, so in April 1988 I offered him a full-time job on *Viz*.

Graham fitted quite comfortably into the new space I'd created by the window, and I bought him a little drawing board and a second-hand typist's chair to sit on. He was a very punctual worker, arriving at 9 o'clock on the dot every day. After a couple of weeks my dad remarked what a coincidence it was that the same long-haired bloke seemed to have called at the same time every morning for several days running. I explained that Graham was now working for me, and called him downstairs to make formal introductions. I was worried how my dad might react to having a stranger coming in and out of the house, but he didn't object at all. In fact he seemed quite chuffed. He'd been a humble employee all his life and I sensed he was quite proud of the fact that I was now an employer. Before that his attitude to my business had been at best mixed. The first time he'd read *Viz* was around Christmas 1986 when I came downstairs and found him going through a copy of *The Big Hard One* which someone had inadvertently left lying around. I stood and watched him for a moment through the glass panels of the living room door, waiting to see if I could gauge a reaction. I couldn't, but he certainly wasn't laughing. When I entered the room he closed the book and handed it to me. 'It's, erm … a bit like the comics I used to read when I was a kid,' he said with a hesitant sort of smile. I *think* he was looking for a compliment, but that was all that came out.

By now there were generally three of us crammed into the bedroom. As well as myself and Graham, each with our own drawing board, there'd be Dolores sitting at a desk in the corner answering the phone, doing all the bookkeeping and still handling mail-order sales of T-shirts and back issues. Dolores had been sacked from her previous job as a nanny after I was rude to her employers, allegedly. She'd been asked to babysit one night and I'd gone around to keep her company, with her employers' permission of course. They were a well-to-do and well-connected local family and they were having a few well-to-do, well-connected friends around for drinks before they went out. They were talking about Joe Robertson, the king of cocktails, and his latest multi-million-pound pub makeover. I hated Robertson for what he was doing to the city centre, but these people idolized him. 'I hear Joe's bought another place down by the station,' said one. 'Yeah, some old boozer called the Trent,' said another. I gritted my teeth. Joe Robertson had just bought the Midland, not the Trent, but being the babysitter's scruffy boyfriend I thought it would be inappropriate to correct him. When they eventually came home to relieve Dolores it was 4.20 a.m., not 1 o'clock as they had promised, and I was fuming. And when they told her to report back for work as usual at 8 a.m. that morning I came over all abrupt.

Dolores was an invaluable asset in the office, but I think from Simon's point of view there was an element of 'Janine joining us on the road' involved. Like Graham, Simon was also working full time – at least in theory – but not in the bedroom. The atmosphere between Simon and myself could get a little tetchy at times. Granted, there was an element of sibling rivalry between us. Steve and I had occasionally ganged up on Simon when we were kids, taunting him with the name 'Coconut Tête' sung to the tune of Suzi Quatro's '48 Crash', for example. But now I felt I had genuine grievances. Deadlines would arrive and Simon would fail to deliver his promised quota of cartoons. Despite his purely nominal title of 'co-editor' his entire contribution was a couple of cartoons per issue, far less than Graham or even freelancer Simon Thorp produced. And sometimes he'd take holidays unannounced, leaving myself and Graham up shit creek. An additional irritation was the fact that

Simon was keeping me awake at nights. Dolores and I had now moved to a slightly nicer flat (it had dry rot, but the carpets were clean) and by chance Jim Brownlow had recently moved into the flat directly above us. By now Simon was much closer to Jim than I was and they would often go out drinking together then come back late at night and watch TV directly above our bedroom. So I'd be at work until late in the evening, often to try and make up for Simon's dereliction of duty, and when I came home to try and get some sleep the sound of him laughing and joking in the room above would keep me awake all night. Simon had a very loud laugh. I suppose they might have kept the noise down if I'd asked them to, but that would have spoilt the irony of the situation, so I didn't.

By total contrast to Simon, Graham was turning out to be a workaholic. The problem with him was finding enough things for him to do. As soon as you gave him a script to illustrate he'd have finished it and he'd want another one. I wasn't entirely happy with the standard of his work. There were still big noses and cowboy boots creeping in, and when he drew someone having their teeth punched out he always drew anatomically correct teeth, with roots, flying through the air. I preferred to see rectangular, unrealistic teeth. They looked less painful. And he didn't draw dog turds in the house style either. He drew the flies circling above too big, and gave them wings. Me, I preferred a few tiny little dots above a turd. That made it look less disgusting, but smellier at the same time. Perhaps I was being too particular. But Graham's advantages far outweighed the oversized flies he sometimes drew above dog turds. With him on board we were able to take on extra work, and in the summer of 1988 John published the *Viz Holiday Special*, a paperback book featuring extended versions of regular strips, including Simon Thorp's graphic masterpiece 'Finbarr Holds His Own'.

Cosy though it was, by the spring of 1988 there was simply no avoiding the fact that *Viz* had outgrown the bedroom. Simon complained that he neither fitted nor felt welcome in the room,

A newly wedded Mum and Dad set off on their honeymoon from Newcastle Central Station, 1956.

Me as Lord Snooty, aged 2, and big brother Steve, Christmas 1962.

A Sunday picnic at the seaside, 1968. Me on the left, Coconut Tête in the middle, and Mr Logic on the right.

Above: Simon looks cute, Steve looks smart and I look indifferent, in the garden of the Heatherlea hotel, Allendale, 1971.

Above: The obligatory embarrassing school photograph.

Right: Jim on the beach at Scarborough 1978. We'd organised a bus trip from school to celebrate leaving, and everybody got pissed.

ove: Arthur 2 Stroke,
...mplete with his Mr Spock
...ircut, and his musical
...complice WM7 pose for a
...blicity shot in a speedboat
...op in Newcastle,
...vember 1979. Moments
...er they were ejected from
...e shop.

ight: Jim and I pose for our
...rst ever press photo on the
    roof of Thomson House,
Newcastle, summer 1980.

Above: Presenting Arthur 2 Stroke with a 'Camouflage Disc' at the Gosforth Hotel, 1981. I'm on the right, wearing my dad's old army hat.

Left: This is me at the Tyneside Free Press, finishir comics in about 1981. Note how I've put paper trimmings on my head for comic effect.

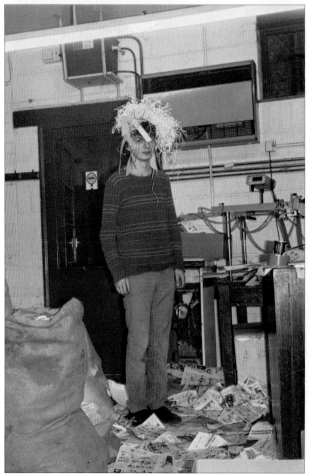

Above right: Me posing at t card table in my bedrooi 1982, and modelling t bloody awful jumper th Karen had knitted me. S must have taken the pictu

Right: Our photograph Colin took this picture of r in the bedroom for posteri just before we moved out 1987. Graham's chair sits the bottom right corn

Right: This is me drunk on BBC2's *Something Else* yoof programme in 1982. The moustache is false, but that's a real cardigan.

Left: Graham, Simon, Ann and I celebrate the news of our 268,000 print run – and overtaking *Private Eye* – with a cup of tea in the drawing studio, September 1988. Thorpy took this Polaroid, so he's not in it.

Right: This picture was going to be used to blackmail *Oink* magazine following the infamous kidnapping of their cake in 1985, but soon after it was taken the cake met a grizzly end.

bove: Simon and I caught somewhere
tween smirking and sneering, outside
e house in Lily Crescent, 1988.

Below: Simon, Andy Pop, Graham, me
and Simon Thorp prior to becoming
drunk and abusive at the Grosvenor
House Hotel, 1989.

The millionth copy of issue 39 is handed over to Emma Wilcock, none too convincingly, by the fat bloke in C&S Supercigs, Liverpool Central Station shopping arcade, November 1989.

Mr Moneybags, aka Arthur 2 Stroke, with 'Ton of Money' winner Emma Wilcock holding aloft the millionth comic sold, outside C&S Supercigs.

so I started looking for office space to rent. I wanted somewhere close to our flat and close to Lily Crescent so I could keep in touch with my parents. I couldn't drive. I found the perfect place nearby but when the landlord found out who I was he backed out of negotiations. He was worried about *Viz*'s 'reputation'. Eventually I found a suitable office with a landlord mercenary enough to take my money. It was the first floor of a large Victorian former terraced house, and I knew it had great comic potential because it was right next door to the local branch of the Conservative Central Office (Northern Area).

To go with our new office I decided to take on a full-time secretary and headhunted Ann from a copy shop in town where I'd been her best customer for several years. As well as moving office in May 1988 Dolores and I were also busy buying our first house, not to mention getting married at the same time.

I didn't have time to buy a ring. I was too busy at work so Dolores had to rush out and buy one herself on the Friday afternoon before the wedding. I hadn't found time to buy a suit either and on the day of the wedding I discovered that the only suit I owned was far too small. As a result to this day I'm still putting off ordering copies of our wedding photographs. The day after the wedding we moved into our new office, and at the same time we were exchanging contracts on the purchase of our first house.

When Dolores and I went house-hunting we'd set ourselves a spending limit of £40,000 and quickly found the perfect place for £39,500. The owner, a rather dim housewife with a permanent smile, showed us around every beautifully decorated room and told us that all the lovely carpets would be staying, before mentioning, purely as an afterthought, that the house had already been sold. Two weeks later we were offered a smaller house (the estate agent himself described it as 'pokey') in the same street for £47,500. The agent said he'd give me five seconds to think about it and then the price would go up to £52,500. That was how it worked at the height of the late 1980s property boom. So I yelled, 'Yes, we'll take it!' then went straight to the bank to arrange a mortgage. In the space of a few weeks I'd got married, got a mortgage, and started a nine-to-five office job. How the fuck did that happen?

CHAPTER NINE

A Ton of Money

The April 1988 issue of *Viz* marked our first six-figure print run, and to celebrate John Brown staged a party for influential magazine distributors at the London Press Club. John and Charlie Harness had gathered together a roomful of the most powerful men in the magazine wholesale sector and our job – myself, Graham and Simon – was to go around the room schmoozing and shaking hands. *Viz* was officially an adult magazine and, unfortunately, most of the guests appeared to be involved in the fleshier end of that market. It was a room full of British Bob Gucciones. The Gold brothers were there, and there was a man in a fur coat carrying a miniature poodle under his arm who looked like he was auditioning for a role in a James Bond movie. There was also a cigar-smoking Arthur Daley-type who told me he had his printing presses and a photographic studio all under the same roof. 'The mags can be printed up and out on the van before the birds have got their kit back on,' he told me. I was impressed. Another jazz merchant told us about a regular customer of his, a rather elderly gentleman as it happened, who'd been in his warehouse buying magazines late one afternoon and had accidentally got locked inside as the place was closing. This frail old man was trapped all night inside a massive warehouse full of pornography. The next morning when they opened the doors they found him lying unconscious in a pile of magazines, his trousers round his ankles. 'The silly beggar had *wanked* himself to sleep!' bellowed the storyteller before sloshing some more of John's free wine down his neck. Introducing us to a room full of eccentric pornographers was an unusual sales tactic, but like everything else John was doing it seemed to work. The June issue had a print run of 145,000, followed by 189,000 in August.

With revenue from royalties growing and a big office at our disposal I decided to take on a fourth member of my editorial team. Thorpy was the only candidate for the job. Those brief, businesslike notes that accompanied his early cartoons had gradually bloomed into long, dry and wonderfully witty letters. Thorpy and I got on very well by post but when he came up to Newcastle, as he occasionally did to help out at deadlines, we could sit in the same room for hours and hardly speak at all. Tim Harrison, from Surrey, who'd contributed to the very first issue, had started off as a pen friend and we'd got on great. Then one day Tim called on me totally out of the blue. He was on his way to Edinburgh with a girlfriend and just dropped by to say 'Hi'. He was clearly disappointed to discover that I was a nerd living in my parents' house, and I was equally unimpressed to find that he was a flashy git with an open-top sports car. He and his bird looked like something off a 1970s Martini advert. I invited them in, we endured a very difficult cup of tea together (during which his bird remained standing), then they left. I never saw or heard from Tim again. But Simon Thorp didn't look or behave anything like a person in a Martini commercial, so in the summer of 1988 I offered him a job.

With four of us now working under the same roof inevitable changes in the creative process started to take place. In the past we'd all written and drawn our cartoons entirely independent of one another, but now that we were in the same room we quickly developed a system of multilateral cartoon creation. Writing took place in a group, often all four of us together. If we were writing a script for an existing character, such as Billy the Fish, then the cartoonist previously responsible for that character – me in that case – would hold the pen and effectively be the editor. We'd all fire ideas into the air and the person with the pen would decide whether to write each idea down or ignore it. All four of us had different contributions to make. Graham was a comedy sergeant major. He was always making us work harder. Thorpy was a comedy sniper. He sat patiently waiting his opportunity. He didn't say much but what he did say was usually funny. Simon tended to be a comedy machine gunner, often going over the top, gun blazing. I suppose I was the comedy colonel, responsible for tactics and overseeing the operation. There were certain unwritten rules when we were writing. For instance, pretending to laugh at something out of politeness was a sin. Honesty was everything. If someone suggested a bad idea it would be met with a wall of embarrassed silence. Once the script was finished the artist concerned would take it away and draw it, a process that would take anything from a day to a month, depending who was doing it. For me drawing in pencil was the hardest bit. I'd often wear holes in the paper with my rubber trying to get a single expression right. Graham had an uncanny ability to draw anything at all, entirely from memory. He was a graphic reference library. For example, a cry would go up of, 'Graham. What does an Anglican bishop's hat look like from the back?' and he'd draw one instantly. The favours were quickly returned. Often Graham would raise a pen above his head and say, 'What colour's this?' 'Green,' someone would shout. Graham is colour blind.

Every now and then Ann would burst into our little drawing studio, her face beaming, and interrupt our work. 'Right. Guess what the latest print run is?' she'd say. We never got close. It was always something ridiculous, two or three times what we expected it to be. We'd overtaken *Punch* in the summer of 1987, and the *NME* in April 1988. By October we'd overtaken *Private*

Eye with a print run of 268,000. That was a special occasion so we all stopped work and had a cup of coffee to celebrate. Little did we know the 268,000 would sell so quickly that John would soon be ordering a 55,000 reprint, bringing the total for issue 32 up to 323,000. When December came around we all stopped again and had another drink. But this time it wasn't coffee. John Brown had sent us five crates of champagne to celebrate a print run of 515,000.

By the end of 1988 John must have been in a state of shock. I doubt whether he ever imagined *Viz* selling more than 150,000. The sales explosion had been pretty amazing, but at the same time it all felt rather familiar. What John had witnessed in the last three years was exactly the same phenomenon that had taken place in Newcastle during the early eighties. But now it was occurring on a national scale. And of course all this had happened without the expense of an advertising budget. *Viz* didn't need that. The *Viz* gospel had been spread entirely by word of mouth.

It would be easy to imagine John Brown sitting in his office, his big feet up on the desk, doing absolutely nothing all day while sales of the comic sky-rocketed, his biggest challenge for the day deciding where to go for lunch. That's how we imagined him anyway. But John had worked hard to establish a distribution network effective enough to pump *Viz* out to the capillaries. He'd had to do it the hard way because from the outset retailing and wholesaling giants WHSmith wouldn't touch *Viz* with someone else's shitty barge-pole. John personally badgered every newsagent he visited to make sure they were stocking *Viz*. Every time I went anywhere with him he'd suddenly bolt off into a newsagent, bound up to the counter and start harassing the poor sod on the till. If they didn't stock *Viz* he asked them why not. If they did stock *Viz* he asked them to display it more prominently. And if it was already displayed prominently he'd tell them they were running out and they should reorder more copies.

Back in 1980 WHSmith's Bournemouth branch manager made magazine retailing history by becoming the first representative of that esteemed organization to turn his nose up at a copy of *Viz*. By the end of 1988 Smith's began to see our comic in a more positive light, possibly due to the fact that sales were approaching half a million and they could now make a tidy profit out of it. On 24 November their News Buying and Marketing Manager, a Mr Bill Rowe, wrote to our distributor Charlie Harness setting out their terms. 'We consider this publication one that we must review very carefully at every issue,' he wrote. He then asked for advance copies of every issue to be sent to both himself and to Smith's Retail Managing Director for close inspection. 'I should also like to point out to you that an increasing incidence of "Anglo-Saxon" expletives or depiction of gratuitous violence could lead us to withdraw the magazine from both Wholesale and Retail sale,' he added ominously. I was quite happy to do sensible things, like dropping the word 'Comic' from the title to prevent short-sighted old ladies buying *Viz* for their grandchildren. But there was no way I was going to tailor the editorial to an individual distributor's requirements, I didn't care how many they might sell. WH bloody Smith wouldn't move their wank mags to keep one customer happy, so why should I alter my comic just for them? I said WHSmith were welcome to see the comic in advance, but if they objected to anything they could stick their almighty wholesaling and retailing empire up their arse. As a matter of principle we wouldn't alter a thing. John agreed.

With half a million copies of the magazine now being pumped out to the capillaries every two months John became worried about our veteran ticker and decided it was time for a transplant. At the end of 1988 he surgically removed Charlie Harness, rewarding him for all his efforts with the sack, and replaced him with Seymour, a much larger distributor. It was a pity to see Charlie go. He'd helped take our sales from 5000 to 500,000, and he'd also introduced me to some very interesting figures from the world of pornography. But there was no room for sentiment in John Brown's business planning.

Sales continued to soar and the first print run of 1989, issue 34, was a whopping 651,000 copies. When was it going to stop? Not in April. For issue 35 John printed 861,000 copies. As anyone with a big enough calculator may already have worked out, in a little over a year sales had increased by 1000 per cent.

In issue 34 *Viz* readers were introduced to a new character, Spoilt Bastard. He was the result of a three-way writing session between Graham, Thorpy and Simon. Graham's original idea was inspired, allegedly, by the behaviour of his elder brother. But everyone knows a spoilt kid, or has wanted to smack one around the head at one time or another, so the insufferable, sailor-suited Timmy Timpson tapped into a rich comic vein. This was a standard formula for us – taking a recognizable stereotype and exaggerating it – and we used it over and over again with varying degrees of success. They were what I called 'Category A' characters, like Sid the Sexist, Biffa Bacon and Mrs Brady. These were based in reality, and their popularity was sustained as a result. Another formula was characters parodying comic characters, rather than real people. These generally had a silly name and amusing appearance, no roots in real life, but were amusing none the less. These I classed as 'Category B' cartoons and their popularity wouldn't generally survive as long as a Category A. There was a splendid example of a Category B cartoon in that February 1989 issue.

When we wrote it we were expecting big things from Tommy and his Magic Arse. In fact, so confident were we that this new character would become a massive hit we started printing Tommy and his Magic Arse T-shirts before the strip was even published. But Tommy turned out to be a turkey, our Gary Birtles if you like, the big-name signing who never lived up to his promise. The key to Tommy's success, as I saw it, was the fact that his arse 'wasn't magic all the time – only when he talked in rhyme'. I think we laughed more during the writing of that script than we did during any other in the history of the magazine. But the readers weren't impressed and John Brown probably still has a few hundred Tommy and his Magic Arse T-shirts stowed away in an attic somewhere.

John liked merchandise. In fact he preferred selling T-shirts to selling books and magazines. That dodgy, Arthur Daley world of

Tommy and his Magic Arse

fast bucks and non-colourfast T-shirts appealed to the rebellious side of him. He was constantly pushing us to produce more T-shirts and other spin-off products, and by April 1989 our mail-order merchandising advert had spread like a rash to cover three pages of the comic, featuring eighteen different T-shirt designs, three pairs of boxer shorts, five different button badges plus various postcards and four *Viz* books. John had taken over the mail-order business from Dolores in 1987 but it wasn't long until his office couldn't cope with the volume of business. So everything was farmed out to a specialist mail-order contractor in a warehouse somewhere down south, and for the next ten years I would receive a constant flow of complaints from dissatisfied readers who hadn't received their orders, or who had been sent the wrong items, or whose subscription had failed to materialize. *Viz* was big business now.

The more money John made the more money he wanted to make. The idea of *Viz* becoming a monthly was raised on a pretty regular basis and I was always under pressure to make production of the magazine more efficient. 'What are you doing?' he would ask when he came on phone. 'We're working on the next comic,' I'd say. 'No, *now*. What are *you* doing right now?' If I told him I was inking a cartoon he'd snap back at me, 'You're not supposed to be *inking* any more! Tell Graham to do that. You should be *writing*.' His view was that we could turn the creative process into a more efficient production line by introducing specialization. I'd already handed over many of my cartoon characters to other people to illustrate. First Thorpy had wrestled a screaming Billy the Fish from my arms, then Graham had come to take Biffa Bacon away. Soon Mrs Brady and Postman Plod would also be up for adoption.

One domain which remained very much my own was design. It was a fairly unusual situation, the editor of a national magazine doing all his own page design and layout, but I'd always done it and I enjoyed it. Besides, when you're writing your own headlines, finding your own pictures, writing your own captions and sticking the whole page together, you get loads of opportunities to add extra jokes along the way.

Another area of specialization was office cleaning. Doreen was an elderly cleaner whom we'd inherited along with our new office. She usually came in late when the place was empty so most of our communication was by written notes, instructions left for her to follow. But frequently jobs weren't getting done. One night when she was alone in the office she'd used a key to scrape the letters off the sign on our office door. We were baffled until a few days later when we saw her and she explained. 'Oh aye ... I've cleaned them aald letters off the sign so youz can put your own name on it,' she said. She thought the sign on the door was the name of the previous occupants. It wasn't. It had said 'reception'. It was only then the coin dropped and we realized that Doreen couldn't read.

She later confessed she could neither read nor write, and offered a less than plausible explanation. 'When a was a bairn someone left the windee owpen, an' I caught the Jorman measles, so I couldn't gan to school, y'see.' I had a soft spot for Doreen. In the brief time she'd been with us she'd proved invaluable, not for her shoddy cleaning, but by introducing us to the term 'fling tits', her unaffectionate nickname for Shirley Bassey. But at the end of the day I needed a cleaner we could communicate with so I decided she had to go. To soften the blow I gave her a very generous redundancy package. As she left the office for the last time she stopped in the doorway and turned back. 'Eeeeh! I'm glad youz give us this,' she said, raising the wad of money in her hand. 'Cos if youz hadn't me husband would have come roond here and put yer fuckin' windees through.' A salt of the earth Geordie was Doreen.

While I was sacking my cleaner, in London John Brown was recruiting staff by the busload. In the summer of 1989 he'd invested some of his burgeoning *Viz* profits in his own office building, the Boathouse down by the river in Fulham. 'The Boathouse' conjured up images of a charming Victorian pavilion perched at the water's edge, with a terrace balcony on which John could stroll, dressed in a stripy blazer, plimsolls and straw hat. But it wasn't like that at all. In the many years since the building had last contained a boat the course of the river appeared to have changed dramatically, and planners had taken the opportunity to build a high-rise council estate between it and the river Thames. The Boathouse was a big, brick-built, three-storey building and extremely spacious inside, due in no small part to there not being any staircases. Unusually, and rather impractically for an office building, all access from one floor to another was by means of an external fire escape. But John liked his boathouse and he lavished a great deal of money on it. The interior décor alone, which was conceived and executed by a foppish French-looking designer called Fabien, was rumoured to have cost John £200,000. Why it cost £200,000 to coat the bare brick and plaster walls and ceilings in gaudy blue and red emulsion I never understood, although I gather there were also some light fittings included on the bill.

John now employed a team of dedicated sales staff whose job it was to fill up the advertising pages in *Viz*. All of a sudden we were one of the best-selling magazines in Britain, and we had a unique and easily defined readership to boot. Where better to advertise bank accounts, beer and premium rate masturbation telephone services to young, gullible men? To begin with there was only one ad salesman, a nice little bloke called Ronnie Hackston who was originally from Gateshead. But soon there would be an entire roomful of young, ambitious and highly motivated twats. As sales went up, so did page rates, squeezing out traditional advertisers like the Mandala wholefood shop. In their place came national advertisers, but the problem with these new ads was that none of them were funny. I insisted that I have approval over all new adverts. Having someone advertise in your comic is a bit like having guests staying in your house. There's certain people you wouldn't allow in. I didn't want David Sullivan's sleazy *Sunday Sport*, for example, wanking away in my spare bedroom. They were rejected, along with another ad featuring female nudity. *Viz* may have been ostensibly rude and vulgar but it always displayed a subtle degree of taste and sensibility.

The fact that I was pooh-poohing a lot of potential sponsors didn't go down well with the ad sales team, who were all on commissions. There was constant friction between us. They were always pushing for more pages to be devoted to advertising, and for better placements. Advertisers would ask for their advert to be on the right-hand page, opposite a specific cartoon. I'd say 'Fuck off!' and bury it in a graveyard (two pages of adverts facing each other which the reader can totally ignore). To me advertising was a cancer, and it would take over the magazine if I didn't fight it. One virulent strain was the premium-rate phone line advertisement. Not just wanking service providers – we were being inundated with tacky adverts for so-called 'comedy phone lines'. At the end of 1989 *Viz* put a blanket ban on all premium rate telephone service advertisers, and our bold stance earned us a commendation of sorts from anti-premium rate phone line campaigner, MP Terry Lewis. 'Other magazines should follow suit. If a magazine as crude as *Viz* can do it, they all can,' he told the London *Evening Standard*. But John hadn't been entirely happy with my decision.

There were always tensions between myself and John. Basically our roles were totally disparate. He had an instinctive urge (and, to be fair, a contractual obligation) to exploit *Viz* for all it was worth. His aim was to make money. But I was the editor of a subversive, anarchic magazine. I couldn't be seen to be adhering to capitalist principles. There was a massive North–South divide between my office and John's. My staff often felt that John was being greedy and unscrupulous, and sometimes I agreed. But remembering Mr Hart-Jackson's three-legged race analogy – you can never afford to fall out with your publisher – I played piggy-in-the-middle and tried to keep both sides happy. It was a bloody difficult balancing act at times. As I explained it to John, from our office he was viewed as the Sheriff of Nottingham, the villain of the piece, and I was Robin Hood with my band of Merry Men. Our job was to oppose his cruel price increases and exploitative merchandising, and to give the good readers value for money. I actively encouraged the poking of fun at John, and snide comments at his expense would often appear in the comic. John was quite happy to take the stick because he understood the complexities of the situation. He was greedy but quite bright with it.

Like pop records, rich people and the world's sexiest women, magazines have their very own Top 100 charts which publishers watch anxiously to see how their titles are performing. This chart is published every six months and figures are compiled by

ABC, the Audit Bureau of Circulations. To put *Viz* sales into some perspective, in the six months between January and June 1989 *Private Eye*, previously Britain's best-selling humour magazine, was selling on average 209,000 copies per issue and was at No. 33 in the Top 100. Its ailing rival *Punch* – selling around 30,000 – didn't even make the chart. Magazine of the Year *Q* was in like a bullet at No. 58 selling 133,000 copies, and *Woman's Realm* and *People's Friend* were battling it out for the No.13 slot with sales of around 550,000 each. *Viz* had come from absolutely nowhere and overtaken them all, with an audited average sale of 680,000 for the same period. We were now going where no men's magazine had gone before. The only titles thought to be capable of surviving at this publishing altitude were the housewives' glossies like *Prima* (853,000) and *Woman's Own* (931,000). Above them, up at the very summit of the magazine publishing mountain, were the unassailable *TV Times* and *Radio Times*, with their exclusive rights to TV listings, un-limited access to cover stars and consequent sales in excess of two million each.

As well as comics we were selling tat by the ton. 26,125 *Viz* T-shirts by mail order alone during 1989, not to mention badly made boxer shorts, beach towels and baseball caps. T-shirt sales peaked that year, and for a while it looked like comic sales had done so too when in the summer of 1989 we suffered a minor sales slump. The print run for the June 1989 issue – 833,000 – was actually 30,000 down on April's. *Viz* had been performing way above its limits. We were like a Sunday league team play-ing in the Premiership. It looked like we'd been found out at last. Sales were slowing and the print run dropped again, down to 817,000 for the August issue. Rather than a disappointment this came as a slight relief to me. It had been a hell of a ride but at last sales were beginning to settle down and I was look-ing forward to getting my breath back. Besides, there were far more important things on my mind than sales of *Viz*. In early 1989 Dolores had managed to get herself in the family way, and we were expecting our first child in the autumn.

The June 1989 issue had featured the début of two new 'Category A' characters who were soon to become household names, as well as popular playground insults. They were Sandra Burke and Tracey Tunstall, better known as the Fat Slags. The Slags were such an instant success they were immediately

The Fat Slags

promoted to the cover of the following issue, and over the years San and Tray have become arguably the comic's most popular characters. Their name has certainly become synonymous with *Viz*, which riles me a little, because frankly I never liked them all that much.

The Fat Slags were very much Graham and Thorpy's babies, despite the fact that their conception was a gang-bang in which all four of us took part. We were aware that our cartoon pages were largely male dominated. Two of my earlier attempts to redress the balance – Tina's Tits and Miss Demeanour and her Concertina – had proved unsuccessful, so we decided to sit down and write a strip based on the stereotypical Geordie good-time girls who used to inhabit Joe Robertson's wine bars. (Joe Robertson's 'hay clarse' wine bar business had, I'm relieved to say, gone bust by this stage and Joe had sloped off to his yacht in Monte Carlo.) These women were obvious targets for parody, with their ill-fitting all-weather mini-skirts, their precarious heels, their orange tans and their unbecoming language. One minute they'd be the picture of elegance and refinement, tottering into a bar and ordering a posh cocktail. The next they'd be outside, shagging a total stranger against a wall or scratching a love-rival's eyes out at the bus stop.

Graham was extremely enthusiastic about the new characters, not because he was particularly familiar with the stereotype, but because he felt he had fewer characters in his stable than the other cartoonists and he desperately wanted some new ones. When it came to cartoon characters there was always a slight element of rivalry among us, especially among Graham. When the first script was finished Graham laid claim to the drawing rights and Thorpy helped him with the initial design of the two girls. The result was one of the strongest new strips we'd written in a long time and I confidently placed it on page 3, the show-case page that was always reserved for something strong or particularly eye-catching.

Whether the Fat Slags had anything to do with it I don't know – it has certainly been suggested in some quarters – but following their appearance sales took off upwards again. The print run for our October 1989 issue was an enormous 974,500 copies, and John rang me to say that demand was so high that for our December issue he would be printing over a million.

I could hardly believe my ears, but John was very calm and keeping his business head. He wanted to maximize the opportunity for publicity that a millionth sale would present and asked me for my thoughts. 'If we're selling a million what do we need publicity for?' I asked, sensibly I thought. Media coverage of *Viz* had already gone haywire. Simon Bates was plugging the comic almost daily on his Radio 1 show, calling it 'the new *Private Eye*'. And even as John and I spoke a three-page feature on Biffa Bacon and company was appearing in *Vanity Fair*, for crying out loud. I had what I thought was a pretty rational idea. We should stop when we got to a million. Print one million comics, and no more. The first million people to the newsagents would get one, the rest would miss out. But John didn't like it. I think he'd already set two million as his next target. So we had a think about it and came up with a suitably cheesy PR gimmick to celebrate our first million-selling issue. The customer who purchased the millionth copy of the December issue would be stopped as they left the shop and presented with a 'Ton of Money'. A ton of money, in copper of course, only equates to about £2,500, but it sounds good. I thought it might also be a good joke if we left someone standing in the street lumbered with a massive mountain of copper.

Press coverage of *Viz* had not been limited to *Vanity Fair*. Even the *Daily Telegraph* had peered down its nose at us. In January their concerned columnist Martyn Harris likened reading *Viz* to watching the Australian soap *Neighbours*, and he diagnosed the growing cult of student *Viz* readers as suffering from *nostalgie de la boue* – literally, a 'yearning for the mud' – a self-conscious slobbishness, if you will, which had been prevalent in students and intellectuals throughout the ages. I thought he was talking out of his arse. Yes, *Viz* was popular with those trendy, intellectual student types, but we had a much wider social base than that. We had crossover appeal between all sorts of social groups and classes. *Viz* appealed broadly to anyone with a sense of humour.

The *Daily Telegraph* may not have liked us but elsewhere in the media establishment *Viz* was becoming accepted. Well, almost. At the dinner-jacket-and-bow-tie-only *Media Week* Awards held at London's plush Grosvenor House Hotel in November 1989, *Viz* was nominated for top prize in the category for the magazine achieving the biggest circulation increase. They won't need judges to work that one out, I thought. Just a calculator. So myself, the other three cartoonists and distributor Andy Pop joined John Brown and his staff at the award ceremony, confident of collecting the prize. But we didn't. *Auto* fucking *Express* magazine – which was selling less than a third of our total – won it because, in the words of the judges, it had been 'performing in a more competitive market' than us. The announcement was greeted by spontaneous booing from all around the hall, not just our table, where it was particularly loud. But there was a consolation for me when the *Sun* bestowed on me the honour of 'Celebrity Behaving Badly' the following week. Under the headline 'BIFFA BOSS GETS IN BOVVER' the *Sun's* showbiz columnist Piers Morgan reported how Chris Donald, 'creator of the outrageous comic *Viz*', had 'caused chaos' at the *Media Week* Awards by 'turning into his own most disgusting character, skinhead yob Biffa Bacon'. The paper accused me of knocking back huge amounts of wine before reeling across to the table where the *Auto Express* staff were sitting, and shouting 'You're going home in a f***ing ambulance!' This was another breathtaking example of tabloid inaccuracy and lies. It was my brother Simon who did that, not me.

In 1979 an obnoxious DJ called James Whale was a hate figure on Tyneside where he baited callers on a local late-night radio phone-in. Ten years later he'd risen to the status of national hate figure and was baiting late-night TV viewers on a chat show broadcast live from Leeds. I'd been invited to appear as a guest and was expecting Whale to give me a hard time as Anti-Pop had orchestrated a prolonged hate campaign against him in his Metro Radio days, and an obscene call to his *Night Owls* show had been recorded and used as an intro to the title track on Wavis O'Shave's album, *Anna Ford's Bum*. But when I got to Leeds it was another guest – smug, spangle-suited, mockney-mouthed funny man Ben Elton – who had a go. I'd met Elton once before at the Jewish Mother in Newcastle back in 1988. On that occasion he'd been very complimentary about *Viz*. But in the green room prior to the James Whale show he decided to give me a lecture in his capacity as self-appointed shop steward for the National Union of Right On Comedians. Elton criticized me for having granted an interview to *Mayfair* magazine a few months earlier. I wasn't really listening to the politics of his argument – I was too busy wondering how on Earth Ben Elton had spotted our interview in *Mayfair* magazine. It conjured up quite an unpleasant image of him down on his knees, wanking away furiously, and then stopping, eyes agog, as he came across our interview. Fortunately Ben Elton didn't read *Escort*. If he had done no doubt he would have spotted my earlier transgression. In 1983 I submitted some cartoons of scantily clad women playing pool to a 'readers' drawings' feature in that magazine. They were offering £125 for every submission used, and at the time I was desperately in need of money. By the time my cartoons were published, two years later, I wasn't. As best I recall, these 'sexy' drawings did nothing but expose my embarrassing ignorance of hosiery design and female anatomy. I bitterly regretted having sent them off, but fortunately I've been able to keep their publication quiet thus far.

In late September 1989 Dolores gave birth to our first child, Dale. I took a couple of days off work for the event, but within six weeks both mother and child were on the road with me and the other cartoonists promoting the upcoming, million-selling December issue of *Viz*. We were wined and dined at the Savoy by the *Evening Standard* (they bought us lunch anyway) and we stayed at fashionable media watering hole the Groucho Club where Honor Blackman stopped in the bar to say hello to Dolores and child – and cantankerous, chair-wetting journalist Jeffrey Barnard went out of his way to be rude to them. He didn't approve of children in the club, or women by the sound of it. An official press conference was staged at the New Connaught Rooms and the 'Ton of Money' was put on display with two totally unnecessary security guards standing by. It took six of us an hour to get the money up all the stairs and it would have taken any opportunist thief acting on his own at least two working days to make off with it.

A hectic nationwide publicity tour then took us all over the country, talking to newspapers and doing radio interviews. All four cartoonists were on the road, splitting up at times to cover more ground and more late-night local radio shows. Eventually we all rendezvoused early one morning at a grotty little news-agents in Liverpool city centre called T&S Supercigs.

Precisely 1,251,356 copies of our December issue had been printed and the millionth copy to come off the presses had supposedly been tracked until it was delivered in a bundle to this particular shop, conveniently situated in a shopping arcade near both our hotel and Liverpool's main railway station. As part of this stunt our old friend Arthur 2 Stroke was hired to play our equivalent to Chris Tarrant, 'Mr Moneybags'. 2 Stroke had swapped his career as an unsuccessful pop singer for a career as an equally unsuccessful seaside guest-house owner, and needed the work. His job was to wait until a customer bought the comic and then spring from nowhere, dressed in a tasteless gold lamé suit, and ask the lucky purchaser three simple questions (for the purposes of the Gaming Act). Then he had to give them the money. The original plan, to run away and leave the poor victim standing in the street with an immovable pile of copper, had by now been lost somewhere in the wheels of the PR machine.

The shop had yet to open as the cash arrived from London in a hired van and was loaded onto a large trolley and wheeled round the back out of sight. Meanwhile the editorial team, John Brown, publicist Eugen Beer and a host of invited press onlookers all huddled together in a storeroom at the back of the shop as the proprietor opened for business. Rather fortuitously the millionth copy just happened to be the one sitting on the top of the pile next to the till. We still could have been there for hours, or conceivably days, waiting for someone to buy it, but, surprise surprise, within minutes of the doors opening a customer walked purposely into the shop and made straight for the comic. Unusually it was a girl, by the name of Emma – the vast majority of *Viz* readers are male. Equally unusually all she bought was a single copy of *Viz*. No newspaper, no cigarettes, no sweets. And perhaps even more unusually than that, this was the first time in her life she'd ever bought a copy of *Viz*. This is what she told reporters after the surprise had been sprung and Mr Moneybags had presented her with the money. But perhaps most unusually of all, Emma appeared to be on first name terms with the shopkeeper. Upon making enquiries I received a personal assurance from organizer Eugen Beer that nothing untoward could possibly have gone on. Security had been airtight and there was no chance whatsoever of it having been a fix. Absolutely none at all.

In any event the stunt proved to be a waste of time as it got barely any coverage in the press. It may not have occurred to John and Eugen, but the fact that *Viz* was selling over a million copies was actually newsworthy in itself. There was no need for them to embellish it with a tacky PR stunt. The million-selling rag-mag story was seized upon by press, radio and TV, and I was whisked from studio to studio, from dawn till dusk, for two or three days solid. I even popped up live on *Sky TV News* to talk about Buster Gonad, Johnny Fartpants and the Fat Slags. We didn't make *Newsnight* though.

We ended 1989 on a massive high. The comic was selling over a million copies and our fourth annual, *The Dog's Bollocks* was right up there in the *Sunday Times* best-sellers list, alongside Prince Charles's *A Vision of Britain* and Stephen Hawking's *Brief History of Time*.

CHAPTER TEN

An Inspector Calls

An unavoidable consequence of the comic's startling success was that all of a sudden I found myself rich. I'd never had any wild dreams to be rich beyond, but if I had done then, by 1989, I almost certainly would have been rich beyond them.

The money didn't appear completely out of the blue. There were a few signs of gradually accruing wealth along the way. One day I was discreetly taken to one side in my local bank and told that I had too much money in my account. They suggested I put some of it into a deposit account instead. A few months later my accountant looked grim-faced as he studied my books. 'What's the matter?' I asked. 'Your house is too small,' he replied. 'You'll have to buy something bigger.' Our new house was a touch on the small side, and Dolores had been a bit peeved when I put a pool table in the only decent-sized bedroom. But it was a nice little house in a nice little neighbourhood. It would never have occurred to me to buy a bigger house if my accountant hadn't opened his mouth and unsettled me.

When I was in my early teens every weekend throughout the summer, and most of the winter too, my dad took the family for picnics in Northumberland. Dad considered his car, which came with his job, an asset we were fortunate to have and he was determined that we should make the most of it – by driving as many miles as we possibly could every Sunday. He seemed to think that the amount of enjoyment we'd get from these trips was directly proportional to the distance we travelled. These expeditions were planned meticulously the night before. The picnic basket, folding chairs, tartan rug, windbreak, Wellington boots and binoculars would all be made ready in the hall, and our intended destination would be marked with a coloured pin on an old Ordnance Survey map which Dad kept especially for this purpose. Our route would always be dictated by the availability of disabled access public toilets for the use of my mum, so we had to stick strictly to both the map and a timetable. During the journey I would chart our progress on a map of my own and pester Dad to make diversions to follow the routes of old railway lines. Meanwhile my big brother Steve would moan constantly. He hated these outings and was working on the theory that if he ruined every single one of them by endlessly arguing he would eventually be left behind. 'What is the point of going on a picnic if you aren't enjoying it?' he'd ask Dad at the height of a blazing row. 'I *am* bloody well enjoying it, you awkward bastard!' Dad would say before stopping the car, red faced, temples bulging, waving his fist and threatening to make Steve walk the forty miles or so home.

Occasionally I'd get my way and we would drive close to derelict, overgrown railway lines.

There was something that fascinated me about these remote, abandoned places, and the idea of living in an old, rustic railway station was a dream of mine. A dream as opposed to an ambition. Other dreams included scoring for Newcastle in the Leazes End, and going to bed with Julie Christie in 1967. But in 1989 it suddenly dawned on me that at least one of those dreams could become a reality.

There were still a few practical problems to overcome. I'd need to find a station and that would almost certainly involve the use of a car. I didn't have one and I couldn't drive. I'd also have to wheedle Dolores into thinking it was a good idea. Fortunately she was distracted at the time. This was the spring of 1989 and she was not long pregnant with Dale. Perhaps it was her hormones, but she seemed remarkably susceptible to the idea. I mentioned the fact that I was in the market for a disused railway station to John Brown too – not in the hope that he or anyone in his circle of London media pals might know of one for sale, but as luck would have it one of them did. A TV producer friend of John's knew of a station for sale in the far north of Scotland, so Dolores and I set out to view it. We travelled by train and taxi to Kinbrace, a charming little hamlet in the middle of nowhere. The station was so remote the nearest pub had an entry in the *Guinness Book of Records* as Britain's most remote hotel. We liked Kinbrace station a lot but it had taken us two days to get there, with an overnight stop in Inverness, so it was going to be hellish for commuting. Ideally I wanted something a little closer to Newcastle, so, imposing on anyone we knew who could drive a car, we continued our search in Northumberland. We looked at a station up on the moors near the Scottish border but it had rising damp which had risen all the way to the roof, and it was full of cows. Eventually a lovely old station house came up for sale in north Northumberland at the foot of the Cheviot Hills. It was a beautiful building that had already been converted into a house, with a lovely woodland garden. So we bought it, and every weekend we'd invite friends to come up with us and stay for the weekend, on the condition that they drove.

I'd never felt an urge to drive a car but, by 1989, with Dolores pregnant, and having just bought a house fifty miles from Newcastle, I decided it was time to learn. I passed my test at the third attempt and bought myself a second-hand VW Golf. The benefits were immediate. Dolores and I could escape from the hectic world of *Viz* and spend lazy weekends alone together tucked away in rural isolation. Unfortunately the central heating boiler died during our very first weekend in the house, but there was something romantic about boiling your water on a wood-burning stove and keeping warm in front of a coal fire. The other cartoonists were all buying houses or flats too, but generally a bit closer to the office. My secretary Ann was also clambering onto the property ladder and, for a bizarre period of several months – or was it years? – office chit-chat turned almost exclusively to property prices, damp treatment, structural surveys and mort-gage rates.

Another sign of our success was the emergence of legal claims against the magazine. When I had published *Viz* myself I'd never given a thought to legal considerations. I made up a story claiming Paul McCartney had had sex with every girl in the Cavern Club five times over in a single night. And in another we'd claimed that the floor in snooker player Tony Knowles's hotel bedroom had collapsed from the sheer weight of groupies he was having sex with one night. I'd parody adverts using real product names and logos. The 'Black Hole' advert, for example, featured a man stuffing John Player Special cigarettes up his arse. But from the moment Virgin took over, each comic had to be read by a solicitor before it went to press. And as our sales increased *Viz* became a much bigger and fatter target for any predatory lawyers who happened to be swimming nearby.

Our first legal problem came to light in July 1989 when we received a letter from a firm of solicitors in Newcastle. Their client, a Mr Stephen Dixon, was complaining about an article that had appeared in issue 37 of the comic under the heading 'I made love to myself – while I watched'. This was a spoof news-paper story I'd written about a man called Reg Thompson who claimed to have had sex with himself in his own front room. It wasn't about wanking – I find wanking a tasteless subject for humour (unless, for some reason, monkeys are involved). This was a surreal story intended to take tabloid sex revelations to a nonsensical, inverted extreme: 'I'd had a few drinks and was feeling quite relaxed. Next thing I knew I felt my hand on my shoulder. Seconds later I was rolling around naked on the floor with myself. It seemed like the most natural thing in the world,' said Mr Thompson. And so it went on. The story was accompanied by an anonymous-looking photograph of a semi-detached house which I'd nicked from a local estate agent's brochure. And this was the problem. According to the solicitor's letter the house in the photograph belonged to their client, Mr Dixon, and they were demanding a 'proper and suitable sum of damages for the injury to his [Mr Dixon's] reputation and for the embarrassment and distress caused to him'. The final, and in my view ridiculous, outcome was that John Brown Publishing agreed to pay Mr Dixon £100 including costs. It was a paltry payout but it gave Mr Stephen Dixon a historic victory as he became the first person ever to receive damages from *Viz* magazine. If it had been up to me I'd have just told him to fuck off.

While that case was still in progress another, slightly more serious problem arose. On 14th December 1989 John was taken in to New Scotland Yard for questioning by the Anti-Terrorist Branch. They were making enquiries into an item that had appeared in issue 38 (October 1989), namely a Top Tip on the letters page that the police felt might constitute an incitement to commit an offence. John's solicitor faxed me the transcript he had taken of the interview. As we all huddled around my desk to read it John's first answer was greeted with howls of derisive laughter.

> 15th December 1989
>
> At the request of John Brown of John Brown Publishing Limited I attended at Scotland Yard on 14th December at 6.00 p.m. when John Brown was interviewed by Detective Inspector Hodges and Detective Constable Mayson who took a verbatim note. DI Hodges asked the questions and the interview took the following course.
>
> Hodges produced a copy of No. 38 of *Viz* magazine. Hodges asked John Brown whether he was responsible for the contents of the magazine and John Brown replied that he was the publisher and responsible only for the

promotion and physical distribution of the magazine and
the people responsible for the content were Chris and
Simon Donald, Graham Dury and Simon Thorp …

John sang like a canary on an ornithological version of
Opportunity Knocks. It's a wonder he didn't reel off our addresses
as well. But blaming us hadn't got him off the hook. Not long
into the interview the police read him his rights and on the
advice of his lawyer he declined to answer any more questions.

Following John's interview I was expecting a pull from the old
bill at any moment. Fortunately they decided against kicking
down my door and pulling me out of bed at five in the morning
while Dolores covered herself with the bedsheet. Instead DI
Hodges rang me at work and politely invited me to come down
to London to assist him with his enquiries. So a few days before
Christmas I set off to kill an unusual brace of birds with one
stone. I'd do a spot of Christmas shopping in the morning, and
then be interrogated by the Anti-Terrorist Branch after lunch. I
felt quite relaxed about the whole thing on the train but when I
arrived at New Scotland Yard and saw that famous revolving
sign outside the door I began to wonder. It was only five days
before Christmas. Dolores was at home, alone with our three-
month-old son Dale. What if they arrested me and threw me in
the cells? What sort of sentence could I expect for inciting a
terrorist act? And how old would Dale be when I got out?

John must have felt guilty about squealing, so he provided me
with a lawyer. There was some sort of incident underway in
London at the time and the Anti-Terrorist Branch were busy.
When the two officers eventually came down to see us they
apologized for being late. 'As you can hear, we're a bit busy
today,' said DI Hodges. There were sirens constantly wailing in
the street outside. We were taken to an interview room where
DI Hodges asked the questions and his young colleague DC
Mayson took notes. Because DC Mayson wrote at a painfully
slow pace DI Hodges had to punctuate his questions with long

pauses and was constantly turning to his colleague to see if he was keeping up. I … joined … in …, answering … one … word … at … a … time. This made the whole interview rather comical, but it also gave me extra time to think about what I was going to say.

Once again DI Hodges produced his copy of issue 38 of *Viz* magazine, and referred me to a Top Tip on the letters page. Top Tips were the amusing but ridiculous suggestions of thrift and ingenuity which appeared regularly in the magazine. I can't go into specifics for fairly obvious reasons but the gist of what the letter said was that carrying out a bomb hoax at a certain place at a certain time would, under certain circumstances, be a good idea. It must have seemed funny to me at the time I was editing the letters page, but it didn't sound so funny now, being read aloud to me in a deliberately sombre manner by a Detective Inspector from the Anti-Terrorist Branch. Hodges asked if I'd written it. I said I couldn't recall who'd written it but I'd edited the page and it would therefore have been my decision to include it in the comic. At this point the atmosphere changed and he read me an official caution. 'You have the right to remain silent' and all that jazz. This wasn't my first police caution. A transport copper in Carlisle once read me my rights after he'd stood and watched me walk across a disused railway line. The bastard had been disguised as a train-spotter. Hearing those words read out had been a terrifying ordeal for me as a twelve-year-old child, and it didn't feel a lot better aged twenty-nine. At this point my solicitor leaned forward and advised me to say nothing further. 'Hang on a minute,' I thought. This was ridiculous. By procrastinating all my lawyer would achieve was a bigger fee. Common sense told me they wouldn't bring charges as that would only generate publicity for us. So I ignored my brief and said I'd be happy to continue. Thereon the name of the game was for the police to try and get me to say something incriminating. DI Hodges started by talking generally about *Viz* and its success, getting quite matey at times. But I'd seen enough police interviews on TV to know what he was up to. After a protracted preamble – delivered at DC Mayson's pitiful writing pace – Hodges finally made his move. He asked how many readers *Viz* had. I said I didn't know precisely but it was well over half a million. 'Out of all those people, don't you think there might be one idiot daft enough to take that letter seriously?' he asked lightly, with a smile. 'Definitely not,' I said, and I heard my lawyer breathe a sigh of relief behind me.

The file was referred to the Crown Prosecution Service and I was eventually let off with an official caution and a warning that the letter in question must never be published again. Unfortunately, two years later, I'd completely forgotten the episode and without thinking I included it in the 1991 Christmas annual, *The Sausage Sandwich*. For a man who had just printed 250,000 incriminating books John Brown took the news quite well. He told me not to worry about it and then hired a specialist firm to apply an over-sticker, by hand, to every single copy. The sticker carried a new Top Tip, which read as follows:

PUBLISHERS. Always make sure your editors have
proofread your books before you print 250,000 of them.
  J Brown, London

Following our million-selling December 1989 issue the print run rose yet again to 1,366,350 for the February 1990 issue. *Viz* had reached its peak in terms of both sales and public profile, and our four-man writing committee was probably at its most productive. In the first million-seller we launched another strong character, Millie Tant. She was a crude parody of a stereotypical, boot-ugly feminist, the type of gal commonly found outside the gates of Greenham Common or campaigning to be elected Women's Officer in the Students' Union. This was another team effort by four of us, and Simon was allotted the task of illustrating the strip.

The Fat Slags and Millie Tant were both very funny, but they were also taking political incorrectness to extremes. In the past *Guardian* readers had given *Viz* the benefit of the doubt. In 1985 I'd even received a postcard from Billy Bragg in Nicaragua. How much more socialist can you get? But *Viz*'s contents were now becoming conspicuously popular and populist. The comic was also fashionable with the masses, and so, by definition, it was no longer going to be trendy with the trend-setters. I woke up one morning and found that *Viz* was no longer hip. It was mainstream. To make matters worse we were becoming part of the *establishment.* Awards were starting to roll in. *Viz* was named Medium of the Year for 1989 by *Campaign* magazine, the advertising tosspot's bible. In March 1990 we won first prize in the consumer magazine section of the British Press Circulation Awards and I was named Youth Editor of the Year 1989 at the British Society of Magazine Editors Awards. Alas I wasn't there to collect the prize. I was too busy. John Brown's office hoovered up all the trophies. None of the silverware ever made it up to Newcastle.

In 1985 John had asked whether I'd be interested in moving down to London, but only out of curiosity. But I was happy to remain at arm's length from him and the 'let's do lunch' culture of London's media world. John did lunch round the corner from the Boathouse at the River Café, where the young Jamie Oliver was still washing dishes. Occasionally John would ring me on his mobile and tell me to guess who was sitting at the next table. Once it was Sarah Ferguson, another time Bill Wyman. Meanwhile in Newcastle we bought our lunch at the Esso garage round the corner; horrible sandwiches, pop and crisps. Occasionally I'd ring John and ask him to guess what flavour crisps I was eating.

John's principal business strength was his bullying. I pity anyone who went to school with him. He was often frustrated by the distance between us because it made bullying me a lot more difficult. I would agree to anything John said on the phone, then send him a fax ten minutes later saying I'd changed my mind. So he'd come up to our Newcastle office to pin me down on really important issues, and during one such visit in 1989 he bumped into our landlord in the corridor downstairs. The next thing I knew John had bought the building. It wasn't for sale, he just asked the landlord how much he wanted for it. John considered it an investment, but I considered it an affront. My feeling of independence was important, and having John as my landlord considerably weakened it. John saw it the opposite way. He wanted me in his pocket. John made plenty of other mistakes, one of which was to try and export *Viz* to the most humourless country on Earth. In 1990 he licensed some material to a German magazine called *Irre Cool* without even mentioning it to me. But alongside our cartoon strips translated into German *Irre Cool* also reproduced news features, adding their own photographs and jokes, and making up their own letters for the letters page. I was incensed, as were the other cartoonists who passed an impromptu vote of no confidence in John. I had a workers' revolt on my hands so I hatched a scheme to defuse the situation. I told John to send the four of us £250 each, in cash, or we would put our pens down and stop work. It was petulant and most unbusinesslike, but it worked. John sent the money, albeit reluctantly, and as we counted our loot the Merry Men were happy again.

During 1989 we had an approach from an agency eager to hire the services of the Fat Slags for a poster campaign advertising Tennent's Pilsner lager. I told John to demand the same money Mel Smith would get if he appeared in a similar campaign, as I saw some similarities between Smith and our characters. John came back with what he described as a Frank Bruno offer instead, but it was still a lot of money so I put my artistic principles to one side for a moment and allowed the ad to go ahead.

The billboard poster itself was awful. It featured a scene from TV's *Blind Date* with one of the Fat Slags having just revealed herself to her prospective date. Only the man's foot can be seen as he disappears off the other side of the poster at high speed, leaving behind him a bottle of Tennent's Pilsner lager. The slogan was 'It's good, but not *that* good'. The fact that people don't drink lager on *Blind Date* obviously hadn't worried the creative director. Neither had the issue of PC. The Advertising Standards Authority received thirty-six complaints about the campaign which coincided, rather unfortunately, with the February 1990 publication of 'Herself Reappraised', the ASA's survey on attitudes to women in advertising. Talk about bad timing – it was Rag Week at the ASA. The complainants said that the advertisement was grossly offensive in its portrayal of women and in its implication that fat women could not be attractive. Inevitably the ASA case report upheld these complaints and described the advertising approach as 'crude, vulgar and not to be condoned'. They also said that the advert could *not* be justified by its humour, which I took to mean that it wasn't funny. On that point I agreed. Ironically the ad had been the work of a female executive called Kate Murphy, of Grays agency. But all credit to the Millie Tants of this world who shot it down in flames. I'd never received a single complaint from them about the Fat Slags cartoon strip – in the context of a banal comic for boys they didn't deem the Slags worthy of attention – but the moment a Slag popped her head up above the parapet in a public advertising campaign they opened fire. Mind you, the Fat Slags sexist sell-out controversy was nothing compared to the storm that erupted in October 1990 over what turned out to be the most controversial cartoon ever published in *Viz*.

The story of the Thieving Gypsy Bastards began in Nottingham way back in the early 1970s when travelling folk who were in town for the annual Goose Fair plundered an old washing machine from Graham Dury's back yard. Graham had been given specific instructions to guard the house against marauding travellers while his mother ran an errand. The washing machine was virtually worthless, but its theft left a deep psychological scar on the young cartoonist-to-be. At around the same time the annual Hoppings event was taking place on Newcastle's Town Moor and a huge population of travellers were encamped nearby. My dad had often warned me to beware of thefts during Hoppings week and for that reason my bike, along with my brothers' bikes, had been locked away in a coal shed in the back yard. A few days after the Hoppings left town I went to

Thieving Gypsy Bastards

open the shed and to my horror found the lock had been forced and all three bikes were gone. It wasn't much of a bike – bought second, third or quite possibly fourth-hand by my dad – but its theft left a deep psychological scar on me too.

Many years later Graham and I were sitting in the *Viz* office exchanging childhood back yard traveller theft anecdotes when we suddenly hit upon an idea for a new cartoon.

The Thieving Gypsy Bastards was the story of a family of miscreant caravan dwellers called the McO'Dougles who travelled from town to town, camping in private gardens, burgling houses, picking pockets and placing malicious curses on anyone who refused to buy their lucky heather. But it wasn't just the 'Gypsies' who were the butt of the joke. An innocent victim who complains about their behaviour to the police is himself arrested for harassing the 'friendly, harmless, traditional Romany travelling folk' who throughout the story are blatantly patronized by the local council. Looking at it now, the editorial undercurrent of the strip looks more compatible with the *Daily Mail* than *Viz*. Apart from the obvious fact that it was reinforcing the idea that all Gypsies are thieves, it was also propagating the notion that they get preferential treatment from left-wing authorities.

I knew we were batting on a sticky wicket so I let John Brown read the strip prior to publication. John was rarely given this privilege. We'd run another by him once – The Milky Bar Yid – and he'd said no to that, pointing out that his partner Claudia was Jewish. Generally speaking I applied my own levels of censorship, and there was only one hard and fast rule. I forbade the use of the 'C' word. I didn't like the word, perhaps because it was the only one that had never cropped up in my dad's heated argument vocabulary. Dad never swore unless he was furious. Mum never swore at all. So in the early days the 'C' word was definitely out of bounds (until I received a cartoon called Bertie Blunt – His Parrot's a Cunt, from a Belfast cartoonist called Sean Agnew, and I simply couldn't resist it).

John thought the Thieving Gypsy Bastards would raise more problems than laughter. He rang me at home and asked me to reconsider using it on the grounds that it would create an enormous stink, and that some less bright readers might take it as encouragement to taunt Gypsies. Graham, Thorpy and myself had a meeting the following morning and discussed the issue at some length. Then I gave John my decision. I acknowledged that the cartoon might cause offence to a small number of people, and in the worst-case scenario some ignorant readers might be encouraged to taunt Gypsies. But I put it to John that the same rules had not been applied to the Fat Slags. How many overweight women had been called 'fat slags' since that strip became popular? But that didn't stop him from publishing it. If you analysed the comic enough we were effectively playground bullies, poking fun at one or two individuals in order to entertain the crowd. Of course there were limits to what I would do or say, but they had always been instinctive, not reasoned. In this case instinct told me that this strip was much funnier than it was offensive, and I overruled John. Reluctantly he agreed to be overruled.

In order to placate John a little and deflect some of the inevitable criticism we wrote another short strip, The Nice Honest Gypsies, and put it on the following page. It began with the words, 'Like the vast majority of itinerants, travellers and showmen, the Nice Honest Gypsies are honest law-abiding citizens.' I don't think it helped very much. I gave the Thieving Gypsy Bastards top billing on page 3 of issue 44. In the small print of the publishing credits a special address was given for Gypsies to send their complaints to. Complaints duly arrived, but not from Gypsies. There were only four written complaints to my office and they were from an academic, a Romany organization, and two from racial equality councils. The charge was racism. Gypsies were a race, and we were inciting racial hatred. T. A. Acton, a Doctor of Philosophy and Reader in Romany Studies at Thames Polytechnic, wrote to me saying that 'photocopies of the strip are being passed around among Gypsies and are exciting the same kind of outrage as The Satanic Verses have among Muslims'. He concluded what was a very serious letter by calling us 'a bunch of lazy-minded, chicken-shit Geordie wankers', which I thought was rather a neat touch. The other complainants were less engaging. The President of the Romany Union (the 'Romano Internacionalno Jekhethanibe') wrote to me from Texas accusing Viz of a breach of the Race Relations Act and threatening legal action unless a retraction and apology were forthcoming. Tyne and Wear Racial Equality Council wrote to complain about the volume of complaints they were having to field from offended Gypsies, and Essex Racial

Equality Council took their grievance directly to the Press Council who contacted me as part of their formal complaints procedure.

The tabloid press were quickly on the case. On 23 October 1990 the *Sun* ran a story claiming, 'Furious Gypsy leaders have sent the cartoon to Attorney General Sir Patrick Mayhew – demanding legal action.' They quoted one Hughie Smith, 'boss of the 50,000 strong National Gypsy Council', who according to them described the strip as 'disgusting'. Later I received a long letter from Hughie Smith himself, writing on behalf of the National Gypsy Council and denying the *Sun*'s claims. Smith said he wanted to set the record straight. In his very long letter he wrote: 'In the first instance, when we became aware of the cartoon strip in your magazine, we at once recognized it as a piece of humour in the true satirical fashion, and as such it works; in fact, I found it highly amusing. There are, however, certain self-styled "Gypsy protectors" and other do-gooders in this country who take the view that the Gypsy is always right, and who jump and shout discrimination immediately anyone tries to use the name Gypsy in conjunction with anything they might disagree with.' Mr Smith accompanied his letter with a thick wad of documents which related to a number of 'so-called Gypsy organizations' which had been set up in this country, 'all of which need us more than we need them', as he put it. He drew a distinction between genuine Gypsies and what he termed 'pretend Gypsies', many of whom he accused of living in houses. Mr Smith blamed 'so-called Gypsy organizations' for squandering hundreds of thousands of pounds in Government and EEC funding on projects designed to benefit Gypsies but which had in fact benefited only the people responsible for running them. He suggested we might want to run a strip in the future called the 'Thieving Do-Gooder Bastards'.

The dossier Hughie Smith enclosed was fascinating, if not a little on the heavy side. There were photocopies of correspondence, press clippings and other literature, all of which detailed – and I do mean *detailed* – a long-running feud between himself, Hughie Smith – 'President of the National Gypsy Council incorporating the Romany Kris and the Western European Council of Gypsies' – and a man called Thomas O'Doherty whose official title appeared to be 'Principal of the Society of Travelling People in co-operation with the International Gypsy Council', but whom Mr Smith referred to as the 'self-styled King of the Gypsies'. Among the copied letters were legal threats, long lists of alleged criminal convictions against both men, unsubstantiated accusations and counteraccusations of defamation and libel, and letters from their respective organizations each accusing the other of a multitude of sins, including illiteracy and, once again, that most despicable of Gypsy crimes: house-dwelling.

This comical inter-Gypsy feud was a pleasant distraction from the problems that the cartoon itself had been creating. We had been trying to sit tight and weather the storm, but the storm simply wouldn't go away. There was a constant bombardment of press enquiries, and 'told you so' phone calls from a harassed John Brown. Graham, who had drawn the strip, was getting particularly worried about the various curses that were being bandied about in the press. Then, in December, I got a phone call from the *Sun*. Graham begged me not to take it – we were in a writing meeting at the time – but I did. The reporter was conspiratorial in his tone, and he tipped me off that one of the Gypsies involved in the protest about our cartoon was due up in court in Oldham later that week on a charge of handling stolen goods. If he was convicted they were planning to run a story accusing him of hypocrisy. Did I want to comment?

Accusing someone of hypocrisy was a bit hypocritical, I thought, coming from a tabloid journalist. He obviously wanted me to gloat and come up with some witty put-downs to complement his story, but I wasn't going to. The Gypsy in the dock was none other than Hughie Smith, who had not complained about the strip, and in any case the last thing I wanted was to be making flippant jokes in the *Sun* while an argument was still raging about racism. So I told the reporter that the strip had been discontinued following complaints of racism and that an apology would appear in the next issue. He went ahead with his story regardless and on 13 December 1990 the *Sun* revealed that Hughie Smith had been convicted of handling two stolen generators and fined £120. The story may have been inaccurate, but the *Sun* wasn't going to let a minor detail like that get in the way of a good headline: 'Don't brand us all thieving gypsies – says thieving gypsy.'

CHAPTER ELEVEN

The TV Comedy of the Nineties

Back in 1986, in the footnote of a letter to John, I casually mentioned that we were busy writing a sitcom called 'Too Many Cooks' about three chefs who all got divorced and ended up sharing a house next door to their three ex-wives. John got very excited about this and I had to let him down gently when telling him it was just a joke.

John was always very keen to make a *Viz* TV programme. It wasn't an idea that had occurred to me, but John envisaged films and TV shows, and all the money and showbiz kudos that came with them. He was constantly on the phone reminding me to write a *Viz* TV show, as if it was something we could do in our lunch break.

In 1987 I met someone else who also had visions of *Viz* on TV. I'd never heard the name Harry Enfield until September of that year when the man himself rang me up and explained that he was a comedian and a big fan of *Viz*. He wondered if he could come up to Newcastle and meet me. He brought with him a producer friend called Andrew Fell and we went to Willow Teas for lunch. Harry was a big sniggerer – he laughed and chuckled a lot – but he was also smarmy. He'd studied politics at York University and seemed to be employing the tricks of that trade to further his career in entertainment. At one point he whispered that I should just ignore his friend Andrew as he'd only been invited along to pay for the train tickets and lunch.

Harry said he was interested in doing a television equivalent of *Viz*, a sketch show based around lots of different characters. Would we be interested in helping to write it? As with Jonathan Ross, I nodded politely and said I'd think about it. Not long after that meeting Harry was on tour and performing at Newcastle Polytechnic along with the Scottish comedian and writer Craig Ferguson, who in those days was fat and went by the stage name of Bing Hitler. I'd never seen Harry perform, but from what he'd told me his act was made up of various characters, a bit like *Viz*. I was amazed at how much like *Viz* it was. One of his jokes, about him being so sexy that a taxi he was travelling in exploded, had been lifted straight out of our Tony Knowles story in issue 11.

Offstage, Harry did a hysterical range of impressions (Windsor Davis, Donald Sinden and Bob Monkhouse being among the best) but on stage he seemed uncomfortable and his characters were very hit and miss. He didn't come across as a natural entertainer; more like someone who'd chosen comedy as a career in the same way that a graduate might opt for accountancy or law. But his career appeared to be going according to plan. Before long two of his characters – Stavros and Loads of Money – became huge hits on ITV's *Saturday Night Live* show and Harry also became a regular voice impressionist on *Spitting Image*.

In December 1987 Harry invited me and Dolores to stay at his flat in Muswell Hill. We were down in London for John Brown's wedding to the lovely Claudia Zeff, daughter of a very wealthy tailor. At the wedding party I spoke to Claudia's wealthy dad. He asked me how sales of *Viz* were going. 'Not bad,' I said, 'but we're having trouble getting the magazine into the big shops like WHSmith.' 'Have you tried bribing the store managers?' he asked, apparently in all seriousness. John's wedding party was held at Claridge's, and the minute we walked in the door I knew

Dolores and I were way out of our depth. There was no sign of a disco or karaoke. In the corner a string quartet was playing classical music, and blokes dressed up like the footmen in Cinderella were gliding about the room carrying trays of champagne and posh sandwiches back and forth. I'm not one for champagne – it gives me wind – so afterwards Harry took us to a pub for a drink, then we went back to his flat where he kindly put us up in his basement bedroom, while he slept in the living room above. Unfortunately, in the course of the wedding-do, Dolores had partaken of a touch too much champagne, plus a touch too many egg and cress sandwiches. During the night I was awoken by what I thought was the sound of splashing water. Alas it wasn't. It was the sound of Dolores being sick into her lap.

She was sitting on the edge of the bed, and, not wishing to stain the bed or the carpet, she had somehow managed to retain the vomit in a makeshift reservoir between her thighs. By the time I awoke this reservoir was almost full to capacity and I desperately looked around for a watertight container to catch the inevitable overflow. I couldn't get to the kitchen without waking Harry so in a panic I decided to make do with an empty fish tank that was in our bedroom for some reason. Alas it was too late. By the time I got back to the bed a flash flood of egg, cress and champagne spew had poured down the side of the bed and formed a lake on the newly carpeted floor below.

In the morning I paced around the room nervously, dreading the prospect of having to tell Harry Enfield, TV's Mr Loads of Money, that my wife had just spewed all over his nice new carpet. Eventually I took a deep breath and went upstairs to break the news. Harry was absolutely charming. He gave a perfect demonstration of how an English gentleman host should react when a lady house guest throws up all over his bedroom. He wasn't in the least bit concerned about the damage or the smell. His only concern was for the welfare of the lady in distress. 'Oh, the poooooor darling!' he said at first in a deliberately loud voice intended to reassure Dolores in the room below. When she'd recovered sufficiently he made her a stomach-settling breakfast of goat's yoghurt with honey.

Despite this unfortunate incident Harry remained a friend and he called me again not long afterwards. He'd come up with a new TV character called Bugger All Money, a Geordie designed to counteract his boastful, flash Cockney character Loads of Money. Harry had some dialogue already but asked if I could write some more and work it all up into a script. Oh, and there was one other thing. Could he possibly have it in time for his TV rehearsal which was in two hours? I cobbled something together as best I could and then read it down the phone to him, spelling out phonetic versions of all the Geordie phraseology. Then he read it back to me and I corrected him at the points where he was getting the accent seriously wrong. Harry performed it live on TV the following night. It wasn't perfect, but I have to say that for a posh southern twat he made a pretty good job of the Geordie accent.

Harry had, and still does have, extremely short and stumpy fingers which he somehow managed to conceal from his adoring female fans. But his ambitions stretched farther than his fingers. Harry seemed unusually well connected in the TV world, introducing us to producer John Lloyd with whom John Brown, myself and the entire editorial team vaguely discussed ideas for Harry's '*Viz*-style' TV show. Nothing came of that. Then in September 1988 he took me for tea at Maureen Lipman's house in a very leafy suburb of London. I don't recall why we went to Maureen Lipman's house, but we did. Clearly she hadn't been expecting us, and the poor woman didn't have a clue what *Viz* was, but she was very nice anyway and made us a cup of tea.

Harry also introduced me to one of my greatest heroes, Peter Cook. To my delight Cook *had* heard of *Viz* and said he was a fan of Roger Mellie in particular. Harry, Dolores and I went out for a meal with Peter and his wife Lin at an Italian restaurant somewhere in Hampstead. Cook looked pretty dreadful compared to when I'd last seen him – in the 1960s film *Bedazzled*. He was white-haired, overweight and drunk, but at the same time entirely alert to everything around him. And he was amazingly, effortlessly funny. I wanted to write down every casual aside he muttered, but alas I didn't. At the end of the evening as we were leaving Peter's house Harry suggested that Peter and I might get together and write something one day. The audacity of this remark took me by surprise. I looked down at the great Peter

Roger Mellie the Man on the Telly

Cook, sitting there on his gigantic settee, and was totally lost for words. Despite the empty vodka bottles on the table in front of him Peter was entirely *compos mentis* and could see that I was a little embarrassed. He said nothing, but smiled at me in a 'let's not get too carried away' sort of manner. It was a lovely smile.

Quite why I was being carted around all these comedy icons I wasn't sure, but I suspect Harry was trying to rope all of them into his proposed TV show. He wanted me to help write it, but writing comedy with someone you don't really know is impossible. You need to have an empathy with someone first. Despite spending time with Harry I didn't feel like we were empathizing. We'd sit in pubs not saying much and Harry would occasionally break the silence by asking how much money *Viz* was making. He was very money-minded. John Brown, who had his own *Viz* TV aspirations, was actively encouraging my relationship with Harry to the point where I began to feel a like a specially imported panda at Moscow Zoo. And I wasn't getting wood. Harry and I just didn't spark. There was one defining moment when he took me to a new house he'd just bought in Primrose Hill and introduced me to two mates, Charlie Higson and a bloke called Paul Whitehouse. They were dressed in overalls and were engaged in a very workman-like conversation about light fittings that hadn't arrived, but Harry assured me these were his comedy writers. We all sat there for a while on the floor (there wasn't any furniture) and I remember feeling an enormous pressure to say something funny. But I couldn't.

In the Soho circles that he moved in, John Brown met many of TV's movers and shakers and he seemed to be on very good terms with a posh bloke called Stephen Garrett who was Channel 4's Commissioning Editor for Youth Programmes. Garrett was a TV industry bright young thing – the Channel 4 equivalent of Janet Street-Porter, but with a less adventurous set of incisors. The son of a wealthy advertising mogul, Garrett's principal qualification for dictating what Britain's yoof should be watching on TV seemed to be a law degree from Oxford. In 1989 a production company called Millennium put forward a proposal to John for a TV documentary telling the story of the comic's remarkable success. John was very keen on the idea, and so was Stephen Garrett. John told me the exposure would be useful, but the way he described the programme made me weary. I thought this might be a surreptitious attempt to rope us into making a TV programme ourselves.

What Millennium had in mind was exactly that. They wanted to make a *Viz* investigative documentary, taking the piss out of shows like the po-faced *Cook Report*. John talked me into meeting up with Millennium's producer Pete Ward and director Phil

Morrow. They came up to see us and pitched their idea over a meal at Sachins, a Punjabi restaurant in Newcastle. Morrow did all the talking. He seemed like a nice enough bloke but he was a bit boastful about his contacts in the TV world. At one point during the meal he dropped the name of Janet Street-Porter. With unbelievable timing Janet Street-Porter then walked into the restaurant with another group of diners. It was uncanny. 'Look, there she is now,' we pointed out. 'Aren't you going to say hello?' 'She looks a bit busy right now,' Morrow replied, looking a trifle embarrassed. I felt sorry for him. The chances of Janet Street-Porter walking through that door, bang on cue, must have been billions to one.

He may have exaggerated his show-business connections a little, but we liked Phil and eventually he talked us into cooperating with their documentary, saying we didn't have to contribute anything to the script if we didn't want to. It was a hideously vague arrangement. By now I realized that the idea had been sold to Channel 4 entirely on the strength of our involvement. Stephen Garrett wanted a *Viz* TV show on Channel 4. But he wasn't going to get one. Now that they'd got their commission Millennium were perfectly happy to make the programme themselves, and we had no idea what we were letting ourselves in for.

The only input I had was when Morrow asked who I thought should present the programme. I suggested my old mate Arthur 2 Stroke (aka Tony O'Diamond and Mr Moneybags). Since we last heard from him he had swapped his unsuccessful career as a guest-house proprietor (the guest-house burnt down the week after the insurance expired) for a spectacularly unsuccessful career as a bus driver. (He crashed into a parked car at high speed on his first day, then remonstrated rudely with his elderly passengers, accusing them of making a fuss over nothing when he failed to stop.) I was certain this man would be a star when I first saw him on stage at the Gosforth Hotel. Ten years, four flop records, one gutted guest-house and a written-off VW Beetle later, Arthur 2 Stroke still harboured showbiz ambitions. So I was surprised and delighted when, despite a total lack of experience, he was handed the job of TV presenter.

In the autumn of 1989 2 Stroke took time off from crashing buses to film the *Viz* documentary. We took no part in the planning of the show and merely went along with anything Phil Morrow asked us to do. For example, I was interviewed driving to work in the cab of a railway engine which I had supposedly bought with the proceeds of the comic, and Thorpy was filmed at the wheel of 'his' vintage bus. The film-makers spent quite a bit of time interviewing *Viz* fans, but only celebrities of course. To their credit they did try to speak to a few detractors, too, in order to give a more balanced view, and in this regard I pointed them in the direction of Mrs Stella Shacklady, a combative Bristol housewife who had been quoted saying some uncomplimentary things about *Viz* in her local newspaper. Unfortunately when interviewed on camera Mrs Shacklady turned out to be disappointingly reasonable. The star of the programme was without doubt TV presenter Keith Chegwin who claimed that *Viz* had ruined his career by printing a story about him having no talent. Chegwin gave a magnificent performance as a down-and-out, wearing tramps' clothing and rummaging around at low tide on the dirty banks of the river Thames, looking for junk to sell. Unbeknown to us at the time of filming, Chegwin's performance was heavily ironic. His career had, at that time, hit an all-time low and he was in the depths of alcoholism.

In January 1990, with filming in the can, Phil Morrow and Pete Ward came back to Newcastle to moot the idea of a series of six further documentaries covering different, diverse subjects. Were we, as *individuals*, interested in contributing to such a project? This would be nothing to do with *Viz*, they said, and we wouldn't have much input either. We could leave all the work to them. John was furious when I told him about this approach which he felt had been made behind his back. He was still expecting us to lay him a golden TV egg – 'the TV comedy of the nineties', as he used to call it – and he didn't want us going off to sit on someone else's nest. He said Millennium would be using the *Viz* name to get the series commissioned, and no matter how far we officially distanced *Viz* from the proposed documentaries, if we were involved the series was bound to be regarded within the industry as a *Viz* product. And if the final products were shit, said John, it would reflect badly on the magazine. This was a very valid point, and one that John might also have applied to the original *Viz* documentary proposal. Unfortunately he didn't, and unfortunately the *Viz* documentary was shit.

Director Phil Morrow made an elementary mistake. He tried to make a funny documentary about a funny subject; and in comedy, just as in O-level Physics, two positives equal a negative. The programme fell awkwardly between the documentary and comedy stools. After it was transmitted, in May 1990, *Guardian* TV reviewer Adam Sweeting summed it up rather well:

'*Viz* – The Documentary' (Channel 4) purported to be a hard-hitting documentary, in the style of *This Week* or *World in Action*, exposing the sinister conspiracy to undermine the British way of life which is the ultra-successful *Viz* comic. Spurious witnesses were interviewed, embittered ex-friends of the *Viz* squad appeared in silhouette, knowledgeable commentators were sought out. For all that, the effort to counter *Viz*-style humour with deadpan pseudo-reportage was never much better than clumsy ... The *Viz* documentary never seemed clear about its objectives, and apparently mixed straightforward factual bits with jokey set-ups ... Dismally, the *Viz* men came across as a particularly dull rock group from any anonymous northern city. They had nothing to say, and revelations that Chris Donald is an avid train-spotter while the others tinker with old Mini Coopers and veteran omnibuses proved that inventors aren't always as interesting as their inventions.'

All press criticism stings at the time, but with the benefit of hindsight Adam Sweeting was entirely right. Jokingly or not – you could never tell – the programme focused far too much on us as individuals, trying to generate some sort of aura or mystique around us. Fortunately by this time plans for the six subsequent documentaries had already been scrapped, but the damage to our reputation had already been done. Just as the *Sparks* programme on BBC2 had launched *Viz* onto the national stage six years earlier, the *Viz* documentary on Channel 4 made one of the first holes in its hull.

The blindingly obvious way to adapt *Viz* for TV was of course to animate the cartoons, and I first proposed this idea in March 1988. In those days animation was still a hugely expensive, labour-intensive process and, John being a tight bastard, we were bound to be looking at a bargain bin production. Bearing this in mind, I suggested that the low-budget, cut-out style of animation used on the Captain Pugwash cartoons would suit a strip like Billy the Fish, as the clumsiness of the animation would add to the intentional cheesiness of the script. It wasn't until two years later, after John Brown had clambered into bed with Channel 4's Stephen Garrett, that the idea was finally taken up. By 1990 football had become highly fashionable among London's media fops and so the idea to animate Billy the Fish was rekindled by John and Stephen Garrett over lunch in a Soho brasserie. Their brilliant idea was for it to be screened on Channel 4 to coincide with the June 1990 World Cup finals. The only problem being that it was already March.

Despite the disappointing *Viz* documentary, John had taken a shine to Phil Morrow and appointed him as producer for the Billy the Fish animation. There was no script to write – the animators would use my old cartoons as storyboards. The only problem was finding some poor bastard to animate it all – as cheaply as possible – in less than two months. A suitable poor bastard was located in Cardiff. His name was Tony Barnes, of Fairwater Films, and he already had one hit TV animation under his belt. I'd never heard of *The Shoe People*, but John Brown was impressed by Tony's credentials. He was the cheapest animator outside of China – and prepared to work for the ridiculously low figure of around £3,600 per minute. (That's per minute of finished animation, not his rate of pay.)

Before they could start making my pictures move, the soundtrack had to be recorded. The animator synchronizes the lips to fit the soundtrack, so the voices are always recorded first. Again there were severe budget restrictions in place so we asked Harry Enfield if he'd help out, not mentioning that we wanted him to do every single voice. He agreed and we then booked a ridiculously short slot at a London recording studio in which Harry had to invent, rehearse and then record every single voice in the cartoon.

Tony Barnes and his team then worked night and day to get the animation ready. It was such a rush job there were inevitable errors made along the way. Unfortunately the animators didn't know a great deal about the geography of a football pitch, so a strange penalty kick was taken from the 18-yard line, but apart from that it was pretty much okay. Five short episodes were broadcast on Channel 4 late in the evening on consecutive nights between 30 June and 4 July 1990. An omnibus edition was then shown twice on Friday 6 July. Somehow someone in the TV industry calculated that between them they were watched by 3.4 million viewers, but how they worked that out I'm not entirely sure.

Creatively I rated it 'okay', but from a commercial point of view *Billy the Fish* was a big success. Channel 4 commissioned two further batches and they were screened in December 1991. The TV money paid John's production costs, on top of which PolyGram then paid a generous six-figure advance for the video rights. This came as a delightful surprise to me. John's reaction was fairly predictable. 'Which cartoon shall we animate next?' John proposed that Roger Mellie should be next up into the make-up chair, but this was different. Roger Mellie was my pride and joy. Despite the onset of multilateral studio practices I'd always refused to let anyone else draw him. Roger had come quite a long way since his first, inspired but rather one-dimensional appearance in 1981. He was now a much fuller character, although not entirely original. Physically, Roger's frizzy sides and comb-over hairdo were modelled on George House, a 1970's BBC North-East anchor man, while his bulky body belonged to House's on-screen partner Mike Neville. His jacket – the pattern totally unsuitable for television – was inspired by Stuart Hall. And although I didn't know it at the time, Roger's personality was also on loan. Looking back at him now I think Roger's stupidity, comically counterbalanced with his jovial, bluff self-confidence ('Don't worry, Tom, I'm a professional') originally belonged to Ted Baxter, the similarly inept newsreader on the *Mary Tyler Moore Show*. I would always watch that show for Ted Baxter's brief appearances alone, and I guess Roger was simply Ted Baxter with Tourette's syndrome.

I was very precious about Roger and I wasn't keen to see him animated in the same style as Billy the Fish. With all due respect to Tony 'Give me enough money and I'll make you *Fantasia*' Barnes, his Poundstretcher style of animation had been perfect for Billy the Fish. But Roger Mellie was different. A lot of the jokes and nuances were in Roger's facial expressions. It was a bit more subtle, I thought. I wasn't at all keen on the idea … until Peter Cook agreed to do Roger's voice. At that point I cancelled all my reservations.

This was a chance to work with my greatest living comedy hero. And with the great Peter Cook involved, how could we possibly fail?

CHAPTER TWELVE

Chocolates? Maltesers

One of the more difficult aspects of a publisher's job is estimating how many books to print, especially in the run-up to the busy Christmas period. Print too few and you lose sales, print too many and you wake up on Boxing Day with a warehouse charging you rent for an unwanted mountain of books and a massive printer's bill that you can't pay.

In 1989 we produced the *Viz Book of Crap Jokes* – a little Christmas stocking-sized rehash of the single-frame jokes which were John's favourite part of the magazine. Before deciding how many he should print John licked his finger and held it in the air. Taking into account the facts that (a) sales of our Christmas annuals had been rising as sharply as those of the comic, (b) the new joke book was small enough to sit alongside the till in shops, and (c) it would appeal broadly to people of all ages – it wasn't rude at all – John made the confident decision to print 350,000 copies of the book. 350,000 was a fuck of a lot of books, even by our best-selling standards. In the event the *Crap Jokes* book did very well indeed, but it didn't do a *fuck of a lot* well, which was the level of success John had been hoping for. So on Boxing Day he woke up with an estimated 150,000 *Crap Jokes* books left on his hands.

Another difficult part of a publisher's job is deciding what to do with 150,000 unwanted books. John's first idea was, by his standards, brilliant. 'Why don't we give them away as a competition prize in the magazine?' he said. 'First prize: 100,000 copies of the *Crap Jokes* book! Second prize: 50,000 copies.' Alas that wasn't practical, so John pulped the vast majority of the books and gave tens of thousands away to the Richer Sounds retail chain. (Anyone who bought a hi-fi system in 1990 for £9.99 may recall getting a free book with it.) The Crap Joke was on John, but in more ways than one. I suppose it was inevitable really that, having pulped and given away so many books, sales would subsequently take off. They did, of course, and by the following Christmas poor John was paying to have the book reprinted.

Another book scheduled for publication in 1989 was the *Bumper Book of Shite*, a spoof of the classic British adventure comics of the 1950s. Unfortunately it wasn't ready in time – we hadn't even started it – so it was rescheduled for a 1990 launch. By 1990 we still hadn't started it so the *Bumper Book of Shite* was once again postponed and in its place a *Billy the Fish Football Yearbook* was hastily thrown together. This was another flimsy rehash of old material, intended to capitalize on young Billy Thompson's simultaneous TV début.

Billy the Fish had never been that popular with our readers. Despite the signing of numerous big-name players (Shakin' Stevens, Mick Hucknall, Norman Wisdom, Cardinal Basil Hume, leader of the Catholic Church in Britain, the Archbishop of Canterbury Dr David Runcie and Her Royal Highness the Queen Mother) Fulchester United were in the doldrums. The strip was perpetually on its last legs, and it descended into farce when Go! Discs record label became Fulchester United's official shirt sponsors (two years before SEGA announced their ground-breaking sponsorship of Roy Race's Melchester Rovers). As blatant plugs for records by The Beautiful South and Beats International began to appear in the dialogue as well as on shirts and hoardings, what little plot there had been went out the window. Bearing in mind this and the fact that readers had already been given two opportunities to buy the cartoons – first in the comic and then in the Christmas reprint annuals – the *Billy the Fish Football Yearbook* was not one of our bestsellers. But our annuals were proving massive money-spinners. In 1988 the initial print run for our *Big Pink Stiff One* was 65,000. Twelve months later John ordered 375,000 copies of *The Dog's Bollocks*.

The way to promote a book according to conventional PR wisdom is for the author or editor to appear in the media at every available opportunity. The theory was that if I appeared as a guest at 1 a.m. on Bob Roberts's late-night local radio show in Blackburn, for example, sales of *Viz* books would increase. With all due respect to Bob Roberts and his erstwhile colleagues in the world of late-night local radio, I doubt very much whether all my appearances on their various late-night radio shows put together resulted in the sale of a single *Viz* book.

In 1989 our rags-to-riches story had been newsworthy, but a year later the fact that *Viz* was *still* selling a million wasn't quite so interesting. So we needed something else by way of a gimmick to stir up media interest. The idea we came up with was to stage an exhibition of modern art.

The plan was for the cartoonists to knock up a few pretentious abstract paintings, put them on show at a top London gallery, and claim that we were bored with producing *Viz* and wanted to be taken seriously for a change. This plan was inspired by *Beano Boy*, a huge, ugly painting of a full-length figure that John had (presumably) paid a fortune for, and the painting hung on the wall behind him in his garishly decorated Fulham office. It was 'naïve' in style, or 'crap' as an art novice might prefer to call it. It looked as if the artist had started at the bottom of the canvas, painting the feet first, and by the time he'd reached the shoulders he'd realized he was running out of room. So the neck and head were tilted sideways to cram them into the remaining space. It was painted in vile colours, all applied in thick layers, like Polyfilla. To us this picture came to symbolize John's extravagant and pretentious use of all the money we were earning for him. So I guess our exhibition – 'The Other Side of *Viz*' – was, subconsciously at least, our way of taking the piss out of John.

The Vanessa Devereux Gallery in the Notting Hill area of London agreed to stage the exhibition. Vanessa was the wife of Robert Devereux, a friend and former Virgin Books colleague of John's. She was also the sister of Richard Branson and she shared her brother's unmistakable bone structure and prominent teeth, while at the same time managing to look rather attractive. Fancying a woman who so closely resembled Richard Branson was an extremely unsettling sensation, as Thorpy confessed at the time.

A date for our exhibition was set and we frantically set about producing the twenty or so paintings required to fill the space. We had less than two weeks to do the lot. Myself and Simon had both dabbled with painting in the past, Simon Thorp has studied fine art for three years so he had a pretty good idea what he was doing, while Graham could paint flowers and knew all their Latin names. So we each had an art pedigree of sorts. The paintings we came up with varied enormously in style. There was the enormous *Beano Boy*-style *Rock and Roll*, a full-length painting of Jerry Lee Lewis sitting at the piano surrounded by numerous rock'n'roll references (a hot dog, and a hound dog failing to catch a rabbit, to name but two). There was Graham's naïve portrait of Shakin' Stevens, and a rather splendid quartet of abstract oils entitled *The Four Seasons*. (A fifth picture in the series – *Frankie Valli* – wasn't completed in time). There was my own portrait of Princess Diana in a Francis Bacon Screaming Pope-style, and a figurative expressionist portrait of Kylie Minogue, painted using a cassette box lid as opposed to a brush. I called that one *Sexy Bitch*. Then there was my bold yet minimalist abstract: a big white canvas with a box of Milk Tray glued to one corner, and a box of Maltesers glued diagonally opposite.

With this challenging juxtaposition I set out to pose the profound question 'Chocolates?' and simultaneously provide the viewer with the answer, 'Maltesers'.

Our plan had just been to exhibit the pictures, but publicists Beer Davis wanted us to go a step further. They arranged interviews with leading art critics who came and talked to us about our work. As always seemed to happen with these PR scams, it all got a bit out of hand. We flippantly mentioned to one reporter that we were planning to stop drawing cartoons, fold the magazine and turn our attention to painting instead. Within hours the publishing trade press was reporting the imminent demise of *Viz*, much to John Brown's consternation. Then a reporter from the *Sunday Times*, a Ms Ruby Millington, travelled all the way from London to see us. The interview was a total disaster. To begin with Ms Millington seemed uncomfortable merely being at such a northerly latitude. She also seemed to form an early impression that we were taking the piss. Despite all our attempts to cajole her into good humour, and our earnest answers to all her difficult questions, Ms Millington was not a happy girl. So much so that when she got back to London she registered a formal complaint with Beer Davis, accusing us of being uncooperative and monosyllabic. I'll never forget that word *monosyllabic*, because I had to look it up at the time. And yet, when she wrote her report our flowing, lucid quotes simply poured from the page.

'Art is the underlay beneath the carpet of life,' I told her, 'but because there's a minority of prats who get a little bit of underlay one foot by one foot and hang it on their wall, so they can stand there looking at it, sipping a glass of wine and saying "Oh this underlay is fantastic," the majority of people don't want underlay because they think it's pretentious rubbish, instead of realizing it's just something you put under the carpet to make life more comfortable.' Monosyllabic? I don't fucking think so.

In November 1990 we attended a private viewing at the gallery to which all of London's heavyweight art critics were invited. Unfortunately only freeloading rent-a-toff Brian Sewell turned up. 'It was utterly dreadful,' he summarised in his review with plummy aplomb. Dreadful our paintings may have been, but that didn't stop one unnamed buyer forking out £400 for 'Chocolates? Maltesers'. I never found out who the buyer was, but it may well have been either Jimmy Nail, or Roger Taylor out of Queen, both of whom turned up to dip their snouts in the free buffet.

I hadn't known Jimmy Nail was a *Viz* fan but he was, apparently. Nail had been a well-known figure on the Newcastle pub rock and cowboy double-glazing scenes during the 1970s. I didn't know him, but I knew lots of people who did. And I knew at least a dozen who all claimed to have chinned him on one famous occasion when his band, the King Crabs, played a gig at the Black Bull in Wooler. The first time I met Jimmy had been earlier in 1990 when he called into our Newcastle office unannounced. I was in the drawing studio when I got a phone call from Ann saying that Jimmy Nail was in reception … and he was bleeding from a serious head wound. Sure enough, when I walked into the room there was Jimmy Nail, dressed rather scruffily, with a mucky face and with what appeared to be a big, bloody gash on the top of his head. Jimmy had enjoyed a certain reputation for fightiness in his pub rock days and I immediately assumed he'd been in some sort of street brawl and had come in to seek shelter and medical attention.

'Divvun mind this,' he said in his best Jimmy Nail drawl, smiling and pointing at the bloody mess on his crown. 'It's just *mayyyyk*-up,' he explained, putting that peculiar, prolonged emphasis of his on the word 'make'. He said he was only in town briefly, having arrived in a helicopter direct from filming the TV series *Spender*, in the course of which he had just theatrically banged his head on the steel hull of a boat while rounding up criminals. But that was purely incidental. The reason he'd come to see us was to talk about, or '*taaaaak* aboot' as he put it, Sid the Sexist. Jimmy said he thought the character would adapt well to television and he was interested in making a TV dramatization of Simon's cult cartoon.

Not long after our first meeting Jimmy invited me and Dolores round to his house for tea. At the time he was living in a big detached house in Cricklewood with his Welsh wife and their two boisterous young boys. When we arrived at the house one of the boys was being reprimanded for sawing up the furniture with a bread knife. As the children wreaked havoc in an adjoining room we sat down to eat. As it happened Jimmy wasn't very happy with his lamb. 'What are *theeeeez*?' he asked, poking the pieces of meat around his plate with the end of a knife. They were lamb noisettes, explained his wife, patiently. Fortunately Jimmy was distracted by a phone call. A transatlantic phone call. 'It's *Iaaaaan* calling from Californ-*yaaaa*,' Jimmy announced with visible pride. The caller was none other than Ian La Frenais, half of a living legend in the North-East for his work with Dick Clement on *The Likely Lads*. There I was having lamb chops in Jimmy Nail's living room while he was on the phone to Ian La Frenais. How much more Geordie showbiz mafia could you get?

In the course of that evening Jimmy struck me as both a difficult man to cook for and a difficult man to work with. He was very sure of his own opinions, dismissing one local actor that I tentatively nominated for a part in Sid the Sexist with a single word – 'wanker'. I wondered what he would be like to work with if his Sid the Sexist idea came off. But that was going to be Simon's problem, not mine. Simon and Jimmy met up back in Newcastle and they got on like a house ahad. On the business side a high-powered meeting then took place at the Boathouse between all four cartoonists, John Brown and an entourage of men in suits who escorted Jimmy Nail into the building. These were Jimmy's 'people', one of whom was Roger Bamford, an acclaimed TV director. Jimmy and his 'people' looked like they'd come to complete a multi-million-dollar drug deal. Various formalities were discussed, including money. I seem to recall John Brown nearly shat himself when he heard how much it would cost to shoot a TV drama on film. Jimmy's plan was for Jimmy to write, Jimmy to direct and Jimmy to star in a series of Sid the Sexist shorts, but no deal was agreed at the meeting so we kept the project under wraps. Jimmy didn't, though, and he mentioned that he was adapting Sid the Sexist

Jimmy Nail as Sid the Sexist

for television in an interview with the *Evening Standard*. That was in February 1991. Not long after that Jimmy pulled the plug on the project. A second series of *Spender* had been commissioned by the BBC. This time *Iaaan* La Frenais, his co-writer, was unavailable to work with him, due to other commitments, and as a result Jimmy was going to have to write the new series all by himself, as well as directing it and starring in it, of course. So sadly the world never got to see Jimmy Nail's interpretation of Sidney Smutt.

The audited sales figure of *Viz* from July to December 1990 was 1,128,151, making us officially Britain's third best-selling title. Ahead of us lay only the *Reader's Digest* (which didn't count), *TV Times* and in top slot the *Radio Times*. *Viz* was outselling every other magazine in the country. And, as if I wasn't already having enough trouble counting money, our *Spunky Parts* annual reached No. 2 in the bestsellers list. Add to that the income that was pouring in from our merchandise, plus revenue from the Billy the Fish animation, and it all added up to some very large numbers indeed.

When I'd gone to see my accountant in 1984 with my first end-of-year books the receptionist had given me some mildly condescending looks for my scruffy appearance then shown me to a tiny, no-frills meeting room – more of a cupboard really – where I had to wait fifteen minutes for Mr Thornton to appear. Six years later I was still dressed like a tramp but now the receptionist greeted me as 'Aaah! Mr Donald', and ushered me into the boardroom where I was offered tea or coffee in delicate china cups and saucers. Before the tea was even poured Mr Thornton appeared at the door, extending a hand and obviously delighted to see me. So what was the reason for this sudden change in attitude? About one and half million pounds was the reason.

He read through my accounts for 1990 like a schoolmaster reading out an end-of-term report. Turning to the second last page he said, 'And as you are no doubt aware the net profit for the year is slightly over the one and a half million mark.' As I was no doubt aware? I hadn't got a fucking clue. I did look at bank statements, but I never did cash flows or quarterly accounts. I had no idea how much money I'd invoiced that year, or what my costs had been. So the news that I'd made more than a million in profit came as something of a shock. But I tried not to look too surprised.

Simon, Graham and Thorpy were all employed on fairly modest salaries but by 1990 I was paying them six-figure bonuses on top of their wages and my accountant was advising us all on tax avoidance schemes. With so much money sploshing about it would have been easy to go on a Porsche-crashing spree, or start sniffing coke off the arses and tits of Brazilian supermodels. But there was never any danger of us lot going wild. Never mind partying, we didn't even go out for a quiet drink any more. We saw each other every day at work, so what was the point of socializing? Besides which we were all too busy nest-building in our new homes with our respective partners. People used to say, 'I bet you *Viz* boys have a wild time together,' but I can honestly say that our office was duller than the DHSS. At least at the Ministry we went out for a pint on a Friday lunchtime. Even if a spectacular set of sales figures came through the most extravagant thing we'd do at the *Viz* office would be go out and get a McDonald's for lunch.

A typical day in the office would begin at 9.30 a.m. with everyone sitting around reading the day's papers, drinking coffee and discussing the previous night's TV. Then I'd probably disappear into my little room to deal with the business of the day while Ann opened cartoon contributions and readers' letters. Ann was a gem. When I first took her on it was impossible to make any calls in or out of the office as she spent most of the day on the phone to her sister Elaine talking about her baby Adam, how well he had slept the previous night and what his nappies had been like that morning. I resolved this problem by installing a second phone line for Ann's own personal use. But in the brief periods when Ann came off the phone she was great at her job. She could spot a decent cartoon from a mile off, and would sift the wheat from the chaff before handing me all the readers' submissions.

Often Graham and Thorpy would sit down at the writing table and write cartoons on their own, and in the February 1991 issue they came up with two notable newcomers, Victorian Dad and Nobby's Piles. Victorian Dad was an anachronistic, puritanical parent who constantly forced his antiquated Victorian values on his poor young son. The irony was that Graham, who drew the strip, was something of a Victorian parent himself. He wasn't a puritan, but he was a lot closer to a Victorian Dad than a Modern Parent. Nobby's Piles was run-of-the-mill slapstick involving a succession of increasingly sharp or hot objects getting stuck up an unfortunate pile-sufferer's arse. This wasn't particularly ironic because, so far as I'm aware, Simon Thorp, who drew it, did not suffer from haemorrhoids. The antithesis of Victorian Dad is of course the Modern Parents, and they first appeared in the very next issue, April 1991, and were the work of an Edinburgh cartoonist called John Fardell. I don't know what sort of parent John Fardell is, only that he looks a little bit like Jeremy Clarkson.

I was gradually becoming less involved with cartoons but was still doing all the written editorial. The ideas for the newspaper spoofs would usually come from a group writing session and I'd then take the notes away to the calm of my office and go through the drafting process. Once it was typed up I'd read out the first draft to whoever was in the studio. Different people would laugh at different things. If only Thorpy laughed, it might be too clever. If only Simon laughed it might not be funny enough. If Ann laughed that was a very good sign. And if nobody laughed it was shit, no matter how good I thought it was. Taking note of their reactions, I'd then go and do a final draft before sending it off to be typeset.

Various types of tabloid feature had become standard by this stage. The exclusive revelations of somebody not very inter-esting, for example. Like the confessions of the TV weatherman, the most exciting of which was that his map nearly fell over on one particular occasion. Or the exclusive revelations of someone with an implied mental problem. And there was also the '20 things you never knew about ...' formula, a *Sun* gimmick that I'd applied to dull or ridiculous subjects like car parking. We'd pick on dull and ridiculous places too, like Tipton in the West Midlands which became a running joke. And we took occasional pot shots at Filey, a small seaside resort on the Yorkshire coast. For some reason Filey was funny, and I think it gave us a feeling of power knowing that from our command bunker in Newcastle we could launch futile little attacks in the magazine that would send shockwaves through the council chamber of a crummy little seaside resort over 100 miles away.

As well as towns we targeted people. Celebrities who for some reason seemed ripe for attack, in much the same way that Filey was. Shakin' Stevens for example. At one point we produced a special 'Wakey Shaky' alarm clock in his honour, with his legs as the pointers. It didn't sell very well. One day in about 1988 Shakin' Stevens was appearing at Newcastle City Hall and members of his road crew called in at our office to buy some of our post-modern ironic (i.e. deliberately crap) Shaky T-shirts. We later heard that his backing band had worn them during a sound check in Yorkshire the following night and Shaky had stormed offstage in disgust. But by 1990, when the hits were starting to dry up, Shaky's record company turned to us and asked if we would design a record sleeve for him. They were hoping to capitalize on his 'cult popularity among students', as they saw it. They were grasping at straws as I saw it. Thorpy drew them a sleeve design featuring numerous *Viz* characters but it didn't help sales a great deal. The single, 'I Might', only got to No.18 in the charts.

In the course of touring late-night, Alan Partridge-esque radio programmes to promote our *Viz* books I'd met a DJ in Leeds by the name of Martin Kelner. Thorpy had originally alerted me to Kelner's highly entertaining radio shows which were networked from his Leeds studio to BBC stations throughout the North of England. A regular guest on these shows was a character called Mrs Merton who ran a sort of radio problem page. Mrs Merton was the invention of a bright young Manchester comedienne called Caroline Aherne. Caroline had several other alter egos including a nun, Sister Mary Immaculate, and a Jewish country-and-western singer by the name of Mitzi Goldberg. But it was as Mrs Merton that she was best known and, spotting her great potential, Martin Kelner arranged for her to make a low-budget

TV pilot of her own show. Clearly struggling for guests, he rang me up and asked whether I'd like to drive down to Yorkshire at my own expense and be interviewed on the show. I drove to Sheffield's Meadowhall Shopping Complex as fast as I possibly could.

It was a low-budget affair, hence the bizarre location. The TV studio was in a tiny room in the middle of a shopping mall. It was so small it may well have been a CCTV monitoring room. My fellow guests on this bargain bin line-up were the Radio 1 brother and sister duo of Liz and Andy Kershaw, who presumably had come cheap as a pair. There was no audience, and no green room – we had to go and stand outside in the shopping centre until our turn to come on.

After the recording Martin took us for a meal at a newly opened 1950s-style American diner that was entirely deserted apart from our small group. Period music was playing loudly, and at regular intervals the under-occupied waiting staff would clamber up onto the tables and start performing choreographed dance routines with a breathtaking lack of enthusiasm. I seem to remember Andy Kershaw asking me repeatedly whether this was really happening, or was it a dream. Each time I had to repeat the bad news. In the end both the BBC and Yorkshire TV turned their noses up at the *Mrs Merton Show*, one famously saying that Mancunian girls dressed as old ladies were on the way out. But as I sat there eating my 1950s-style American food I could hear a gentle ticking sound. For I knew that the quiet, self-conscious girl sitting opposite me was a TV comedy time-bomb just waiting to go off.

Whilst I was assisting the young Caroline Aherne on the road to TV stardom, John Brown was setting up his very own television production company. Following the success of the *Billy the Fish* animation John was now more eager than ever to exploit *Viz* on TV. But three years of reminding me almost daily to write 'the TV comedy of the nineties' had failed to produce so much as an idea, so in the summer of 1991 John tried a new tactic. He despatched the four of us – me, Simon, Graham and Thorpy – to a remote hotel in Devon for a week, during which time we were to work exclusively on producing ideas for a television script. To us it sounded like an opportunity for a free holiday and we jumped at the invitation. But John had other ideas. He'd recruited a television producer, a stranger to us by the name of Miles Ross, and was sending him to Devon to keep an eye on us and make sure we got some work done.

Our holiday got off to a bad start when the guard on our train insisted that there was no station at Tiverton, which was where we'd planned to get off. 'Tiverton's closed,' he said with the confident smile of a man who enjoyed disappointing his customers. When we pointed out that the word 'TIVERTON' was clearly printed on all of our tickets he shook his head and took out a large timetable in order to prove his point. Then he went quiet, clipped our tickets and walked away without saying another word.

We were picked up at the station in Tiverton by Mogens Bolwig, half of the weird couple who ran Huntsham Court. Mogens drove us along narrow country lanes at such terrifying speeds that when we finally got to the hotel alive we were in a state of jubilation. Huntsham Court was a rambling Victorian gothic revivalist mansion which belonged in part to the late Douglas Adams but was run by Mogens and his wife Andrea. At weekends it was a popular haunt with London media and showbiz types, but through the week it appeared to be blissfully quiet.

Andrea Bolwig was an attractive and very Greek-looking Greek lady. She did all the cooking, and offered no choice of menu whatsoever to her guests. At mealtimes everyone sat down together round one big table, and got what they were given. There was no room service either. If you wanted any-thing to eat between meals you were told to help yourself to bread and cheese in the kitchen. Andrea's husband Mogens was a laid-back Dane, and about as far removed from Basil Fawlty as a hotelier could get. Despite its architectural grandeur Huntsham was the antitheses of the pretentious country house hotel.

John's newly recruited TV producer Miles Ross was there to greet us when we arrived. Miles was a smiley-faced, quick-witted and extremely talkative Cockney, and John obviously saw him as the catalyst he required to get a TV script-writing reaction out of us. But the chemistry wasn't quite right. Having spent the best part of his childhood sharing a small bedroom with chat show king-to-be Jonathan Ross and three similarly noisy siblings, Miles had learnt the hard way how to get a word in edgeways. As a result he could talk faster than anyone I had ever met, and consequently he tended to dominate all our writing sessions. But, worse than that, he insisted on holding the pen. How could we possibly write a TV script with a stranger holding the pen? Before long the work ground to a halt and it became obvious that we were wasting our time. So the four of us went back to plan A, which was to have a holiday. Being on John's payroll Miles was reluctant at first, but he soon came round to our way of thinking. We played snooker in the library, and out in the garden we invented Stick Bongo – a game for two to six players involving six cricket stumps and a football. We spent hours developing the game, which was simple but addictive. By the end of the week we may not have had a TV show, but we really did think we were onto a winner with Stick Bongo. Even Miles agreed that the game had real potential.

At the end of the week John Brown drove out from London in a brand new bright-yellow Porsche to collect his finished TV scripts and pay the hotel bill. The bill was a bit larger than he'd expected, due in no small part to a dispute between Miles and Mogens, who had been wine waitering at the time. On our last night Miles had ordered champagne ('Why not, eh? It's on John.') and Mogens had recommended an Australian sparkling wine. Miles interrupted him with a wave of a finger and pointed out that Australian sparkling wine was *not* champagne. A silly point-scoring argument about wine ensued. Miles was no match for Mogens and, realizing he was out of his depth, tried to end the conversation abruptly by raising the stakes. 'Right!' he said, banging his fist on the table. 'Give me a bottle of the most expensive wine you've got!' A slightly anonymous-looking bottle of red wine was delivered to the table and carefully uncorked. After sniffing it ceremoniously Miles offered us all a glass. I'm not normally a wine drinker, but I must say this stuff was nice, although not nearly nice enough to justify the ridiculous money John paid for it.

John's dismay at the drinks bill was compounded when Miles presented him with the 'scripts' we'd produced during our stay. These were basically a handful of ideas, stretching out to precisely one and a half sides of A4. The best of the bunch was a series called the *The Pond Makers*, a bit like *Dallas* but with two large garden pond-building corporations competing for business in a sleepy English village. Alas, John couldn't spot a golden comedy nugget when he saw one. And he also failed to spot the potential of Stick Bongo. I'm convinced that, given the right marketing and promotion, Stick Bongo could have been bigger than *Viz*.

Just before we left Huntsham a group of young advertising executives arrived from London and we had the misfortune to spend a short period of time in their company. The loudmouthed little yuppies were full of themselves and very keen to brag about their respective CVs. They all seemed to be in awe of one particular bloke, a short-arse called Beesley Beesley – honestly, that's what they called him – whom a colleague described as a 'bladdy clever guy'. 'This is the man responsible for Mars Ice Cream,' he said, as if we were in the presence of a god. We tried to look suitably impressed but were having difficulty keeping straight faces. 'Did you *really* invent Mars Ice Cream?' Graham asked. 'No!' one of his colleagues snapped with obvious frustration. 'He was the guy responsible for the Mars Ice Cream *advertising campaign*.' In their eyes that was clearly far more important than the product itself. When we got back to Newcastle we set to work on a new character called Dickie Beesley, schoolboy advertising genius.

As well as a TV series John was always on the look-out for other potential spin-offs, and in the autumn of 1990 he received an offer from Virgin Games to produce a *Viz* game for PCs. John was a mate of the man at Virgin Games, Brynn Gilmore, so by the time the proposal got to me it was already weighted in favour of acceptance. When I saw the draft plans for the game I was alarmed. It was fucking dreadful. Not the game itself – that was just a bog-standard obstacle race between characters – but the language. They'd been putting words in the characters' mouths and it was all out of tune with *Viz*: inappropriate and unfunny. I wanted to pull out but John was having none of it. He said Virgin had already invested huge amounts in programming and it was too late to pull the plug. Then in December Virgin sent a draft copy of the instruction manual to accompany the game. It was irredeemably awful. They'd produced their own *Viz*-style magazine, full of their own in-jokes and attempts at *Viz* humour. It was fucking pap. John pacified me again and assured me that he'd 'clip Virgin's creative wings', as he put it. He'd have needed a bolt cutter to do the job properly. In March 1991 the final product arrived at our office in Newcastle and we huddled around a hastily borrowed computer to watch it. As the programme rolled, suddenly Top Tips started popping up on the screen. Not Top Tips from *Viz*, but Top Tips written by Virgin Games' own in-house jokers. We had never seen any of this before. The Virgin game was crap, total and utter crap. And there it was all neatly packaged in a green and red box with our name on the front.

We were all furious, feeling John had let us down so badly. First he'd told us we had a veto on the game, and then he'd told us we couldn't use it. So I turned to blackmail again to try and calm the situation. We were due to meet John in a few days' time to discuss a new animation project and I told him we wouldn't be at the meeting unless he sent us £2,500 in used banknotes. This time John dug his heels in and refused to be blackmailed, for about half an hour. Then he rolled over and sent us the cash. This time we got £600 each, in used £50 notes, and we shared the rest between Ann and Maddie.

Maddie was the latest addition to my staff, a former John Brown employee whom I'd appointed office manager. Maddie's job was basically to count the money, freeing up my time for creative duties. But John Brown wanted me to take on cartoonists, not office managers, and he was constantly badgering me to offer a full-time job to freelancer Davey Jones who'd been sending in excellent cartoons on a regular basis for three years now.

Jonesy, as we referred to him, was producing wonderful cartoons such as Tinribs, Roger Irrelevant and various surreal Blyton-esque adventure yarns set in burrowing churches, or schools that were housed in giant electronic woodlice. The first time I'd met Jonesy was at a Comic Art Convention party in Glasgow in 1988. (The UK Comic Art Convention is an annual get-together of American-style fantasy comic artists – muscles and big tits men – which is organized annually by sad comic fans hopeful of stalking guest artists like Alan Moore for the weekend.) Jonesy had been very drunk and I'd asked him, out of genuine concern for his welfare, where he was stopping for the night. 'I don't know,' he said in his yokel, Herefordshire accent. 'I'm just going to drink so much that it doesn't matter.' His three years at university studying philosophy had obviously paid off. A man of his word, shortly after that he passed out and fell face down onto the floor. I liked Jonesy. He didn't say much. In fact, he took not saying much to extremes. He was totally immune to that strange social pressure that forces most people – my mother-in-law in particular – to say something, anything, in order to break a silence. Getting to know him was difficult, but I found the few things that he did say hugely encouraging. For example, on recreation: 'I don't play any sport unless you can smoke while you're doing it.' I valued Jonesy's freelance contribution to the comic immensely, but John seemed to believe that bringing him to Newcastle and giving him a job would increase our overall productivity by 25 per cent. I wasn't sure. I doubted he'd be any more productive sitting at a desk in Newcastle from 9 till 5 than he was sitting in his little cottage on Anglesey from where he was currently posting us a steady stream of consistently brilliant cartoons.

In contrast some of my cartoons were looking a bit jaded. The Pathetic Sharks, for example, looked tame alongside the Fat Slags, Terry Fuckwitt, Bertie Blunt and co. In 1991 I had a notion that some of them could perhaps rekindle their flagging careers by finding a new, younger audience. The plan was to do a *Viz* book aimed entirely at children. Many of my characters were

Captain Morgan and his Hammond Organ

not rude or violent and would be ideal for kids, I reckoned. As well as the Crap Sharks there was Felix (and his Amazing Underpants), Albert O'Balsam (and his Magic Hat), not to mention Captain Morgan (and his Hammond Organ). Captain Morgan had been a surprise hit when he first appeared in August 1990 – a dotty old sea dog who pretended to have one leg and preferred playing easy-listening music on his Hammond organ to more traditional cut-throat activities.

We didn't have time to devote to a children's book so John suggested we delegate the work to outsiders. This is common in most of the cartoon industry, but for us it was a revolutionary experiment in working practices. I wrote some of the stories myself, but a lot of the writing and all of the illustration was farmed out to freelancers. The *Pathetic Sharks Bumper Special* was launched in summer 1991, but this bold attempt at cross-over marketing failed and Captain Morgan's comic career was tragically cut short soon afterwards. The repertoire of songs which he burst into during cartoons included 'Puppet on a String', 'It's Not Unusual', 'Raindrops Keep Falling on My Head' and 'Waterloo'. Believe it or not spoilsport music publishers actually wrote in and complained about him using their lyrics without permission. John's solicitor suggested we get round the problem by making the Captain sing traditional songs that were out of copyright. 'How about hymns or negro spirituals?' he suggested. That's fucking solicitors for you.

In a bid to promote the *Pathetic Sharks* book Beer Davies tried to get me on the *Wogan* show. They didn't have much trouble. By this stage in his TV career Terry Wogan was on BBC1 three nights a week and frankly he was running out of people to talk to. I'd already been 'auditioned' by a researcher with a tape recorder who'd visited me in Newcastle a few days earlier to find out whether I could answer questions, and I was on standby when I got a call asking if I could come down to London and be a guest on the show the very next day. The fee was £150 plus my train fare. I would have taken Dolores down for the occasion but by now she was heavily pregnant with our second child, and she'd already arranged to sit her driving test the very same day. I was sitting next to Danii Minogue in the make-up department when I got a call from Dolores saying she'd passed. I was so delighted with the news that all my nerves vanished in an instant.

In the run-up to the show one of the producer's assistants – some bird with headphones and a clipboard anyway – suggested I draw a cartoon of Terry which they could show during the closing credits. They provided a pad and pens and I drew a picture of your man surrounded by Pathetic Sharks, one of whom was *syrup*-ticiously lifting his hairpiece with a fishing line. My drawing was taken up to the production suite for approval. It came back a few minutes later with the comment that the hairpiece was rather a delicate subject, and would it be possible to lower it slightly, a bit closer to Terry's head. I was given a bottle of Tippex with which to make the necessary alteration. Reluctantly I obliged, this time leaving only the tiniest gap between hair and head. This version was taken away for approval but once again it was rejected. 'Could the hairpiece be lowered even further?' I was asked. So low that it was in fact sitting on Terry's head, just like real hair. Eugen Beer was in stitches as I took out the Tippex once again and duly brought the syrup down to a safe landing on Terry's head, albeit at a slight comedy angle.

My prime-time TV appearance did no good for sales of the book but it did get me my fifteen minutes of fame. A couple of days later Dolores and I took the ferry to Ireland and an excited police detective recognized me as we went through the security check. 'Hey! You're the man from *Viz*, aren't you?' he said. I wondered if he greeted terror suspects the same way. 'Hey! You're the man from the IRA, aren't you?' A few minutes later the boat set sail and we were looking for somewhere to sit in the crowded lounge when there was a public announcement asking me to go to the bursar's desk. When we got there a smiling stewardess greeted us and handed us the keys to our own luxurious cabin suite, with compliments of the captain. The star-struck policeman had obviously tipped them off.

It's always irked me the way that people give freebies to celebrities. Millionaire footballers who get complimentary cars and supermodels who wear free designer clothes. Stars get their names on guest lists, they're offered the best tables in restaurants and they're given privileged treatment everywhere they go, despite being the last people in the world who need it. On this occasion we were tired, Dolores was pregnant and we had Dale with us, so I reluctantly accepted the perk. My conscience wasn't troubled for too long though. By the time we made our return crossing a week later I was a nobody again as far as the security staff at Holyhead ferry terminal were concerned.

CHAPTER THIRTEEN

A Night at the Welsh BAFTAs

You always remember where you were when you first heard a momentous piece of news. I was on my way down the stairs in Lily Crescent when Simon told me John Lennon had been shot. I was delivering newspapers on Jesmond Road when I heard that Malcolm MacDonald had signed for Arsenal. And I was sitting in our office reception drinking coffee when I heard that Peter Cook had agreed to voice our Roger Mellie animation.

Unfortunately the budget for the animation did not reflect John Brown's TV ambitions. Once again the Welsh miracle-worker Tony Barnes would be making the film on a shoestring, and once again the all-important sound recording which would form the backbone of the whole thing was to be made in one short studio session without any prior rehearsal. When I arrived at the studio somewhere in Chelsea Harbour I was extremely apprehensive. I would never have had the nerve to write these crummy cartoon scripts if I'd known they would one day be spoken by my all-time comedy hero. I was also worried that Peter might turn up drunk, or that he might not turn up at all. I seem to recall having diarrhoea that morning. But then the great man rolled into the room and I was quickly put at ease by one of his opening remarks. One of the studio engineers had greeted him slightly sycophantically. 'Hi, Peter. You're looking well. Have you lost weight?' Cook looked pretty awful and I'm sure he knew it. 'Oh, yeah,' he muttered beneath his breath. 'A few more stones and I'll be a sixties icon again.'

Harry Enfield was there too. His recent rise to stardom had been meteoric and he was now the star of his own successful *Viz*-like TV show. Despite his celebrity status Harry kindly accepted our invitation to do all the voices except Roger's (including females) for peanuts. Well, cashew nuts at any rate. There was no time for a proper run-through, there'd been virtually no preparation and I think it was a bit early in the morning for Peter. Someone went out and got him a beer and he eventually began to get into the part a bit, but the pressures of time – and possibly the fact that Tony Barnes and myself were both in awe of him – meant that we couldn't be as fussy as we wanted to, often settling for takes that weren't nearly as good as they could have been. But I did pull Peter up on one thing. For some reason he insisted on pronouncing the word twat as *twot*. I had to stop him and insist he say *twat*. I even had to coach him through the intercom until he got the emphasis right. It was bizarre, me trying to tell Peter Cook how to make a rude word sound funny. When we were finished I kept Peter's empty beer bottle as a souvenir and asked him to sign my copy of the script. I treasure both of those artefacts to this day, but I don't own a copy of the video.

When I saw the finished product I felt sick. I turned it off and for the next twelve years pretended it had never been made. Drawing a Roger Mellie strip cartoon in the comic was easy. I was just providing a few key reference points in the story and the reader filled in the gaps with their own imagination. But when you watch a moving animation those gaps are filled in for you. We hadn't expanded on the cartoon scripts at all, and poor Tony Barnes's priorities were, as usual, to meet a difficult dead-line and do it within a tight budget. Despite working under such trying conditions Tony's studio artists had managed to faithfully reproduce all the shortfalls in my original drawings, and now these had been complemented by clumsy, sub-Pugwash-style movement. The sound track was barren. One money-saving tactic was to spend ten seconds at a time zooming in on an office window in total silence, as a kind of a post-Hitchcock scene-setter. The whole thing was flat, and worst of all the punch lines, which had always been a weakness in my original cartoons, became painfully exposed on film. I switched off at the lowest point in the tape, when Roger punches Paul Daniels. I could bear no more.

There was no reason for us to animate our cartoons unless we were going to improve on the originals in some way, apart from money of course. *Roger Mellie* was another commercial success, with Channel 4's broadcast fees entirely covering the production costs and a stream of pure profit flowing in from subsequent video sales. Fortunately for us in the late 1980s and early 1990s people in their hundreds of thousands would go out and buy any old shit masquerading as a comedy video, including ours. In fairness to Tony Barnes and his team of animators I should point out that their earlier effort – *Billy the Fish* – was now receiving the highest form of critical acclaim. Well, it was being nominated for a Welsh BAFTA anyway.

I'd never heard of the Welsh BAFTAs either, until Tony Barnes received a nomination in the Animation category, and I got the distinct impression that, had any other cartoons been made in Wales during 1990 – any cartoons at all, they would have been nominated ahead of us. Tony's only competition for the prize was Nick Park's groundbreaking *Creature Comforts*, also made in Wales, so I knew right away we wouldn't win and I wasn't planning on going all the way to Cardiff to spend an evening in a stiff collar listening to heartfelt acceptance speeches being made in Welsh. The organizers had obviously anticipated a certain level of reluctance on the part of their invited guests so, as an incentive, they'd strategically placed a celebrity guest on every table and the celebrity's name was mentioned on your invite. When I realized that Catherine Zeta-Jones would be sitting at our table my attitude towards the Welsh television and film industry became a lot more positive.

I drove to Cardiff at high speed and met up with Tony Barnes, John Brown and producer Phil Morrow at the Great Western Hotel where we donned our tuxedos and had a couple of

Phil Morrow

extremely expensive drinks in the bar. Then we headed off to the university sports hall where the televised awards ceremony was being held. All we talked about on the way there was Catherine Zeta-Jones. Would she really be sitting at our table?

We were sipping free champagne in a reception area adjoining the hall when she first appeared, sweeping straight past me. I noticed her, but I didn't recognize who she was at first. For a few seconds I was standing looking at this lady with sparkling jewellery, bluey-black hair and a black off-the-shoulder dress, wondering why everyone else was paying her so much attention. She didn't look anything like Catherine Zeta-Jones to me. Perhaps that was because I had a sideways view. From that angle her face seemed rather big and flat, like Weed from *Bill and Ben*. It was only when I got a frontal view that the penny dropped and I turned to tell John Brown. 'That's her over there!' I whispered, nudging him excitedly. 'I know,' he said through gritted teeth, kicking me on the ankle equally excitedly. We were like a pair of gibbering schoolboys.

When we found our table, which was unoccupied so far, we noticed that there were no place names marked so John, Phil Morrow, Tony Barnes and myself all hovered about in a non-committal, musical-chairs fashion. The stakes were high. Whoever made the right move would end up sitting next to Catherine Zeta-Jones. But as other guests arrived our options were rapidly diminishing. Eventually Catherine came over, said hello to everybody and sat down *almost* next to me. Just one seat away: so close and yet so far. I was closer than John, who was miles away, sitting virtually opposite her. But Phil Morrow had hit the jackpot. The spawny bastard was right next to her and on her other arm was a beaming Tony Barnes.

The awards ceremony took bloody ages to get started due to problems with the TV recording, and extra bottles of free wine were delivered to the tables to keep everyone happy. We couldn't have been happier, guzzling the free booze and chatting away to Catherine Zeta-Jones. Everyone was vying for her attention, including Tony Barnes who had by now given up on any attempt at conversation and was instead holding two empty wine bottles to his forehead and making loud mooing noises. Catherine was very polite, putting up with this and an increasing amount of giggling. Then, after the meal had been served, she got up from the table and went off to present an award.

The quality – and indeed the Welshness – of the other celebrity guests varied considerably from table to table. There was Sian Lloyd the weather girl, for example. And that bloke from Liverpool who did *Grange Hill* and *Brookside*. To my amazement as I looked around the hall I realized that not only was I dining – sort of – with my 1980s TV-crush-of-the-decade Catherine Zeta-Jones, but my two sex idols from the previous decades were also in the room. Representing the seventies, my dream-girl Angharad Rees from *Poldark* was there, she of the compacted bosom and delightful, perky eyes. And from the sixties, my all-time No.1 pin-up Julie Christie was also present. Alas, it was now the 1990s and both Julie and Angharad were old enough to be grandmothers, barely recognizable as the women of my adolescent dreams. But if I'd had some sort of time-machine to whisk them back to my hotel room in circa 1970, along with Catherine Zeta-Jones at her current space/time co-ordinates, what a fabulous foursome that would have been.

Phil Morrow was having similar, if slightly less ambitious thoughts. He'd taken considerable encouragement from the fact that Catherine Zeta-Jones had been polite to him throughout their conversation. Like Tony Barnes, who was still mooing, despite Catherine having left the table, Phil was pretty well gone with the free wine. So far gone that he began to hatch a plan to get Catherine back to our hotel. He took me to one side, with some difficulty, and explained his plan, which was to locate Catherine and invite her back for a few more drinks. Then we would 'take it from there', as he put it. 'You never know ...' he slurred, smiling, closing his eyes and raising his eyebrows simultaneously. Perhaps he was right. There was an unreal atmosphere in the hall. The ceremony was over by now and people were standing up only to discover that they were fantastically pissed. They'd been slowly pickling themselves with free wine for almost five hours, and it made them all drunk in an old-fashioned, silent movie sort of way. Respectable-looking men were falling over and laughing. I'd never been as drunk before in my life and I was game for anything, even a three-in-a-bed sex session with Catherine Zeta-Jones and a ginger-haired, male TV producer. Somehow Phil and I managed to relocate Catherine and got chatting to her again. Again she was incredibly polite, especially when you consider what we must have looked and sounded like by this stage of the evening. Phil was just getting on to the subject of our hotel and drinks when veteran actor Victor Spinetti, one-time Beatles TV director and Pink Panther hotel concierge, appeared from nowhere. Catherine introduced us. 'This is Victor. He's my chaperone for the evening,' she said as they exchanged luvvie smiles. Spinetti looked at me the same way he'd looked at Peter Sellers when he walked up to his desk and asked, 'Do you hev a rurm?', then he turned and walked away with Catherine on his arm.

I may not have shagged Catherine Zeta-Jones that evening, but over a few glasses of wine and a lukewarm chicken dinner I did manage to learn a little bit about her. We shared a common ambition, Catherine and I. We both dreamed of having a hit record. She had serious plans to be a pop star and was in the process of recording an album with Justin Hayward. My plans may not have been so ambitious, but I too had a yearning for chart success. As I explained to Catherine, next to having sex with people like herself, wanting to have a hit single must be one of man's most basic instincts. (I may not have been quite so specific at the time, but I recall making the general point.) Despite the comic's success I somehow felt that my life would never be complete without a hit record. Andy Partridge and John Otway's 1986 *Viz* single hadn't had a hope in hell of making the charts but, now that *Viz* was right up there in the public eye, with millions of readers at our mercy, I felt a Top Forty *Viz* record was a genuine possibility.

In the early days Simon's attentions had been far more focused on becoming a pop star or an actor than drawing cartoons. And now, with *Viz* a million-selling success, nothing much had changed. A Geordie club musician called Davey Baird had written and recorded a song called 'Friday Night' (aka 'The Geordie Rap') which had been a minor hit in local clubs in the early 1980s. In 1989 a local musician friend and studio owner suggested Simon record it and release it as a Sid the Sexist single. The song was duly recorded, the tape got around a bit, and in 1990 MCA Records expressed an interest in releasing it. I was all in favour and I thought there was a very good chance the single might work. But John Brown put a stop to it, saying Sid the Sexist's name could not be used. Simon was keen to put the record out under the name Miami Tab Machine, but without the

Viz association MCA's interest waned and in the end 'The Geordie Rap' was never released.

So instead of Sid the Sexist it was Billy the Fish who was given the task of spear-heading our second assault on the pop charts. We needed a novelty record, and who better to record it than our fictional football team Fulchester United? Real football teams were always having hits with crappy records, so why not ours? I reckoned there was a simple formula for success. All popular football chants have one thing in common – they steal a very catchy, familiar tune from somewhere else. All we needed to do was find a very catchy tune, and steal it. I reckoned 'Annie's Song' would be perfect, so I told Arthur 2 Stroke to go away and write a new lyric to the John Denver classic, and record us a hit record.

When Arthur played me the tape I was gobsmacked. It was brilliant. Stealing John Denver's tune had been a stroke of genius. In an instant it made our song just as catchy as his. Everyone I played the tape to was whistling it straight away, and I was singing it on my way home in the car. Instead of Denver's lyrics, our chorus went like this:

Ful-chester U-ni-ted, we'll always su-pport you.
We'll never de-ssort you, on that you can count.
We'll follow you al-ways, up and down mountains.
You're crap but we like you, our Fulchester squad.

'It's a sure-fire hit,' I told John Brown. John had already been cajoled into paying for the studio time and wasn't happy with the idea of releasing it at all, cheerily pointing out that it would have to sell 5000 copies just to break even. He also pointed out that we'd need John Denver's permission before we could use his tune. We hadn't thought of that. Selling 5000 would have been no problem. It was that good. But getting John bloody Denver to approve of a fictional football team from a vulgar British comic singing their cup final song to his precious tune was going to be a bit more difficult. Unfortunately – from a purely selfish point of view – John Denver was still alive in those days and he listened to a tape of our song before refusing outright to let us borrow his tune. So at the last minute we had to remove 'Annie's Song' from the mix and replace it with a mediocre melody of our own. We released the record anyway, on our own Fulchester label, publicizing its launch in the Billy the Fish cartoon strip. Just to confuse any intending buyers it was released under the name 'Billy Vanilli Ice Cream T Featuring the FU Posse', and the title of the song was 'Sing-a-long-a Fulchester United'. In the first eight weeks of its release we sold one single copy by mail order and, despite professional plugging it received one solitary late-night radio play, on Two Counties Radio, wherever that was. Rather ironically, as it happened, John's main argument for not releasing the Sid the Sexist track was that it might have detracted from sales of our Billy the Fish single. All one of them.

Despite the record flop and the other disappointments of 1991, the mood in the Newcastle office was still jubilant due to the fact that our unreal comic sales were holding up. For our Christmas party I booked Caroline Aherne to come up to Newcastle and perform live for us as Mitzi Goldberg. As we danced the night away to her unique Jewish country-and-western sound, the future was looking pretty damn good.

CHAPTER FOURTEEN

If It Ain't Broke ...

Shakin' Stevens's request for us to design a record sleeve for him was symptomatic of a major problem we now faced. Previously when we'd taken the piss out of someone they got annoyed or irritated. But now our victims were starting to laugh along as if they were in on the joke. People in the media whom we'd seen as contemptible figures of fun were now beginning to embrace us.

Radio 1 DJ Simon Bates had publicly crowned himself the nation's number one *Viz* fan. During one trip to London, Bates invited all four of us into his studio for a chat while he was live on air and, between fielding his slightly sycophantic questions, we'd marvelled at his bizarre body shape. He seemed to have two bellies, one above his belt and then another, just as big, below. This bizarre underbelly arrangement became known as 'a Batesy bilge tank' in our office parlance. On another occasion Bates rang our office in Newcastle and conducted a live radio interview with me down the phone. While technicians were setting things up and a record was playing on air, Bates was extremely chatty. He asked if I had kids and I told him a boy, Dale. He also asked what kind of car I was driving, in a very informal, bloke-ish kind of way. Naïvely I told him about the new BMW that had recently replaced the old VW Golf. A few moments later as the interview got underway I realized why he'd been asking all these questions. 'So how is Dale anyway?' he boomed across the airwaves, sounding every bit the long-time family friend. 'And how's that new Beamer of yours driving?' He'd probably call it professionalism, but I'd call it a cunt's trick.

We had other celebrity fans too. Loopy Irish songbird Sinead O'Connor was pictured in *Rolling Stone* magazine wearing a Fat Slags T-shirt, ironically I would venture to suggest. Carrot-topped fanny rat Mick Hucknall recorded a special video message for us on our TV documentary saying he was proud to be playing for Fulchester United. Bends-both-ways-allegation, asymmetrical-eyed rocker David Bowie was pictured in the *Sun* reading a copy of *Viz*. But worse was to come. In the summer of 1991 the Mayor of Filey, Councillor Dave Murton, told the *Scarborough Evening Gazette* that he was 'highly delighted' after we claimed that Kylie Minogue was buying a six-berth static caravan in the unfashionable Yorkshire coastal resort. 'Kylie can be sure of a *neighbourly* welcome at Filey – the gem of the Yorkshire coast,' said the mayor, adding that she'd be welcome to attend the town's Edwardian Fair on 26 June as guest of honour.

It's a common phenomenon in comedy, the victim declaring himself in on the joke. In the office we called it 'Nicholas Parsons Syndrome' as Parsons was the prime example of self-parody. At some point he'd realized that he was becoming a figure of fun and rejuvenated his career by going along with it. When Keith Chegwin appeared in the *Viz* documentary the same thing was happening. Suddenly your victim is turning round and offering you a wink and a handshake. Your natural reaction is to feel flattered. 'Why shouldn't we design a Shakin' Stevens record sleeve?' we asked ourselves. 'It won't do us any harm.' But if you're not careful, before you know it, you aren't mocking celebrities any more, you've joined their little club, you're playing by their rules, and you're not a rebel any more.

Another simultaneous problem was the turning tide of the press. Up till now we'd been darlings of the media, particularly the music press who'd given us their unreserved adulation. But *Viz* had burst into the publishing party so quickly no one had really had time to check our invitation. Now that we'd rudely established ourselves at the head of the table, critics were starting to examine our credentials a little more closely.

On 10 March 1991 a snooty columnist called Nicholas Farrell took a pop at us in the *Sunday Telegraph* comment pages. He said that *Viz* lacked grace, and wit and nerve (we didn't make fun of blacks or Arabs, for example – a criticism that would only have occurred to a *Telegraph* columnist). He also accused us of being silly, not serious – and at the same time of missing our targets by miles. Two days later, while I was still trying to get my head round Farrell's contradictory ramblings, another *Telegraph* writer, James Delingpole, sprang to our defence: 'The true humour of *Viz* lies beneath its puerile veneer, as is demonstrated in cartoon strips like Farmer Palmer. Ostensibly just an excuse to trot out a few well-worn jokes about rutting bulls and in-bred country bumpkins, Farmer Palmer is in fact a brilliant satire on the power of the farming lobby,' Delingpole wrote (although I might say this was news to Graham and Thorpy, who wrote the cartoon). Delingpole's flattery then soared even higher. 'Those who doubt the ingenuity of *Viz* should ask themselves why it is that it has a circulation of a million, while its imitators – all of which are filled with schoolboy humour and foul language – do not. The simple reason is that *Viz* is much subtler than anyone had hitherto acknowledged. Its smut and innuendo are just a very clever front.'

Delingpole's piece was flattery to the point of sarcasm and I suspect it may have been written purely to annoy Nicholas Farrell. One nose it certainly did get up was that of Richard Ingrams, the godfather of satirical magazines. In 1991 Ingrams, co-founder and former editor of *Private Eye*, was embarking on a new publishing venture, *The Oldie* magazine. Quoted in the

Independent on Sunday, Ingrams cited Delingpole's piece in the *Telegraph* as one of the reasons for starting a new magazine aimed fairly and squarely at the reactionary old fart end of the market. 'Part of the reason for starting *The Oldie* is that the *Telegraph*, which used to be a repository of the oldie spirit, has started printing articles about how wonderful *Viz* is,' he told Zoë Heller in September 1991. I expected, indeed welcomed, criticism from certain musty quarters of the press, but when previous allies turned their guns on us it made me feel uncomfortable. We'd always enjoyed a good relationship with *Q* magazine. Humour was an important part of their editorial blend and a lot of their writing (the photo captions at any rate) was clearly influenced by *Viz*. In 1989 *Q* had run a big feature on *Viz* pretty much singing our praises, but two years later they despatched their ace hatchet man Tom Hibbert to Newcastle. Scraggy-arsed music journalist Hibbert wrote the highly amusing but rather cheap 'Who the hell does ... think he is?' feature in *Q*. Every month he would politely interview an irritating public figure, such as Eddie 'The Eagle' Edwards, then he'd sneak away with his notes and mercilessly take the piss out of the poor bastards in his write-up. I was an avid reader of this cruel form of public humiliation and was somewhat dismayed to learn that Hibbert now had us in his sights. Nevertheless we granted him an interview, as an act of bravado I seem to recall, knowing full well what his intentions were (which gave us a considerable advantage over some of his earlier victims). Hibbert interviewed all four of us at once and did his utmost to make us look stupid. But our interview technique had always been one of appropriate modesty and self-deprecation and this counteracted Hibbert's bubble-bursting approach. He was saying that we weren't funny, and so were we. As a result, neither was his article. I hadn't realized it at the time but Hibbert was in fact running out of victims. People were getting wise to him and his two-faced, pre-Martin Bashir journalistic approach. Not long after that the feature disappeared from *Q*.

It wasn't just the press that were starting to scrutinize *Viz* more closely. In the summer of 1991 five police officers marched into the Islington newsagents of Mr Shashi Shah and seized fifty-three copies of the comic which they then handed over to the Obscene Publications Branch. Fortunately the police's subsequent attempt to bring a prosecution was thrown out by magistrates and, after two months, the comics – or back issues, as they were by now – were returned to Mr Shah. Head of the Obscene Publications Branch, Chief Superintendent Michael Haines, later admitted the charges should never have been brought.

Bad language was no longer obscene, or so it seemed, and the British Board of Film Classification confirmed this when they ruled that our Roger Mellie animation – which had been screened on Channel 4 well after the watershed over Christmas 1991 – was only a 15 certificate, despite the best efforts of Roger Mellie and Peter Cook combined. PolyGram had been so confident of lining the tape up alongside those of their best-selling blue comic Roy 'Chubby' Brown, they'd already printed 40,000 sleeves marked 'Certificate 18'.

Despite the liberal views of the censors our media bombardment continued. Writing in the *Guardian*, Judith Thomas of New Malden said: '*Viz* magazine is a symptom of a subtle but evil trend in society to show complete disregard for the feelings of others … What this magazine is feeding young people should concern us all.' The *Guardian* in question was of the *Wimbledon* variety, where a heated *Viz* debate among concerned residents of the South London borough had been raging on the letters page. *Viz* was being talked about in the most bizarre publications. Solicitors had voted us Magazine of the Year in *Lawyer* magazine, and a prominent Knightsbridge estate agent named the comic as his favourite read in *Chartered Surveyor Weekly*. Who said there's no such thing as bad publicity?

As if to confirm our establishment credentials, in autumn 1991 the Conservative Students' Association decided to place an advert in the comic. They wanted to sell amusing Tory T-shirts by mail order and thought *Viz* the best place to do it. They'd obviously done their research. Thinking it might be a sensitive issue John Brown called me and asked whether I would allow the advert. In the past *Viz* had been perceived as left-wing by a lot of people – Billy Bragg at any rate – even though it never was. I didn't like Tories particularly, especially our next-door neighbours, but as a Liberal voter myself I couldn't use a petty dispute over office car parking as justification for censorship.

Our next-door neighbours at the Conservative Central Office (Northern Area) had recently taken delivery of a set of brand spanking new traffic cones, dark blue in colour and complete with a pompous Conservative Party 'Olympic torch' logo. Parking was scarce enough around our office without them blocking off half the street with their snooty traffic cones every time a high-profile visitor came to see them. We tried to annoy the Tories whenever we could – we felt it was our duty. For example, during the first Gulf War we put masking tape crosses on all of our windows to prevent them from shattering in the event that Iraq started firing back. And we'd occasionally shout rude names through our intercom as visitors to their office passed our door. But as a matter of principle I wasn't going to let my own political views affect our advertising policy, so I said the Young Conservatives could advertise in the comic – as long as they paid full price. Absolutely no discounts.

Some of our readers weren't so liberal. A reader from Wales wrote:

Fuck the Poll Tax and fuck you, you cunts! I've been buying *Viz* since issue 18 and although a lot of people say it's been going downhill, I reckoned it was as good as ever. Then in the latest issue, No. 47, I saw the advert for the Conservative Students. These evil bastards have been screwing the people of this country for 10 years, and to see *Viz* taking adverts from them made me fucking sick.

You can count on the fact that I'll never buy your Tory-loving 'comic' again, and I'll be getting my mates to do the same.

Fuck you and your Tory mates.

    Giles B

      Powys

I wasn't bothered about upsetting bigots like Giles, but I was regretting having run the Conservative Students' ad. The cunning shits had used the ad as a PR opportunity and leaked word of it to the press, proudly announcing their association with the new, trendy *Viz*. If nothing else it demonstrated how out of touch they were. The daft sods were attempting to jump on the *Viz* bandwagon a couple of years too late. They'd well and truly missed the bus. By the end of 1991 *Viz* had become officially unfashionable and, just to confirm it in those ubiquitous 'ins' and 'outs' features which lazy, hung-over journalists produce every Christmas, *Viz* started to appear in the 'out' column for 1992. The trick to remaining fashionable is, of course, never to become fashionable. Unfortunately *Viz* had become the Clackers of 1990 and our fortunes were inevitably going to wane. But the figures didn't look too bad at first. Our audited average sale for July to December 1991 was 1,080,411, down only 4 per cent on the previous year. Our sales were still the envy of our competitors. Take *Punch*, for example. In the last twelve months we had lost more sales than they had got in total.

I still found *Punch* very amusing, but not the magazine itself. It was the desperate advertising campaign they'd recently embarked on that I was laughing at. At the start of the 1990s *Punch*'s problem seemed to be that most of its hard-core, traditional readership had either been buried or cremated, and those who remained alive no longer had the presence of mind to renew their subscriptions. Sales had dwindled from 175,000 per week in the 1940s to around 30,000 by the late 1980s. Clearly envious of our 1,000,000-plus sales figure, *Punch*'s dynamic new editor David Thomas had radically altered the magazine, trying to make it cool and trendy. *Punch* had also launched a press advertising campaign aimed at the 'typical' student, the sort that exists nowhere but in the minds of marketing ignoramuses. Some clown had come up with the awful slogan 'Not as funny as it used to be ... Funnier', and the ads themselves, placed in magazines like *Q*, looked so pretentious they could easily have been mistaken for a bank's. The change of editorial direction and the advertising campaign were abject failures. It was the equivalent of the captain of the *Titanic* telling his flooded engine room to reverse engines and handing out brochures for next year's Caribbean cruise to passengers as they threw themselves overboard. In March 1992 Britain's oldest and best-known humour magazine went bow up and then slowly slipped beneath the waves. There was a great deal of creaking and groaning as she went down. Former *Punch* contributors began an acrimonious public enquiry into the tragedy, and in the absence of any other suspects we were allotted much of the blame. I didn't dare visit my dentist for months. On the day *Punch's* closure was announced we spent a fairly solemn lunch break trying to decide whether or not it really *was* our fault. My dad had been a *Punch* subscriber and I had some fond memories of the magazine in the 1970s. Thorpy still was a subscriber, and at his behest I sent John a fax that afternoon suggesting he buy *Punch* and reinstate Alan Coren as editor. Funnily enough John did later enquire about the availability of the title from the owners, United Biscuits (or was it Newspapers?), but they refused to even discuss the possibility of a sale. They seemed to think that selling *Punch* to the publisher of *Viz* would be like putting Princess Diana's coffin on display in Harrods shop window ... although I don't believe those were the actual words they used.

John had been serious about taking over *Punch*. He realized that John Brown Publishing relied far too heavily on one title and wanted to expand, so he'd been going through a phase of rapid magazine acquisitions. There was *Sticky Wicket*, for example, a small but established cricket fanzine which John had plucked from obscurity, *Viz*-style. And *Fortean Times* – 'the world of strange phenomena' – a small but established UFO, Loch Ness Monster and yeti magazine which John had plucked from obscurity, *Viz*-style. Then there was *Electric Soup*, a small but established Scottish comic which John had plucked from obscurity, again somewhat *Viz*-style. I think it would be fair to say that John was trying desperately to repeat the successful formula he had followed with *Viz*, plucking a small magazine from obscurity, nourishing it and waiting for it to grow. But so far he wasn't having much luck with his new titles. None were sprouting shoots and, to make matters worse, his impressive *Viz* beanstalk was now starting to wither.

I used our print run as my major indicator of how sales were going, and they seemed to be holding up well. John was still printing over 1.2 million copies for the first half of 1992, and this dropped back to just over 1.1 million by Christmas. Little did I know that, as the year progressed, John was being snowed under with huge numbers of returns. Sales of merchandise had also started to dip, and subscription rates were falling too.

The reverse in our fortunes was so pronounced that John came up to Newcastle to tell me in person. He suggested we go for a little walk on the Town Moor, a large, grassy space near the city centre. John liked to go for these little walks when there were momentous decisions to be made. He also liked to try and trip me up with his enormous feet. It was a childish joke he never tired of, no matter how many times he did it. He also liked to dislodge your gear stick as you were driving your car. I noticed that John was not his usual highly strung, hyperactive self this time. He was in a slightly sombre mood. Sales were well down, he told me. Our next ABC figure was going to show a substantial drop from over a million to somewhere nearer 850,000. He felt that we had reached a critical point. *Viz* was in decline and we could either continue as we were and 'gracelessly flog the magazine to death', to use John's own expression, or we could stop the rot. What he actually meant was that *I* could stop the rot. He was proposing that I might 'somehow reinvent' the magazine, to use his own words again.

Fuck me, I thought. I've already made him a multi-millionaire once. And now, not content with that, the greedy bastard wants me to do it all over again. John said the choice was mine – whether to reinvent, or flog gracelessly – and he'd go along with whatever decision I made.

Despite the falling sales figures things weren't looking that bad. *Viz* was a relatively inexpensive magazine to produce and I assured Graham that we could afford to lose another 700,000 sales before he should start worrying about his job. Graham was a natural worrier, quite absurdly pessimistic at times. When the first Gulf War broke out we'd had to work very hard to allay his fears that he would be called up to serve as a tank spotter in the desert. Apparently colour-blind people, who are not easily fooled by camouflage, are very good at spotting tanks. Spotting tanks was, in previous wars, a very dangerous front-line occupation (particularly if they spotted you first) and, despite his age, and the advent of considerably more efficient tank-spotting technology, Graham was convinced he would follow in his colour-blind grandfather's footsteps and receive his call-up papers any day. As Graham worried about conscription and we all worried about sales the mood in the office became a little gloomy. It was the first time this roller-coaster ride had actually stopped and for one scary moment we were able to look around us and admire the view. We seemed to have reached the brow of a very steep incline and were about to go plummeting down the other side. It was impossible to see what lay ahead. Would there be more ups and downs and thrilling loops ... or were we looking at a single, trouser-soiling vertical drop that would take us bombing straight down to the end of the ride?

John's ambiguous proposal that I should 'somehow reinvent' the magazine was a non-starter. I was already beginning to get fed up with the workaday routine of producing the comic. Editorially I felt we had got stuck in a bit of a rut. Because everything had been going so amazingly well the tendency had just been to keep on repeating formulas. Even in office conversation, people were repeating the same jokes, conversations would go off on familiar tangents and I was constantly suffering from déjà vu. Whenever I'd suggested shaking things up a bit Graham would always pipe up with his favourite saying, 'If it ain't broke, don't fix it.' He wouldn't have got far in the aviation maintenance industry. For the first time I was starting to get irritated with my workmates. The relationships between the four of us were changing. There were tensions involved, and not just the sibling variety. I was starting to find Graham and Thorpy too dull and predictable, and Simon too bright and unpredictable. There were other fault lines too. In terms of personality Graham and Thorpy were like chalk to Simon's cheese fondue. They were both modest, quiet and totally unassuming, introverts by nature. Simon was an extrovert and, despite being the least prodigious worker, he had a tendency to arrogate over-enthusiastically on his own behalf whenever plaudits were up for grabs. That could cause a bit of resentment, during press interviews in particular, but things never boiled over. Thorpy and Graham were far too placid to make their feelings known. If either of them got *really* angry they'd simply fold their arms and shuffle slightly in their chair.

I agreed with John in principle that something drastic needed to be done. But I didn't want to reinvent *Viz*. I wanted to scuttle it. In May 1992 I wrote to John telling him we should call it a day and stop producing *Viz* with effect from the end of the year. Instead of grinding out six comics every year we'd produce three or four books instead. This had actually been Thorpy's idea, not mine. In one of our more contemplative moments he'd cited the example of Monty Python, who had stopped making weekly television programmes long ago, but still made the odd hugely successful film. We would hopefully make quite a few odd, hugely successful books, but our other hope was that this drastic new way of working would give us more time for getting properly involved in other projects, like animation, film and TV. We felt that opportunities in those areas were being wasted or were simply passing us by.

Rather than shoot this idea down in flames John bombed it while it was still sitting on the runway. There was no way he would stop publishing *Viz*. In that case, I told him, I would happily step aside and let someone else try to reinvent the magazine for him, and I proposed the now-unemployed *Punch* editor David Thomas as a candidate. But John would not even contemplate my departure. He saw me as the lynch-pin of his money-making machine. At one point he even tried to take out 'Key Man' life insurance to cover his own arse just in case anything should happen to me. I refused to go along with that because I knew that if business took a downturn he was the type of bloke who wouldn't think twice about having me bumped off to collect the insurance money.

And so we ended up going for the first of John's two proposals, by default. The comic would carry on and I would carry on as editor. And although John never used the phrase again, we would continue gracelessly flogging the magazine to death.

CHAPTER FIFTEEN

Pftt! Pftt! Pftt!

Selling our animated cartoons twice – first to Channel 4 and then to PolyGram – was proving to be very profitable indeed. But not profitable enough for John. In 1992 he wanted to double the amount of money he was making.

His greedy plan was to make two animations simultaneously. The Fat Slags were an obvious commercial choice, even though the joke was starting to wear a bit thin by now. And Sid the Sexist was another obvious choice, now that Jimmy Nail had taken the 'get off the pot' option on his ambitious television project. San, Tray and Sidney Smutt were not exactly renowned for their political correctness and I wondered whether this package might be a bit much for Channel 4 to swallow. But John said our TV sugar daddy Stephen Garrett was still on board and was in negotiations for both of them. So we split into two teams: myself, Graham and Thorpy working on a Fat Slags script, and Simon taking sole charge of the Sid the Sexist project.

John wanted Tony Barnes, our overworked and underpaid Welsh animator, to make both animations. But that was never going to work. Apart from the fact that he couldn't perform miracles, another weakness of Tony's was a slight tendency to go over the top with any animation involving breasts. Tony had a touch of Benny Hill about him and I'd had to cut a couple of his awful add-ons out of the previous videos. (For example, he'd got a little bit too excited about Brown Fox, Fulchester United's large-breasted redskin winger.) Giving Tony the Fat Slags to animate would have been like locking an alcoholic in an off-licence.

Graham and Thorpy felt that foam-model stop-frame animation would be a far better idea, like *Postman Pat* on kids' TV. At the other end of the animation scale from Tony Barnes was Nick Park whose award-winning Plasticine zoo animals had trounced Billy the Fish at the Welsh BAFTAs. We couldn't afford Park for the Fat Slags – and I very much doubt he'd have wanted to do it – but there was an economy brand alternative available. Working Media Co. had been set up by a former collaborator of Park's, so it was to them we turned to get the Fat Slags moving. Sid the Sexist was left in the hands of Tony Barnes, and weeding out the inevitable tit jokes was left to Simon.

There was considerable debate about who should do the voices for the Fat Slags. I suggested over-the-top male voices, with *Monty Python*'s Terry Jones top of my wish-list. John wanted French and Saunders but I warned that if he asked them I would resign. In the end actress Kathy Burke, who had recently sprung into the public eye on Harry Enfield's TV show, agreed to play Sandra while Jo Unwin, who had an impressive CV in advertising voiceovers (including the annoying 'We want to be together' building society ad) took the part of Tracey. Simon Day did the Slags' mate Baz and all the other incidental voices.

When we sat down to write the Slags scripts I had trouble remembering which was Sandra and which was Tracey. Apart from their hairstyles there was virtually no telling them apart, which made writing dialogue very difficult. So I suggested we flesh out the characters a bit, get inside their heads and give them some depth and personality … by making one clever and the other one thick.

Just as the animation was getting underway at a studio in

North London I had a phone call from a very excited John Brown. He rang me at home on a Sunday morning to say that he'd just come up with a *brilliant* idea, and he couldn't wait until Monday to tell me: 'The Fat Slags ...' he said, pausing for dramatic effect, 'singing "Summer Holiday"!' Then there was another gap as I wondered what the fuck he was on about. I was confused. 'Uuh?' I said. John explained that he wanted to release a record featuring the Fat Slags singing the Cliff Richard song 'Summer Holiday'. I knew instantly that this was the worst idea anyone, anywhere had ever, ever had. Including the Sinclair C5 and Hitler's invasion of Poland. And yet John was bouncing around on the other end of the phone thinking he was a genius for having had it. I tried to let him down gently. Rather than simply saying, 'Fuck off, John,' I pointed out that our last record had done rather badly, selling only one copy. I told him there was no point in making another record unless it could be guaranteed a hit, and the only way to *guarantee* a hit in 1992 would be for Stock, Aitken and Waterman to produce it. I knew there was no way the Hit Factory team would waste their time on a *Viz* novelty record, so I was effectively saying 'no' to John's idea, but in the most diplomatic way possible. The next day John rang me at work and said Pete Waterman had agreed to produce the single.

As the full horror of what we were about to do gradually sank in I consoled myself with the thought that at the end of it all we would at least have a hit record to tell our grandchildren about. I was wrong about that too. In the end all we had was an instructive lesson to give them on how *not* to make a pop record.

The first step was to go and meet Pete Waterman at his Hit Factory studio. John was driving around in a new Porsche – a green one this time – so he gave me a lift. The Hit Factory had gold and platinum discs lining the walls pretty much as you would expect at a recording studio, but these were far out-numbered by model steam locomotives. I was surprised to learn that a fair amount of the profits from Kylie Minogue, Jason

Donovan and Rick Astley's successes were being used to employ a railway modeller whose full-time job was to make trains for Pete Waterman. Whether Waterman was able to claim a model-maker's wage as a tax-deductible expense I don't know, but the man was certainly earning it. Judging by the sheer volume of models on the walls he must have been churning them out almost as fast as Waterman was turning out shit records.

As a fellow train buff I was expecting to hit it off instantly with Pete Waterman, but we didn't get off to an ideal start. To break the ice a little I told him my funny anecdote about the last time I visited a record company, EMI in Manchester Square. That was the occasion when has-been pop stars Tight Fit had been standing at the door, yelling at the security guard to let them in. ('Don't you know who we are? We're Tight Fit!') I'd told this story many times before and it always raised a laugh. But not this time. 'Tight Fit, yeah?' said an un-amused Pete Waterman. 'That's my wife you're talking about.' As luck would have it Pete Waterman was now happily married to one of the has-been pop stars in question. We quickly moved on to the next item on the agenda, our Fat Slags single.

When asked how long it would take to actually make the record Pete Waterman said he could do it in a day, the only problem was that his studios were fully booked for the next couple of months. Part of John's plan was for Working Media to produce an animated pop video which would accompany the single to the top of the hit parade and precipitate massive sales of our Fat Slags video. But it was going to take a hell of a lot longer to make the video than it would to make the record – about the duration of an ice age compared to a mammoth's fart – and the animators needed to get to work straight away if they were going to finish the pop video in time. The solution John Brown and Pete Waterman arrived at was simple, and staggeringly stupid. The animators would begin work using the Cliff Richard version of the song for lip-sync purposes, and when Waterman eventually found ten minutes to make our record he would simply position his vocals to match exactly the original Cliff Richard version. Talk about making a rod for your back. Before we'd even started to think about the record itself we were already committed to copying exactly the Cliff Richard version. The question of who would sing on the record was quickly dealt with. 'I've got some backing singers who can do it,' said Waterman. Sorted. As for the accents, 'vague northern' was deemed to be the order of the day.

At the meeting John seemed to be in awe of David Howells, the Hit Factory's money-man. John saw the music industry as glamorous and exciting and what he really wanted to be was a pop mogul, not a publisher. After our meeting he invited Howells to the animation studios in North London to see our Slags film in production. 'You can hop in my Carrera,' said John, casually name-dropping his snazzy new car. John's car was very smart, but it wasn't very big. John's legs were, however, and even on his own he tended to fill the tiny little vehicle as he folded himself into it like a collapsing bed-settee. I was already sitting in the front passenger seat, so John tipped his seat forward and invited Howells to get in the back. There then followed a hilarious sequence in which John tried to cram his celebrated passenger into this tiny bucket seat. At one point Howell's foot was on the handbrake while at around the same time his arse appeared to be on the back window shelf. Most of the time his head was pushed up against my headrest. There was clearly no way he would fit, but the longer it went on and the more embarrassing it became, the harder John tried to shoehorn him in. It reminded me very much of Laurel and Hardy attempting to elope with Ollie's girlfriend in a tiny car, and it was made all the funnier by the fact that John's prime objective had been to impress his would-be passenger. Eventually John accepted that it wasn't going to work and backed away, allowing David Howells to carefully extract himself from the vehicle. He said thanks but he'd take his own car.

The finished record sounded even worse than John's idea had

when I first heard it on the phone, and I was extremely grateful for the fact that its shameful release went virtually unnoticed by the music industry and the public as a whole. I think it spent one week at No. 99 in the charts – not quite long enough to trigger a torrent of Fat Slags video sales. The Working Media team, under producer Eira Ellis and directors Martin Pullen and Gary Kachelhoffer, did a pretty good job of animating our scripts on a very tight schedule, but to me the films looked rather slow and cumbersome, and I couldn't understand why Tracey and Sandra were constantly made to jiggle their enormous tits with their hands every time they laughed. Perhaps all animators have breast fixations.

The Slags' accents had become a bit of a sore point with me. When we'd first conceived the characters the idea was very much Geordie lasses in the Bigg Market. It naturally followed that they should have Geordie accents. But Graham, who had by now adopted the characters as his own, decided that they would have Nottingham accents and say things like 'Ay up duck'. This he justified by saying that we (Simon and myself) already had our fair share of Geordies in the comic, and now it was his turn to have some Nottingham characters. I eventually gave up caring but when it came to recording their voices Nottingham was out of the question, so the ugly compromise of 'vaguely northern' was arrived at.

Stephen Garrett, the man in charge of the youth purse strings at Channel 4, was also unhappy with the Fat Slags. And he wasn't too keen on the Sid the Sexist animation either. After seeing the scripts he complained to John that they 'lacked narrative' and he wanted to see some extensive rewriting. John tried to broker a compromise. He suggested making 'minimal' changes that would not 'fundamentally alter' the scripts. We saw this editorial interference as an outrage and immediately saddled up our high horses. Indeed, to demonstrate the strength of our feelings we wrote a brief, revised version of the Slags script which we sent to John:

Slags at Large – Garrett Mix for Channel 4

It is morning and we find the Slags huddled around a small kitchen table. They are both smoking (dope) and drinking tea. Empty syringes litter the floor. In the background a baby cries.

TRACEY: Ten years of Thatcher and there's still no light at the end of the tunnel.

SANDRA (*opening letter*): Another Poll Tax summons. Can't pay, won't pay!

TRACEY: Right on sister!

SANDRA: Tray. There's something that I've never told you. That I've never felt able to tell you. Or strong enough to tell you.

TRACEY: Strength. Take strength through your pain. Talk. And don't be ashamed to cry.

SANDRA: Tray. I've been raped. A man monster. A penis-wielding oppressor has soiled me.

TRACEY: Rape. It's a rabbit in the vegetable garden of womanhood. It nibbles our carrots, and plunders our parsnips. Our celery is decimated.

SANDRA: I feel dirty. And guilty. Almost as if …

TRACEY: As if what?

SANDRA: As if it was my fault!

TRACEY: Don't think that way. That's what men want you to think. That's what the Tory media want you to think.

SANDRA: Guilt is a two-edged sword. A pendulum. An uncomfortable bedfellow.

TRACEY: Bed? What bed? A flowerbed?

SANDRA: No. A bed of nails. Like tiny daggers piercing my heart.

TRACEY: Let's share the pain. Let us cry together. As women.

The Slags sob hysterically for ten minutes, embrace, rocking back and forth. Suddenly the picture turns to grainy black and white. The Slags begin to talk in French, subtitled in English.

TRACEY: Je suis une lesbian.
SANDRA: Moi aussi.

There follows a 45-minute, artistically filmed, tender, gentle love scene where there is explicit sex (licking, tongues, shaven haven) but with the emphasis on the emotional rather than the physical relationship. Afterwards they light up Gitanes cigarettes. Through the curling grey smoke, light from the louvre blinds dances across their naked breasts. And hairy pussies.

SANDRA: I never knew that love between two women could be that strong. So passionate, yet tender.
TRACEY: Wild, like a hungry lion. Yet timid, like a tortoise, or a shrew.
SANDRA: Stronger than any love between a man and a woman.
TRACEY: Will you marry me … in Holland?
SANDRA: Yes.

THE END

We may have been joking but for John this was an extremely serious situation. He depended on Channel 4 stumping up to cover the cost of the animations. In this case a not inconsiderable £300,000. If we stood our ground and refused to 'add narrative' to our scripts, Channel 4 were not going to buy the videos and we could kiss all that lolly goodbye. If that happened John would have to go cap in hand to PolyGram and ask them to bump up their advance against video sales in order to cover the production costs. The profitability of the entire project hung in the balance. Despite John's pleas we were adamant, stamped our feet and refused to budge, and to give the man his due he accepted our decision. John waved goodbye to his half of £300,000 just to keep us happy, and I waved goodbye to our half.

The Fat Slags animation consisted of three fifteen-minute

films. For our first-ever attempt at writing spoken dialogue it wasn't too bad, but it wasn't brilliant either. Garrett was right about narrative, although we mocked him at the time. It was all very cartoon-like in structure and relied entirely on the same old shagging punchlines. *Slags at Large* was basically a trip to the pub followed by a visit to a Chinese restaurant (cue Chinese jokes) and ending with a shag in a taxi. *Working Girls* was an interview at the dole office interspersed with shagging flashbacks and ending with a shag at the dole office. And *Dirty Weekend* was a trip to the countryside featuring a cameo appearance by Farmer Palmer, with lots of shagging. Neither the Fat Slags nor Simon's Sid the Sexist videos were deemed suitable for broadcast until eleven years later, by which time television standards had lowered sufficiently for the Men and Motors satellite channel to give them their first airing, providing their viewers with a bit of light relief between sessions of hand relief.

£150,000 may sound like a lot of money to chuck away, but in those days I was raking in that much from a single issue of the magazine, or so I thought. By the time the videos were released at Christmas 1992 our audited sales figure was down 20 per cent year-on-year to 875,408 for the period July to December.

But our sales weren't *falling*. That was not a word we used. I preferred to describe them as 'settling' while John stuck with the commonly used publishing verb 'plateau', meaning to level off. As our sales *plateaued* John Brown began to think in terms of promotion. One obvious solution to the problem of losing a fifth of your readers in the space of a year was to go out and sponsor Fulham Football Club, or so it seemed to John. To be fair I think it was Fulham who approached him – they were near neighbours of his – and proposed a shirt sponsorship deal. At the time Fulham were languishing near the bottom of the old Third Division and I think the sum of £20,000 was mentioned. I told John to forget it. There was no way *Viz* could be associated with a London football team, especially one whose nickname was 'The Cottagers'. If he did want to sponsor a football club it would have to be a small, unglamorous North-East side. Whether our telephones were being bugged or not I cannot say for sure but within days of that conversation I received a letter from Blyth Spartans, a non-league club famous in the football world for their FA Cup giant-killing exploits. In 1978 Spartans had come within one game of reaching the quarter-finals of the FA Cup. The club had since fallen on hard times and the letter explained that if they didn't find a new sponsor within weeks the club would go out of business.

As a twelfth birthday treat my dad took me to see Newcastle play Everton, and I've been a Newcastle fan ever since. (Fortunately the score that night was 0–0, leaving me with a low level of expectation.) I'd never been a fan of non-league football but I had seen Blyth once, in their 1978 fifth-round replay against Wrexham, which was staged at St James Park. I told John we should go for it. John had no idea where Blyth was but he loved the name 'Spartans' and readily coughed up £10,000 to make *Viz* their official club sponsor.

A few weeks later John and our publicist Eugen Beer travelled up from London to take in a Blyth match and enjoy some of the benefits of corporate football sponsorship. They looked a little disappointed with the pre-match buffet. It was strictly soup and sausage rolls – not a prawn sandwich in sight. During the game one of our corporate guests, my mate Walter, tried to attract the attention of Eugen, who was sitting several seats away. 'Eddie! Eddie! Eddie!' he kept shouting. Later Eugen asked him why he'd called him Eddie. Walter explained. 'Well I'm not going to shout *Eugen* in Blyth, am I?'

Producing the comic had become a bit of a chore, and it was starting to show. More and more uninspired cartoons were being thrown into the mix. The only way I could stop that was by coming up with something better myself and, frankly, I couldn't. So cartoons like 'Euro School' (in issue 55) and 'Sherlock Homo' (issue 56) went in despite the fact that I hated them. Then there was 'Little Old Man' – about a young boy who behaved like an old man, and 'Playtime Fontayne' – about an old man who behaved like a young boy. These were formulaic nonsense, brilliantly drawn of course, and occasionally quite funny. But they were Category C cartoons, not A. Signs of boredom and distraction were there for all our remaining readers to see. For example, in 'Roger Mellie' (issue 56, October 1992) Roger and his director Tom start the cartoon speaking each other's lines by mistake; and in issue 59 Billy the Fish's manager Tommy Brown stands up on his desk, drops his trousers, bends over and has a shit. The object of this exercise, he explains to Fulchester coach Syd Preston, is to prove that nobody is reading. Self-parody had always been a vital ingredient in *Viz*, but now we were starting to take the piss. Increasingly our readers were not amused, and it wasn't just Tommy Brown defecating on his desk that got them going. In our August 1992 issue I gave pride of place on the letters page to a damning dispatch from a little miss called Jenny Marlow of Camden:

> Judging by the overt misogyny that appears in your boysie comic I can only assume that you all have hang-ups about the size of your cocks, and probably feel threatened by females of all ages. Your evident hatred of women makes your comic as low grade as the *Sun* and the *Sport* and other papers you pretend to ridicule.
>   Jenny Marlow, aged 14
>   Camden, London

I had a policy of loudly ignoring this sort of criticism, and it was this policy that formed the basis for an ill-judged and wholly unsuccessful campaign to promote our videos in the run-up to Christmas 1992. We were also hawking a calendar, an annual plus a hurriedly compiled Fat Slags 1993 desk diary (a last-minute replacement for *The Bumper Book of Shite*, which was now three years late), but our main priority was to push the Fat Slags and Sid the Sexist videos which were now operating on a very

226

narrow profit margin. To do this publicists Beer Davis came up with the idea of a *Viz* roadshow, sending us on a whistle-stop tour of the country to meet the provincial media during the day and then visit Students' Unions at night to play our awful videos in front of live audiences. The plan was that after the screenings myself, Graham, Thorpy and Simon would do a question-and-answer session during which we would be lambasted by outraged feminists over the content of the videos, and this rumble of criticism would then become an earthquake of publicity which would in turn lead to a volcanic eruption of video sales. So off we went on our first live tour.

At the first Students' Union we visited I couldn't stay in the room to watch the videos. I hid until it was over then braced myself for the terrifying ordeal of being confronted by a room full of hundreds of appalled feminists. In fact, any sensible person who saw the videos would have been appalled, not just feminists. The planning of these events had been virtually non-existent and there was nobody to chair the question-and-answer session. We were plonked on four seats on a stage in front of an audience still reeling from what they had just seen, and left to fend for ourselves. I mumbled a few words of introduction then we just sat there with a crowd of two or three hundred students sitting staring at us. There weren't any feminists. There was no anger in anyone's eyes, just a great deal of disappointment. I think they'd been expecting some sort of comedy act. Occasionally people did punctuate the awkward silence with questions, but there was no debate, no controversy. Thorpy, Graham and myself hated every minute of it, but my brother Simon was in his element. He enjoyed being on stage and he started to fill the awkward silences with awkward monologues while the other three of us shuffled in our seats, arms folded, staring at the floor. As far as Simon was concerned we were on the road – gigging – and this was as close to being a rock star as he was ever going to get. I thought we were wasting our fucking time. Tensions were mounting as our tour bus pulled in to

Coventry and headed for the offices of the *Coventry Evening Telegraph* to do a local press interview.

We tended to come up against two types of provincial journalist on our travels. One was the junior reporter who was often a fan of *Viz* and would generally give us an easy time. The other was the older hack who probably didn't like the comic but had been lumbered with the job of talking to us. The latter might dig about a bit to try and amuse themselves. Peter Walters fell pretty neatly into the second category. He was a hack all right, and most of his questions revolved around money. How much was I making? What was my financial relationship with John Brown? How much were the others paid? Where did we all live? How big were our houses? In fairness to the reporter you can't wander into a newspaper office and expect them to plug your books and videos without asking you any questions. I had no objections at all to people asking questions about my personal finances, providing they were from the Inland Revenue. But this bloke wasn't. He was from the *Coventry Evening Telegraph*. Midway through our grilling, a photographer turned up to take our picture. Provincial press photographers also tend to fall into two categories. The first is the no-nonsense cliché man who goes for the obvious shot, usually of us peering over the top of an open comic. I've been patiently peering over the top of open comics ever since Jim and I posed on the roof of Thompson House, Newcastle, way back in 1980. The other type of photographer is the artistic individual who likes to come up with something original to show his editor. He'll have you posing in any number of fucking ridiculous positions and take several reels of film just to get one poxy black-and-white shot in the paper. I've met a few of these in my time, the most extreme example being a freelance Scottish photographer called Murdo McLeod. He once made me take off my shoes, roll up my trousers and stand in an icy cold river in my bare feet, cradling my baby son in my arms for fifteen minutes while he tried to get the lighting right. Needless to say the paper didn't use that picture.

Paul Gilroy of the *Coventry Evening Telegraph* was an artistic individual too. First he went for a shot of us poking our heads through vertical louvre window blinds. That took an eternity. Then he had an even better idea. *Viz* is toilet humour, so let's have a shot of all four of us crowded into a lavatory cubicle, photographed from above. Wearily we marched into the toilet followed by the reporter Peter Walters. He was still asking questions so we had to pull silly poses and provide sensible answers simultaneously. One question directed at me was, 'How long do you think *Viz* will last?' Bearing in mind that it had been a very long day, I was hating this 'tour', dreading that evening's 'performance' in Birmingham, and as he spoke I was being forced to cram into a toilet cubicle and pull silly faces with Graham, Thorpy and Simon, my answer was probably a touch on the optimistic side. 'Two years at the most,' I said. The other three weren't at all happy with that and as we left the building an argument began. They didn't think I should be talking so negatively. Was there something I hadn't told them? What about their futures? It wasn't a particularly loud or animated argument but it seemed significant to me at the time. To make matters worse, in an interview with *Today* newspaper three days later I continued my negative theme. 'Some mornings when I wake up I just want to give it all up,' I told their reporter Jane Moore. 'It started off as a laugh but it has become a job to me. It's not as much fun any more.' I concluded this depressing rant – the purpose of which, you'll recall, was to sell our new books and videos – by offering *Viz* for sale. 'If someone said "Here's £10 million" I'd sell like a shot,' I told her. This quote was of course picked up on by the sub-editors who ran the giant headline 'I EN-*VIZ*-AGE SELLING OUT' the following day. Then came the domino effect and a rash of less contextual '*Viz* for sale' stories appeared in all the other papers.

Nobody came forward with an offer but I knew full well that nobody would, even at £10 million, which was actually quite a good price. A year earlier John had looked into the possibility of selling *Viz* in some detail, and in a slightly more discreet manner too. It was me who had first suggested the idea in June 1991. John subsequently approached a firm of city analysts to find out what *Viz* was worth and, more importantly, to see if anyone would be interested in taking it off our hands. John wasn't looking to sell but he thought it sensible that we should be 'aware of our options', as he put it. And I think we were both keen to see how many noughts there would be on the end of that particular option.

Selling at that time – 1991 – would have made sense. *Viz* wasn't going to get any fatter and, if it was going to be slaughtered, then now would be the best time to do it. If there was an absolute fortune to be had I could have divvied it up between the whole team and we could have all fucked off to Portugal to play golf or something. A few months after that John got back to me. The good news was that the comic was worth 'somewhere between £10 million and £25 million' (how much he paid his analysts to come up with such a precise figure I never found out). The bad news was that there were only four companies they had identified as likely purchasers, and none of them was interested. Even if a generous buyer had been found, our retirement would still have been a long way off. The potential value of the magazine was tied inextricably to the editorial staff, so any sale would have to be supplemented with some sort of binding obligation on our part to keep on working. Alas, as the engines began to go 'Pftt! Pftt! Pftt!', bailing out with a bagful of money on our backs was not an option.

CHAPTER SIXTEEN

The Rabbit Hunter

After using our railway retreat as a weekend home for a couple of years Dolores and I eventually decided to move out to the sticks full time. In the autumn of 1991 we'd had our second child, a daughter called Jamie, and our son Dale would soon be starting pre-school playgroup, so we had to decide where home was going to be. In our crowded street in Newcastle we'd only ever met two neighbours, and one of them had only popped his head out of the door briefly to complain that the back of our car was encroaching across the front of his house. But out in the country we'd quickly got to know everybody living within a twenty-mile radius. Newcastle was changing, too, and I wasn't sure that I liked it any more.

I'd had an old weighbridge building in the garden converted into a small studio, and increasingly I preferred to work from home. Whether Dolores was happy having me around all day was another matter. I tended to get rather moody, shall we say, at times. I'd be fine when I was busy or on a deadline, but for a week or two after deadlines I'd be totally insufferable – bored, depressed and foul tempered. 'He's on his publishing cycle,' she would explain to any visitors before they were allowed into the house.

I'd taken to country life like a duck to water, buying myself a plaid shirt and chainsaw, and spending my weekends felling trees in the garden. Soon I found that the length of the cable on my chainsaw limited the number of trees I could fell. We had one and a half acres of wooded garden and, even with a long extension lead, the majority of trees were well out of range. A friendly local called by one day to admire my work and suggested that I might want to try using a 'proper' chainsaw. Mine – a B&Q Black & Decker model – was apparently for girls. So I got myself a petrol chainsaw and thereafter progress was astonishing. Not a tree in the garden was safe.

I'd seen lumberjacks at work on *Blue Peter* so I knew the basic principles already and it wasn't long until I'd perfected the technique of getting a tree to fall in a precise direction. My proudest achievement was bringing down a large pine with pinpoint accuracy so that it fell precisely into a five-foot slot between our electricity power cables and the Calor gas tank. I don't think Dolores truly appreciated that achievement. Then one day I was sawing the remains of a tree into logs when I carelessly lowered the saw before the blade had stopped. The teeth lightly brushed my trousers just as they were coming to rest. Needless to say I wasn't wearing any protective clothing – apart from my plaid shirt, of course. Fortunately the teeth of the saw didn't even break the surface of my jeans, but it suddenly dawned on me how dangerous the tool in my hands was. I looked at my leg, looked at the saw and then looked at my leg again. Then I put the saw away and I've never used it since.

Trees weren't the only problem in our garden. The real bastards were the rabbits. The previous owners had employed a part-time gardener to keep everything in order but I'd assured Dolores that such an expense would not be necessary. I could look after the place perfectly well myself. I bought a sit-on mower and a strimmer to cut the grass with, and, through a combination of bad driving and botanical ignorance, within a fortnight I had wiped out most of the flowers and shrubs. To deal with the rabbit problem I equipped myself with a .22 air rifle and began making regular dusk and dawn patrols up and down the garden. Not long after buying the house I'd been driving along a narrow lane somewhere up in the Scottish borders when I suddenly came upon a large group of rabbits sitting in the road. They seemed to be having some sort of organized family outing. It was too late to stop and I ploughed straight over them, then watched their bodies bouncing and rolling down the road in my rear-view mirror. I lost sleep that night worrying about all the rabbit grief I'd caused and the poor little orphaned bunnies that I'd left by the roadside. I worried about it for several days. But I quickly came to hate rabbits after I watched the bastards slowly and methodically destroy my garden. The bits that I hadn't destroyed yet anyway.

The garden had originally been railway sidings so beneath the shallow turf was dirt, clinker and stones. During the night the rabbits would burrow down through the grass and start drift mining the crap below, leaving irreparable holes in the grass and huge mounds of dirt. Historically part of the garden had been a tip and it was here that the little sods chose to build their rabbit city, drilling a maze of massive tunnels into the earth and throwing up enormous chunks of broken crockery and glass. Soon parts of the garden were no longer safe for the kids to play in.

I vividly remember the first one I shot. I'd come across it on one of my patrols and it had hidden itself behind a log. Tentatively it stuck its little rabbit head up to see if the coast was clear. I squeezed the trigger and heard its skull crack. On an average day I'd kill two or three but it didn't seem to make any difference to the overall population numbers. They just kept on popping out of the ground, like little fluffy zombies. I liked all the other animals, apart from rabbits. One morning I was tip-toeing up the garden, Elmer Fudd style, when I heard something move in the bushes just ahead of me. I released my safety catch and was turning slowly to my left when a deer flew out of the top of the bush and landed not fifteen feet away from me. It was a tiny little thing with skinny legs and it just stood there staring at me. Then in one amazing bound it launched itself high over the fence and away. In all my life I'd never seen such a springy thing.

I told myself that I was only shooting the rabbits because they were pests. I wasn't doing it for sport or pleasure. Then one day a local farmer asked if I fancied coming out one night to go lamping rabbits in his fields. Lamping rabbits means shining powerful torches at them (although a more significant part of the procedure, certainly as far as the rabbit is concerned, is that you then shoot them). Not wishing to appear a soft townie I accepted the invitation and sat on the back of his quad-bike as we set out at dusk on a killing tour of his fields. In theory this was also a pest control exercise but you could tell from the look in Farmer Neil's eyes as he loaded his .22 rifle (a real one, not an air gun) that this was personal. We stopped in a field and he shot a rabbit that was so far away I couldn't even see it. 'Got the bastard!' he said. He passed me the gun and invited me to have a go. I missed. We repeated this sequence in several fields, him shooting one or two rabbits then me missing. Neil picked up all the bodies and put them in a sack which I had the pleasure of carrying on my back. Any rabbits that weren't dead either had their necks broken manually or their heads smashed against the handlebars. It was all a bit grim and not really my idea of a night out. When we got back to his farmyard he emptied the rabbits onto the ground and lined them all up in a row, moving along them with a torch as if to get a good look at their faces. He kicked one over and poked its guts with the toe of his boot. 'Look at that bastard, with its belly full of my corn!'

'They don't grow corn in England,' muttered Graham when I told him about my adventure in the office the following morning. I stormed off to get a dictionary. 'Corn,' I announced seconds later. 'Noun. Grain; wheat; oats; the seeds of cereals. Used to describe maize *chiefly in North America*,' I said triumphantly. Graham didn't like me killing rabbits or winning arguments. And he didn't like farmers either. One had been rude to him many years ago and he'd borne a grudge ever since. That's where Farmer Palmer came from. Graham would often whine on about how greedy and rich farmers were and how they had no right to own their land. 'Most of them are tenants or low-paid farm workers and they don't own any land,' I'd tell him. But Graham could be obstinate when it came to petty arguments – almost as obstinate as me. As well as farmers he didn't like cars. 'How can you possibly enjoy driving something that is potentially a lethal weapon?' he'd argue. He didn't like drink-drivers either and believed that anyone caught drink-driving should receive an immediate lifetime ban. Graham's laid-back, long-haired appearance was totally misleading. Given a cut and perm, a blue rinse and a pearl necklace, he wouldn't have been at all out of place in the front row at a Tory Party conference.

We could argue about anything, me versus the others. In fairness, the others would say that it was *me* arguing, not them. But that was something else I'd argue about. I may have started the arguments, but I seem to recall they would always join in. One day 'Baker Street' by Gerry Rafferty came on the radio. 'Tssch! They must play that song on Radio 1 at least once a day,' said Graham in all seriousness. 'You don't honestly believe that, do you?' I said, jumping up from my drawing board with not entirely justifiable indignation. Graham dug in, insisting that 'Baker Street' was played on Radio 1 *at least* once a day. I rang Eugen, who plugged records as well as books, and asked him to get me the exact figure. 'Baker Street' had been played some-thing like twenty-three times on Radio 1 in the previous year. 'You see! *I* was right and *you* were wrong,' I said. But, as usual, by that stage Graham had lost interest in the argument and gone back to his drawing, denying me my rightful satisfaction.

At the end of 1991 we'd moved to new offices just round the corner from our old one. I'd felt uncomfortable having John as both our landlord and publisher, but my main reason for moving was the hope that a change might be as good as a rest. Moving my desk around and swapping rooms any number of times in the old office hadn't made life any more exciting so I was hoping that a completely new building might make a difference. Unfortunately, for our new home I chose the dreariest, most characterless concrete block in the whole of Newcastle.

For me our production-line system had taken all the fun out of cartooning. Characters were becoming homogenized, and you rarely had the pleasure of being surprised by something someone else had created out of the blue. But Davey Jones's cartoons were still being farmed organically in Wales and it was still a joy when one of his efforts arrived. A cry of 'Jonesy's stuff's here' would go up and we'd all drop whatever we were doing and gather round as the tube was opened and the drawing paper unfurled. Then there'd be a brief silence before the first howls of laughter went up, usually brought on by the title itself. This was certainly the case in March 1992 when Jonesy sent in his defining piece of work – 'The Vibrating Bum-Faced Goats' – which began with this immortal piece of narration: 'High up in the wild and craggy Quantock Mountains was a herd of the most unusual animals you have ever seen. Built by Grandpa Simmons, a brilliant mechanic, they were vibrating robot goats. And each and every one of them had a face like an arse.'

Opening Jonesy's cartoons became one of the main highlights of the entire production cycle, along with the hectic deadline spell which was still a big buzz. But by now I was cramming most of my work into that brief, frantic period. It was like revising for an exam. I'd start work as late as possible and if I still made the deadline then I knew that I could leave it a little bit later the next time. Once I actually got going I'd be as happy as a pig in shit; manically writing, planning and laying out pages, editing the letters, designing the cover and having a whale of a time. At the end of it all we'd be adding the finishing touches to the last pages at three or four in the morning while a courier sat in reception waiting to drive the artwork to the printers in Bristol, the last train already having gone. Those busy spells were still great fun, but for the other five or six weeks I couldn't motivate myself. I'd be bored and constantly looking for distractions outside of work.

There was virtually no limit to the amount of money I had to distract myself with, and I tried buying a few things to cheer me

Davey Jones's Vibrating Bum-faced Goats

up. My first extravagance had been my BMW, but I soon regretted it. To begin with, the salesman was a smarmy git. He'd brought the car round to the office and after a test drive we were finalizing details. As I was going to be paying cash I thought I'd try and get the price rounded down a little. 'I'll tell you what. Knock off that £400 and we'll call it a deal,' I said, extending a hopeful hand. The salesman went into a well-rehearsed routine that they must have taught him at BMW sales school. A look of concern crept across his face, he took me to one side and then whispered in my ear. 'Listen,' he said. 'If you can't afford it I can always put a cheaper radio in for you.' Not only did arseholes sell BMWs, but the general perception out on the road seemed to be that everyone who drove one was an arsehole as well. One day I was delivering a finished comic to the Red Star parcels office at Newcastle Central station. I'd been up all night and by now it was about 7 a.m. The young man handing out the tickets at the entrance to the car park took a sneering, derisive look at the car as I drove up. I was getting used to this by now so I silently took the ticket from his hand and drove on. As I did he leaned out of his booth and shouted, 'Don't bother saying "thank you" then, you wanker.' It wasn't like me at all, but I flew into an instant rage, slammed on the brakes and jumped out to confront him. 'Have you got a *problem*?' I enquired, marching towards his booth. An apology wasn't forthcoming. Instead he stood up, revealing himself to be rather a tall young man, got out of the booth and lumbered towards me. 'You want *some*, do you?' he enquired. Then he pointed to a very specific spot on the road about five yards away. 'Come on then. I'll give you *some*. Over there, now!' At this point he started taking off his yellow fluorescent jacket. The situation had developed rather more quickly than I'd expected, and in a totally different direction. I was now staring at the specific area of Tarmac where he was proposing to kick my head in. If pointing out this piece of ground was a deliberate psychological tactic then it had worked, and I was desperately looking for a way out. Fortunately at that moment the lady behind me in the queue for the car park, who up till then had been sitting quite patiently waiting for her ticket, decided to honk her horn. This gave me an excuse to return to my car to move it, waving a finger at my opponent in a 'Don't you worry, I'll be back' sort of way. By the time I did go back, a couple of weeks later, I was too late. To my great relief the man in question had been replaced by an orange box on a stick which dispensed tickets quietly and efficiently without passing any judgements on you or your car.

I don't think my accountant drove a BMW. He was a very conservative type, his only obvious extravagance being a posh silver pen. When it came to investing money he didn't believe in the stock markets. 'You can't go wrong with bricks and mortar,' was one of his favourite sayings. But I didn't want to buy property purely as an investment. I had no desire to be like Mrs Collins, our penny-pinching old landlady. So I came up with a compromise; I'd buy some property, as he suggested, but only *ex-railway* property. I didn't mention this part of the plan to him.

Buying several railway stations was a tactic I'd often employed in Monopoly, but only with limited success. Now all of a sudden here I was doing it for real. Compared to the one we lived in, the second station I bought was very small. An unmanned halt in fact. It needed a lot of work to make it habitable, so Dolores and I turned architects to redesign the internal layout and supervise all the building work. That station is now a lovely little house and not a bad investment. But my third station was where I really fucked up.

I knew Ilderton station was for sale because I regularly drove past it on my way to work. It was a large and very impressive stone building set above the road, with half-hipped dormer windows and gables, decorative barge boards and ornate iron finials. In other words, it had a fancy roof. I deliberately looked away every time I drove past it because I knew that once I started to think about buying it the temptation would be too much. People don't realize this, but it's every bit as frustrating being able to afford *too many* houses as it is being able to afford none at all. Honest. In fact it's worse, because no one gives you any sympathy for your problem. I'm sure Elton John knows what I'm on about. Anyway, in order to avoid buying this old station house I deliberately ignored it until a 'sold' sign appeared. Only then did I knock on the door and ask the outgoing owner if I could take a look around, purely out of historical interest.

What I saw inside almost moved me to tears. The old station offices had never been converted to a new use, and it was as if nothing had changed in the sixty years since the last passenger train had left. The original brass-rimmed locks were still on the doors. The ceramic chain-pull was still hanging in the lavatory. Enamel doorplates were visible, peering out from beneath the paint. The beautiful glazed brickwork was still intact, and in the waiting rooms there were cast-iron fireplaces bearing the railway company monogram. In the booking office the timber security shutters were still in perfect working order and a luggage label rack hung on the wall, still bearing labels for long-closed destinations like Rothbury, Kelso and Alnwick. But best of all the ticket window, with its gleaming, ornate glazed brick arch above and distinctive cast-iron grille, was entirely intact. I knew there'd been an identical window in our house because I'd uncovered its broken remains buried in the garden. I knew it must have been special but I had no idea just how special until I saw this identical window. It broke my heart. I was furious with myself for not having bought Ilderton station, but rather than sulk I decided to do something about it. So I found out who had bought it, and I bought it off him. The only flaw in my plan was that I hadn't the foggiest idea what I was going to do with it.

When the locals got word that I'd bought three stations more or less in a row speculation mounted that I was about to relay the track and reopen the railway. Word spread well beyond the immediate area, and pretty soon every estate agent in the country had heard about the daft bastard from *Viz* magazine who collects old railway stations. Every time a railway property came on the market anywhere in the UK (and occasionally overseas) I was sent details.

The other cartoonists had also returned to the housing market, but were buying in smaller quantities than me. Graham bought a lovely Victorian red brick villa near the coast, Thorpy a detached stone house overlooking the Tyne Valley, and Simon a big Edwardian terraced house close to Newcastle city centre. With the exception of Simon we were all living entirely domesticated lives. Since moving north Thorpy had met and married a girl who worked for Andy Pop's *Viz* distribution company. (Andy had diversified and was by now distributing a lot more Spice Girls and *Coronation Street* merchandise than *Viz*.) Graham's old girlfriend Karen had left him, unwisely I feared, for a man who looked alarmingly like the cricketer Graham Gooch. But since then our Graham had met his perfect partner and they were now happily married and in the process of starting a family. My brother Simon was the only one of us still single, but he did have a steady relationship with a long-term girlfriend. Most of my early inspiration for cartoons had come from observing people, but now the only people I tended to observe were my work colleagues, my wife, my kids and of course my accountant. And frankly there wasn't much mileage for a cartoon in Mr Thornton.

We had changed, our circumstances had changed, and the world outside our window had changed too. Since the 'alternative' comedy boom of the 1980s, stand-up was now all the rage in pubs and clubs around the country. Comedy was the 'new rock'n'roll', by all accounts, and kids who in the past would have dreamt of being pop stars now subscribed to the far more attainable ambition of wanting to stand behind a microphone and be a smart-arse. The rules of comedy engagement had changed too. Despite Sir Ben of Elton's brave attempts to rescue fair maidens and mothers-in-law from sexist comedy – and holding Benny Hill's severed head aloft on his sword – political correctness was actually in recession. Laddism had arrived – chauvinism neatly repackaged for the 1990s. The magazine world was undergoing serious tectonic activity too. *Viz* may have been flagging, but by the beginning of 1993 an entirely new magazine market was opening up in our wake.

CHAPTER SEVENTEEN

Honk if You've Shagged Catherine Zeta-Jones

In the early days, when *Viz* was just beginning to break through, I'd had a recurring dream that someone else had brought out a magazine that was funnier than ours. Surely it was just a matter of time until someone did. After all, what we'd been doing was nothing special.

During the late eighties and early nineties a hell of a lot of people tried. Newsagents' shelves became littered with crappy *Viz* lookalikes. It had taken us ten years to get *Viz* into WHSmith's – ten years of hard labour, building a road through seemingly impenetrable terrain. And now any Tom, Dick or Harry could cruise along that road and straight onto the shelf marked 'Adult Humour'. I hated that word *adult* – it implied pornography to me. I'd have much rather they called it 'Lavatory Humour', or 'Shit' perhaps. Call them what you will, but a rash of clones appeared: *Ziggy, Smut, Poot!, Toxic, Acne, Blag, Gutter, Brain Damage, UT, Spit*. There was even a Christian comic called *The Winebibber* which, in 1991, brought out a Christmas annual called *The Big Holy One*. Some of these comics were the work of aspiring cartoonists, clearly inspired by our success. I wouldn't say I was flattered, but I had no great objections to them. But the ones that irritated me were those that were started up by cynical publishers who looked at our success and came up with the following equation:

(CRUDE CARTOONS + SWEARING) = ENORMOUS PROFIT

The most annoying of these cynical publishers was Russell Church of Brighton-based Humour Publications. He was the man responsible for our most persistent rival, *Zit* magazine. I first got wind of his activities in January 1991 when an illustrator who had been working on *Zit* prior to its launch fell out with Church, jumped ship and sent me copies of some of the work he had already produced. It wasn't very good. Not long after that an ad appeared in *Journalist's Week* offering 'excellent freelance rates' and 'an opportunity to become part of a success story of the nineties'. It read like a double-glazing sales recruitment campaign, but Church was actually soliciting for journalists to write for *Zit*, people who, as he put it, could 'write stronger, funnier, more biting editorial than *Viz*'.

My initial impression of Russell Church was based on a photograph I saw of him in a newspaper. He was wearing a striped jacket with the sleeves pulled up, in a Don Johnson style and looked like a fucking arsehole. There's something about people who pull their jacket sleeves up that annoys me (I harbour an irrational loathing of the singer Daryl Hall for the self-same reason). Irrational my loathing may have been, but everything I've since discovered about Russell Church has merely confirmed my initial impression.

Church marketed *Zit* aggressively against *Viz*. He tried to stir up a public rivalry between the two comics by taunting us in the press and hoping we would respond. He tried to make it personal too, getting hold of our fax number and sending us congratulations every time our sales figures went down. I made the mistake of replying to one of his faxes with a rather curt, handwritten reply – 'FUCK OFF, YOU STUPID CUNT' – but that served only to encourage him. *Viz* may have been losing readers but they sure as hell weren't going over to *Zit*. Church's magazine was so bad he couldn't give the thing away. On a Saturday early in 1991 he sent a team of dolly birds to Newcastle to hand out free copies of *Zit* in the city centre. By the end of the day the street was littered with them. He even got his team of glamour girls to distribute free copies on the doorstep of our office. Church spent a great deal of time and energy trying to antagonize us. I wouldn't say he got to me, but in quiet moments I did consider taking some sort of revenge.

The plan I came up with was to have him followed by a private eye. I don't know why, but hiring a private eye sounded like fun, and John Brown was very keen on the idea too. We decided to get our private eye to take lots of big black-and-white photographs of Church as he left buildings, got into his car or met people. We had no possible use for these photographs, but we thought it would be fun having them delivered to us by a private detective in big brown envelopes. Unfortunately the private eye we rang – I got his number from the Yellow Pages – was a drearily practical sort of bloke.

I asked him if he could follow someone for me. 'How far do you want me to follow him?' he asked. What a stupid question. 'Everywhere he goes, of course,' I said. 'So, if he gets on a plane to South America you want me to follow him there?' 'Erm ... not necessarily,' I replied. 'Well, what about Europe?' After a couple of minutes on the phone to this bloke all the novelty of the idea had worn off. Then he mentioned his fee, and at that point I lost interest completely. £2000 would only have bought us two days' surveillance, plus expenses of course. And so Church continued his nefarious activities unsurveilled.

In February 1993 Church had the audacity to sue another *Viz* clone, *Spit*, accusing them of passing off their magazine as *Zit*. Passing off is the legal term for making your product look like someone else's in order to benefit from their product's success and reputation. 'We'll take on the winner,' I said to John. But we already knew there was no case for passing off between similar comics. Our lawyer had already told us the charge would never stick. You have to be a counterfeiter rather than a copycat to be guilty of passing off. But Russell Church's legal advice wasn't as good as ours and he pursued *Spit* all the way to the High Court where the judge ruled that nobody 'with reasonable apprehension and proper eyesight' could confuse *Spit* with *Zit*. Church was landed with his opponent's legal bill, estimated at £32,000, on top of his own costs. And he was in even bigger trouble months later when TV presenter Ann Diamond took legal action over a reference *Zit* had made to her child's tragic cot death. That particular 'strong, funny and biting piece of editorial' pretty well summed up *Zit*'s level of humour.

Pint-sized wank-magnate David Sullivan had tried to jump on the bandwagon too. He published a comic called *UT* which was put together by an ex-*Viz* contributor called Kevin Sutherland. I came face-to-quiff with diddy porn millionaire Sullivan late one night while making my second appearance on James Whale's controversial TV chat show.

This was the most ridiculous TV programme I'd ever found myself in the midst of. On one side of me sat David Sullivan, the diminutive pornographer, wearing high heels; and on the other side of me was an extremely disturbing elderly gentleman who appeared to be campaigning for the legalization of child sex. If not that, then he certainly wanted the age of sexual consent lowered. I just sat there thinking, 'How the fuck did I get here?'

I'd got there by car, driven by Arthur 2 Stroke, who'd volunteered his services for the night because he was anxious to reacquaint himself with James Whale. As I've already mentioned, Anti-Pop orchestrated a hate campaign against Whale in Newcastle some years ago, and 2 Stroke was hoping to rekindle their relationship. During the live broadcast he started shouting what might best be described as 'persistent abuse' at Whale from the back of the studio. Unfortunately David Sullivan's minder interpreted this as some kind of threat to his employer's safety and laid into 2 Stroke, giving him a firm but discreet punch in the kidney as he bundled him out of the studio door. At around the same time I made some unkind on-air comment to James Whale who by this stage was getting quite agitated and he told me to shut up or I'd be thrown off the show. That sounded fine to me so I made another similarly unkind comment, at which point Whale ordered me out of the studio. I took off my microphone and left gladly. On my way out the producer approached me in the corridor. 'Don't mind James,' he said. 'You realize it's all a bit of fun. He'll be delighted to have you back on in a minute.' The show was taking a commercial break and James Whale appeared from the studio door. He wasn't looking particularly delighted, and he warned me, in no uncertain terms, about the consequences of any further misbehaviour. He was trying to look macho and aggressive but he didn't succeed, largely because he was wearing red clogs at the time. Outside the front door of the studios I came across David Sullivan's minder and driver, both of whom were having a fag. The minder looked and sounded like Arthur Mullard, while the driver was a younger man with a similar suit and East End accent. I got talking to them briefly and asked how their 'adult' comic *UT* was going. 'Nyyaaaaaaaah,' said the minder, exhaling smoke and dismissively shaking his head, all of which I took to mean 'not very well'. 'But you've really cracked it with *Viz*,' he said. He spoke like a villain congratulating a rival on a particularly ingenious wages snatch. 'You done well there, my son.'

Fortunately most of the engagements I was offered in my capacity as a 'D' list celebrity were more civilized than the James Whale show. Possibly the most civilized of all was an invitation to speak in the hallowed debating chamber of the Cambridge Union Society. My natural instinct was to turn this down. Cambridge was daunting. Previous speakers in the Union Society's 180-year history had included Churchill, Attlee, Roosevelt, Reagan, King Hussein of Jordan, the Dalai Lama, South African premier F.W. de Klerk and German chancellor Helmut Kohl. These were going to be tough acts to follow. But I was quietly confident that on a good night, and with the right material, I could get more laughs than F.W. de Klerk and Helmut Kohl put together. So I accepted, and in February 1993 I drove down to Cambridge to make my public speaking début.

I'd been to Cambridge once before during a publicity tour and had been struck by the radiant appearance of the students. They all looked so healthy with their bright white teeth, their clean, glowing complexions and their rosy red cheeks. Perhaps it's the country air that does it, or maybe it's the fox blood. Or more likely still, eating veal and smoked salmon instead of Pot Noodles and crisps. Dolores and I were put up in a poky room overlooking the Union Society on Bridge Street. I remember feeling terribly nervous looking out onto the busy street below as I struggled to fasten my bow tie. The motion for the evening's debate was 'This house would rather have a degree from the University of Life,' the familiar academics versus non-academics argument which I occasionally engaged Graham and Thorpy in to brighten up a dull lunch hour. So at least I was on familiar ground. I'd prepared a speech about my own career ambitions and my academic failures and tried to learn it all off by heart, but I couldn't. Former public schoolboy John Brown warned me not to take any notes – that would be seen as a sign of weakness – but I didn't give a shit how weak I looked, so I stuck my comforting wad of paper in my inside pocket, and as we made our way out of the building and across the road I checked it with a firm pat every ten seconds or so to make sure it was still there.

At the Union Society we were ushered upstairs into a grand dining room where the President, Ben Elkington, and a large group of his associates greeted us. Then we sat down for an uncomfortable meal. The room seemed dark and the vast dining table was lit by candles, their warm, glowing light reflecting on the pressed shirts and immaculate teeth of the toffs who surrounded me. Dolores and I were separated. She was on the other side of the table being interrogated by an eccentric Iranian mathematician while I was struggling to understand a single word the plummy young man on my left was saying. Luckily there was a softly spoken Asian gentleman on my right, the Union Society treasurer I think he was, and I was able to communicate much more easily with him. Everyone was terribly polite but irritatingly talkative. I hate people who talk while they're eating, but at dinner parties it seems to be a common practice. People balance a fork full of food below their mouth, ask you a question and then shovel it into their gob. While they chomp away it's your turn to talk. You then load up your forkful and conclude a point before shoving the food into your mouth, giving them an opportunity to respond. It's a bit like sex in so far as you need to get a rhythm going for it to work properly. But I don't even try. I just wank my grub down, keeping my head low and trying to ignore the conversation around me. During the first course I remember getting into a prolonged tussle with some resilient and foul-tasting vegetables that Dolores later identified as asparagus. Later still – ten years later, to be precise – I discovered that you're only supposed to nibble the ends, not eat the whole thing. By the end of that meal I was actually looking forward to my speech. Not to the speech itself, but the prospect of escaping from the table in order to make it.

The boisterous crowd in the chamber made me feel most welcome as I was introduced. As I took my seat I remember thinking that from now on I'm going to support Cambridge in the boat race. I can't remember much about the debate itself. Despite being read less than fluently from the page, my speech was very well received by the audience. (This might have had something to do with the fact that bitter had been reduced to 60p a pint in the bar beforehand.) Supporting the motion alongside me was a man off the telly whom I'd never heard of, Michael Gove, while on the opposite side were a strait-laced university professor and a careers expert. Michael Gove was extremely witty and sharp and, from the moment he stood up to the moment he sat down, the entire crowd were pissing their over-privileged pants. Between the two of us we won the debate hands down.

Afterwards I felt euphoric. The combined feeling of relief and achievement was incredible, and for a brief moment I knew what it was like to be a performer coming offstage on a high. When you've drawn something funny you sometimes sit back and allow yourself a quiet moment of smug satisfaction, and you might occasionally let off a Mutley-type snigger at something particularly funny you'd written. But all those little moments of self-satisfaction put together were nothing compared to the feeling of total exhilaration I experienced that night. I was on cloud fucking nine as we trooped off to celebrate on a late-night wine bar crawl with some of my new toffee-nosed mates.

Confirmation of my minor celebrity status arrived shortly afterwards when I was invited to appear in a celebrity football match. The big game, in aid of the Imperial Cancer Research Fund and a local charity radio station, took place at Gateshead International Stadium in May of 1993. The organizers were struggling to find twenty-two players, let alone celebrities, because when they rang me they asked if I could bring along as many people as possible. Myself, Simon and Graham instant-ly agreed to play, and I offered them a bonus celebrity in the shape of Arthur 2 Stroke, promising that he'd be dressed up as Fulchester United boss Tommy Brown for the occasion. As part of the pre-match publicity we were invited to a press conference at a local McDonald's restaurant where we found ourselves in the unusual position of posing for press pictures in Imperial Cancer Research hats with Big Mac beefburgers in our mouths. This wasn't the ideal pre-match preparation. I'd put on more stones than I'd kicked footballs in the last ten years so in the days leading up to the game I set about some serious training. I bought a pair of football boots and spent a few evenings drib-bling a ball up and down the garden, trying to avoid the broken glass and rabbit holes.

When we arrived at the stadium it soon became apparent that

it wasn't just celebrities who were in short supply. There was a conspicuous lack of spectators too. According to the programme there was supposed to be a 'crowd sing-a-long' twenty minutes before kick-off, but twenty minutes before kick-off there wasn't a crowd. The situation had not improved much by the time the teams emerged from the tunnel. There were more people on the pitch than in the stand. The poor turn-out was hardly surprising when you consider the level of celebrity that was on display. Shane Ritchie had not been able to make it, so the only real star present was *Blue Peter* heartthrob John Leslie. The rest of the sides were made up of local radio DJs, ex-footballers and assorted minor cast members from *Byker Grove*. Oh, and Eddie 'The Eagle' Edwards. Arthur 2 Stroke stood on the touchline wearing a sheepskin coat and a rather pathetic pink rubber bald patch, looking nothing whatsoever like Tommy Brown. I'd promised to make him an inflatable Billy the Fish to carry about on a string, but I hadn't got round to it.

My side was captained by the recently deposed Sunderland manager Malcolm Crosby and we had a couple of Sunderland players as our backbone. In goal Eddie 'The Eagle' Edwards was wearing his skis for comedy effect. Tactics weren't discussed at any great length so I decided to play wide left, out of the way of things. The word in our dressing room was that, despite being an ex-choirboy, the opposing captain John Leslie took his football very seriously. This was immediately apparent out on the pitch. Leslie was almost Souness-like in his drive, his enthusiasm and his mistiming of tackles. Malcolm Crosby was a far more laid-back skipper, giving us gentle words of encouragement rather than yelling war cries. Early in the game Crosby collected the ball in midfield and went on a mazy run down the right, leaving a trail of disorientated, overweight local disc jockeys in his wake. Cutting inside to the edge of the penalty area, he looked up and spotted me lurking about ten yards from goal. Crosby threaded a pinpoint ball through the crowded penalty area and I turned and hit it first time with my right foot then watched with delight

Graham caught schmoozing and sipping Champers at the 'Other Side of Viz' art exhibition, 1990.

Simon Thorp explains art to some woman off the radio, at our fine art exhibition.

Thorpy and Graham stop to contemplate *Winter*, one of our Four Seasons paintings. Significantly perhaps, both have attended the opening of their art exhibition, in fashionable Notting Hill, wearing anoraks.

Haughty Channel 4 Youth Commissioning Editor Stephen Garrett holds his glass like a girl and baffles Graham with a few big words at the opening of the exhibition.

Above: Harry Enfield and chums – me and Peter Cook – at the recording of the Roger Mellie animation soundtrack, 1991.

Below: A Fat Slag on the game. A billboard poster for the Tennent's lager campaign.

his picture was taken during our ill-fated university tour in 1992. Clockwise, from
Simon (bottom left), Graham (partially obscured), some bloke with a daft haircut,
Thorpy (with a beard), a clock-watching Eddie from Beer Davies, and me.

Catherine Zeta Jones not talking to *Viz* animator Tony Barnes at the Welsh BAFTAs in 1991. She was probably talking to me at the time.

John Brown gets in Davey Jones's face – and probably spits at him while he's talking – at the Porchester Hall party in 1993.

A fresh-faced senior police officer talks to John Brown while the bomb squad search the Porchester Hall for any trace of explosives or unconsumed alcohol.

Bargain-bin celebrity Lionel Blair gives an ironic interview to highbrow Radio 4 show *Loose Ends* after being classified as a £100 celebrity.

The lovely Dolores and the not-quite-so-vely me at some party or other, circa 1992.

The man behind Roger Mellie: local TV anchorman, the late Rod Griffiths, opening an exhibition of *Viz* artwork in Newcastle, November 1999.

One of the many faces of John Brown. Here he is *(left)* coming at me with a length of seaweed on the windswept beach at Bamburgh, 1989 and *(below)* walking ten yards ahead of me, as usual, in Barbados, 1994.

Below: Here's me as I appeared in *The Dandy*, August 1995. This was *Dandy* editor Morris Heggie's retaliation for 'D. C. Thompson – The Humourless Scottish Git'.

Left: Another exciting day at the office. Crestina House, circa 1996.

Below: Issue 70, February 1995, featuring 'short-arsed twat' Danny Baker.

low: In 1996 my Station House
staurant was awarded an Ian Allan
ational Railway Heritage Award, the
ghest possible honour that can be
stowed on a failing business that has
avily overinvested in the renovation
 a remote former railway property.

FREE TAKE THAT!
BICYCLE SEAT COVER INSIDE
Issue 70
Not for sale to children

Girls! It's your big chance to sit on our faces!

VIZ

£1.25
STUDENTS £1.50 ON PRODUCTION OF S.U. CARD

TITS OFF FOR THE LADS

Baywatch beauty Pam in knocker shocker!

HOLLYWOOD HIGHS!

You won't believe some of the things the stars stick up their arses

ISSN 0952-7966

COCKNEY WANKER
STUDENT GRANT ★ FAT SLAGS
ROGER MELLIE ★ SID THE SEXIST
Plus PAUL WHICKER THE TALL VICAR!

IAN ALLAN 1996 NATIONAL

THE BRITISH RAIL AWARD
ILDERTON
STATION HOUSE RESTAURANT
PRESENTED BY THE RAIL REGULATOR
JOHN SWIFT QC

RAILWAY HERITAGE AWARDS

© Northumberland Gazette

Right: Tony O'Diamond and Top Group Fantastic. They could have been huge, if only they'd got the breaks.

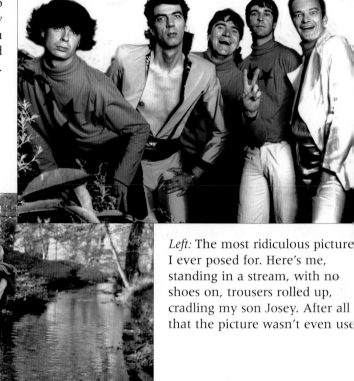

Left: The most ridiculous picture I ever posed for. Here's me, standing in a stream, with no shoes on, trousers rolled up, cradling my son Josey. After all that the picture wasn't even use

Below (*left to right*): Jonesy, Jim Brownlow, Simon, Graham and Thorpy rest on top of a hill during a hike in the Cheviot Hills, 1997. I'm not in it 'cos I took the picture.

as the ball sailed beyond the flailing arms of former Newcastle keeper Kevin Carr – who'd elected not to wear skis – and into the net. I couldn't believe it. I'd scored! I raised a triumphant single arm, turned away and began walking towards the tunnel. For some reason I had it in my mind to walk straight off the pitch, like Denis Law did after he scored for Manchester City to condemn United to relegation in the early 1970s. I knew that my inexplicably disappearing down the tunnel fifteen minutes into a nondescript charity football match wouldn't have quite the same dramatic effect, but that was my plan anyway. Alas there were no substitutes – there were no spare celebrities at all – so instead I had to dig deep, find that extra reserve of energy and somehow manage to avoid the ball for the remainder of the game.

In the showers afterwards I took the opportunity to gaze at the multitude of celebrity cocks that were dangling all around me. I'd never seen a celebrity's cock before and now all of a sudden they were everywhere. They were mainly minor celebrities' cocks, of course, and some of them a lot more minor than others. John Leslie's, for example. In fact the only cock that was worth mentioning was that belonging to Sunderland reserve footballer Martin Gray. Even on the soft it was dangling down like quarter of a bicycle tyre. He seemed quite proud of it too, walking it round the dressing room like a proud owner walking their dog around the ring at Crufts. But more impressive even than the length of Martin Gray's cock was the length of Graham Dury's hair. He always wore it in a pony tail at work, but there in the showers I saw it fully unleashed for the first time, and it was half way down his arse.

In the bar afterwards John Leslie and a local DJ called Nicky Brown were huddled in deep conversation in the corner of the room. All the other local radio jocks were casting envious eyes towards Leslie's table, and the rumour going around was that Brown and Leslie were hatching an audacious plan to take over the Radio 1 breakfast show. It seemed an unlikely pairing to me.

Brown was only a medium-sized radio fish in a small broadcasting pond, and his most noteworthy talent as far as I could tell was an ability to permanently talk as if he had his lungs full of helium. But Leslie was certainly in line for bigger things. By that time the strapping Scotsman was simply becoming too sexy for *Blue Peter* and was being linked with every big job going, from *Dr Who* to the next James Bond. He was also being linked with lots of ladies, among them Catherine Zeta-Jones. As we left the ground me and Simon stuck an improvised window sticker on the back of Leslie's flashy little Peugot car, saying 'Honk if You've Shagged Catherine Zeta-Jones.'

Early in 1993 the *Viz* print run dipped below one million, never to resurface. There were precisely 1,003,850 copies of the February issue printed ... but 290,589 of them would soon be pulp again. In the first half of the year our average sale had tumbled dramatically to 713,261. John was starting to think in terms of advertising and promotion, something he'd never had to contemplate before.

In the summer of 1993 Matthew Bannister was appointed controller of BBC Radio 1 and was setting about his infamous cull of prehistoric disc jockeys. People like Dave Lee Travis and Simon Bates (the latter a great *Viz* fan and a very good friend of my family) were facing the axe. The reactionary old farts in the *Viz* office, myself included, didn't approve of the changes that were taking place. We hated dance music and the irritating new voices of Simon Mayo and Danny Baker. We'd stopped listening to Radio 1 in our drawing studio, while the rest of the nation had stopped listening to it in their droves. Audience figures had fallen from 20 million listeners to 8 million in six months.

At around the same time Richard Branson launched Virgin Radio, a barely audible AM station dedicated entirely to the music of Bruce Springsteen. To advertise this innovative new concept Virgin placed a full-page ad in our June 1993 issue, and instead of paying they offered us some commercials on their new station.

John asked us to come up with some scripts for radio ads, and to try and make them funny just in case anyone was listening. Here are two that we came up with:

Viz ad – Virgin Radio,
December 1993 – No. 2: Gifts for Jesus

[Choral church music plays gently in background. After a few seconds a vicar speaks in warm, patronizing, religious tones.]

VICAR: Imagine if Jesus Christ had been born in this year, 1993. What sort of reception could the Son of God expect in today's greedy, commercial world? And what sort of gifts might the three wise men bring unto him?

[His voice speeds up and develops an American twang like Christopher Timothy's Sun ads.]

VICAR *continues*: Well, they could do a lot worse than buying him the latest issue of *Viz*, available NOW priced just £1.25. If Jesus came back tomorrow he'd love it!

Viz ad – Virgin Radio,
December 1993 – No. 8: Scotch the Noo

[To be spoken by a neutral, well-spoken, non-Scottish actor, in a confident and friendly manner.]

Sound of crude bagpipe music. Stops on a flat, prolonged note. Speaker is out of breath, having been playing the pipes.

SPEAKER: Ock. Hello there lads an' lassies. A'm a wee Scotch person wi' ginger hair an' a kilt. An' I appreciate a bargain when a see one. So, lads an' lassies, this year a'll be buyin' the noo *Viz* annual – *The Porky Chopper*.

[*Slight pause*] Hoots mon. At airnly £6.99, y'canna get brawer value fer money. If y'ken what a mean. [*Clears throat*] Ahem ...

[*Dreadful bagpipe music begins again, and fades out quickly.*]

These two scripts were rejected by the Independent Broadcasting Authority on the grounds of religious content and racism. Another innocuous advert included the line '*Viz* – now with added fizz', and they sent that back too, saying we couldn't claim *Viz* had 'added fizz' unless we could actually prove that the comic was fizzy. The IBA knocked back ad after ad until eventually, out of sheer frustration, I submitted the following:

Virgin Radio Ads,
December 1993 – No. 10: The Censor

[*Spoken by an upper-crust, elderly gentleman, with a military twang. Officious, but not used to public speaking, so a slightly uncomfortable delivery.*]

CENSOR: Hello all you people out there listening to the radio. I am one of the crusty old farts whose job it is to censor radio advertisements before you hear them. I regret to announce that the advertisement for *Viz* magazine which was to have been broadcast at this point has been banned on the grounds that it was offensive to miserable old cunts like myself. As a result the advertisement for *Viz*, available now priced £1.25, is not being broadcast.

They banned that one as well. Early the following year John Brown decided to try advertising on Capital Radio after his research had shown that we were losing readers in the South-East more rapidly than elsewhere. But again there were problems getting our scripts past the censors. This was the first attempt:

Capital Radio ad Viz 64, Draft 1

[Fast, dynamic jingle plays in background with blasts or crashes to highlight key lines. The male voice is punchy, professional. The woman is hesitant, unprofessional and sounds dim. She's clearly reading her lines, and with some difficulty.

MAN: Why do the Scotch *love* shortbread? Find out in the new *Viz*!

GIRL: And what makes good-looking girls like me have ... an orgasm.

MAN: See for yourself, fellas, in our sizzling sex survey starting this week! Part one – tits! Plus, is it true what they say about men with big feet?

GIRL: We look inside ... Britain's underpants ... to find out.

MAN: Does cheese *really* make you sexy? We're giving away a *million tons* of Edam – only this week in your extra-fizz *Viz*. It's Britain's biggest *organ* ...

GIRL [*slight pause as she misses cue*]: Sorry ... And I've got it ... *in my hand.*

MAN: So why not *pull it off* ... the shelf *now*! Only one pound ... twenty-five.

That ad was rejected by the IBA when we confessed that we weren't actually giving away a million tons of cheese.

While we were trying to attract radio listeners to *Viz*, Matthew

Bannister was trying to attract *Viz* readers back to Radio 1. The nation's floundering former favourite took out a full-page ad in our February 1994 issue. Part of a national press campaign, it was a cartoon drawing of a denim-clad bottom and below it a drawing pin on a seat. The slogan read: 'It's sharp. But it's not the *Danny Baker Radio Show*.' We ran a spoof of their advert in the following issue, featuring another cartoon drawn in the same style. This time there was a naked, hairy arse and below it a large turd. The slogan read: 'It's a pile of shit. But it's not the new Radio 1.' Our ad sales people in London were furious as the Radio 1 contract was a big one. We'd already lost them one major client with a similar piss-take of a student banking advertisement that Barclays had placed in the comic.

In June 1993, to coincide with John's radio promotion, we gave *Viz* a new glossy cover, but it was inside the magazine where change was needed most. There was one new character, Graham and Thorpy's old-fashioned thespian caricature Luvvie Darling. But there were too many tired old characters like Billy the Fish. In that issue an appeal fund was set up by Fulchester manager Tommy Brown to raise money to end the strip. Readers were invited to send in 10p to the fund, and if enough money was raised – £10 was the target – the strip would be discontinued. In truth Billy the Fish would have been discontinued long before then if we'd had anything better to replace it with.

In the autumn of 1993 our 1989 book project, *The Bumper Book of Shite*, finally saw the light of day. Its repeatedly delayed publication had become a running joke among book distributors. We'd eventually got round to writing the thing in 1990, during a blissful week of isolation at a remote cottage in Millom, Cumbria. These were the days before I/we had started to argue about corn, 'Baker Street', etc., and Graham, Thorpy and myself had spent a few thoroughly pleasant days strolling in the hills overlooking Duddon Sands and writing stories around a big kitchen table in front of a raging Aga stove. (Actually the stove was turned off, but it still added to the atmosphere.) The fruits of that week away had been the scripts for *The Bumper Book of Shite* which John had been optimistically scheduling for publication every year since 1989.

We finally got the book illustrated in 1993, thanks largely to our decision not to make any animations that year. John had

The cottage at Millom

wanted Student Grant to receive the next low-budget video makeover and PolyGram were still waving their chequebook at us, despite our falling-out with Channel 4. PolyGram were keen on another Fat Slags video for Christmas 1993 and an advance of £150,000 was waved under our noses. But I was getting pissed off with the depressing spiral of effort, expectation and exasperation that animation produced. We did want to do another Fat Slags video but it wasn't going to be a rush job. So in 1993 there were no videos, but there were still lots of other moneymaking opportunities to mull over.

At the height of *Viz*-mania we received all sorts of stupid offers for product licensing, and the vast majority of them we turned down flat. My favourite suggestion was for a *Viz*-flavour soft drink. The company who came up with the idea even sent a mock-up of the bottle which had a label on it saying '*Viz* soft drink'. 'What would it taste like?' we asked them. They didn't know. We were told that the idea was only at the marketing stage – they hadn't got a product yet. Most people just wanted to tap into the popularity of the comic to shift whatever shit they happened to be making at the time. *Viz* key rings, *Viz* temporary tattoos, *Viz* mobiles (the dangle from the ceiling kind), *Viz* glove puppets, *Viz* bubble gum, *Viz* pasta shapes. In financial terms these licensing deals were usually insignificant, but sometimes we'd go along with a tacky idea purely for the kudos that it would bring. Like when Meltis PLC asked us if they could do a *Viz* chocolate Easter egg exclusively for Woolworths. All our efforts to get a record in the charts may have failed, but getting an Easter egg into Woolies would be just as good, so I said yes. It appeared that Meltis PLC and Woolworths hadn't got a clue what *Viz* was, and didn't realize that our audience was slightly above Easter egg-eating age, but they went ahead with it and the *Viz* Easter Egg appeared on sale briefly in 1994. One for the collectors. That wasn't the only *Viz* chocolate spin-off. There was also a *Viz* Drifter bar featuring free Top Tips on the inside of the wrapper plus a chance to win a *Viz* T-shirt (we couldn't give our T-shirts away by that stage so we thought we'd let someone else have a try).

John and I were well aware of the potential harm chocolate might do to our readers' teeth, and that cheap spin-offs might do to our reputation. But now that our reputation was shot and sales were heading downwards we started listening to offers a lot more carefully. Or *less* carefully, I suppose. There was decent money to be made from some of them. In October 1993 Smirnoff vodka offered to run a *Viz* promotion giving away 'mini-*Viz* comics' with their booze. We thought it would be a good bit of promotion for us, and when they offered to pay £75,000 for the privilege we were absolutely delighted.

One idea I got very excited about was a *Viz* fruit machine. The moment it was suggested, I pictured Finbarr Saunders saying 'Hold my plums!' 'Nudge my melons!' and 'You've got a big pear!' (Fnarr! Fnarr!) I imagined the *Viz* fruit machine sitting in the corner of a pub making farting noises when it wasn't in use, or wolf-whistling at passers-by. The possibilities seemed limitless so we arranged a meeting with Barcrest, the company who had proposed the idea.

Barcrest's unassuming headquarters were alongside a grimy canal somewhere in the backwaters of Manchester. The gaming machine industry is traditionally associated with gangsters so when we arrived we were amused to find several ageing Jaguars occupying the prime spaces in the company car park. Inside the single-storey factory unit blokes in suits took us on a brief tour of the shop floor where rows and rows of slot machines were being assembled by blokes in overalls. Then we were shown into a small room right in the middle of the factory and suddenly found ourselves in a miniature nightclub. This tiny little hide-away was extravagantly decked out with state-of-the-art bar fittings: chrome handrails, sumptuous built-in seating, a miniature bar, mirror ball, you name it. Building their own scaled-down nightclub for testing slot machines *in situ* was obviously a tax-deductible expense in the gaming industry so not a penny had been spared in fitting it out. It seemed like a joke to us but our hosts were obviously very proud of their miniature nightclub and I think they expected us to be impressed with our luxurious if slightly cramped surroundings.

We got down to business and I started reeling off my wonderful ideas for Finbarr's 'Hold My Plums' fruit machine. I hadn't got far into my first sentence when I was cut off. 'Sorry, we don't want any new games,' one of the blokes explained. 'We just want to put the *Viz* name onto one of our existing game formats.' He explained very frankly that so many hundreds of thousands of people in the UK were already 'familiar' with this particular game format. So their policy was to keep the format the same, but occasionally change the theme to try and widen their net. By doing a *Viz* game they hoped to get a few thousand *Viz* readers who hadn't previously wasted money in slot machines to give the pastime a try, and hopefully become hooked. After that they might try a *Gardener's Question Time* game to penetrate yet another untapped slot machine market. So we had no input at all into the fruit machine that finally emerged, apart that is from the voices. Various characters spoke as the lights flashed and your money disappeared into the slot. Simon did most of them but I seem to recall it was Graham who said, 'Get orf moi laaaand.'

Finbarr Saunders

Away from *Viz* I was developing other business interests. I'd been sitting watching a band play in a pub one night when it suddenly dawned on me where every pub band I'd ever seen was going wrong. It was all a question of presentation. There they were hanging around the bar, chatting to their mates, then a moment later they were up and playing their guitars. That was no good. Bands had to distance themselves from the audience. They should wear different clothes, be aloof, have an air of mystery about them. There and then I decided my next project would be to create my own pop idols, and manipulate them to the top. Not the top of the charts, just the top of the local pub circuit. So in 1993 I had a word with Tony O'Diamond and suggested we re-form Top Group Fantastic, the act that had gone down so well at the Jewish Mother party in 1988.

Top Group Fantastic were a pretty scruffy bunch. Tony himself (aka Arthur 2 Stroke and Mr Moneybags) was tall, skinny but not bad looking. He was pushing fifty, but that didn't matter. The lad had charisma coming out of his arse. Archie Brown, on sax and guitar, had once been a real heart-throb – Tom Watkins had signed him and the rest of The Young Bucks up some sixteen years earlier – but now he was back on the pub circuit and losing his hair. The rhythm section – Ian Thomson on bass and Neil Ramshaw on drums – were a bit younger but both had seen better days. But my real problem was the keyboard player, Patrick Rafferty. Most bands get away with having one ugly bloke hidden away somewhere near the back of the stage, but with Pat I was really pushing my luck.

The first thing I did was get them some decent outfits. I dressed them all in bright pink, roll-neck sweaters with big black stars stitched on the front, and black jeans. For their first gig, at the Free Trade pub in Byker, I told them they weren't allowed into the bar until it was time for them to go on. I didn't want them mingling with the punters. Instead they would walk straight into the pub like a band walking on stage, pick up their instruments, play the set and then walk straight out again, leaving the fans gagging for more. There weren't many people in the Free Trade that night but for the lucky few it was a night to remember.

As Top Group Fantastic's reputation spread so the gigs got bigger. First the Free Trade, then the Live Theatre, then the foyer bar at the Newcastle Arts Centre. And finally, the dizzy heights of the Shieldfield Social Club. Up till now Top Group Fantastic had played largely to small groups of bewildered, non-paying pub customers. But a social club packed with fully paid-up CIU members was going to be a different proposition. It would be tough, but it would be worth it. At the end of the night we would be looking at a fee of £125.

When the band first appeared on stage in their bright pink outfits and wigs there was no laughter. Through the silence I could hear 200 Geordies think, 'Are these fuckers taking the piss?' But musically my boys were as tight as a gnat's chuff, and once they struck up some familiar tunes, albeit in a comedy style, people began to relax and enjoy it a bit. Then they started to enjoy it a lot. By the end of the night the audience had been completely won over, the dance floor was packed and girls were screaming ironically at heart-throb Tony O'Diamond. But their success was short-lived. A few weeks later, while performing a sell-out concert at the Westerhope Excelsior Working Men's Club, the band were heckled. Tony O'Diamond's reaction was, to say the least, ill-judged. 'I see we've got some cunts in tonight,' he said. A riot ensued, the band were paid off, and Top Group Fantastic never played again.

Sadly Top Group Fantastic never made it onto record, but in 1993 I did release a CD on my own House of Viz label by Archie Brown. Archie's career had been a string of near misses, first with The Young Bucks, then The Upset, then a band called The Bureau and, of course, more recently Top Group Fantastic. Clearly Archie had far more talent than me and I thought it was a bit unfair that *Viz* was making millions while he was playing in pubs for beer money. So I gave him a job as our Office Songwriter and paid for him to record a CD. I was getting a wee bit frivolous with my spending at the time. Another project was to have been fitting saloon doors to our office kitchen and installing a piano for Archie to play during our lunch breaks. Unfortunately I couldn't find anywhere that sold swinging saloon doors. But Archie did record an album for me, called *Young Bucks in Fancy Shirts*, and I sent out review copies to various magazines in the misguided hope that it might help his cause. It got a couple of decent reviews, but the one that sticks in my mind was in the *Record Mirror* where poor Archie took a terrible slagging. The writer then turned his pen on me, accusing me of having 'lost my marbles' for being daft enough to release the record. Archie very kindly bought me a bag of new marbles to make up for it.

I'd blown a couple of hundred quid managing Top Group Fanstastic and a couple of grand trying to help Archie. But that was peanuts compared to my next business venture. When I first told him about the idea my accountant, Mr Thornton, explained to me in very great detail why I should *not* convert Ilderton station house into a restaurant. He said that over 90 per cent of new restaurants fail, and an even higher percentage of new restaurants that are in the middle of nowhere fail. But I knew all that. I'd heard Sir John Hall, the man responsible for Gateshead's MetroCentre, say that the three main factors to consider when planning a business are location, location and location. In other words, it doesn't matter how fucking shit your shopping centre is, as long as you put it in the right place you'll make a killing. But that wasn't a business philosophy I wanted to follow.

The location of Ilderton station seemed okay to me: right alongside a busy-ish road, within forty-ish minutes of Newcastle, in a fairly touristy area. It might get a bit quiet in February when the place is two foot deep in snow, but that didn't matter. I was working on the assumption that trade would be fairly quiet anyway. In fact, in my original business plan, I estimated *zero* sales in the first year. Not one single customer. If someone did wander in and buy a sandwich, all well and good. But I wasn't banking on it. Customers weren't a part of my plan. My only concern was the building, preserving the railway atmosphere and getting the fixtures and fittings just right. I employed a firm of top architects, restoration specialists Spence & Dower, who drew up the plans and put the building contract out to tender. The building work alone was going to cost me £170,000, but love is blind and I ploughed ahead with it. Before the building work got underway I'd drive past the empty station house on my way to work and I'd talk to it. 'Don't worry, everything's going to be all right,' I'd whisper reassuringly. And who said I was losing my marbles?

Splashing out hundreds of thousands on a restaurant might seem pretty flash, but at the time I didn't think I was spending *enough* money. Despite being a millionaire I didn't really do anything millionaire-ish. I just sat at home and watched telly. I began to think I was missing out on something, and it was time that Dolores and I started living the high life.

To begin with we went shopping at Harrods and bought a bit of ridiculously expensive bedroom furniture for the kids. A red bus bunk bed that cost £2,000, for example. I knew we were on the right lines because a few months later I read an interview with footballer John Barnes and discovered that he had bought one too. Then we decided to book a lavish holiday. I'd often read big-nosed *Deathwish* moneybags movie mogul Michael Winner harping on in his newspaper column about the Sandy Lane Hotel in Barbados. Apparently this was one of *the* poshest hotels in the world, frequented by all the biggest names in showbiz, like Cilla Black. What the fuck, I thought. Let's give it a try. It's got to be better than St Agnes in Cornwall, in the winter, which was where Dolores and I spent our last holiday together. So in the autumn of 1993 we took our two young children on what was to be the holiday of a lifetime.

I may have been a millionaire, technically speaking, but in reality I couldn't hack it. Sandy Lane was so posh it was intimidating. I was scared to touch anything, scared to talk too loud, scared to pick up the wrong cutlery or order the wrong wine. You couldn't relax because there were so many staff running around after you, opening doors for you, pulling out chairs for you, and all of them dressed in silly uniforms with shiny buttons. Walking into the restaurant at night was like walking onto a Paris catwalk. All the other guests were dressed immaculately in their elegantly sophisticated designer evening wear, and there was me – holidaymaker at C&A – red-faced and sweaty, trying to get our children aged four and two to choose something from the incomprehensible menu. The waiters were like dogs. They sensed my fear and singled me out for special attention. That was part of their job – identifying the nouveau riche, new money scum like me – and making them feel uncomfortable. After a couple of nights I was so hacked off by it all I decided we'd eat in our room for the rest of the holiday. The next morning I was looking forward to a peaceful breakfast in the sanctity of our suite when there was a sharp knock at the door. Dolores opened it and in marched a seemingly endless procession of uniformed waiters pushing trolleys of food and carrying trays of crockery. Once inside they began moving furniture, unfolding table linen and laying out silver place settings on our coffee table. Then they began to serve our breakfast, pouring the tea and ceremonially lifting the silver domes off the salvers to reveal our bacon and scrambled eggs. I bolted into the bathroom and locked the fucking door.

There was nobody at the hotel we could talk to. No families or scruffy couples like ourselves. Michael Winner and Cilla Black never showed up. There were just lots of Italian-looking, middle-aged couples in stylish clothing who sat quietly at their tables, their tasteful jewellery sparkling *just* enough to impress, without being vulgar.

One evening, to escape from the hotel, Dolores and I went on a romantic sunset cruise. It was about as romantic as a gondola ride over the Niagara Falls. Just as our small yacht left Bridgetown harbour the sky went grey and a tropical storm engulfed us. The captain said the only course of action was to sail out into the storm to avoid being washed up or smashed against the harbour walls. Riding out the storm was like being on the Waltzer beneath a waterfall, without a safety belt. It was absolutely terrifying. There was some sort of semi-celebrity rally driver on the boat with us who had been racing in Barbados that week, and I distinctly remember wondering which of us would get the bigger obituary in the English newspapers the following day.

But our holiday teething troubles faded to nothing when we got a fax from England telling us that Soo Sidall, Dolores's best friend, our matchmaker and the chief bridesmaid at our wedding, had died. Soo had always been a party animal, God bless her, but recently she'd got herself into serious trouble. She'd been undergoing treatment for addictions, getting help and support, and everyone thought she was through it. But we were wrong, and Soo had died of an accidental heroin overdose.

I did a lot of thinking in what remained of our dream holiday. Sitting mournfully in the hotel bar one evening I had a rare flash of lucidity, quite possibly my first of the decade. 'What the fuck am I opening a restaurant for?' I asked Dolores. But it had come too late. The contracts had already been signed.

CHAPTER EIGHTEEN
A Tale of Two Parties

'The worst party you'll ever have' was how the invitation described a soirée Peter Cook had arranged to celebrate the launch of a Derek and Clive video in the summer of 1993. I was privileged to be among the guests, and in the event Peter's party turned out to be one of the *best* parties I'd ever had. But the worst was just around the corner.

In keeping with my attempts to lead a millionaire lifestyle I decided to check in to the fashionable Portobello Hotel on the night of Peter's party. This is where it was alleged Michael Hutchence had ordered a bath full of champagne to perk up a romantic weekend with Kylie Minogue. I asked at reception if we could have the Kylie bubbly bath suite. They put us in the attic. If this pokey little room was where it all happened then I hope the poor bugger who carried the crates of champagne up the stairs got a decent tip.

The official video launch party was at the Cobden Working Men's Club in Kensal Road, after which it would be back to Peter Cook's house. The club's function room was noisy and boisterous and heaving with party people. It was awful. I caught a glimpse of Peter Cook being pursued around the room by a flotilla of press and friends, and Dolores spotted Julian Clary leaning on a wall in the corner. Still mindful of not having spoken to her other hero Mick Hucknall all those years ago, off she went in Clary's direction. I passed *Private Eye* editor Ian Hislop in a doorway. As I stopped to say a cautious hello a waiter squeezed between us carrying a crate of champagne. I met Hislop again a few years later and said, 'Last time we spoke it was over a crate of champagne.' I thought that was rather clever, but because he hadn't noticed the champagne, or me talking to him, it fell rather flat. Heads turned when Rolling Stones Ronnie Wood and Keith Richards arrived. 'Hide the booze!' cried Wood as he tottered into the room looking a lot like a *Spitting Image* puppet of himself, waving a bottle of Jack Daniel's in his hand. Dolores dragged me away from the wall to introduce me to her new acquaintance Julian Clary, who, to his credit, had been chatting away to her for a good five minutes without once mentioning fisting or any other form of anal sex. I was getting bored and almost on the verge of going back to our hotel when at last I spotted a familiar face, that of Ian Dury out of Ian Dury and The Blockheads. I knew Ian through Blockhead keyboardist Mickey Gallagher, who happened to be Arthur 2 Stroke's brother-in-law. Ian was a bit fed up with the party too and he suggested we go to the bar downstairs where we could get a quiet drink, or whatever the up-to-the-minute Cockney rhyming slang for a quiet drink would have been in the summer of 1993.

The bar of the Cobden Working Men's Club was like the bar in any social club in Britain, except that everywhere you looked there were famous people. It was a bizarre mix of London taxi drivers relaxing at the end of their shifts and partied-out celebrities trying to escape the mayhem upstairs. When Michael Palin appeared in front of me I felt compelled to say something. I'd never met him before but he was my favourite Python and he'd written us a very kind and totally unsolicited letter a few years earlier: 'Your organ has given me greater pleasure these last few years than my own,' he'd said, among other things. That letter was pinned proudly to our office notice board for years, until I stole it and took it home. And now, here was my big chance to thank its author. I stepped forward and introduced myself rather nervously. Michael Palin looked at me, startled, as if I was going to shoot him. Then he dropped his head and mumbled something like, 'Yes ... hello,' before darting away, very quickly indeed. A little disappointing, perhaps, but at least he hadn't told me to fuck off.

The room was an autograph hunter's paradise, but there was no way you could go around asking for autographs. And besides, I didn't collect autographs. So instead I let my train-spotting instincts kick in. Unfortunately celebrities don't have a recognized system of sequential numbering, so instead of numbers I started scribbling down their names as they passed by. Ian Dury introduced me to Ronnie Wood, who'd finished his Jack Daniel's and was now trying a pint of Guinness. 'Is this the man who does *Viz*?' Wood said to Ian, referring to me in the third person. The wizened, slightly jaundiced-looking rocker shook my arm joyously and launched into an enthusiastic rant about how much he enjoyed the comic, quoting sections from a recent story I'd written about Elton John's handyman. As he rambled on at me I stood there thinking how ridiculous this situation was. There was me out for a quiet drink and I was being pestered by bloody rock stars.

Later we hitched a lift in the Blockheadmobile to Peter Cook's house in Hampstead. By now the celebrities had been breeding and they were everywhere. After a while I realized that I'd lost Dolores so I began a methodical search of the house, adding new celebrities to my list as I went. Sam Torrance in the kitchen. David Gower in the hallway. Robert Powell in the airing cupboard. They were everywhere. There was no sign of Dolores downstairs, so I continued upwards until I came to the top of the house. Still no sign. Then as I glanced up the attic stairs I saw two pairs of legs, one of which I recognized. I rounded the corner and there she was sitting on Keith Richards's knee, sharing a joint with him. 'You don't wanna come up here. This is where the bad boys hang out,' said Richards in his unmistakable Keith Richards voice. He offered me the joint, but held on to Dolores for the time being. It was practically burnt out, so I thanked him and popped it into a nearby wine glass.

When we left at about 4.30 a.m. the party was still in full swing. Peter Cook waved us bye-bye and Keith Richards, who was by now my best mate, gave me a smile and a wink. It had been a weird and wonderful night. But the next day when I woke up in our pokey attic hotel room I was kicking myself. I should have kept that joint he gave me and had it framed.

Peter's party was a success by any standards, but there is only one standard by which PR party events are normally judged, and that is the number of famous people who show up. An 'A' list celebrity will get invited to every party in town but if they accept too many invitations then by the end of the week they're on the 'C' list for having overexposed themselves. It's a tricky business. Meanwhile 'C' list celebrities will go to as many parties as possible in a misguided attempt to raise their profile. At the bottom of the celebrity food chain are the 'D' list celebrities who gate-crash parties just to get at the buffet and the free booze.

On our rare business trips to London John Brown would usually put us all up at the Groucho Club, and at night all four of us would sit in the bar spotting celebrities. 'Stephen Fry at 3 o'clock,' Thorpy would whisper loudly and all our necks would turn. 'Michael Elphick at 12 o'clock,' and so it would go on. John Brown would be mortified by our plebeian behaviour, spluttering into his Kir Royale with embarrassment while we all arched our necks to get a good look at Joanna Lumley. In John's circles you didn't *look* at the famous people. That would be acknowledging that they were somehow more important than you.

It seemed to me the whole business of celebrity was a snobbish game, so when it came to launching that year's books – *The Porky Chopper* annual and *The Bumper Book of Shite* – I had a terrific idea. We'd hold a launch party and cut through all the bullshit by simply paying celebrities to turn up. John and Eugen made all the arrangements, booking the Porchester Hall in Bayswater for our grand event. Then we placed the ad *(on page 272)* in *Variety, The Stage, Television Today* and *Music Week.*

I'd tried to make it as much like an advert for a cheap carpet warehouse as I could, but this was potentially a very expensive joke. You'll notice that only the *first* Royal gets £5,000. That was in case the Queen turned up with her husband and her sister Margaret and tried to claim £15,000. We didn't know what to expect, but John set a budget of £20,000. That was how much money he was prepared to hand out on the night.

The invitations had some rules of celebrity snob etiquette printed on the back for the benefit of guests who might not be used to mixing in such circles:

DO NOT
- STARE at celebrities
- POINT at famous people
- ASK for autographs
- GAZE conspicuously

DO
- LOOK unimpressed when celebrities enter the room
- IGNORE celebrities as if they were normal people
- PRETEND not to recognize them
- CLAIM not to have heard of them if they are pointed out to you

As a PR stunt it was an instant success. Reporters spotted the adverts and there was a flood of press stories trailing the event. Demand for tickets soared, but not from celebrities. It was *Viz* fans who wanted to go. All my staff were invited, plus their partners, friends and relatives. I even put on a coach from North Northumberland so that friends and neighbours could come

down for a big night out in London. All John's staff would be coming too, as well as scores of *Viz* wholesalers, retailers, advertisers and goodness knows who else. As the big day approached I wondered whether there'd be room left over for any celebrities.

In the foyer of the Porchester Hall a tacky booth was set up with a sign saying 'Celebrities! Sign on here for cash!' Behind the counter stood Eugen and a security man with a sizeable float of £50 notes. Hidden in a nearby safe was the rest of John's £20,000. My job was to greet the celebrities as they arrived, decide how much each one was worth, and hand them their money and a badge. As 8.00 p.m. approached a gaggle of press began to surround the booth ready to record the first potentially humiliating celebrity valuation. The delightful Emma Freud from Radio 4's *Loose Ends* was there, the less attractive Rod McKenzie from *Radio 1 Newsbeat,* and a host of press reporters including Piers Morgan of the *Sun.* Outside large crowds of people were waiting for the doors to open. I couldn't see any celebrities among them.

Unfortunately hundreds of people had turned up without invitations so when the doors opened the bouncers were in their element, rudely pushing people back into the crowd or pulling them out if they were waving an invitation. Through all this mayhem the first of our celebrity guests eventually began to stagger: the late Gertrude 'comedy hats' Shilling, who was alive at the time, but only just; Mike Fabgear, a self-publicist in a wig; Neil Murray, an old bloke who reckoned he used to play bass guitar in Black Sabbath; someone out of The Christians, but not the bald one; Screaming Lord Sutch, together with his own official photographer; Viv Stanshall, out of The Bonzos; the bald bloke who used to be on Vic and Bob's TV show. At the cash desk business was brisk. Most of these marginal celebrities were handed fifty quid together with a badge saying 'I'm a £50 celebrity'. Harry Enfield strolled in wearing shades and collected £100 before strolling straight out again. And Emma Freud got

£100 too, because I liked her. It was great fun giving out someone else's money, but John was going through hell as he watched the cash being snatched away, fifty quid at a time. Strangely, I think John would have been much happier giving Sarah Ferguson £5000 than giving Nathan out of Brother Beyond fifty quid, which I did. When I gave a one-time extra from the TV show *It Ain't Half Hot Mum* a £50 note John snapped. He couldn't take any more. 'You'll have to stop being so generous or soon we'll have no money left,' he said. 'Oh come on, John,' said Eugen. 'Enjoy yourself. There's still fifteen grand in the safe.'

The calibre of celebrities had thus far been disappointing; so much so that when Lionel Blair arrived he caused something of a stir. Lionel put on a dazzling display of camp for the cameras, trousered his £100 and then headed for the free booze and buffet. But before he'd had a chance to grab his first free glass of champagne police officers swarmed in and started to clear the hall. At first I thought it was a stunt, but these coppers were too young to be actors. They were the real thing. John Brown scooped up his money and we made our way out onto the street where hundreds of people were now milling around in the cold. A senior policeman, in his early twenties, told John they'd received a bomb threat and it might be some time until we could go back inside. Some folk waited patiently in the nearby streets while others went off in search of food and shelter. Journalist Auberon Waugh led an expedition to a nearby Pizza Express restaurant. Actor Keith Allen led another party to a pub. I stayed in the street exchanging bomb scare stories with Lord Sutch and Jools Holland, who was our turn for the night. We'd recently been evacuated from our Newcastle office block when an eagle-eyed employee of our upstairs neighbours, the Prudential Insurance Company, spotted a suspect device in the stairwell. After an hour and a half standing in the street the Army arrived and sent in a robot. The suspect box turned out to be full of strawberries.

The dreaded summer fruits terrorist had not struck this time. The only thing the police found in their search of the hall appeared to be our supply of alcohol, which mysteriously vanished during their brief tenancy. Faced with the problem of vetting crowds of guests as they returned, the bouncers simply gave up and let anyone in on a first come, first served basis. When the hall was full the doors were slammed shut, leaving scores of invited guests outside on the pavement, many of whom had left their coats and other belongings inside the hall. Some of my friends, who'd travelled 350 miles on a coach to be there, were locked outside despite having invites in their hands. The bouncers weren't budging. The scene was ugly, contorted faces were pushed up against the glazed door panels and fists were banging on the doors. It was like a scene from a 1973 Donny Osmond concert. At the height of this drama the bloke out of The Christians, not the bald one, came running up behind me. 'Is there anything I can do to help?' he said. Whether he was proposing to sing to the crowd, or whether he just thought they would listen to him because he was in The Christians, I don't know. But his kind offer was turned down.

I'd had nothing to drink all night, nothing to eat and I'd missed the band. When we got back to our hotel, the Columbia, all I wanted was a quiet drink before bed. I couldn't even have that. I'd block booked all of my guests into the hotel, and one of them, my office manager Susan's husband – a bricklayer called Michael – had just strangled the barman moments before we arrived. There'd been some sort of dispute over change, the outcome of which was that the barman had a large purple mark on his neck and was now cowering behind his shuttered bar and refusing to come out. In a calm voice I offered him twenty quid to reopen the bar. He refused. 'Fifty,' I said. Still no joy. 'One hundred.' 'Two hundred.' That was how much I wanted a quiet drink before bed. But the poor man was petrified and he wasn't going to budge. At that point another of my guests, a highly respected Newcastle art gallery owner by the name of Rashida, bowked up all over the floor behind me. This was definitely the worst party I'd ever had, and at that point I decided to go to bed.

By the end of 1993 offers of media work were coming thick and fast. Well, I had two anyway. One was to review the Sunday papers on television in Birmingham at 5.30 every Sunday morning. I turned that one down as it would have meant missing *Match of the Day* the night before. The other was to write a weekly column for the *Sun*. I didn't turn that one down. Not exactly.

In the autumn a *Sun* reporter by the name of Clare Morrisroe had met me on the pretence of talking about *The Bumper Book of Shite*. She was a dark-haired, slim, smartly dressed and rather attractive girl, and she wore spectacles – a bit like a smouldering secretary in a porn movie. The sort of secretary who takes off her spectacles, shakes down her hair and then gives her boss an unconvincing blowjob under his desk. Unfortunately Clare kept her specs on and her hair up during our interview, during which she asked if I'd be interested in doing a column for the *Sun*. Whether it was the thought of her removing her glasses at some point in the future, or whether I was just being a mercenary fuckwit, I really don't know. But I said 'yes'.

As well as a column the *Sun* also wanted a '*Viz*-style' cartoon, so Thorpy and I unashamedly rattled off a terrible thing called 'PC 69 – The Bobby with the Big Helmet' (featuring Inspector Knickers). I did a couple of dry runs so that Kelvin McKenzie & Co. could test my topicality, my wit and my ability to express entertaining right-wing opinions under pressure. Sometimes Clare, my handler, would ring and ask me to make changes, and give me only fifteen minutes to do it. Or she'd pay me the ultimate *Sun* compliment, 'Garry loved that one.' Looking back, it was ridiculous. I'd started out parodying the *Sun*, and now here I was going through hoops for Garry Bushell. Was I the one who'd changed, or was the *Sun* now becoming a parody of itself? Why was I doing this? Eventually Clare got back to me with a starting date. 'By the way, we haven't talked about money,' she said. I hadn't given much thought to the money, I'd just assumed there'd be rather a lot involved. It was, after all, my soul I was selling. 'The figure we've budgeted for is £150 a week,' she said. 'I want £2,000,' I said. 'I'll ask, but I know what Kelvin's answer will be.' Kelvin McKenzie's answer, which was relayed to me by Clare shortly afterwards, was 'fuck off'. At that point I decided I didn't want to work for the *Sun* anyway, on political grounds.

CHAPTER NINETEEN

A Minor Problem with
Our Reservations

Comic sales had held up remarkably well in 1993. In fact we were heading for a slight increase in our average sales, up to 733,707 for the second half of the year. Things were looking up, and to celebrate John Brown booked the stately Ettington Park Hotel in Warwickshire for a lavish corporate Christmas bash.

John was very much aware of the North–South divide that existed between my staff and his, and he thought the problem could be overcome by arranging team-building breaks, or 'bonding sessions' as he called them. When they came together the two groups were polite to each other but there was always an undercurrent of mutual disrespect. In a nutshell my staff thought that John's staff got paid for doing nothing, and John's staff probably saw us as a bunch of precious, mollycoddled tossers.

The bonding sessions didn't work. Every year John's staff would end up sitting in one side of the hotel bar and we'd be sitting in the other. John's highly motivated ad sales gang tended to be the life and soul of these events, and when they got drunk they became truly obnoxious. In the early hours of the morning at the Ettington Park one of them waved a bottle of premium lager under my nose and said, 'We don't need you, but you need us!' He was having an argument about the relative merits of advertising and editorial content in our magazine, and what he was saying was that the adverts were more important than the cartoons or any of the other stuff we did. He actually believed it.

The drinking at these parties would go on until dawn, and that sharp sorted the men from the boys. The inebriated, feather-puffing ad sales gang would gradually run out of steam and stagger off to bed, often in hopeful pursuit of a female colleague, leaving the more melancholic drinkers in the bar. Last ones to bed at Ettington Hall were myself, Dolores and freelance cartoonist Davey Jones. They say that drink loosens the tongue, but not in Davey's case. He'd just sit there and drink quite happily. The first visible sign that he was under the influence would be when he got up to go to bed, and fell over.

Paying for all of his staff and all of my staff to stay in a posh hotel for the weekend was just the tip of John Brown's hospitality iceberg. In April 1994 he invited me to Barbados to watch a test match. The idea of sitting on my arse all day talking business with John while someone played cricket in the background didn't particularly appeal, but when he mentioned we'd be flying First Class and he would pay for everything I suddenly came round to the idea.

After eight hours of consuming free food and drink under the nose of a ridiculously overattentive air hostess I was glad to get off the plane and into the back of an uncomfortable taxi for the bumpy ride to our hotel. John had booked the trip at the last minute and had only just managed to find us rooms because the small island was brimfull of cricket fans on top of the normal complement of holidaymakers. By the time we arrived at the Glitter Bay Hotel on the west coast of the island it was evening. It was dark anyway. I was knackered and jet lagged, and the heat was getting to me. I just wanted to sleep. Unfortunately there seemed to be a minor problem with our reservations. We didn't have any.

'Don't be ridiculous! Of course we have!' said John loudly. John had a domineering style when it came to dealing with receptionists, waiters and the like – presumably something he'd been taught at public school. I tended to go for the more timid, apologetic approach. The receptionist was joined by another member of staff, but after flicking through the paperwork for a second time their answer was the same. 'Sorry, we don't have any rooms for you.' John's voice went up a couple of decibels and he demanded to see the Duty Manager. It was only then, as I stood and watched him barking at them, that I realized how much he looked and sounded like Ian Faith, manager of the well-known pop group Spinal Tap.

By now John's tactic was to deliberately cause a scene, and heads were turning all around the lobby. The Duty Manager had been a disappointment, and now John demanded to see the General Manager. I tried to distance myself from his shocking behaviour by smiling at people as they walked past, and shrugging my shoulders. In the restaurants and hotels of West London John's imperious approach may well get him results, but in laid-back Barbados it seemed to be going against the grain. While one senior member of staff tried to pacify him, all the others were giving John dirty looks. We hadn't even got our room keys yet and already the waiters were planning to wank in our soup.

Eventually John started getting some satisfaction. The mystery of our missing rooms was solved. They'd given them to somebody else. By sheer coincidence another man by the name of J. Brown had walked into the hotel earlier that evening and asked for two single rooms. The receptionist had assumed this was John, and given him ours. 'Don't worry,' I said to John. 'I know another J. Brown – James Brown. It's probably him. I'm sure he'll let us kip on his floor.' It was a pretty feeble joke, and neither John nor the receptionist laughed. The Duty Manager, or General Manager, or President of the company – whatever level of management John had got up to – invited us to relax in the bar while he arranged two new rooms for us. So we wandered into the bar and there, sitting on a stool right in front of us, was James Brown. 'It *is* you, you bastard!' I said.

James Brown was far from the typical tourist, dressed in a Jack Lord shirt, Ronnie Barker glasses and Leo Sayer haircut. Alongside him was Derek Ridgers, a weird photographer dressed all in black, with a beard and ponytail. James told us they were on the island to interview England cricketer Phil Sutcliffe for *Loaded* magazine.

Loaded was a high-profile magazine for men which James had launched the previous year, claiming *Viz* was one of his main inspirations. But I didn't think the magazines had much in common. In fact my initial impression of *Loaded* was that it was a magazine written by drunks and bought by wankers. After James had left I asked John if he knew how sales of *Loaded* were going. He said they'd been very high for the launch issue, but he didn't think they'd be able to sustain it. He was wrong, of course. *Loaded* would prove to be the publishing phenomenon of the nineties.

James was living the *Loaded* lifestyle. He came back from one shopping trip to Bridgetown and slammed a brown paper bag down on our table by the pool. Big enough to hold a football, the bag was stuffed full of skunk. 'What's all that for?' I asked him. 'It was the smallest deal he'd do,' said James. 'Twenty dollars. Not bad, eh?' John asked him to move it off the table. 'Do you want some, John?' said James, offering it like a bag of popcorn. John declined but I helped myself to a small handful and crammed it into my sunglasses case.

John was an insufferable holiday companion. Every day was strictly timetabled in order to cram as much into the week as possible. When we weren't watching cricket we went sightseeing or shopping, rushing from one place to the next at a hectic pace. Whenever we walked anywhere John would be ten paces in front of me, occasionally turning his head and shouting, 'Come on, hurry up!' We arrived at the island's heliport for a sight-seeing helicopter ride half an hour early. 'Where's the helicopter?' John demanded to know. 'It's in the air at the moment,' the lady explained. 'Can you ask the pilot to come down now because we're in a bit of hurry?' John said, seriously suggesting that someone else's sight-seeing tour should be abruptly halted so that we could get on with ours. John wasn't always pushy and unpleasant. He could be good fun too. One night the two of us dressed up and went for dinner at the posh Royal Pavilion Hotel next door. It had a particularly grand terrace restaurant overlooking the beach and there was a sophisticated jazz ensemble playing live music, giving the joint a terribly exclusive atmosphere. There was no sign of Michael Winner or Cilla Black, but newsreader Peter Sissons was sitting at a nearby table, which was pretty impressive. (It was certainly better than George Layton out of *It Ain't Half Hot Mum*, who was the only celebrity staying at our hotel.) After we'd paid for our meal John dared me to leave via the palm-filled flowerbed at the edge of the terrace, and jump down onto the beach some considerable distance below. Much to the bemusement of Mr and Mrs Sissons and the other diners, we both got up, casually strolled across the floor past the bemused band, waded through the palms, paused for a second and then jumped off the edge of the terrace, disappearing into the darkness below.

Watching the cricket wasn't too painful, due mostly to the amount of rum we drank in the process. On the last day of the test England bowled out the West Indies to win, and between us John and I drank most of a large bottle of rum. Anticipating this famous victory John had booked a table at the island's most exclusive restaurant, La Cage aux Folles. (No matter where you are in the world, John will always know where the most exclusive restaurant is.) He invited James Brown and Derek Ridgers to come along with us, but he soon wished he hadn't.

When we called at James's room the air was thick with cannabis smoke. James was sitting at a typewriter, working, drinking and smoking all at the same time. In his hand was a huge comedy spliff, and on his face was an equally big grin. 'I've decided to use it all up before we go,' he said by way of explanation. His paper bag full of weed was lying on the coffee table, half empty. He handed the joint to John, who accepted it with a nervous smile and took a tiny, token drag before quickly passing it to me. I took a bigger and slightly more convincing token drag before handing it on to Derek. 'I think we ought to be going soon,' said John. 'The taxi will be waiting.' James carefully extinguished the large, carrot-shaped joint and slipped it like a pen into the breast pocket of his shirt. 'I'll have that later,' he said rather ominously.

The restaurant was up on a hill somewhere in the middle of the island and looked like an old plantation house. Inside, the dining room was humming with the sound of ceiling fans and refined conversation, punctuated by the clinking of wine bottles on glass rims. Voices were kept low, and there were no bursts of laughter like you'd hear in a normal restaurant or pub. Wafting in through the louvred windows was the rhythmic creaking of tree frogs. Normally John would be at home in a place like that, but this time it was different. Throughout the meal he couldn't take his eyes off the cannabis joint that was protruding slightly from James's breast pocket. Every now and then James would reach for the joint, take it out of his pocket and toy with it, slowly putting it to his lips before returning it to his pocket. John was on tenterhooks watching this, and James knew it. Eventually James got as far as putting the joint in his mouth and tantalizingly raising a cigarette lighter towards it. 'No!' snapped John. 'Not here!' James just smiled and put it away again.

James was totally immune to embarrassment himself. While we waited for our food to arrive he decided to take a stroll around the room. He walked from table to table, stopping occasionally and rudely leaning over people's shoulders to see what they were eating. Nobody said or did a thing to stop him. They just kept their heads down till he'd gone, then gave him a cautious sideways glance after he'd moved on to the next table. When James finished his surreal walkabout he just sat down again as if nothing had happened. I couldn't decide whether I admired his nerve or thought he was being a complete twat.

Meanwhile back in England PolyGram had commissioned a new Fat Slags video for 1994. Thorpy, Graham and myself were determined to make a better job of it than the first one. This time we wanted to write a proper script as opposed to a jerky series of sketches. Our new office was an uninspiring place to work. We had a dedicated writing room equipped with state-of-the-art table and chairs, and plenty of pens and paper. But it was a stuffy, small and unpleasant place to sit in for any length of time and it looked out onto a cramped, shady quadrangle of tall, grey, prefabricated concrete façades. Our office was a shithole, so when it came to writing our video script we took off to a hotel in Northumberland for a few days in the hope that more pleasant surroundings would help. We booked a small conference room at the Linden Hall Hotel – 'the library', they called it. It wasn't much bigger than our own writing room, but it was better decorated and had a much nicer view. It was apt that we should be writing a Fat Slags script at Linden Hall. This massive country house was originally the home of the Bigg family, from whom Newcastle's bawdy Bigg Market takes its name.

Thorpy had heard about the method John Cleese and Connie Booth used to write *Fawlty Towers*, so we began with a large flow chart on which the various plot strands could be drawn out, eventually developing into an intricate, overlapping series of storylines. We also developed the characters a bit so that once the plot was contrived we were able to drop them into the situations, at which point the dialogue would more or less write itself. We called our Fat Slags 'film' *Blue Honeymoon*. Once again Miles Ross was in charge of production but this time John Brown discreetly distanced himself from the project by allowing Miles to credit his own company, Peckham Films, as producers. We gave Miles a wish-list of voiceover artists and he went out and got the lot. Kathy Burke was recalled from the first Slags video as Sandra, and Jenny Eclair was recruited to be the voice of Tracey. *The Fast Show*'s John Thompson and Simon Day were booked to record all of the male voices between them, and

Caroline Aherne agreed to be Thelma, the Slags' prudish love-rival.

Our script was jam-packed with plot and sub-plot – it had shitloads of narrative – but it was nevertheless largely a pastiche of pastiches. Rather than creating new characters of our own we borrowed existing ones, such as Thelma from *Whatever Happened To The Likely Lads*. I suppose it was our attempt at a British sex farce, a sort of *Confessions* film meets *Postman Pat*. We also sampled *Psycho* and *The Graduate*, and included a parody of blue comic Roy 'Chubby' Brown. Trying to exaggerate Chubby Brown for comic effect is a dangerous business. The character we came up with was Chubby Arse, who was, out of necessity, somewhat crude. *Blue Honeymoon* turned out to be our last video animation. It wasn't perfect by any means, but it was far, far better than the first Slags video. And for my money John Thompson's brief performance as Chubby Arse was the closest we ever got to reproducing *Viz* on videotape.

Encouraged by positive sales figures for the second half of 1993 – up 2.9 per cent on the previous year – John got well and truly carried away. If a tiny bit of radio promotion could increase our sales by 2.9 per cent, just think what a *lot* of promotion would achieve. And so he did the unthinkable. Without consulting me John put word out to advertising agencies that a *Viz* account worth £250,000 was up for grabs. I only found out when a couple of Newcastle agencies contacted me and started touting for the business. John tried to placate me. He said nothing was decided, but he was arranging a day of presentations at his office where various creative teams would come along and put across their clever ideas for promoting *Viz*. He said I was welcome to sit in on these presentations, and even suggested that it might do me some good. 'It might inspire you,' he said. I felt betrayed. John had either lost confidence in me, or in *Viz*, and now he was looking to market it like soap powder.

Meanwhile in our Newcastle laboratory we were still trying to come up with a new improved formula. At the start of 1994 the

Pop Page was dropped, thus severing the magazine's last lingering connection with its fanzine roots. In the same issue two new characters appeared. The first of them, Tarzan in my Pubes, was immediately stamped on by eagle-eyed lawyers representing the estate of the late Edgar Rice Burroughs. But the second new boy, Cockney Wanker, became a huge success. Like the Fat Slags, Wanker was the result of a brain-storming session by all four of us, a new character built to order rather than inspired. And, like the Slags, Wanker could be summed up by his name alone.

The plan was to turn the usual 'luvverly jubberly' Cockney stereotype on its head, exposing some of the less attractive

Cockney Wanker

qualities of certain East End folk. So Wanker became a right-wing, racist taxi driver who drank at the Blind Bigot pub and slapped his wife about when he got home. I didn't want him to become a latter-day Alf Garnett. I definitely didn't want Cockneys liking it and saying, 'Oh yeah, that's me, that is!' And

I knew we were onto a winner when the *East London Advertiser* kicked up a stink about the first strip, accusing us of unfair stereotyping of Blitz-resistant East End folk. A new character, controversy – you'd think our readers would be delighted. But no ...

> Was issue 64 (February 1994) some sort of warped marketing experiment? I refer not to the pink and yellow 'Mr Blobby' cover, but to the crud behind it. Whilst the decline of *Viz* had been well documented and is widely accepted, issue 64 set an unprecedented low point. Was the idea to measure the effect of a particularly poor issue on subsequent sales? I for one will not be reading *Viz* again.
>
> Peter Phelan
> Dublin

Criticism from cynics like that was starting to get through to me and I published this frank reply underneath his letter, under the heading 'Fuck off, bastard':

> Hey, if we could think of a better way of making a living we would. Meanwhile it's thanks to miserable cunts like you that we have to keep putting the price of *Viz* up.

Up till this point I'd always used self-deprecation to deflect criticism. I'd even adopted the common criticism 'It's not as funny as it used to be' as our sales slogan. In truth Viz could still be just as funny – and unfunny – as it always had been. The problem was that people expected it to have the same impact it had when they first read it. And even if we were getting it wrong now, and it wasn't funny any more, when they changed the recipe for Quavers I simply stopped buying them – I didn't write smart-arse letters to the manufacturers telling them they'd 'lost it' and calling the new Quavers 'shit'.

Late in 1994 I finally allowed computers into the Viz studio. A couple of times I'd allowed people to come in and demonstrate AppleMacs to us, stressing that if they wanted to make a sale they would have to keep it simple. But they never did. It was like being in a physics lesson back at school, everything making sense for the first two minutes then suddenly I was lost and didn't understand a word that was being said. Eventually I realized that the only way to get our studio computerized was to employ a computer-literate person who could take over the design side of the magazine.

I interviewed a few candidates and was particularly impressed by a girl called Sheila who spent the entire interview telling me how she'd injured her hand – it was heavily bandaged – rescuing a cat from a derelict house. Her surname was Gill, the name of my favourite typeface, so despite the fact that she talked far too much I gave her the job.

I gave Sheila carte blanche to go out and buy as many computers as she wanted. I think she bought four to start with. Then there were scanners, printers and other grey things all joined together with wires. Sheila's high-tech work station in the middle of the studio grew like a futuristic city out of a jungle of primitive drawing boards, rickety shelves and battered wooden tables covered in litter. Every now and then she'd come and ask for permission to buy something else. 'I need some more memory,' she'd say. 'Fine,' I'd say. 'How much is that?' 'About £300.' So Sheila would make a phone call and in would come a man with a briefcase, presumably containing this 'memory' that she needed, which he then put into the computer. It couldn't have been a messy operation because he always wore a smart suit, never overalls. Sheila got me a computer, too, and put another computer in the writing room for general use. She showed me how to use a word-processing program and store things in folders and I was surprised how easily I got the hang of it. Within a few weeks we were entirely dependent on computers.

In September 1994 a new cartoon character made a controversial début on the front cover. Sweary Mary wasn't so much a cartoon character, more a device for taunting WHSmith's, and on the front of issue 67 she swore twenty-nine times. Intrinsic to the storyline, each swear word had been obliterated using a blue Biro pen, supposedly by a prudish shop assistant in WH Smith's. But when the comic returned from the printers every single swear word, and a couple of other words besides, had been blocked out in solid black ink. This ruined our rather complex and subtle joke entirely. As part of our new computerized production regime the artwork for the cover had been sent to John Brown Publishing early, not directly to the printers as had always been the case in the past. Clearly while at the Boathouse it had been altered. I was furious and immediately made a hollow threat to resign. John, who was in France at the time, relaxing in his newly acquired vineyard chateau, responded with a hollow offer to recall the entire issue and reprint it. The next day when I'd calmed down a little he started pointing out how expensive it would be to recall the whole issue, and how we'd lose a great many sales if we did. So I came up with another idea. Instead of withdrawing the issue, John would have to take out a full-page advertisement in *The Times* newspaper apologizing to us and the readers for the editorial interference. He agreed, in a hollow sort of way.

The next day John rang me up again. People were going to read this apology and think we were a bunch of wankers, he said. He was right, of course. We were taking petulance to new heights. But at the same time we did feel extremely aggrieved. So instead of demanding a public apology I reverted to the tried-and-tested tactic of blackmail, this time asking John to send us ten grand in cash to compensate for the distress we had suffered. He refused and then reluctantly agreed, as usual, and despatched his ad sales man Ronnie Hackston to Newcastle with a suitcase full of money. Ronnie made a big effort, wearing a smart suit and dark sunglasses for the occasion. 'Mr Hackston. I believe you have something for me,' I said when I met him at the airport.

In the summer of 1994 we'd published *The Big Fat Slags Book* as a follow-up to *The Bumper Book of Shite*. This was Graham and Thorpy's pet project and they'd industriously written and illustrated almost the entire book outside of office hours, working late nights and weekends in order to get it done. They had great faith in the Fat Slags and high hopes for the book, but a subdued summer launch didn't help their cause. Viz book sales were slipping also. During our brief boom period we'd been selling well over a quarter of a million annuals and riding high in the best-sellers charts, but by 1994 sales had returned to more realistic levels. *The Big Fat Slags Book* was a more modest success, selling around 60,000 copies.

A more successful venture was the *Top Tips* paperback published in October the same year. In the nine years since it began Top Tips had become one of the most popular features in the comic. I'd nicked both the idea and the name from the old *Titbits* magazine which I always bought just to read the inane readers' letters. The style of these letters was uniform and ridiculously brief, due no doubt to extremely harsh newspaper editing, and I'd adopted this for our letters page. Top Tips varied from the vaguely practical to the totally ridiculous. Readers were quick to get the hang of the formula and we received hundreds of Top Tips in the post. Perhaps the definitive Top Tip was this one from a reader from Lincoln, who wrote:

> Save the expense of having to buy costly personalized number plates by simply changing your name to match your existing plates.
> Mr KVL 741Y
> Lincoln

Throughout 1994 building work had been underway on my spectacularly remote restaurant at Ilderton in the windswept Cheviot Hills. The project was already the talk of the area, with several shepherds and passing RAF pilots having noticed something was going on. We weren't due to open until November, but by the summer I was already starting to reap the rewards of being a celebrity restaurateur and was cordially invited to officiate at the opening of the Ilderton church fête. So as not to go into the catering business completely blind I'd read most of the first chapter of a book called *The Idiot's Guide to Opening a Restaurant*, or something like that. One thing the author stressed was never to employ front-of-house staff who are in relationships with your kitchen staff as that can lead to all sorts of complications. Immediately I chose to disregard this advice and hired a couple to act as my chef and manageress.

Maddie had been in charge of counting money at the *Viz* office in Newcastle, but there wasn't as much money to count these days so I asked if she fancied running a restaurant instead. Her best qualification for the job was that her boyfriend Steve happened to be a chef. I hadn't given much thought to staffing the place and it turned out I'd underestimated the numbers required. I'd naïvely imagined that one determined couple could manage the place with the help of a few part-time staff, but the first thing my newly appointed management team did was to request a second tier of management beneath them – an assistant manageress and a second chef.

My second chef had a slightly disturbing Gary Rhodes haircut and a far more disturbing obsession with firearms. One day he took me on a walk to demonstrate a new gun he'd bought to shoot rabbits. As we strolled through a field he concealed this frightening-looking weapon beneath his long raincoat, then walked forward a few yards and pulled it out dramatically in a one-handed, gun-slinging action. He repeated this movement several times, clearly expecting me to be impressed by both the quickness of the draw and the emotionless, Clint Eastwood style expression on his face. 'That's very good,' I said. 'But why do you have to hide it under your coat? The rabbits don't know it's a gun.'

As far as I was concerned chefs, just like the food, were no more than an awkward necessity in the catering trade. All I cared about was my precious building, which, by the time it was finished, looked absolutely amazing: the gents' toilets, fully restored with their original slate urinals; the ladies' waiting room

The Station House Restaurant

with the original timber-boxed WC beyond; the old booking office, now the manager's office, and outside it the bar with the beautiful ticket window as its centrepiece. My £170,000 had been well spent. The Station House Restaurant officially opened for business on 5 November 1994, and our opening night was a triumph. We even had customers – loads of them. And I invited the old man who'd been custodian of the building for the previous forty years to come along and unveil a commemorative plaque on the wall.

The next day was a Sunday and I'd gone in to work early because a deadline was approaching. I hadn't been there long when Simon's girlfriend came knocking at the door. 'Your mam's died,' she said.

It was a shock, but at the same time it wasn't. We'd had the best part of thirty years to prepare for it. Mum's condition had worsened considerably in recent years. Despite her immobility she'd remained *compos mentis* and had got to know Dale, her first grandchild. She'd always wanted a daughter herself so she was delighted when Jamie, a granddaughter, came along in 1991. Mum and Dad had visited us in our new home in the country where we had a ground-floor toilet she could use, and I'd designed the restaurant with disabled access as a priority. But she never got to see it.

The health workers and volunteers who'd been helping Dad with care at home eventually recommended that for my dad's sake as well as hers she should go into a residential care home on a permanent basis. She'd already visited the Leonard Cheshire home at Matfen Hall in Northumberland for respite periods, and in 1992 she became a permanent resident. The staff there were absolutely wonderful, but the building was antiquated and inappropriate. It was like the setting for a Hammer horror film – a huge, run-down country pile with creaking floors and oak-panelled walls and ceilings. There were even suits of armour and old family portraits littered about in the grand hall where many of the residents spent their days sitting almost motionless in wheelchairs. We took the kids to visit every weekend, meeting up with other family members, and if the weather was good we could take Mum outside and sit on the ha-ha, watching the swans on the pond below. But her mental as well as her physical health was deteriorating. Then in 1993 she suffered a fit and nearly died, and was in intensive care for several days. After that she lost all of her movement, became permanently bedridden and was more or less unable to communicate. All we could do was sit by her bed and talk to her while the kids played around in the room. Sometimes we'd get a reaction, a smile perhaps, but other times there was nothing. Mum had only just been moved to a new, purpose-built home in Jesmond – the suburb of Newcastle where she'd been born and had always lived – when she died.

CHAPTER TWENTY

Me 1, Martin Peters 0

Simon and I missed the 1994 promotional jaunt to London for our latest book. An exhibition of Top Tips was staged at the Alternative Art Gallery in Marylebone High Street. Four students from St Martin's College of Art in London had volunteered to put some of our Top Tips into practice: manufacturing an improvised microwave oven, using a toaster and an old TV; giving scruffy old shoes a stylish 'patent leather' look by wrapping them in Sellotape; and creating a personal address book by simply crossing out the names of all the people they didn't know in their local telephone directory. The centrepiece of the exhibition was a selection of motoring Top Tips demonstrated on an old Citroën 2CV. For example, it had Rice Krispies glued to the tyres – to produce the sound of an expensive gravel drive on ordinary Tarmac.

At the same time PolyGram were attempting to promote the launch of *Blue Honeymoon*. We begged them not to, but their PR team went ahead and made two piss-awful Fat Slag costumes and paid out-of-work actors to wander around tourist sites in London wearing them, Disneyland-style. With ideas like that it's a wonder there aren't more PR people out of work.

The eagerly awaited ABC sales figures for 1994 showed that,

following a flicker of a recovery in the previous year, sales were now back on the slide. In the first half of 1994 they were down 12 per cent to 625,062. That performance earned us a slot in the *Media Week* Top Ten Circulation Decreases chart, in like a bullet at No. 10, making us Britain's tenth best *worst*-selling magazine. In the second half of 1994 we sank further to an average of 571,295. It was bad news, but there were two ways of looking at it. Sales were either down 50 per cent on four years ago, or up an impressive 11,425 per cent on ten years ago.

It was clear that my half-hearted efforts to reinvigorate the comic weren't making a ha'p'orth of difference to the number of people buying it. In October 1994 I'd gone to the considerable expense of recruiting Rodney Bewes – former TV Likely Lad and one-time *Basil Brush* host – for a spectacular cover promotion. I'd used Rodney Bewes in the comic often before. In August 1991 he opened the village fête in the middle of our Summer Special issue; he'd made a brief appearance in 'Billy the Fish'; and I'd often turned to him for quotes when making up stories about the UK walnut-growing industry. But on those occasions Rodney Bewes had not been aware of his involvement. Now I was making an official approach, through his agent, for Rodney to host our new '£5 Snap' promotion, a spoof on the *Sun*'s big-money 'Play Your Cards Right' game. On page 3 of *Viz* every reader was to be given a snap card to cut out and keep, and they would have to match their card with the cards a smiling Rodney Bewes held up at various points throughout the comic. The competition itself was a fix, of course – I wasn't handing over a fiver to anyone – but I did fork out a considerable sum of cash to get the real Rodney Bewes to pose for the pictures. When I met him at a London photo studio he seemed slightly uncomfortable, especially when I asked him to put on a scruffy old 1970s suit and look like a tramp. I wanted it to look as if we'd been scraping the bottom of the barrel for a celebrity, and come up with him.

When my 'Play £5 Snap! with Rodney Bewes' promotion failed to make any impact on sales I did the decent thing and offered to resign. I knew changes were probably necessary and I certainly didn't have the enthusiasm to make them. My 'publishing cycles' were getting worse. Finishing a comic was like running off a cliff in a cartoon. I'd be frantically busy, then suddenly the comic was gone. For a day or two my feet would still be moving and I'd be frozen in midair. Then I'd stop running, slowly look down and see that the ground was no longer there. Then, woosh! Down I went into a mental abyss. I'd be morose and miserable and sit around at home doing nothing, dreading the prospect of starting the whole comic production process all over again. Meanwhile Graham and Thorpy would bounce back in to work bright and early on the Monday morning, sit down at the writing table and start churning out scripts again. When I eventually slouched back in to work it didn't always help. I was sick of the writing routine we'd got into. 'We haven't done the Slags for a while,' Graham might say. Then someone would suggest a situation. 'How about a skiing holiday?' Bingo! There's your plot. Sometimes this worked perfectly well, but when my own characters were nominated for this treatment I'd get annoyed. 'Has Roger Mellie done *Changing Rooms* yet?' someone would suggest. I'd get my back up and start shooting down their ideas, but without suggesting any better ones of my own.

Around this time I started drinking to help me feel more morose. It was only in the evenings, but it was quite unusual for me. I'd never kept drink at home before. Drinking had always been something I did socially, in the pub. But now I was doing it anti-socially, on our settee. Nothing excessive, just two or three cans of beer at night after the kids had gone to bed, and a large whisky chaser or two. I was on the slippery slope and I knew it. If I didn't act fast one day soon I was going to wake up and find myself drinking vodka in the shower first thing in the morning, talking with a Scottish accent and pawning Dolores's jewellery to pay for drugs. So in November 1994 I told John I wanted to quit. On any other magazine quitting would not have been a problem

– with sales figures like ours I'd have been sacked at least two years earlier – but *Viz* wasn't any other magazine. *Viz* was still my baby – or problematic teenager by now – and, more importantly, John still believed I had a crucial role to play in expanding his own personal wealth. He said he'd look into finding a replacement, but he felt a lot of my problems could be solved by better organization. He suggested I take some pressure off myself by putting Sheila in day-to-day charge of running the magazine. I said I'd give it a go.

Sheila Gill

Sheila was from Cumbria and had a slightly grating, crow-like voice. I gave her the job title of Production Editor and told her to think of the studio as a classroom where she was the teacher. Her job was to shout at everybody, myself included, and make sure we got our work done on time. There was friction at first as Sheila tried to knock us into shape. Sheila was a bundle of nerves at times and tended to talk in long, unpunctuated sentences which began in a fairly structured way but in the space of a few seconds descended into garbled chaos. She was not a calming influence by any means, and John quickly nicknamed her Corporal Jones. It took us a while to get used to Sheila's unique management style of stringency and incoherence, blended with occasional panic, but gradually we began to adapt and the studio became more efficient. Her presence also opened up new seams for us to exploit. With an AppleMac and skilled operator in the room, suddenly we could accurately mimic the colour pages of Sunday supplements and produce adverts for exquisite collectibles such as 'Gold! The Tony Hadley Fabergé Pineapple' or the 'Elvis Presley Dambusters Clock Plate of Tutankhamun'. But while our range of potential targets was expanding, the majority of our munitions were still raining down on the big, soft variety.

The rationale behind our campaign against Danny Baker was, I suppose, the fact that by 1995 he'd become seriously over-exposed on both television and radio. He was actually past the peak of his popularity, but was still on Radio 1 at weekends, his BBC chat show seemed to be on every night of the week and he'd even started doing Daz commercials. Baker had got where he was deservedly, by being witty and sharp and entertaining. But now he was overdoing it, talking too much and becoming an irritant. It also seemed to be the case, on a more general note, that any Cockney gobshite who'd ever watched *The David Letterman Show* could now walk into their own chat show on British TV.

Danny Baker appeared in a Cockney Wanker cartoon in January 1995. In the strip he was Danny Wanker, an everyday working-class Cockney chat show host who wanted his son to follow him into the traditional family business. But the young-ster didn't want to be just another Cockney TV chat show host. He was ambitious and wanted to better himself by starting up his own business … as a barrow boy, selling cockles, mussels and whelks.

I don't think Baker could have had any complaints about the cartoon, but the T-shirt that we launched in the same issue wasn't quite as satirical. It featured Thorpy's caricature of a fat, balding Baker holding up a packet of Daz, with the slogan 'DANNY BAKER IS A TWAT' in very big, bold lettering. Especially the word 'twat'. The manager of the HMV shop in London's Oxford Street was reluctant to stock it. 'He's one of my best customers,' he told our distributor Andy Pop. Baker himself responded by dismissing us as 'college boys' on his Radio 1 programme. Graham and Thorpy might have been college boys, but I wasn't. On the Monday morning I sent Baker a fax pointing this out:

Dear Danny Baker
    I refer to the current issue of *Viz*, and the mention you gave it on your one remaining Radio 1 slot on Saturday. You called us 'college boys'. College boys my arse. I never went to university. Academically I'm every bit as thick as you are, thank you very much, and twice as proud of it.
    Regards, Chris Donald

I got a reply straight away.

Dear Chris
    The reason I said the magazine reflected the college boys' paranoia of the proletariat is I had this wild idea it might cause raised hackles and lots of indignant blustering.
    And you a humorist too ... for shame ...
    Your pal in the South, Danny Baker

He was using big words again, like he did on his TV show, and that annoyed me. So I scribbled a note on the bottom of his fax and sent it back.

Cut the waffle and the big words will you. You're killing television. Look at Leonard Sachs. What good did it do him?

I was referring to the similarity in presentational styles between Baker and Leonard Sachs, host of *The Good Old Days*. Baker sent my note straight back again with his own final comment appended.

Ooh. Fax war, luvvie!

Baker may have had the last word in that exchange, but as far as I was concerned all it did was prove our original point – that he was a twat. So *there*. I've had the last word now.

Another victim of our childish taunting was the Scottish comic publisher D. C. Thomson. *Viz* owed a great deal to the *Beano*, the *Dandy* and other traditional British comics as our stock in trade was to lampoon their contents or hijack their formats for our own purposes. D. C. Thomson, publishers of both the *Dandy* and the *Beano*, had a reputation for being an outdated, Victorian institution. I imagined their offices in Dundee were like a giant mill, with rows and rows of low-paid cartoonists slaving over their drawing boards. A lot of our strips were spoofs, exaggerations or derivations of their cartoons, and some bore a closer resemblance to their inspirations than others. From some angles Black Bag, the *Viz* Wonder Bin Liner created by Scotsmen Dave Smith and Graham Murdoch, bore more than a passing resemblance to the *Dandy*'s Black Bob. And while there was no physical resemblance between them, their Three Bears and our Three Chairs had other similarities. Following hot on the heels of the Three Chairs, in 1988 we produced Desperately Unfunny Dan. This time there wasn't even a token attempt at disguising the character. It was simply Desperate Dan, but in our totally unauthorized strip he was trying desperately to be funny, by bending lamp-posts, etc. He failed abysmally then suffered the indignity of eating a cowpat pie.

D. C. Thomson were not amused and their lawyers fired off a formal warning which John relayed to me. For a while after that we steered clear of D. C. Thomson piss-takes, but inevitably they began to creep back in. First Barry the Cat, and then, in April 1990, a surreal skit of Oor Wullie in which a Scottish Jimmy Hill, in dungarees, got up to some high jinks and ended the story sitting on a bucket, eating sweets. (We'd wanted to call it 'Oor Jimmy' but on legal advice had changed it to 'The Adventures of

Jimmy Hill'.) In the following issue came the less surreal and far more blatant McBroons. Thorpy was a great fan of Dudley D. Watkins, the legendary D. C. Thomson illustrator, and did a fine job of imitating his drawing style. The parody of a typically lightweight Broons plotline had been suggested by T. Bam, a *Viz* reader from Newcastle. The McBroon clan all got into a panic when they heard that Grandpa was going to have a 'fight'. But they were mistaken, and in the final frame it turns out he is actually having a *shite*. John received another formal warning from Dundee about that one.

John kept on giving D. C. Thomson assurances that he'd put a stop to our taunting, but they were worthless. We paid no attention to John, who never saw the comic before it went to press, and our solicitor, who did, knew nothing about the *Beano* or the *Dandy* and didn't recognize any of their characters. And so Roger the Lodger, then Little Plumber, both got through. But in November 1994 D. C. Thomson failed to see the funny side when Arsehole Kate – our variation on their nosey mischief-maker Keyhole Kate – got shit on her face after peeking up her dad's bumhole. This time they issued a *final* warning. If we ever did it again we would be in big trouble.

Then Graham and Thorpy came up with Wanker Watson, the story of the champion masturbator of Greytrousers public school. 'Oh … go on then,' I said. I couldn't resist it. It was published in issue 71, April 1995, and this time the combination of copyright theft and sexual depravity was more than D. C. Thomson & Co. Ltd could take. As usual John promised them that it would never, *ever* happen again, but his words fell on deaf ears. Their lawyers came down hard and said they'd sue unless we withdrew the issue from sale and made a formal, written undertaking never to plagiarize any of their comic strips again. John capitulated and signed the following document to get himself off the hook, then sent a copy of it to me.

Undertakings by John Brown Publishing Ltd and Viz Comic to D. C. Thomson & Co. Ltd.

Undertakings not to:

i) Publish in any future edition of *Viz* (i.e. after issue 71), or in any future *Viz* compilation or book, any cartoon strip which is a copy of or a derivation from any cartoon strip, or any characters from such cartoons, which has or have appeared or shall appear in the *Dandy*, the *Beano, Topper, Beezer*, the *Sunday Post, Wizard, Twinkle, Bunty, Mandy* or *Judy*.

ii) Reprint issue 71.

iii) Distribute or sell any back copies of issue 71.

These undertakings were offered and agreed between 10 and 25 May 1995.

John Brown

John told me he'd had no choice in the matter, but I thought he'd been gutless. Surely a court case would have been fun, good for PR. But all that was immaterial now. If we broke the undertaking then suing us would be a formality. This really rankled with me. Not only were we losing our sales, now we were losing our spirit too. John had gone soft.

After brooding on it for a month I came up with a plan. We might not be able to take the piss out of their cartoon characters any more, but there was nothing to stop us taking the piss out of D. C. Thomson personally. So we hit back with a new character called D. C. Thompson – The Humourless Scottish Git. This was a miserable, miserly old Scotsman in a kilt who wandered around complaining about breaches of copyright. At the fruit shop he complains because a 'little plum' is advertised in the window. In the sweet shop he takes exception to a mother calling her son Dennis a 'menace'. And at the pet shop he asks for a sign offering 'Three bears for the price of one' to be removed from the window. The shop assistant refuses to remove the sign but then the pet shop owner, Soft John, appears. 'How about a compromise whereby we give in altogether?' he says. 'After all we don't want to upset Mr Thompson.' Finally D. C. Thompson ends the cartoon sitting on a bucket and pissing his kilt.

D. C. Thompson The Humourless Scottish Git

Our solicitor, a posh girl called Caroline Addy, didn't like it at all. 'Can't you change the initials?' she asked, missing the point entirely, as only a solicitor can. I said I knew that Thomson's would be annoyed – that was indeed the point – but what I wanted her to tell me was whether or not they could take any legal action. Eventually I got word from Caroline that the cartoon was legally okay, although she did ask us to remove the bucket from the last frame. We didn't. Instead Thorpy rather cleverly put a slot in it, then retrospectively slipped it into a display cabinet in the hat shop one frame earlier. If D. C. Thomson were going to sue us for drawing Oor Wullie's bucket, then we were going to stand up in court and say that it wasn't a bucket, it was Ned Kelly's hat.

'D.C. Thompson – The Humourless Scottish Git' was

published in August 1995, and we braced ourselves for a response. It came the same month, and from a totally unexpected direction. 'The Jocks and the Geordies' was one D. C. Thomson strip we'd never got round to parodying. It was about two feuding gangs from either side of the Border and was a regular feature in the *Dandy* from 1975 until 1990. But it made a surprise comeback on 26 August 1995. In a highly unusual edition of the strip (which must have baffled regular *Dandy* readers) a comic publisher called Don Christopher challenged the two gangs to a drawing competition. The Geordies' efforts were all crap (some badly drawn fish, a boy with big underpants, two fat girls and a bloke farting) so they stole the Jocks' drawings and won the competition. But in the end the Geordies were exposed as cheats and Don Christopher announced, 'The Jocks are the winners – and that's a *real* comic punch line.' This good-humoured act of retaliation was the work of *Dandy* editor Morris Heggie, with whom we had always been on very good terms. From that point onwards our relationship with the Jocks in Dundee became a lot more relaxed ... and on the cover of our next issue we featured a brand new character, Corky the Twat.

Caroline Addy read everything before the comic went to press, cartoons as well as news features. As a rule of thumb the more ridiculous a news story, the more likely we were to get away with it. For example, we could say that Bruce Willis got his sexual kicks by swallowing giant snakes while high on a cocktail of drink and drugs, and getting his wife Demi Moore to shove a mongoose up his arse. Caroline raised no objections to that. Some celebrities are more litigious than others, and part of her job was to warn us if we were poking fun at someone who was known to be that way inclined. Jimmy Nail, for example. Calling Danny Baker a twat was fine. It's what lawyers call *low abuse*. But inaccurately labelling somebody a tart, for example, as we did on one occasion, is not a good idea. According to the dictionary 'tart' means only two things; either a pie containing fruit, or a prostitute. And because the lady in question was neither a prostitute, nor a pie containing fruit, legally we didn't have a leg to stand on.

By now we were haemorrhaging readers at the rate of 16,300 sales per issue. In the first half of 1995 our average was down to 527,030. And it wasn't very encouraging to learn that a lot of these remaining readers were in prison and therefore not the most selective members of our audience. We'd always received a lot of mail from prisons, but lately I'd started getting some heavy letters from people pleading their innocence and claiming to be the victims of miscarriages of justice. I felt a lot of sympathy for some of them, but as the editor of Britain's number-one toilet humour magazine there wasn't a lot of power I could wield to get their cases reopened. So instead I decided to give away free pardons to any serving prisoners who wrote in and asked for one, for a limited period only. I printed up an Official *Viz* Pardon certificate, stating that the person named 'didn't do it, honest' and expected to have to send out a few dozen at most. But the response was frightening. Within weeks hundreds of prisoners had written in asking for a pardon. We were snowed under. Apparently the certificates – which included a polite but non-obligatory instruction to prison guards to release the prisoner – became a must-have item in prison cells all across Britain, and demand was so high we had to reprint it several times.

In the autumn of 1995 Eugen Beer suggested we launch a website to publicize our annual crop of books and a slightly unusual calendar called 'Bygones of Yesteryear' – a parody of classic advertising images from the past. Our website was supposed to be a send-up of pretentious advertising agency sites but, never having seen one, I didn't really know what I was supposed to write. Eugen said that if I launched a vitriolic tirade against the advertising industry – as I was known to do from time to time – it would trigger a storm of publicity for the website. But it didn't. Instead it triggered one tiny paragraph in the *Observer* under the headline 'unfeasibly sad site'.

But just when it looked like our publicity bomb had failed to detonate, in stepped Skegness Council to save the day. 'Foul-mouthed jibe at Skegness lands *Viz* in a mess,' read the headline across the top of a half-page story in the *Independent*. 'The anarchic adult comic *Viz* may be sued for the first time in its 16-year history – by Skegness Council.' The fuss was over a page in our calendar, a spoof of the classic 'Jolly Fisherman' poster advertising Skegness. Instead of a jolly fisherman skipping along a sunny beach, Thorpy had painted a Fat Slag skipping past broken glass, dog turds and raw sewage, and the slogan 'Skegness is so bracing' was replaced with 'Skegness is fucking shit'. It turned out that Skegness Council owned the rights to the original poster, by John Hassall, and the Jolly Fisherman was their town mascot.

As sales ebbed away, so advertising revenue became more important. And in 1995 the way to get media types to spend their advertising budget in your magazine was to take them to a football match. Sponsoring Blyth Spartans hadn't provided us with many suitable opportunities. Most of the media buyers whose arses needed to be licked were reluctant to leave Soho, let alone London, and to them the prospect of travelling 300 miles to watch Blyth Spartans play Stalybridge Celtic would not have been an attractive one. So John Brown changed his sponsorship strategy and in 1995 decided to sponsor a single Premiership match instead of an entire non-league season. The cost was about the same.

The match chosen was Spurs *v.* Newcastle on Sunday 29 October, a game broadcast live on Sky TV. As part of the package we got an advertisement hoarding alongside the pitch. Spurs rejected our first-choice slogan, 'DRINK BEER, SMOKE TABS', so instead we went for 'DRINK BEER, SMOKE KIPPERS'. On the match day we turned up early at White Hart Lane for a corporate lunch hosted by former Spurs star Martin Chivers. 'Are you a director here?' John Brown asked him. 'No, I run a pub,' said Chivers. John looked a little deflated not to be dining with the board. After the game, which ended 1–1, I had the great pleasure of winning an argument with an England World Cup winner. I'd been talking to Martin Chivers about the 1976 League Cup semi-final, second leg, when Newcastle had beaten Spurs 3–1 at St James's Park, and I mentioned a player called Chris Jones whom I'd seen playing for Spurs that night. Suddenly big-nosed Martin Peters, who had been hosting another corporate party in the same room, ghosted into our conversation. 'No, no, no. Chris Jones wasn't playing in '76,' he said with all the arrogance of someone who has won the World Cup and can therefore never be wrong in an argument about football. 'Oh yes he was,' I said. 'He was a skinny bloke with long hair, like a thin Chris Waddle.' Martin Peters shook his head and smiled, like a policeman taking pleasure from ignoring a protestation of innocence. 'No, son, '76 was too early for Jones.'

When I got home the first thing I did was reach for my *Rothmans Football Yearbook*, and there it was in black and white. Chris Jones came on as a substitute in that game, replacing Keith Osgood. 'So *there*,' I said to myself. Me 1, Martin Peters 0.

Two weeks later Graham, Simon and myself embarked on a short promotional book-signing tour. Thorpy's wife was expecting so he stayed behind. He was the lucky one. Book signings were interesting thermometers for gauging the health of the magazine. The first signing we ever did was at the Timeslip comic shop in Newcastle in 1986. We graduated from there to record shops, and at one signing at the HMV shop in Newcastle, around the height of *Viz*'s popularity, there was an enormous queue snaking right out into Northumberland Street. We had very busy book signings in London too, although they were far less enjoyable due to the inevitable presence of John Brown.

When John was around us he felt obliged to play a protective, managerial role. He stopped looking like Ian Faith, and actually became him. Instead of just signing books we'd each draw a scribbled cartoon, and if there were four of us sitting behind a table then people would wait while all four of us drew on their book. We didn't mind at all and we had these sketches off to a tee so they only took a few seconds to do. But John Brown didn't like this. He wanted a quick turnaround of customers so he'd stand behind us looking over our shoulders, physically poking us and badgering us with instructions. He'd complain if drawings looked too detailed. 'Hurry it up,' he'd say. 'No more than ten seconds on each drawing.' If a long queue started to build up he'd say, 'Right. Only one drawing per book from now on.' This was John at his bossy, bullying worst, and we'd be smiling at the customers and gritting our teeth at the same time. Afterwards John would make sure we scribbled signatures in any piles of unsold books that remained in the shop. He wasn't doing the shop a favour – he was preventing the books from coming back to him. Once they were signed, the shop could no longer return them as unsold.

Significantly, the majority of people buying books at our early book signings were teenagers, but as the years passed I noticed a gradual change in the clientele. Parents started turning up and asking us to sign books for their teenage children. *Viz* had originally been contraband, bought secretly, smuggled into the house and hidden away from parents. Now parents were buying it for their children in an attempt to get on their good side. *Viz* was becoming acceptable to parents, so inevitably their children didn't want to know about it any more.

By 1995 the parents had stopped coming too. Our quiet book-signing tour reached its anticlimax in Kingston upon Thames. This was not a *Viz* hotbed by any means. Way back in 1979 my Kingston correspondent Tim Harrison had struggled to sell ten copies of our first issue and cut his subsequent order to six. Kingston was not a big college town. A signing had nevertheless been arranged at a big bookshop inside the town's indoor shopping centre. We arrived at the shop – I think it was Waterstone's – twenty minutes before we were due to be signing books, but nobody seemed to be expecting us. No posters advertising the event, no table piled high with *Viz* annuals. We wandered around browsing at books while our driver tried to locate the person in charge. Eventually he returned with a rather embarrassed-looking member of staff and a table was hastily set up and a pile of books placed on top of it. The three of us sat down at the table. By now it was 11 o'clock on the dot, the scheduled time of our book signing, and there wasn't a single person in the shop. The man who was supposed to have organized the event was pacing around anxiously. 'I can't think what's wrong. There's definitely been ads in the local press,' he assured us. He didn't invite us to kick his ass, but he was becoming increasingly apologetic by the minute. Then he rushed out of the shop leaving us sitting alone at our table. A few minutes later the shopping centre PA crackled into action. 'Anyone wishing to buy a signed copy of the latest *Viz* annual please make their way to Waterstone's bookshop on level one where the artists from *Viz* are currently signing books.'

As we sat there alone at our table I started thinking of a story Thorpy had told us. He'd once seen Don Estelle sitting alone in a shopping centre in Leeds, waiting in vain to sign copies of his latest LP. As people walked by they looked at him with pity. Now I knew how Don Estelle must have felt. Well, almost. A small consolation for us was that we weren't dressed in oversized safari suits and pith helmets at the time.

CHAPTER TWENTY-ONE

You Can't Tie an Ice Cube
to Your Beard

At the beginning of 1996 I got a postcard from Prince Charles inviting me to a party at his place. Actually, it was a formal invitation from His Royal Highness the Prince of Wales requesting the pleasure of the company of me for dinner at St James's Palace, on 22 February, 8.00 p.m. for 8.15. I knew Charles was a fan of the Goons, but I'd never had him down as a *Viz* reader.

On closer inspection the RSVP address on the card was that of a charity, WaterAid, and it dawned on me that the invitation was nothing more than a postal scam to get wealthy businessmen like myself to part with their cash. The thought of an expensive after-dinner conversation with the Prince of Wales didn't much appeal to me, and in any case Dolores and I had already booked a holiday on the date in question. So I dropped Charles a note saying sorry we couldn't make it, and promised to pop in for a chat next time we were passing.

At around the same time I got a call from John who told me that an independent television producer by the name of Nicholas Sercombe had come up with an idea for a *Viz Top Tips* video to be presented by comedians Vic Reeves and Bob Mortimer. I thought this sounded like a brilliant idea. Vic and Bob liked it too, so contracts were signed by the three parties – Viz, Nicholas Sercombe's production company Screen Machine and Reeves and Mortimer – and a major distributor called Pearson New Entertainment signed up to buy the finished product and release it on video. It all seemed too good to be true, and of course it was.

I got my first whiff of shit when Nicholas Sercombe announced he was bringing in his own writers to rewrite our Top Tips for the video. John said this was perfectly normal, they couldn't simply work from a book. It went without saying, he said, that they'd have to bring someone in to write a bit of dialogue. But that someone wasn't going to be us, and it wasn't going to be Vic and Bob either. That someone turned out to be a pair of comedy writers called Paul Minett and Brian Leveson, whose past credits included pantomime and Russ Abbott's TV show.

John assured me that the contract he had just signed gave us 'script approval' so I had the power to veto anything I didn't like. At a meeting in London John, Vic, Bob and I, Nicholas Sercombe and Messrs Minett and Leveson all got together for the first time. Vic was aloof, saying little at the meeting. Bob was their spokesman and he briefed the writers with a few ground rules. Minett and Leveson were a contrasting pair. One was a short, fat and rather excitable bloke who looked like Bernie Winters, but without Schnorbitz the dog. The other was a tall, more reserved and contemplative-looking fellow, clearly the moderating influence in the partnership. They seemed to be a bit of an Abbott and Costello double act. I expressed a few of my concerns about handing over the material to them and they appeared most receptive. After that meeting I felt a lot better … then I saw the first draft of their script.

In all my time at *Viz* nothing pissed me off more than sitting reading that script, and the infuriating sequence of events that followed still rankles to this day. Our Top Tips had been completely fucked over. Changes had been made for no apparent reason, totally disarming the jokes. It may sound pedantic, but I'll give you an example.

One Top Tip was the recommendation that applying Tippex to your beard would make you look like an Arctic explorer. Minett and Leveson had changed this to 'tying an ice cube' to your beard will make you look like an Arctic explorer. That doesn't work for two reasons. Firstly, you can't tie an ice cube to your beard. At least not without some considerable difficulty. And secondly, an ice cube wouldn't look like frost and snow on a beard. Tippex would. I found it annoying having to explain the mechanics of the original jokes to two comedy writers, but it had to be done to show why their revisions didn't work. The majority of Top Tips consist of solutions to problems. In the Tippex joke, for example, the solution is entirely practical. It's the problem that is the joke. Nobody would want to make themselves look like an Arctic explorer.

As well as tampering with the mechanisms of existing jokes they had also added their own, throwing smut and innuendo into the mix. They had written jokes that they thought were in the 'wacky' *Viz* style, and come up with 'zany' material which they thought would suit Vic and Bob, but they were way off the mark. Knowing that Vic and Bob were largely improvisational comics who made up their own stuff, I wondered how they would react to having old-fashioned gag writers putting words into their mouths. I already knew how I felt having our work rewritten.

I went through their 69-page script highlighting a hundred or so examples of our jokes that had been defused and their jokes that I found unfunny. At another meeting in London Minett and Leveson thanked me for all my comments and assured me that the recommendations I'd made would be implemented. But when I saw their second draft it was clear that they hadn't been implemented. At the next meeting I arrived on time only to find that a script read-through was already finished. I was starting to get pissed off by this stage. Still none of my suggestions seemed to have been taken up and their own smutty jokes remained. For example, the appearance of a topless model had been written into the script. *'Viz* has never been smutty,' I tried to explain. *Viz* has always been arse, but never tits and bum. The more animated of the two writers – clearly a tits and bum man – found that hard to comprehend. 'Are you serious?' he asked. Basically he didn't get *Viz*, in much the same way that I didn't get Russ Abbott. We were on different comedy wavelengths. But once again I was given a friendly assurance that all my comments would be taken on board when it came to the final

Me by Vic Reeves

drafting of the script. I never even saw a copy of the final script.

Filming took place in June 1996 at the Elstree studios, near Watford, and Graham, Thorpy, Simon and I all went down for a couple of days to watch the video being made. On the first night we met up with Vic and Bob and the film crew at their hotel and had a meal and a few drinks. When we awoke the next morning Vic and Bob and the crew had already gone off to the studios so the four of us made our own way there. Filming was already underway when we arrived and we were taken to a conference room that was acting as the nerve centre for the operation. Yet again, I was assured by the writers and the producer that my recommendations had been followed up. They even thanked me, saying that as a result the script was now much improved. Then we were shown to the studio floor where Vic and Bob were in action.

We were very much spectators and, as we were ushered in, we were told to keep still and stay quiet while filming was taking place. Watching from the sidelines it quickly became apparent that the scripts they were using still contained a great many – if not all – of the things I'd objected to, and I got the distinct impression that Vic and Bob were not comfortable with the material. At one point filming came to a stop and a conference took place between Vic, the floor manager and the director – a sullen Everton fan called David Croft – who was up in the gallery above. Vic was politely declining to do one particular joke, a smutty alteration to one of our Tips that I'd specifically asked to be removed.

The original Top Tip, which was sent in by a reader called P. Turner from Liverpool, read thus:

ALWAYS keep tubes of haemorrhoid ointment and Deep Heat rub well separated in your bathroom cabinet.

This was a solution to an unstated problem, and the joke was in deducing what the problem was and imagining the conse- quences. Messrs Minett and Leveson rewrote it along these lines:

ALWAYS keep tubes of KY Jelly and Deep Heat rub well separated in your bathroom cabinet to avoid getting sore bollocks during sex.

They'd defused the joke by stating the problem rather than implying it, and of course the subject matter had been altered to sex. In the studio Vic was now being asked to illustrate the new version by holding an ice pack to his groin. He was uncomfortable with the idea and, via the floor manager, was involved in a discussion with the production gallery. I was furious and couldn't resist joining in the argument. The moment I did, orders were issued from the gallery and our group was suddenly asked to leave the studio. We were marched up some steps and along a corridor to a small holding cell, where we were told to sit quietly and watch the rest of the proceedings on TV monitors.

I felt like James Bond being held prisoner inside the high-tech HQ of an arch villain, and that villain was Nicholas Sercombe who was directing operations from the production gallery nearby. The debate about the smutty joke was continuing. One of the writers – the chirpy, short-arsed one – flew past our room towards the gallery announcing in a temperamental fluster that Vic's refusal to hold an ice pack to his groin would 'ruin the whole gag'. I was incensed. It wasn't his fucking gag, it was *ours*. And he'd already ruined it. Sercombe was backing him up, but I felt that neither of them should have been interfering at that stage. Once the script was approved by me the writers should have exited the picture and it should have been left to Vic and Bob, and their approved director, to film it. But the final script had *not* been approved, the writers were interfering with the filming, and the evil mastermind Sercombe was now holding us prisoner as his plan to destroy our reputation reached its climax. Ideally I'd have liked to overpower the floor manager and the cameramen, rescue Vic and Bob from Sercombe's clutches and then escape from the building seconds before it exploded, leaving Sercombe and his gag-writing henchmen trapped in the burning gallery. But instead we decided to walk out in a huffy protest.

On our way out we went into the conference room to pick up our bags and the less excitable of the two writers asked us if everything was okay. We told him exactly what we thought and, before long, we found ourselves involved in a heated argument with both writers and Sercombe himself. After shouting at them fruitlessly for a few minutes we left, and slammed the door on our way out.

Sercombe wrote to me the following week, defending Minett and Leveson's interpretation of our material and more or less dismissing my concerns as a predictable writer's strop. He was basically saying that they knew better than us when it came to putting comedy on video. He said that my comments had been taken on board, but he and the writers were using their own 'skill and judgement', as he put it, 'in a medium and genre in which we are highly experienced'. He said he'd already seen the first edit and he assured me that it was looking 'very good'.

When I first saw the tape I quickly used my own skill and judgement to conclude that it was a load of shit. I thought it was flat and unfunny, and shortly afterwards I got a phone call from Vic and Bob's agent saying that they, too, were unhappy with it. There were two tapes, each of around fifty minutes' duration, and these were intended for separate release as *Top Tips 1* and *Top Tips 2*. The first tape was bad, it went on too long and it wasn't funny. The second tape was so bad I could only watch twenty-five minutes of it before giving up. Vic and Bob weren't to blame, although the script had clearly failed to inspire their performances. But now that it was finished there was little we could do. Bob Mortimer suggested that we might be able to salvage something with a last minute re-edit, so he and I started going through time-coded copies of the tapes, making notes for a possible savage re-edit. It was purely a pruning exercise, nothing new could be added, although the use of sound effects and captions gave us some scope for improvements. In the end we concluded that one half-decent forty-five-minute tape was all that could be salvaged from 100-odd minutes of footage. But a re-edit on the scale we were proposing would have meant the distributor, Pearsons, having to accept only one tape, whilst paying for two. Sercombe could have sued Pearsons if they didn't pay him in full for the two tapes he had already delivered.

To put it in a nutshell, we were fucked. And so our dream collaboration became a damage-limitation exercise. I asked for my, Graham's, Thorpy's and Simon's names to be removed from the script-writing credits, and we refused to have anything to do with promoting the video. So did Vic and Bob. Our hope was that the first video would sink without trace, and the second would be shelved indefinitely as a result. The first one came out for the Christmas market in 1996. The only review I saw was in *Q* magazine:

> On paper this stuff can be daftly endearing ... but, hard to believe, the puerile pair (Vic and Bob) manage to deflate the foolish humour, via flat-as-pancake delivery that spells A-U-T-O-C-U-E. They fluff some lines too, but due to the obvious farthing-scraping budget, either there wasn't the time to re-shoot, or no one could actually be bothered. Here's a Top Tip for Vic and Bob: not everything you do is funny, so don't accept everything offered your way, especially TV after-the-pub material that even Roger Mellie would find oiksome.

Nicholas Sercombe's Screen Machine production company went bust shortly after the videos were made and – as well as the artistic disappointment – Vic and Bob ended up out of pocket, a substantial amount of their fee remaining unpaid.

With the benefit of hindsight I don't blame Sercombe for the mess. Or the writers, Minett and Leveson. They were all doing their best. We were to blame ourselves. We got involved because Reeves and Mortimer were involved, and Reeves and Mortimer got involved because we were involved. But neither side thought to check what exactly they were letting themselves in for. We saw it as an exciting opportunity for us to do something different and to engage in a TV production process with people we admired. But the opportunity was pissed up the wall on an ill-conceived, cheap sell-through video. I think John Brown would agree that it wasn't the best deal he ever did for us.

Meanwhile somebody else was also bringing Top Tips to the nation's TV screens. In August 1996 I was sitting watching telly one night when an advertisement came on for McDonald's fast food. I thought for a minute I was dreaming. There on the screen was one of our Top Tips jokes being demonstrated on a commercial for hamburgers. Renamed a 'McDonald's Money-Saving Tip', it was the joke about gluing carpet tiles to the bottom of your shoes to make supermarkets feel as comfortable as your own living room. I wasn't the only one who saw it, and McDonald's TV ads were already the main topic of conversation when I arrived in the office the next day. Gradually reports came in of more and more McDonald's 'Money-Saving Tips' commercials, many bearing remarkable similarities to jokes that had previously appeared in our Top Tips columns.

All credit to the advertising people involved. They had made a much better job of televising Top Tips than we had ourselves, and they were very funny commercials. But we weren't the only ones who spotted the similarities to our own Top Tips, and we started getting complaints from readers accusing us of selling out to the McDonald's corporation. Some of McDonald's jokes were so close to ours people were jumping to the natural conclusion that we'd sold them. One reader fashioned his letter into a sarcastic Top Tip:

> Geordie magazine editors. Continue paying your mortgage and buying expensive train sets ... by simply licensing the Top Tips concept to a multinational burger corporation.

In five cases the similarities were unmistakable. For example, one of our Top Tips read:

> Save a fortune on laundry bills. Give your dirty shirts to Oxfam. They will wash and iron them, and then you can buy them back for 50p.

McDonald's equivalent Money-Saving Tip was:

> Save a fortune on laundry bills. Give your dirty shirts to a
> second-hand shop. They will wash and iron them, and
> then you can buy them back for 50p.

Common sense suggested to me that we had been ripped off, but
the law and common sense are two very different filets-o-fish.
Our lawyers told us we had two problems. Firstly, proving ownership of the copyright (it's hard to prove you own the copyright
in a joke); and, secondly, they said we'd have trouble convincing
a judge that the theft of our Top Tips, if proven, had done us any
material harm. So even if we did sue and win, we might get
nothing for it. Nevertheless, we decided to launch an attack, and
in the first wave our solicitors issued a formal complaint
accusing McDonald's and their advertising agency, Leo Burnett
Advertising, of a breach of copyright.

We expected McDonald's to simply put their hands up, say
'Oops, sorry', and offer to give a couple of grand to charity. But
they didn't. Instead they totally denied the allegation. So we
launched a second wave of attack which was to call in Beer
Davies, our spin doctors. They alerted the press to the alleged
thefts, and a rash of stories began to appear in the papers, com-
paring the nearly identical tips. Under headlines like the *Mirror*'s
'burger all difference' and the *Evening Standard*'s 'burger off',
McDonald's staunch denial was mocked by the papers. The story
even made it onto *Have I Got News for You*. McDonald's PR
woman was quoted in the press saying that the inspiration for
their Money-Saving Tips campaign had actually come from an
ancient Japanese form of wit known as *Chindogu*. She said that
the campaign writers had never even heard of our Top Tips
feature, and, quoted in the *Independent*, she summarized their
defence as follows: 'They are suggesting that we have perhaps
taken the idea from Top Tips. We say we haven't … We just took
the concept of weird and wacky ideas. Our creative people went

to a number of books and publications to get the ideas. *Viz* was not one of them.' McDonald's solicitors were equally staunch in their denials. In correspondence with our solicitors they explained that some of the jokes in question had been 'overheard in a pub, seven or eight years ago'. And yet, remarkably, two of the tips in question had appeared alongside each other on the same page of *Viz* published in April 1996. The 'creatives' at Leo Burnett had written their campaign in May.

Although we were winning the PR battle hands down, our legal challenge was largely a bluff. So I was seeking revenge in other quarters, by goading McDonald's in the magazine. In October 1996 I altered our regular small print credits paragraph so that it read:

© House of Viz/John Brown Publishing. No part of this publication may be 'overheard in a pub seven or eight years ago' by a creative employee of Leo Burnett Advertising Limited and then coincidentally appear in an advertising campaign for McDonald's Restaurants written in May of this year, the very month after it was published in this comic. You fucking little wanker.

I didn't know who the individual responsible was but I knew he'd be reading that, so writing it made me feel a little bit better.

Issuing a writ wasn't a serious option for us – we had a weak legal case and McDonald's were renowned for their tenacious lawyers and abundant reserves of money. But John Brown instructed his lawyers to shake their stick one more time and see what happened. They wrote to McDonald's solicitors demanding financial compensation and threatening to issue a writ. To our surprise they immediately started talking terms. The sum they finally agreed to hand over was 'undisclosed', at their insistence, and was donated to Comic Relief. But they still maintained that the tips had *not* been stolen. As part of the settlement they issued the following statement. 'McDonald's steadfastly maintains any similarity between its commercials and any *Viz* Top Tips was not the result of copying.' That was, and remains, their final word on the matter. Mine is 'arse'.

Despite all the hoo-hah surrounding televised Top Tips we still managed to produce comics throughout 1996. And the latest celebrity to appear in our photo-love strips was the Princess of Wales. 'Princess of Hearts' was the life story of Diana, and rather than trouble Diana to pose for the pictures herself I put it all together using old photos out of magazines and books. We had the computer technology to do it properly but I preferred using scissors and glue as the resulting images always seemed much funnier. A couple of new cartoon characters had appeared on the scene, too. First there was 8 Ace, an alcoholic of Graham, Simon and Thorpy's invention, who was named after the notoriously cheap Ace lager brewed by the Federation Brewery in Gateshead. And shortly afterwards came Ravey Davey Gravy, also the work of Graham and Thorpy.

Ravey Davey Gravy generated a great deal of excitement at the time, in particular from John Brown. Sales of the comic had continued to decline, down another whopping 19 per cent, to a figure of 428,872 for the first six months of 1996. Even Graham had now accepted that something might be broken and in need of repair. We'd attempted to analyse the situation and the general conclusion we came to was that most of our characters had become old and dated, as had many of our references which remained firmly rooted in nostalgia and the 1970s. The feeling was that *Viz* was losing touch with the young generation and we needed new characters and material relevant to the 1990s. Then, in April 1996, along came Ravey Davey Gravy, a raver with a funny hat who danced to repetitive noises, like car alarms and road drills. John hailed Ravey Davey Gravy as the new messiah who would lead us back into seven-figure sales. But was this really a character that a new generation of ravers could identify with, or just a reactionary dig at dance music culture by a bunch of ageing old farts? Statistics suggested John's optimism was justified. For the last three years sales had been falling sharply, but in the second half of 1996 they actually went up, albeit by only 2,532 to a new figure of 431,404. Had we finally pulled out of our nose dive?

Ravey Davey Gravey

During the summer of 1996 John came up to my house in Northumberland to talk about the future and we went for our obligatory long walk. John very generously bought me an expensive pair of walking boots and we set off together up the College Valley, a remarkably peaceful and unspoilt little corner of Northumberland. Having spent almost his entire life in central London John found open spaces hugely appealing – he'd have been happy walking around all day in a B&Q car park. As we walked, with John inevitably setting a hurried pace and me struggling to keep up, we agreed that it was time for me to step down as editor. We'd agreed this several times before but nothing had happened. This time John seemed prepared to let me go.

I would have broached the subject with all the others, but only Thorpy and Graham were in the country at the time. Simon had just shot off to France on holiday, unannounced, despite the fact that his soon-to-be-published book, *The Joy of Sexism*, hadn't been started yet. Thorpy and Graham didn't raise any strong objections to the idea of my leaving, and John taking over as their employer, but they didn't seem particularly enthusiastic either. Perhaps the prospect of working directly for John didn't appeal.

I'd been making noises about leaving the comic for several years and now that I finally had a finishing date – 31 November 1996 – I promptly did a U-turn and announced that I'd be staying on for another three years. Ostensibly the reason I changed my mind was that I wanted to score a century. I think it was Thorpy who did the maths, pointing out that our 100th issue would be the first comic of the next millennium, in February 2000. That would be quite an occasion, and the perfect point at which to quit, I thought. I would also be able to complete my ton and walk back to the pavilion, bat held aloft, raising my cap to the applause. That's what I thought anyway.

Late one night in 1996 I arrived home from work tired and in a bad mood to be greeted by the shock news that Dolores and I were expecting another baby. The imminent arrival of our third child meant we would have to move house – our railway station only had three small bedrooms and there was no scope for gracefully extending it. At the time I was already in the process of converting a twenty-seven-bedroom hotel in Northumberland into a block of flats, as well as trying to run my restaurant. My life was in a bit of turmoil.

Heatherlea, a four-storey hotel in the middle of the small Northumbrian village of Allendale, had been my Utopia as a very young child. It belonged to Uncle Tommy, my mother's cousin, and our family went there for holidays and day trips throughout the 1960s. I loved the place. It had a billiards room where I first picked up a cue, a putting lawn, a table tennis room and a sun lounge that was always full of old ladies. There were huge corridors to run along, lounges to play in, and – one of the main attractions – Aunty Margaret's meringues at tea-time. The hotel's reputation had been built largely on the consistency of these meringues, and regular, returning guests stood the business in good stead throughout the 1960s, despite the increasing trend towards Spanish beach holidays. But as those regular guests eventually died – quite often on the premises – so did the business. The hotel closed down and was put up for sale in 1992.

I was very tempted to buy it but I didn't. 'Never invest in property for sentimental reasons.' These weren't the words of my sage-like accountant. They were a lesson I'd learnt, indirectly, from Errol Brown, the singer out of Hot Chocolate. On my first-ever trip to London, for the *Something Else* TV programme in 1981, someone had mentioned that Errol Brown grew up in the house next door to the BBC Community Programme Unit's offices, and when he'd made a bit of money he'd bought his old house for sentimental reasons. But Errol Brown had later come to regret it, and I made a mental note never to make the same mistake myself. Unfortunately, by 1996 I'd lost that note and I bought the crumbling hotel – all four floors and twenty-seven bedrooms of it – for £85,000. My building surveyor concluded his damning report by describing the hotel as a 'gigantic white elephant', but it still seemed like a bargain to me.

For a while I considered reopening it as a hotel. It was in a terrible state, riddled with dry rot, and located well off the beaten tourist track. But it did have one thing going for it – my blind optimism. Mr Thornton, my accountant, sighed in desperation and said that opening a restaurant was a potential mistake, but opening a hotel would be a potential disaster. Financially speaking I'd be better off producing a *Viz* musical on the West End stage. Fortunately I saw sense and decided not to reopen the hotel. Instead I embarked on a scheme to save Heatherlea by converting it into a block of flats. This property-developing lark kept me away from the *Viz* office for long periods of time, as did my restaurant.

Business at the restaurant had been better than expected, and in our first year we'd had sales of £156,000, way above my projected figure of nil. We'd even won an award, but not from Egon Ronay. It was from Ian Allan. In 1996 I was invited to the Royal Institute of British Architects in London to collect the Ian Allan National Railway Heritage Award for the 'restoration and sympathetic conversion' of the building. But while the building itself was winning awards, inside it things weren't going entirely according to plan. Dining out in my own restaurant was not how I'd imagined it. When I took the family there I could never relax and enjoy myself. I was too worried about the food and the service and constantly looking about to see if all the customers looked happy. I worried about little things that I thought were important, and both Dolores and I constantly complained if things weren't right. Maddie, my manageress, got fed up with our persistent nagging and resigned. Her partner remained in charge of the kitchen, where a power struggle developed between him and the shotgun-wielding second chef. An impossible uncooperative chefs situation developed so I paid off the first chef and put the second chef in charge. Then the new first chef walked out when he found his partner, my new manageress, in bed with his brother, the recently appointed kitchen porter. Rather than too many cooks, all of a sudden I had no cooks at all.

Finding good, hard-working, reliable, low-paid staff in the middle of nowhere – and keeping them – isn't easy. I managed to locate another chef but he turned up to the job interview with a list of twenty-one dates that he couldn't work because he also ran a mobile disco. I took him on anyway. In the light of all these complications in our second year trade at the restaurant was well down on the first.

John Brown was sticking to publishing. He was investing his profits in a variety of new magazines. Following his early rash of unsuccessful titles, in November 1991 John won a prestigious contract to publish an in-flight magazine for the Soviet national airline Aeroflot. Alas, John's groundbreaking, glasnostic publishing deal went up in smoke a month later when the USSR – and Aeroflot with it – ceased to exist. At the *Viz* office we all laughed at John's rotten luck/judgement. As our sales fell, so John would lavish more care and investment on his new titles, and we held the lot of them in unsporting contempt. They were like newly arrived step-brothers and sisters to us, and we didn't get on with them at all.

In the summer of 1993 John launched a big-budget, up-market gardening magazine called *Gardens Illustrated*. It was more of a horticultural style magazine than a practical aid for gardeners, and we were particularly spiteful about it because we knew that John's wife Claudia – the grandly titled 'Art Editor' of the magazine – had only recently taken up gardening. It looked to us as if this new magazine, aimed very much at the toff end of the market, was an expensive plaything for John's wife. Somebody else obviously felt the same way because in June 1993 a spoof advert appeared in *Private Eye* for a new gardening magazine called *Sod*. The *Private Eye* joke implied that John was using manure produced by '*Wiz*' to fertilize his haughty new title, and that the new magazine was being published primarily to satisfy Claudia's whim. We weren't responsible for that caustic piece of satire but we wished we had been. In my excitement I hastily wrote a letter to Ian Hislop, ostensibly defending John Brown, but in fact sticking a blatant boot into both him and his wife. *Private Eye* printed it:

Dear Mr Hislop

I was appalled to read in the latest issue of your flagging organ a despicable 'spoof' advertisement for a gardening magazine called *Sod*. This was clearly a pastiche of the similarly titled *Gardens Illustrated* published by Mr John Brown.

The innocent victim of your public-school sarcasm was Mr Brown's talented wife, one of the most gifted Art

Editors in the field of glossy, expensive gardening magazines. To suggest that Mrs Brown's appointment was in any way connected with her being the Publisher's wife is both ludicrous and unfounded. As anyone connected with John Brown Publishing would tell you, Mrs Brown had been keenly interested in gardening for at least three weeks before her husband handed her this gardening magazine on a plate.

Furthermore I refute your suggestion that the magazine was founded on the proceeds of *Wiz*. As anyone connected with John Brown Publishing who values their job will tell you, *Wiz* is only one of a highly valued stable of best-selling magazines belonging to Mr Brown. Others include *Sticky Wicket* (1988–89), the comedy cricket magazine for friends of John Brown, *Electric Soup* (1990–92), the Scottish adult humour comic and best-selling rival to *Wiz*, and *Aeroflop* (1991–91), the Russian state airline's in-flight magazine, bought by Mr Brown the day before the collapse of the Soviet Union.

You have gone too far this time. I will this afternoon be taking out a subscription, and cancelling it by return of post.

The Editors, *Wiz* magazine

A day after faxing the letter I felt a twinge of guilt. I didn't know Claudia particularly well. To be honest she'd always seemed a bit off-ish with me, and I had noticed the uncanny regularity with which she would be otherwise engaged if John was ever taking Dolores and me out for a meal in London. But I didn't want to cause any ructions in John's marriage. It was too late to stop the letter being published so instead I tipped John off about it, apologized in advance, and gave him the chance to lock Claudia in a wardrobe for a fortnight to prevent her from seeing *Private Eye*. John took it all in good spirit. His reply was also published in *Private Eye*:

Dear Sirs
With reference to the letter in your last issue. Fuck off
the lot of you.
Yours truly,
John Brown

Gardens Illustrated gradually took over from the heavily listing *Viz*
as John Brown's flagship magazine, and John's company continued to expand. In March 1996 he announced the appointment of a new director called Peter Norris. Norris was an old
friend of John's who'd been out of work since his previous
company, Barings Bank, had collapsed. Yes, Peter Norris had
been the chief executive of Barings and the man personally
responsible for employing rogue trader Nick Leeson. John
giggled like a schoolboy when he told me this on the phone. He
thought the appointment was rather witty.

A couple of days later a synopsis for another new John Brown
magazine landed on my desk. It described a dreadful, down-
market glossy for ghouls and weirdos called *Bizarre* – a sort of
cross between *Loaded* and *Mortician's Monthly* – which would be
full of tasteless features and graphic images of death, sex and
tattooed penises. Among the proposed features was a 'Top Ten
Serial Murders League'. I was actually reading this proposal
when news of the Dunblane massacre came on the radio, and I
asked John whether the Dunblane shootings might qualify for a
future edition of his entertaining new magazine. It may sound
like a case of the kettle calling the pot black, but I thought *Bizarre*
was a tasteless, vulgar idea. But it wasn't just the voyeuristic,
pervy nature of the magazine that annoyed me, it was the crass
and calculated way John was planning it, using market demo-
graphics and all that bollocks to identify a market and tailor a
product to it. If John had no scruples and just wanted to make
money I'd given him the perfect idea for that years ago. He once
asked me, when *Viz* was first starting to wilt, how he was going
to make his next fortune. I told him the best way would be to

publish an honest pornographic magazine. No features about motorbikes, just tasteful photography. And no ridiculous, made-up quotes from the models about their hobbies and love of animals. Just practical advice on how to wank. Remove the stigma from dirty magazines, I said. Make them clean, legitimate, acceptable purchases, like pile ointment and condoms. Design them to resemble pharmaceutical packaging, using whites and blues and clean, antiseptic typefaces like Optima. Don't try and disguise it as glamour. Market porn as a medical aid and you'd make millions. 'You're right,' said John. 'But Claudia wouldn't stand for it.'

Sid the Sexist's *The Joy of Sexism* book (or *Sid the Sexist Behaving Badly*, as John had originally called it) had been completed in a matter of weeks thanks to Graham and Thorpy helping Simon out with the project. This was the year's most notable book offering and so it was decided, by whom I don't recall, to stage a sexist 'lads' night in' to publicize its launch. Instead of the usual champagne reception and posh buffet we'd invite members of the press to join us on the settee for a few beers and a fish supper, while we watched football and a blue movie on TV.

Arrangements for this dubious event were put in the hands of our publicity maestro Eugen Beer, and I think it would be fair to say that on this occasion he failed to fully grasp the concept. He booked an attic room at the exclusive Soho House, a more voguish version of the Groucho Club, where extremely posh-looking sofas were set up facing a small television screen. As the invited members of the press arrived they were served bottles of chilled Budvar lager, not cans of beer as we'd requested. Worst of all, when the fish and chip supper arrived, delivered to the room by uniformed waiters, it was *nouvelle cuisine*, served in the centre of enormous dinner plates and accompanied by decoratively carved slices of fresh lemon. We'd assumed it would come wrapped up in newspaper. It was a pretty bad idea to start with, but by now it had turned into an embarrassing fiasco. In front of the handful of journalists who'd bothered to attend a row broke out between ourselves, Eugen and the waiters. And as this embarrassing scene unfolded another embarrassing scene – from *Confessions of an Odd Job Man* – flickered away on the TV screen. Two female reporters didn't hang around to watch Robin Askwith in action, they just turned heel and left. Shortly afterwards so did we, escaping to a nearby pub. John Brown had made his excuses and left very early on, and so a rather rattled Eugen was left to launch the book himself.

CHAPTER TWENTY-TWO

Funnier than Petrol

Towards the end of 1996 I finally gave in to pressure from John and offered Davey Jones a job as a full-time cartoonist. I was concerned that working in the studio from nine till five might sap his enthusiasm, but I needn't have worried. Jonesy had no discernible enthusiasm to sap. What made him tick was a complete mystery to me. At script meetings he'd sit in total silence. He may have contributed little in the form of speech, but his presence was still valuable. Getting Jonesy to laugh became my prime objective when we were writing. I knew the others too well by now. I knew what they would say and when they would laugh. But getting Jonesy to laugh was a new and exciting challenge. It was also quite difficult and if you did get him guffawing you knew you were on to something good. Thankfully Jonesy continued to keep his own cartoons to himself. He wrote on his own, in his head, often sitting in silence over a blank piece of paper for hours at a time, occasionally doodling something in pencil, or stopping and strolling outside for a roll-up cigarette. When he did leave the room the rest of us would scamper across to his drawing board like excited children to see what he'd done so far. The thrill of opening up a postal tube and seeing his finished cartoons for the first time had gone, but now we could watch his masterpieces slowly emerge from the paper. Masterpieces like 'Arse Farm', a Blyton-esque adventure set on a traditional Sussex farm where arses grew in the fields.

Davey Jones

As *Viz* had gradually faded out of fashion I'd harboured a hope that one day our time would come again, like Mini cars and Tony Blackburn. At the start of 1997 things were looking good. A trendy young man with a shaven head came knocking at our door and said he wanted to make a documentary about *Viz* for BBC Radio 1. All of a sudden young, fashionable people were showing an interest again. But that feeling of being back in the ascendancy was swept away shortly afterwards when *Viz* received a glowing commendation in the *Evening Standard*, written by former *Sunday Telegraph* editor Sir Peregrine Worsthorne. 'Oh shit!' I thought. If there was one thing we didn't need as we battled to become hip again, it was Sir Peregrine fucking Worsthorne praising us in his newspaper column.

Sir Peregrine had read *Viz* for the first time after visiting my restaurant with his wife Lucinda Lambton, the scatty-but-nice aristocratic TV architecture buff. Darling Perry had been so impressed he was now recommending both the comic and my restaurant to his readers. I very much appreciated his kind remarks about the restaurant, but unfortunately a good review in the *Evening Standard* wasn't going to do much to help the quiet January trade in a restaurant 350 miles from London.

Our new-found optimism for *Viz* wasn't being matched down in London. As *Gardens Illustrated* continued to bloom and grow, and the launch issue of *Bizarre* hit the newsstands in a blaze of publicity, John was spending less and less time and money on *Viz*. Promotional ideas were still being tried to bolster sales, but nothing on the scale of our radio advertising campaign. We tried point-of-sale prompts, like adverts on the back of petrol pump nozzles which said: '*Viz* – Funnier than petrol. Just.' There was no immediate effect on sales. Then in the spring of 1997 we tried illegal flyposting, the very same technique that Jim and I had used way back in 1979 to spread word of our first issue. This time the flyposting was to be on a much grander scale, with city centres across the UK being targeted by vanloads of fly-by-night poster gangs. John asked me to come up with a suitable poster design. For several months a set of bizarre 1960s pornographic magazines had been floating around the studio. They weren't so much soft porn as ridiculous porn. Photographs of a fully dressed woman answering a telephone, for example; a woman in her underwear vacuuming the carpet; and a woman wrapped up in a fur hat and coat warming her bum in front of a period 1960s gas fire. I'd been using some of these images on the subscriptions and back issues ads in the magazine, adding speech balloons and text, and I decided to extend this house style to the fly posters.

The campaign began in June 1997, and on the 17th day of that month an outraged resident of the Borough of Kensington wrote the following letter to the Prime Minister Tony Blair:

Dear Prime Minister

I would like to draw your attention to an advertisement for *Viz* magazine that has been posted in the London area this past month. The bright yellow advertisement posters, which have been posted illegally on signs and walls, display a woman with her naked posterior tilted upwards in a suggestive position. The caption at the bottom of the poster reads '*Viz* – the magazine this woman's arse is talking about'.

I am appalled that a country that prides itself on refinement, education, and respect towards women turns a blind eye to such vulgarity ... There is something awry in the community if these advertisements are allowed to appear. It is surely the duty of all of us, and in particular our leaders, to ensure that such vulgar influences are not permitted to spread. I would be grateful if you could take some action post-haste.

> Yours faithfully
> Ms E. J.
> London SW1

The outraged woman's description didn't really do justice to the poster. Crucially, she'd neglected to mention that there was a speech balloon coming out of the woman's arse, which read, 'Have you seen the latest *Viz*? Very funny. Made *me* laugh anyway.'

As well as writing to the Prime Minister, Ms E. J. copied her letter to me, to *The Times* and to the Kensington MP Alan Clarke (although I doubt Clarke would have been much help – he'd previously pronounced *Viz* one of his favourite magazines). The posters were certainly being noticed but, as in 1979, the most conspicuous effect of the campaign was to annoy the authorities. In 1979 Jim and I had been chased out of the Polytechnic Students' Union building by an irate entertainments officer. Eighteen years later John and I were being threatened with legal action by Westminster, Bristol, Southampton and Birmingham city councils. So the outraged residents of Kensington got their way and the short-lived campaign was aborted.

That woman's arse wasn't the only thing causing offence at the time. SmithKline Beecham had decided to enrol the services of our Fat Slags to promote their Lucozade Low Calorie drink in a high-profile TV advertising campaign. When the offer came along John and I hadn't thought about it for very long before accepting. For my part I wasn't being *entirely* mercenary and hypocritical in taking the advertiser's money. I saw the Fat Slags as has-beens, faded stars that I was happy to sell on for a fat fee to anyone daft enough to want them. Like a football manager I was planning to invest the money in a spot of team rebuilding. Funnily enough, Alan Shearer was simultaneously being signed up to promote another Lucozade drink as part of the same campaign. 'To perform at my best I need to stay hydrated. That's why I drink Lucozade Sport before, during and after training sessions and games,' said Shearer vapidly. The Slags' performance was far more animated. 'Get it out of our fridge!' they yelled after finding a bottle of Low Calorie Lucozade nestling between their cream cakes and lard. Despite his flat performance I suspect Shearer was paid a much fatter fee than Sandra and Tracey.

The Slags' appearance in the TV commercial caused disgruntlement in the office, where Graham and Thorpy viewed them as their babies and were unhappy that John and I were now pimping them to ad agencies on the streets of Soho. There was also disgruntlement from TV viewers, 309 of whom complained to the Independent Television Commission about the use of the caption 'Oh mercy! It's the Fat Slags' on daytime television. It was a record – the highest number of complaints received by any TV advertisement that year. By comparison the notorious Impulse body spray ad, which featured the emergence of an erection in a gentleman's trousers, polled a miserable forty complaints. Most complaints about the Lucozade ad were from parents whose young children had started to adopt the phrase 'Fat Slag' in pre-watershed conversation, although there were also complaints about the 'negative, stereotypical portrayal of the overweight', as you might expect. The ITC overruled the moaning fatties, but agreed that the word 'slag' was inappropriate and banned the advertisement. It later returned to the screens with the introductory caption changed to 'Oh mercy! It's Sandra and Tracey'.

The ITC's ruling was widely reported in the press and a *Guardian* writer called Katharine Viner took the opportunity to launch a feminist offensive on *Viz*. 'For the first time the men behind the Fat Slags have got their comeuppance,' she began with relish. The general gist of her whine was that for eighteen years people had been reluctant to criticize *Viz*. 'We are simply not supposed to object to *Viz*, because if we do, we clearly don't get the joke. It's the same old story – it's ironic, it's satire, stop being humourless and live with it. But by accepting the irony, we are also accepting the premise on which the Fat Slags is founded: that women who enjoy sex are slags, that "slag" is an acceptable term to describe a woman, that women who are fat and enjoy sex are disgusting.' And so she went on. Speaking of irony, by celebrating the Fat Slags' demise Ms Viner was in fact single-handedly responsible for their rejuvenation. If she'd kept her gob shut I doubt whether they would ever have appeared in *Viz* again. Although she described them as 'the most prized characters in *Viz*', at the time of the ad campaign they hadn't made an appearance in the comic for over a year. I was sick of them. But as a direct response to the *Guardian* article they were instantly resurrected in the following issue, and on the cover Millie Tant took a page out of Ms Viner's book, accusing San and Tray of being traitors to the female sex. 'How dare you appear on the cover of this degrading, stoutist magazine, allowing infantile, phallocratic men-monsters to put lesbopohobic words into your mouths, thinly veiled as irony, in order to get a cheap laugh at the expense of wimminkind?' she raged. 'Hey! Watch it, San. That fat fanny nosher's after your chips,' was Tracey's response.

Unaware of the impending tragic death of Princess Diana in a Paris underpass later that month, on the cover of our August 1997 issue I put the words 'Your chance to romp with a naked Princess Di!' in large red letters across the bottom of the page. There was no reference to her inside the magazine, it just seemed like a good line at the time. Diana had featured heavily in recent issues, though, and on the cover of the June issue I'd made a gruesome composite of her as Frankenstein's monster, with the words 'Frankenstein Must Di!' plastered across it. After her death one anonymous reader cut the image out and sent it to me with a note blaming me for the tragedy.

September 1997 was a strange month. Large elements of the press contracted People's Hysteria. Even John Brown was forced to join in when grieving distributors forced him to withdraw the remaining copies of our August issue from sale and reprint them minus the offending cover slogan. I couldn't believe the hoo-hah that was going on in the press, the outpouring of emotion, the tacky poems and the vitriol that was being aimed at anyone appearing to be insufficiently grief-stricken. Diana had died and it was a tragedy, fair enough. But it seemed that every *Sun* reader in the country had suddenly adopted her death as their reason for living, and the papers were full of irrational, sentimental shit. I wanted to write something about it but the mood in the office was one of caution. There was a genuine feeling that if you wrote the wrong thing there'd be a people's lynch mob at the door. So we went for subtlety and wrote a story about an unprecedented display of people power that had been shown for Mickey Dolenz out of the Monkees, despite the fact that he wasn't dead. 'Tributes pour in for the People's Monkee,' said the headline. The story claimed that as a tribute to Mickey Dolenz, a sea of bananas had been laid at the gates of the Hollywood TV studios where the Monkees was filmed. And it ended up criticizing other members of the Monkees, accusing them of being out of touch with public opinion. There was also a Book of Mickeydolences for people to sign.

On the cover of our Christmas 1997 issue we gave away a free pocket-sized, thirty-two-page swearing dictionary called *Roger's Profanisaurus*. In the beginning cover-mounts had been a joke, like the balloon stapled to the cover of issue 2, but now they were serious. We were just another title on the newsagent's shelf desperately struggling to catch the consumer's eye. Having said that, the *Profanisaurus* was a bloody good free gift.

Roger's Profanisaurus evolved out of *Sweary Mary's Swearing Dictionary*, an interactive catalogue of rude words and their definitions which had instantly become the most popular feature on our recently established website. This lewd lexicon grew rapidly in size and it soon became obvious that there was the potential for a book in it. The cover-mount was a taster for a full-size paperback swearing dictionary that I was hoping to have finished in time for publication in 1998.

While I sat and typed wordy definitions to phrases like 'fanny batter' the others continued to churn out cartoons, rarely with any assistance from me. There'd been little in the way of new characters for some time, but there were still the odd flashes of brilliance. Graham and Thorpy's version of Auden's 'The Night Train', starring Postman Plod, for example. In September 1996 Jim Brownlow wandered into the office with a brand new Paul Whicker strip, the first in years. And twelve months later he wandered in again with another one. During one of those two visits I raised the possibility of Jim working with us full time, but he wasn't interested. His attitude had never changed. He drew cartoons when he felt like it. It was as if he'd known all along that drawing them as a full-time job would spoil the fun. It certainly had done for me.

By the end of 1997 our sales were down around 75,000 from the previous year to 356,005. News from my restaurant wasn't exactly cheering either. A poor second year had prompted me to make drastic changes in staff and opening hours. But as our third year drew to a close there were no signs of improvement and I was having to pay the VAT bills out of my own pocket in order to keep the business afloat. I deliberately avoided thinking about how much it had cost me in total to set the place up, but my accountant was always on hand to remind me. For the same money I could have had my pick of England centre-forwards in the mid-1970s. By opening that restaurant I'd been living a dream, but now I was waking up with stomach pains, vomiting and diarrhoea. I had no choice but to swallow my pride, kiss the vast majority of my investment goodbye, and close the Station House Restaurant down. One grey October morning in 1997 I called in on my way to work, took a deep breath, and broke the news to the remaining staff.

In May of that year Dolores had given birth to our third child, Josey, a baby boy, and we were also in the process of moving house. I'd hoped a change of house, like our changes of office, might help rejuvenate me a bit. My bi-monthly 'publishing cycle' moods had developed into almost constant depression. Since the AppleMacs had arrived in the studio, and the Cow Gum fumes had gone, the length of the exciting deadline spells had been compacted down into less than a week. My highs were getting shorter and my lows were getting longer and deeper. By now I'd virtually given up drawing cartoons. I'd relinquished my last character, my beloved Roger Mellie, to Graham (although I always insisted on checking the pencil drawing with a ruler before Graham inked it, to make sure he wasn't drawing Roger's legs too long, or his shoes too big).

At the start of 1998, John demonstrated his diminishing faith in our ability by commissioning an independent marketing company to come up with a strategy to promote *Viz* in the coming year. Their plan revolved largely around the World Cup finals in France. John was kind enough to send a copy to me for my comments.

The main thrust of their plan was that *Viz* would be the self-declared 'unofficial sponsors' of the England football team for the World Cup finals in France. As part of the build-up we'd pay Premier League players £500 to wear *Viz* T-shirts under their strips and reveal them to the cameras when they scored. These T-shirts would have the words 'Oi, Hoddle, what d'ya think of that?!' written on them. We would have *Viz* logos printed on the buses, trains and planes taking fans to the games. We'd make inflatable *Viz* characters. We'd produce a *Viz* football record. We'd also produce a *World Cup Handbook* that would include a piss-taking guide to French public lavatories, 'something about

French letters', and a 'Fat Slags' handy guide to using a baguette'. Another of their ideas was that we could sponsor the physio's sponge and bucket during England games, despite the fact that no physio had carried a bucket and sponge onto a football pitch for decades. And finally – the *pièce de résistance* of this promotional plan – we would sponsor the English football 'yobs' in France and get them to wear our T-shirts.

I was dumbstruck by the sheer stupidity of it. The words 'FUCK OFF' that I scrawled in big red letters across the front of the document before sending it back to John didn't even begin to express my anger and resentment at the fact that he had, without consulting me, paid some outside agency to come up with fuck-witted ideas for *Viz* – not just crass and idiotic marketing ideas, but ideas that encroached into our editorial space. This was the most annoying thing John had done since a recent suggestion that we should invite 'focus groups' of readers to tell us where the comic was going wrong.

John had lost touch. Since 1997 he'd been delegating more and more of his responsibility for the comic to his minions and his marketing men. He'd lost faith in *Viz*, lost interest in it. It was broken and he couldn't fix it, so he had nothing to lose by allowing other people to try. He sent his minions up to Newcastle for marketing meetings. One of them, in all seriousness, suggested we get McDonald's to sponsor Billy the Fish. Then one of John's people, called Andrew, who wore a suit but whose job was always something of a mystery to me, turned up at our Newcastle office and started suggesting ideas for cartoon characters.

John himself was becoming physically as well as psychologically detached from the running of the magazine. In 1998 he moved from the Boathouse in Fulham into a swish, refurbished, multi-million pound office block in Hammersmith, complete with staff restaurant, cinema and IT department. John ensconced himself in a luxurious penthouse suite surrounded by executive gadgets, publishing awards, paintings and framed mementoes. One of these mementoes was the battered Virgin pocket calculator he'd brought with him to Lily Crescent thirteen years ago. I'd sent it to him as a souvenir in our heyday and he'd had it framed. Below John's sumptuous penthouse were several layers of beautifully lit and furnished open-plan office space, the floors filling up one at a time as John's business expanded at a dazzling pace. Ten years earlier Ann used to come into our studio and tell us to guess the latest incredible *Viz* print run. Now the same thing was happening with the number of John's employees. One day he'd have 106, the next it would be 112, then it was up to 120. He called his new building the New Boathouse and unlike the old Boathouse this one enjoyed a very impressive view – of the A40(M).

On my first trip to London since his move I walked into the building's swish reception area and asked to see John. 'What's your name, please?' asked the receptionist. His company had grown so fast I hardly knew any of the staff, and they didn't know me. I was asked to take a seat alongside various couriers, reps and stationery salesmen, and wait until John was free.

I considered storming out of the enormous glass door in a fit of petulance, but decided to stay and flick through a magazine instead. The vast reception hall had all of John's dozen or so titles displayed in arty, modernist racks along the walls. *Viz* was still up there, but not nearly as prominently displayed as his latest signing, *Waitrose Food Illustrated*.

CHAPTER TWENTY-THREE

The Case of the Flying Bin Liner

In special recognition of my lofty achievements in the field of lavatory humour, in 1998 I was afforded the great honour of an appearance on *Through the Keyhole*.

By this late stage in the programme's history the once-popular celebrity home intrusion game show had been relegated to a miserable slot on daytime TV, and judging by the fact that I had been invited to appear they were clearly struggling to find co-operative celebrity homeowners. It seemed like the last programme on Earth I would want to have anything to do with, but I agreed to it out of curiosity.

I was determined not to punch Loyd Grossman in the face when he came calling at our new house. Watching him on TV I'd always found his accent and his manner unbearable and I was worried that instinct might get the better of me when I came into personal contact with him. My black moods and bad temper could descend like a fog at any time. Grossman arrived early in a chauffer-driven Daimler that had picked him up at Newcastle Airport, and breezed into the house like a pompous member of royalty. My wife offered him a bowl of her home-made potato and sweetcorn soup. 'Euuuur neeuuughh!' he said, striking a chord of perfect disdain with two highly affected syllables. The

TV crew and all their equipment arrived half an hour later, crammed uncomfortably into a people-carrier. They'd driven all the way up from Leeds.

As Grossman went through the rooms filming, it became clear that he didn't have many close friends among the crew. He liked our sitting room, though, suggesting that the décor had been inspired by Lutyens, and he filmed in the bathroom too. The clues to my identity that he focused on were some Tintin books in the sitting room ('Peurr-hepps he's the sord of person who *draws* inspiration from these cartooooons for his work?') and of course the lavatory where he suggested I might spend a lot of my time thinking up ideas. But neither these, nor several other less subtle clues, were any use to the celebrity panel whose job it was to identify me.

When Dolores and I went down to Leeds to film the studio segment of the show we were put in a huge, hangar-sized green room packed with celebrities, all of whom were there for the same reason. Yorkshire TV were making something like 144 episodes of the show all in one day, so not only was there a sea of celebrity homeowners all waiting for their numbers to be called, next door was a dressing room jam-packed with about two dozen low-grade celebrity panellists. There was a conveyor belt of homeowners making their way into the studio, and every hour or so they'd swap the panel to give them a break and allow them to change their shirts ready for their next stint.

Sitting next to us in the green room was the young Irish snooker player Ken Doherty. To make polite conversation I asked him if he'd had a good season. 'I won the World Championship,' he said. 'Oh, good,' I said. I hadn't watched much snooker lately. Opposite us, at the other side of the table, was a gaggle of rather quaint-looking elderly people, the sort of old people who used to stay at my Uncle Tommy's hotel in the 1960s. One of the gentlemen introduced himself as Tom Finney, and explained that his wife and their friends had come along to enjoy a day out in Leeds. They asked us if we fancied coming along to Betty's Tea Rooms for a wrap party after the show.

By the time our house came up, the much-shuffled celebrity panel consisted of Les Dennis, Anna Walker from Sky Sports and cartoonist Bill Tidy. Bill Tidy had presumably been hand-picked as he was the only person in the celebrity pool likely to know who I was. After they'd seen the house and heard the clues there was an embarrassing session of prompts and further clues during which it was virtually spelled out to them that I was the editor of *Viz*. It still didn't help. None of them knew my name, although Bill Tidy had it on the tip of his tongue. 'Is it a colour?' he said. 'Is it … Brown?' He was thinking of John, whom he'd once met. Eventually they were put out of their misery and I was led out to shake their hands. Poor Anna Walker still hadn't got a clue who I was, and neither had the show's host, Sir David Frost, whose job it now was to interview me.

I don't know how many celebrity homeowners had passed him on the conveyor belt that day but by this stage he'd given up even feigning interest. There was a lull in our embarrassing chat, at which point he looked down at his notes. 'And erm … you live in a railway station, don't you?' he said. I couldn't believe what a stupid question that was. Everyone else in the studio had just seen a film of my new house and it was obvious to anyone who'd ever caught a train that it was not, and had never been, a railway station. I didn't know what to say, so I just smiled and said, 'Yes'.

An altogether more prestigious TV show was *Have I Got News for You*, and it was Eugen Beer's long-standing ambition to get me on it. I didn't particularly want to be on it, but in PR terms it would have been a feather in Eugen's cap. The closest he came was getting me on a pilot for a show called *Bygones* – a sort of cross between *Have I Got News for You* and the *Antiques Roadshow* – which was filmed at Tyne-Tees in the mid-1990s. Before the recording the director, whose name escapes me, gave myself and the other bargain-bin celebs who'd agreed to take part a bit of a pep talk. 'Remember, think *Have I Got News for You!*' he said, clenching his non-clipboard hand into a fist. And that was it. I don't think I contributed a single word throughout the entire recording – possibly because I was too busy thinking *Have I Got News for You* to pay any attention to the questions. As far as I know *Bygones* was never commissioned.

Years later, in the spring of 1998, I got a phone call inviting me to appear on the real *Have I Got News for You*, but it didn't come through Eugen's office. The show's producers contacted me direct. Eugen was heartbroken. I didn't know whether to do it or not, so I talked it over with the others in the office. 'Don't be a fool!' was the general consensus. They reminded me of well-known cases where guests had gone on, tried to outwit the show's regular panellists and ended up being humiliated. Paula Yates and Ken Livingstone sprang readily to mind. We'd recently published a *Have I Got News for You* board game in which we'd accused both Ian Hislop and Angus Deayton of being smug, self-satisfied smart-arses, and I wondered whether they might be out for revenge. But I accepted the invitation, on the grounds that if I didn't I'd forever wonder what would have happened if I had done.

The show was recorded at the former London Weekend TV studios on the South Bank of the Thames – one of the little buildings John Sanders had pointed out to me from the top of King's Reach Tower fourteen years earlier. I took Dolores along and we were introduced to Angus Deayton and the other panellists over a meal in the canteen. The two teams sat on opposite sides of the dining table. Paul Merton was next to me, and alongside Ian Hislop was the fearsome feminist author, academic and broadcaster Germaine Greer. 'Oh dear,' I thought. But the atmosphere was very cordial. Germaine Greer seemed sedate and grandmotherly, nothing like an intellectual feminist firebrand. She looked more likely to get stuck into her knitting than me.

After the meal the two teams were left alone in their respective dressing rooms for what seemed like hours. Paul Merton and I were given a huge pile of newspapers to read, but

we both ignored them. I'd already read every national newspaper that had been published that week. As I'd read them I'd
tried to put myself in the show-writer's shoes. Which stories
were the most amusing or unusual? I'd made notes on things I
thought likely to crop up, and then revised these for days
beforehand. My game plan was simple. I wouldn't try to get into
any rallies with Hislop. You can't beat a good tennis player by
knocking the ball gently back across the net at him. Instead of
playing smart-arse tennis my aim was to win the quiz by getting
as many answers right as I could.

We often speculated in the *Viz* office about whether or not
Have I Got News for You was rigged, and we'd heard numerous
media rumours about the questions being leaked to guests
beforehand. But none of that turned out to be true. There was a
technical rehearsal where we all sat in our seats for a few
moments while people fiddled with lights and cameras, but no
questions were asked. When we returned to the studio an hour
or so later the audience was in place and the atmosphere was
highly charged. But, to my surprise, as the rounds unfolded
there was no hostility at all from the opposition. It was all very
amicable. My swotting up paid dividends and Paul and I won the
game at a canter. I think I got just about all of my questions
right, including one bonus question which was to name the new
star that astronomers had discovered earlier that week. I knew
the name – BMP37093 – off by heart. At that point Hislop asked
whether I was some sort of a train-spotter. That was about as
vicious as he got all night.

Over the summer of 1998 I'd buried myself in *Roger's
Profanisaurus*, the swearing dictionary we'd been planning for
Christmas 1998. On a bad day I could sit down and find none of
the entries remotely amusing. I'd tell John the whole project
was a waste of time. But on a good day I'd look at exactly the
same stuff and be overcome with enthusiasm. It was then I
realized that I'd become the Dr Jekyll and Mr Hyde of lavatory
humour, and Mr Hyde had been gradually taking over. Only by

being very busy could I avoid slipping into depression, so I took the book home and worked on it non-stop for weeks on end. The marketing men at Comag, who had taken over from Seymour as John Brown's main distributor, decided the name *Roger's Profanisaurus* wasn't suitable. They wanted to call it a *Swearosaurus*. Their argument was that some of our thicker readers wouldn't be familiar with the word 'profanity'. My argument was that if they didn't know what profanity was, then they wouldn't understand what 'osaurus' meant either, in which case they might think the book was about dinosaurs. My dinosaur argument won the day and the book remained *Roger's Profanisaurus*. Meanwhile the name for the 1998 annual was selected from a list of eighteen nominees, including; *The Hairy Pie, The Papal Plums, The Spam Sceptre, The Beef Curtains, The Pink Oboe, The Ham Shank, The Hand Shandy, The Bum Cigar, The Brown Trout, The Camel's Foot* and *The Hairy Arse*. We didn't bother asking anyone at Comag for their opinion. The final decision – to call it *On the Bone* – was influenced by events in the meat industry at the time.

Tragically, recent events in a Paris underpass had put a stop to the enjoyable task of assembling photo-stories using Princess Diana's image. These had made a refreshing change from the tired old teenage romance format that we'd been shagging to death for the last sixteen years. In that time photo-stories had come full circle. Originally I'd been taking the piss out of dated girlie magazines like *Jackie* and *Blue Jeans*. Our photo-stories then re-popularized the format and it started appearing in press advertising. Then the tabloids adopted the format to titillate their problem pages, getting models to illustrate marital problems, dressed only in bras and underpants. Then we started lampooning the tabloid problem page strips, by which time we were chasing our own tail.

In the summer of 1998, with the anniversary of Diana's death approaching, I had an idea for a new Diana photo-story. There was perhaps a way of getting round her tragic demise, and even using it to comic advantage. I suggested a story called 'Diana and Hopkirk Deceased', in which Diana's ghost, dressed in an all-white suit, is invisible to everyone except her former police bodyguard, Jack Randall. This light-hearted crime-fighting duo would be a partnership made in heaven. The immediate reaction in the office was howls of laughter, followed by sharp intakes of breath and some serious ooh-ing and aah-ing. It was borderline. For me getting that borderline reaction was like scoring 180 at darts. In comedy there is a line that you should never cross, but I think it was Peter Cook who said you should always aim to have one foot on the wrong side of it.

Graham was his usual over-cautious self. We'd be strung up if we did the story, he said. The press would crucify us. I wouldn't have minded that at all, but when the strip was published, in August 1998, only the moralistic *Sunday Sport* took offence, condemning it across their front page with an enormous headline 'DIANA GHOST JOKE FURY'. The fury to which the headline referred seemed to come entirely from one 'Blackpool-based computer engineer' whom they quoted: 'I've read *Viz* for years but they've gone too far this time,' he said.

I felt as if the comic had been improving in the last year or so, but this wasn't reflected in sales. During the first half of 1998 we'd lost another 44,000 readers. Like *Punch*, we were losing readers as they got older. Ours weren't dying, but they were falling by the wayside as their lifestyles and their outlook on life changed. To replace them we needed to attract youth. For years we'd been thinking the way to do this was with new cartoon characters, like Ravey Davey Gravy. But now we got to thinking that maybe it was new *cartoonists* we really needed.

One day a young sixth-form schoolboy named Alex Collier came to the office for a few days' work experience, and our eyes lit up. Alex was young, a local lad and a keen cartoonist who'd been producing his own comic at school. He jumped at our invitation to contribute to *Viz*, and his first effort was a strip called 'Kappa Slappa'.

Natasha Slappa was a 'charver' – a skulking, working-class teenager who chewed bubble gum, wore bright orange make-up, tacky track suits and big earrings. Young Alex knew all about charvers and the other social groupings and fashions of the day. He spoke in teenage tongues, and told of all the wondrous current street slang. Most of ours was twenty-five years out of date. As he sat in our kitchen we all gathered around Alex. 'Tell us more about the *young* people,' we said.

We loved his cartoon but 'Kappa Slappa' didn't go down very well in the offices of Kappa, the Italian sportswear manufacturer. In the second strip Alex drew, published in April 1998, Tasha's tracksuit was touched by a cigarette and instantly went up in smoke, so she went to steal a new one. A tiny sign on the clothes rack in the sports shop read 'Dayglo yellow jackets for teenage tarts and the colourblind'. Another, more significantly, read 'Please! No naked flames'. Unfortunately someone in Kappa's legal department owned a magnifying glass and interpreted this as an implication that Kappa tracksuits were highly flammable. When their legal letter arrived we all jumped into my car and headed straight for the nearest sports clothing warehouse to buy the cheapest, most flammable-looking item of Kappa sportswear we could find. Then, back in the office car park we frantically tried to ignite it with a cigarette lighter. The bloody thing wouldn't burn. The others made their way back to the office but I stayed and tried a few more times in desperation. It was no good. The bastard wouldn't burn.

I was already involved in another legal battle at the time – The Case of the Flying Bin Liner. It wasn't about anything we'd published. This was about a real black bin liner, full of scrap paper, that my office environment manager, a girl called Stevie, had dropped out of our first-floor kitchen window into the rubbish compound below. Unbeknown to Stevie, a cleaner from a neighbouring office was in the compound at the time. It was a dark winter evening and, according to the letter I received from the victim's solicitors, the shock of our black bag landing only inches away in the darkness caused her to jump up with a start, jerking her back and causing her a painful injury.

Her solicitors expected me to simply hand their claim over to my insurers so that a settlement could be negotiated. I was prepared to pay up eventually, but first I wanted to make them work for their money. So I wrote them a string of procrastinating letters, knowing that each one would eat up a little of their valuable time. Then I started making derisory offers of a cash settlement, knowing that every time I made an offer the solicitors would be obliged to relay it to their client. My offer had got up to around £200 when they stopped replying. I heard nothing more, and after a few months I forgot all about it. Months passed, and then years, and still I heard nothing. Then, completely out of the blue, in 1998 I received a writ. This was the first proper writ *Viz* had ever received, and it wasn't for a scurrilous libel or outrageous defamation. It was for a flying bin liner.

The cleaner's solicitors were demanding £5,000 in damages and costs. At this point I realized I was out of my depth. I should have referred it to my solicitor when I'd got their first letter three years ago. Then I remembered something. *Three years* ago. I'd once included a letter on our letters page from a reader pointing out how irresponsible Gerry and the Pacemakers had been for advising people to 'hold their head up high' when they walked through a storm, as doing so would surely increase the likelihood of their being struck by lightning. The correspondent wondered whether anyone struck by lightning in such circumstances could sue the singer, Gerry Marsden, for giving dangerous or inappropriate advice. A solicitor responded with a letter in the following issue saying that Gerry Marsden could not be held responsible if the victim had been struck by lightning more than three years ago, as three years was the time limit for making personal injury claims. I checked the date of the original letter about the flying bin liner and, sure enough, three years had elapsed.

My own solicitor confirmed that the claimant was out of time and, when the court case came up, it was a walkover. The case against me was thrown out. Meanwhile the Kappa Slappa case never got to court. John paid them off with a five-figure sum and promised not to imply that their clothing was highly flammable ever again. Thereafter Kappa Slappa was known by her Christian name.

Dolores often suggested I should seek medical help for my depression and moods, but she tended do this when I was least susceptible to that kind of delicate advice. 'What the fuck are you saying? That I'm mad?' I'd scream like a madman. I didn't even go to the doctor when I was properly ill, so the last thing I was going to do was walk into the surgery and say I'd gone mental. But in the winter of 1998 I hit an all-time low. I stayed off work and went for days without talking to Dolores or the children. I couldn't do anything. I couldn't make simple decisions. What to have for lunch, for example. My head would just go into a spin so I'd give up and go back to bed. If I did eventually get up again I'd spend the rest of the day slumped in a chair doing nothing. Not even thinking. I felt as if the fuses in my brain had all blown. Then I just stopped getting up. Eventually Dolores took it upon herself to call our GP and make an appointment.

Our GP happened to be a young and fairly attractive blonde woman, which made going to the doctor with a personal problem a lot more difficult. The only other time I'd been to see her was following my vasectomy, when I'd developed an infection and had to present my weepy, incommensurate knackers for an embarrassing inspection. This time Dolores came along and she did most of the talking. I just sat there in the corner demonstrating my melancholic symptoms as and when required. Depression was officially diagnosed and the GP's first instruction was that I should take at least six weeks off work. Then she referred me to a counsellor.

Dolores had already phoned John and told him that I

wouldn't be coming in to work for a while. Issue 93 was going to press at the time and it was going to be the first deadline I'd ever missed. I couldn't bear to think about it, so I didn't. Then one day in early December a large envelope came through the door. This was the first issue of *my* comic that had ever been produced without me. What would the cover be like? The letters pages? The news features? I couldn't bear to open it. A day or two later I plucked up my courage and was hugely relieved to see that issue 93 looked just like all the previous comics. The others had managed perfectly well without me.

My counsellor was an old-ish woman, a bit like TV's Dr Ruth, but without the funny accent or the fixation with sexual matters. Our sessions consisted of me sitting in a chair while she asked the odd question and then prompted me to analyse my reply at great length. It seemed like I was doing all the work. Over a period of weeks I sat there and unravelled my brain on her carpet while she nodded and smiled. Eventually the final part of the knot came undone. We'd reached the core of the problem. I didn't want to edit *Viz* any more, and hadn't for a long time. I was sick of it, but I was unable to distinguish between the comic and myself. *Viz* had become an integral part of my psyche. I wouldn't let it go because I didn't know what, if anything, would be left without it. And the upshot of it all, she explained, was that I'd gone bonkers.

I followed doctor's orders and stayed away from the *Viz* office for several weeks. Having played and missed on 93, and subsequently left the field for treatment, my century was looking increasingly unlikely. But John and the others were all keen for me to come back. They seemed to think that because my mental problems had come to a head I could now return as the cheerful, carefree Chris of old, and not the obstreperous git I'd become of late. I agreed that when I felt up to it I'd return, but only part time, in what might best be described as a *Dixon of Dock Green* role, until I completed my century. *Dixon of Dock Green* was a reference to Jack Warner's final series when a rather incontinent-looking PC Dixon, aged about ninety-six, returned to Dock Green police station in a purely static role simply to justify the use of his name in the title.

I returned to work in January 1999, and as I walked into the office Simon started to sing 'Welcome Home', Peters and Lee's 1973 chart topper, which was a nice touch. It was certainly nicer than the taunting, playground-style rendition of 'You've Had a Breakdown', accompanied by poking, which John sang when I first saw him again. Back in the office both the air and my head seemed to be a lot clearer, and I got straight back to work. With my eye once again on my century I judged the pace and length of issue 94 to perfection, turning on my back foot and despatching it effortlessly to the boundary. Another six issues – just one more year – and I would declare, having scored an unbeaten century. Little did I know I was going to be out to the very next ball.

CHAPTER TWENTY-FOUR

The Leaving of Fulchester

Since moving office in 1992 we'd tried various things to liven up the dreary surroundings of the carbuncular Crestina House. We shuffled rooms and moved desks and drawing boards around on an almost weekly basis. We knocked out walls and built new ones. We bought new furniture: tons of it. We bought office furniture like fatties buying chocolate, to cheer ourselves up.

We had a little rest room called the kitchen where we'd sit for hours on end, playing the *Viz* fruit machine, drinking coffee and looking through the day's newspapers. A visiting journalist said the room looked like 'a grotesque minicab office'. He was spot on. Following my abortive attempt to convert it into a Wild West saloon I'd decided to go up-market and replace the tatty, white, melamine cupboards and sink unit with some quality, light oak kitchen furniture. But it was all too much fuss so in the end I just got a brown felt-tip pen and drew some wood grain on the white cupboard doors.

By 1998 we'd given up our makeover efforts and were look-ing for new premises. A quick glance at our sales graph (we'd parted company with another 11,000 readers in the second half of 1998, leaving us with just over 300,000) told me we needed something perhaps a little bit smaller. I was also looking for a building with a bit of character, and some zest. By all accounts Newcastle was now a thriving party city and I felt it might help liven things up a bit if we came in from the cold, concrete suburb and boogied on down to the vibrant, buzzing city centre.

Towering above Dean Street and The Side, in the very heart of Newcastle, there is a gargantuan red-brick and sandstone building which has its ground floor virtually on the Quayside and its ornate dormers and attic windows peering down onto the deck of a passing railway viaduct. I used to gaze at those attic windows from the train in my anorak-and-flask days. I envied the people who worked behind them their marvellous view of the passing trains. I'd also marvelled at the architecture, the elaborate roof details, and the incredible foresight of the Edwardians who, in 1902, had somehow managed to name the building – Milburn House – in honour of a legendary Newcastle centre-forward of the 1950s. I made enquiries and found that one suite was currently available, and it was just the right size for us. Alas, when we got there I discovered that it wasn't perched high up in the sunlight on the south-facing side of the building, overlooking the railway and the castle. The vacant office was on the ground floor of the opposite side of the building, and the only view was of the dilapidated graveyard behind St Nicholas's Cathedral, now one of the party city's most popular unofficial public conveniences. It wasn't perfect, but I said we'd take it.

With a move in the offing, a new *young* contributor, and a belief that my bad moods had gone forever, there was an air of great optimism in the office. But I felt detached from it all. It seemed to me that they were being far too optimistic. At one meeting someone suggested doing a poster of John Inman on our website saying 'Are U.S. being served?' in order to promote comic sales in America. 'If *Are You Being Served* can be a hit in America, there's no reason why *Viz* can't,' went their enthusiastic argument. I could think of several reasons, but I kept my mouth shut. Then came the inevitable suggestion that *Viz* could be big in Japan. 'They love anything British over there,' said Simon. Minis, maybe. But *Viz*? Were they going mad? Or was I? Then I remembered, I already had done. And the only cure was to get away from the comic. So I walked out of the meeting in silence and drove home.

That was effectively the moment when I left, although I did limp in irregularly for a few months afterwards. I didn't receive a clock for my twenty years of service, I just got the loan of a fruit bowl for a year. In 1999 John Brown invited me to a posh dinner-do at the Grosvenor House Hotel in London where, in the same room ten years earlier, *Auto Express* had robbed us of the Biggest Circulation Increase award. This time he said I'd been nominated by the British Society of Magazine Editors for their Mark Boxer Award. This was a sort of 'lifetime achievement' award for editors. I'd been to plenty of awards ceremonies before and had always gone home empty handed. In 1989 at the star-studded North-East Personality of the Year Awards in Newcastle I'd been narrowly pipped at the post by Alan Plater for the title of Male North-East Personality of the Year. I'd made *Viz* into the third best-selling magazine in Britain that year, and Plater had written *Z Cars* in the 1960s. The judges were definitely bent that night. Female North-East Personality of the Year was Cockney actress Wendy Richard who, as hostess Angela Rippon had to explain to a baffled audience, was born in Redcar.

Ten years later I turned up at the Grosvenor House and was surprised to see my old mate Harry Enfield sitting at our table. I asked him what he was up to these days. 'I'm making a rubbish series for Sky – for the money,' he said as a joke, but meaning it. Lo and behold, Harry was there to present me with the Mark Boxer Award. I'd actually won it. It took a while to sink in, but afterwards, as Dolores and I staggered out of the hotel and into the taxi queue carrying the cumbersome, on-loan crystal fruit bowl, I began to reflect upon the significance of my victory. In particular on the fact that the award had been decided by a committee, and that one of John Brown's senior employees had been on that committee. Basically it was another fix, but this time I was the benefactor.

While I sat and admired my fruit bowl and contemplated a life without *Viz*, John Brown took over the running of the office from London, and started to take a more hands-on approach. One of his first moves was to give Alex Collier a full-time job. John asked his new gang of five – Simon, Graham, Thorpy, Jonesy and Alex – if any of them were interested in the editor's job, but their unanimous wish was that they should all be joint editors, a system that was already up and running. But John wasn't happy with that arrangement. He felt a committee would lack direction at a time when direction was urgently needed. Mind you, despite there only being one of him, John was un-deniably lacking a bit of direction himself, and once again he was looking to an outside source for guidance. This time he commissioned a strategic study of *Viz* from an independent publishing expert. John didn't know what to do with *Viz*, and he wanted an outsider's overview of the situation. The person he turned to for help was my old mate James Brown.

James Brown

It had been three years since John and I had bumped into James in Barbados, and in that time James had been very busy. He'd left *Loaded*, been controversially appointed as editor of *GQ*, even more controversially sacked as editor of *GQ* (for running a feature on the sartorial style of the Nazis), he'd declared himself a reformed alcoholic, and he was now in the process of setting up his own publishing company, I Feel Good PLC. James had also transformed himself from the fun-loving mischief-maker I knew into an ambitious businessman in a suit – a bit like a butterfly turning into a caterpillar – and he'd smooth-talked investors into financing his ambitious publishing plans. James used his CV – which had 'inventing laddism single-handed' at the top – to good effect, and he was viewed by many as a publishing prodigy and a genius. James wasn't the type to disagree with them.

When John Brown announced that my mate James would be coming up to Newcastle for a few days to do some work as a consultant there was an air of deep suspicion in the office. People were putting two and two together and coming up with the answer that James was about to be foisted on them as their new boss. That was ridiculous. James would never have been accepted in the *Viz* office as editor, and before he could even be accepted as a short-term independent consultant he had three significant handicaps to overcome. One was his dress sense: he wore trendy clothes. Another was his foppish, curly hair. And the third was his brash, self-confident personality. Ever since the very early days of the comic, people with fashionable clothes, remarkable haircuts or any discernible trace of self-confidence had always been frowned upon in the *Viz* office.

James Brown had always struck me as slightly odd. He once complimented me on a coat I was wearing. "Your coat looks really good," he said. That didn't sound right to me. He had 'funny eyes' too, a condition that my dad was always very quick to diagnose in people. James would look straight at you with the impertinence of a staring child, or the naïvety of a retarded adult. He seemed to have no concept of awkwardness or embarrassment. I'd always got on well with him, despite his liking my coat and having funny eyes. But when he came up to see me as part of his consultancy we didn't have any fun like we used to have. I was still nursing my brain back to health, and he didn't drink any more. We were both as dull as fuck and it seemed like a real shame. James talked to me about *Viz* and asked if I could ever see myself coming back to work. I said no. Then he went and spent some time at the Newcastle office talking to everyone there.

When James's report was finished he sent a copy to me. Entitled 'Are You Looking at My Magazine?' it spelled out a whole bunch of obvious things that John and I already knew. But James did have a few perceptive things to say. At 7,700 words it was a bit on the long side, so here is a précis of sixty:

> *Viz* was a unique publishing phenomenon but now sales have declined because of competition from other forms of media, and the *Viz* audience have grown up and had kids. It's still very funny but success had bred complacency and the cartoons have become formulaic. It needs a new editor to give it editorial direction, and new publishing and marketing strategies.

In fairness there was a bit more to it than that. James rather succinctly pointed out that if I had stayed on any longer in my part-time, unenthused editorial role we'd have ended up with a situation more like Brian Clough in his final year at Nottingham Forest than PC Dixon in his final year at Dock Green.

Despite James's recommendation, John took no steps to replace me with a new editor. But there was one personnel change. My big brother Steve joined the team part time as web site designer. Steve had done the odd cartoon for us in the early days, before moving away to work in the special-effects industry, on films like *Labyrinth* and *Little Shop of Horrors*, and briefly on *Spitting Image*. By all accounts he'd remained his irritating, logical self throughout.

I'd first recognized Steve on TV while watching *Star Trek* in the early 1970s, when I diagnosed him as a Vulcan. Twenty-five years later I recognized him again during a documentary about

Asperger's Syndrome. In the programme a despairing woman had been describing her husband's bizarre, obsessive and emotionless behaviour. Simultaneously Dolores and I turned to each other and said, 'Uncle Steve!' Steve had seen that programme too, and diagnosed himself. Now that he understands the condition, he's developed ways of coping with it. Perfectly logical ways of course. Consequently he's become a lot easier to get on with.

Everything seemed hunky dory as the new Millennium dawned. I'd occasionally nip into the office to say hello, and I'd do the odd cartoon if an idea occurred to me. Everyone seemed happy, and sales were on the up as well. In the first half of 1999 – during my final, blotchy, asleep-in-a-hedge management period – they had slipped drastically below the 300,000 mark to 226,869. But in the second half of the year, in my absence, the others seemed to have turned things around and recaptured 34,000 recent deserters, the total figure climbing back up above 260,000.

The future was looking bright... until the day John rang me to say that he'd received an offer from two film producers. Charles Finch and Luc Roeg (the respective sons of actor Peter and director Nic) wanted to make a Fat Slags movie, with actresses playing the Slags. I thought this was a terrible idea, but John said we would only be selling them a *licence* to make the film. It was quite possible that it would never get made and their licence would expire, leaving us a little bit richer and them a little bit wiser. On the flip side he pointed out there was always a possibility that the movie would be made, that it would be an enormous box office smash and we'd make an absolute fortune. The rather large, grey area of probability in the middle – where the film is made and it turns out to be shit – wasn't discussed. I don't know whether it was pure greed, or a touch of *Schadenfreude* coming into play – by now I hated the Fat Slags and seeing them die on screen might give me some perverse pleasure – but I agreed to sign.

It was a hideous mistake. Graham and Thorpy were livid, and they resented the fact that John and I still had control over what they now considered to be *their* characters. Since I'd left they'd been working for John, a situation they were also unhappy with. And it now emerged that they'd been unhappy working for me, too. The analogy they used was that they saw themselves as being part of a band, and that as co-writers rather than session musicians they should own the rights to their cartoon characters. But *Viz* wasn't a band. If we have to use analogies then I saw it more as a Kentucky Fried Chicken restaurant. I'd set up the first little diner in Kentucky all those years ago, and it was *my* original recipe. I'd taken them on as chefs. Admittedly, over the years they'd come up with a few finger-lickin' variations on the menu, but it was still KFC and I was still the Colonel.

As this dispute simmered, early in 2001 John Brown rang me with the shock news that James Brown had offered to buy *Viz*. James's company I Feel Good PLC were offering to buy three of John's titles: *Viz*, *Bizarre* and *Fortean Times*. Because IFG were a listed company the proposed deal was top secret at this stage, but when I told Dolores she wasn't in the least bit surprised. 'James asked whether he should buy *Viz* last time he was here,' she said nonchalantly. James had broached the subject with Dolores, but neither of them had deemed it worth mentioning to me.

Various values had been put on the comic over the years. It had cost me around forty quid to get the ball rolling in 1979. In the early 1990s that investment was worth £10 million, according to the *Sun*. I sold the comic for £10 million to Richard Branson in 1985, according to a carpet fitter who'd been working at Thorpy's house in the mid-1990s. £6.5 million was the comic's tabloid value when the *Mirror* did a business profile on John around 1996. And at our very peak the sum of £25 million had been conjured up by city analysts. Estimates had varied, but now at last we had a definitive figure. *Viz* was worth just £2.2 million, less than a half-decent lottery win in today's money. Harder to stomach was the fact that shitty *Bizarre* magazine was valued twice as highly. The total IFG were offering for all three titles was £6.4 million. Of that money I wouldn't get a penny. It was only John's interest as publisher that was under offer.

John made a few sentimental noises but I could tell his mind was already made up. Sales had been slipping again during the year 2000, down to 200,768 by the end of the year. John wanted rid of it, and I wouldn't be surprised if he'd hired James as a consultant deliberately to put the comic in the shop window, so to speak. Or perhaps I'm giving him too much credit.

Before the sale could go through our simmering dispute over the ownership of rights had to be resolved. As well as Graham and Thorpy, Simon was also unhappy with his lot. Lawyers concluded that due to changing circumstances the original contract which Simon and I signed with Virgin Books in 1985 was now about as relevant as the 1918 armistice agreement had been during the Blitz, so a brand-new agreement would have to be hammered out between all of us before the sale could proceed.

I met John at Newcastle Central Station and we walked the short distance to the new office for a showdown meeting with the other side. It was them and us by now. When we arrived John went into the meeting room, then came out again giggling. 'They've got a solicitor!' he whispered, nudging me excitedly. We had come unarmed. In the end the meeting was all very amicable. I had already offered to give Simon the vast majority of my stake in the comic in order to protect his future position, and give him some leverage when it came to dealing with the new publisher. But he had sided with Graham and Thorpy in the dispute and rather benevolently, and perhaps a little foolishly, he insisted that my interest be divided up between all five co-editors. So the five of them – Simon, Graham, Thorpy, Jonesy and Alex – became partners and set up a new business to produce the comic from then on, calling themselves Fulchester Industries.

With the new deal signed, in May 2001 the sale of *Viz* to IFG went ahead. I retained a minor stake in Viz, enough to give me a small royalty, on top of which James offered me a £25,000-a-year consultancy to advise him on his other publishing projects. It wasn't a perk. I had to earn it.

On my first visit to IFG's London offices I was ushered to an upstairs room to be briefed on their latest project, a multi-million-pound new magazine launch. Rumours had been circulating that James was about to unveil something big. The room was cleared of junior staff, the door was closed and only I, James and two of his top minions remained. Then they dramatically unveiled a dummy version of their new magazine, *Jack*.

I sat there in stunned silence. Basically *Jack* looked like a cross between *National Geographic* and *GQ*. James tried to explain the revolutionary philosophy behind it. 'Lions, not lager,' he said. I thought he was kidding. He repeated the slogan until it started to sound like a mantra he'd picked up at an AA meeting. The dummy magazine did indeed have some photos of lions in it, as well as pictures of semi-naked women and adverts for expensive clothes. James asked me what I thought. My first thought was that I was being filmed for one of those wind-up TV shows. I looked around for a hidden camera. To start with the name *Jack* was a dreadful choice, on a par with Newcastle Bright lagered ale. If Terry Wogan had said 'JACK *blank*' to me my first answer would definitely have been 'SHIT'. But I was a chicken. I couldn't bring myself to say what I really thought. I put my negative reactions down to the fact that I was burnt out. James wasn't. He had endless enthusiasm for his new magazine so I left him to it, and resigned from my consultancy without having been paid a penny.

I was far more excited about another job I'd been offered. In February 2001, David Stonehouse, the recently appointed Chief Executive of Newcastle United FC, got in touch with me. He was unhappy with the football club's match-day programme and official magazine, and he invited me to take a look at them and give him my honest opinion. I seemed a strange choice of consultant, but I told him he'd come to just the right man.

I hated the match-day programmes, which were unimaginative, over-designed and over-priced. And their magazine was a pile of shite too. They were both produced by the same agency and both covered exactly the same ground in the same style. I wrote Stonehouse a report suggesting ways of improving the programme, and recommended farming the club magazine out to an independent publisher, like James Brown's IFG who already published the Leeds United club magazine. A few weeks later James Brown rang me. Stonehouse had taken my advice and offered IFG the contract. And now James was inviting me to edit the new-look Newcastle United club magazine!

For me, editing Newcastle's magazine was the equivalent of playing for the team. This was my dream job. Me, Chris Donald, editing for United! Before contracts had been signed I went to work on the first issue, planning interviews with Tony Green and Newcastle fan Norman Wisdom. My first issue was going to be a corker. Then all of a sudden David Stonehouse mysteriously quit his new job at Newcastle, and my transfer fell through. I was as sick as a parrot. Totally gutted. But I did leave one small legacy from my brief spell 'on loan' at the club. After taking on board most of my recommendations, the club programme was voted the 'most improved programme in the Premiership' the following season.

While I was dreaming of signing for United, back at the *Viz* office Graham and Thorpy were suffering nightmares over the proposed Fat Slags film. After signing the licence agreement I'd heard nothing for several months, then John sent me a copy of a draft film script written by a face from the past, Scottish comic Craig Ferguson. John wanted me to pass comment, but I told him I wasn't interested and suggested he hand it over to Graham and Thorpy. They hated it. They felt that if anyone should be writing a Slags movie script, they should. And, never afraid of a few late nights, they set about writing one themselves. Alas, their efforts were rejected by the film-makers.

By now I wasn't making social visits to the office any more, but I was able to monitor movie developments in the press, as rumours spread that Minnie Driver, Fern Britton and Dawn French, to name but three, were in line to play Fat Slags. Then John told me that a friend of his, Ed Bye, had been asked to direct the film. Bye's track record included Harry Enfield's dreadful *Kevin and Perry Go Large* movie. Even at that stage there was still a glimmer of hope that the entire project would fall through, as Ed Bye was supposedly reluctant to make the movie unless the script had the backing of the original cartoonists. I kept my fingers crossed and hoped for the worst. Then one day I ran into Tony Wadsworth, the Chairman and Chief Executive of EMI, at an exclusive showbiz party in the beer garden of the Blue Bell pub in Jesmond Vale. Tony told me that Geri Halliwell had been in to see him the week before, and she'd been all excited about getting a role in the Fat Slags movie (although not, funnily enough, one of the lead roles). This was the news I'd been dreading. The film was *definitely* being made.

Graham, Thorpy and the others had plenty to distract them from the impending disaster movie. Under IFG's ownership *Viz*'s frequency at long last increased, from six a year to eleven, so they were busier than ever before. I'd always resisted any such change, fearing an inevitable drop in standards. But now it made sense, from a commercial point of view. Sales were continuing to slide, down to 178,745 for the whole year in 2001, and down again to 157,730 for 2002. But *Viz* was in relatively good health compared to some of IFG's other titles. A new-launch movie magazine called *Hotdog* flopped and was sold off at a loss. *Jack* was launched but lager drinkers displayed a predictable indifference towards lions and, as a result, sales were disappointing. James seemed to be losing his golden touch, and in May 2003 *Viz* changed hands again when struggling IFG were bought out by publishing heavyweights the Dennis Group. Dennis paid £5.1 million for the entire business. Two years earlier IFG had paid £6.4 million for John's three magazines alone. Curiously, that leaves *Viz* in the hands of Felix Dennis, formerly one of the reprobates responsible for the notorious *Oz* magazine, but now a totally reformed, cigar-smoking, capitalist multi-millionaire.

It seemed to be a good deal from the point of view of the remaining editorial team whose diffidence had bemused and frustrated James Brown. Their working relationship with him had broken down completely the day James turned up at the Newcastle office in a loud shirt and asked Alex to go out and buy him a sandwich. They never spoke to him again. That the editorial committee should fall out with James Brown was inevitable, I guess. It came as no surprise to me. But I was shocked when, at the end of November 2003, my brother Simon left the magazine.

Expecting five people with contrasting personalities to jointly edit a magazine was always a tall order. Every orchestra needs a conductor. I don't know what triggered the eventual split, but the fault line had always been there; I'd been slapping Pollyfilla into the bastard for years. Young Alex left with Simon, to form Blissna, a TV writing partnership. Their first effort was a quiz show on Tyne Tees TV called The Regionnaires. Simon has always wanted a career in showbiz, and I hope he succeeds.

I'm sure he'll fare better than the Fat Slags. In December 2003 John Brown rang me just as I was finishing this book. He was in an upstairs bedroom of his huge terraced house in Notting Hill. His friend and neighbour Ed Bye had just popped round, with his wife Ruby Wax. Ed was excited. He'd brought with him a rough cut of the Fat Slags movie which he'd just finished directing. He invited John to sit and watch it with him. Halfway through the film John made an excuse, left the room and went upstairs to call me.

'It's worse than our worst fears,' he said in a hushed voice. I wasn't quick enough to write it all down verbatim, but John's flabbergasted description of the film contained the words: 'absurd', 'woeful', 'completely ludicrous' and 'astonishingly bad'. He expressed concern for his poor friend Ed, whom he suspected might never work in the film industry again.

Since then I've heard various rumours. That members of the audience walked out of a test screening, that the film is so bad scenes have had to be re-shot in an effort to salvage it. As this book goes to press there's still no sign of a release date, and I'm clinging to a faint hope that the Fat Slags movie will never be released at all. At least then poor Graham and Thorpy will be spared the pain of having to watch it.

During one frank exchange on the subject Graham had told John that watching the film-makers mess around with his characters was like watching his children getting raped. I thought his choice of simile was slightly ill-judged in the case of the Slags, but I knew only too well what he meant.

I've eventually come to terms with the fact that *Viz*, my baby, has now grown up and is living a life of its own. But I still have paternal feelings for the characters I created. And I still worry about the size of Roger Mellie's feet.

CHAPTER TWENTY-FIVE

The End

Back in 1970, when I was just ten years old, my mum and dad gave me the most perfect Christmas present a boy could ever have dreamed of: a model railway.

There were shiny green engines, brightly coloured carriages, trucks, wagons and station buildings, all arranged around a large loop of track. The railway stood in the window of my bedroom in Lily Crescent, on a big green trestle table that my dad had built specially for it. There was only one simple loop of track, with two small sidings, but I loved that train set and played with it constantly, running timetabled services from the only station, round the loop 144 times, and arriving back at the same station 48 minutes later.

Putting a stopwatch on the trains brightened it up a little bit, but my loop was essentially a bit dull. I often dreamed of expanding the layout, building new tracks and scenery and buying new engines. For years I saved up the wages from my paper round to fund my dream extension, buying new trains and equipment from the model shop in town whenever I could afford to. But the building work never got underway. Eventually I grew out of my railway, boxed it all up and put it away, and I took up drawing as a hobby instead.

The boxes moved from attic to attic after that. I'd occasionally open them, sit and admire the engines for a while, then carefully pack them away again. Then, in 1999, after moving house and quitting *Viz* I suddenly found myself with both the time and the space to build my dream railway. I applied to Dolores for planning permission to build a gigantic layout in a spare room in our new house. My initial plan was rejected – she didn't want it taking up the entire room – but a revised version got the go-ahead. I started by building a table, just like my dad did, but bigger. Then I set about planning and building the train set of my dreams, with main lines, branch lines, engine sheds, tunnels, bridges, a viaduct, spectacular scenery and even a castle perched high up on a craggy cliff. I encouraged my son Dale, who was now ten, to help me. I had this vision in my mind, based on the old Hornby train catalogues my dad gave me, of Dale controlling a speeding train, his face beaming with delight, while I stood behind him, wearing a tank-top cardigan, smiling proudly and smoking a pipe.

But it soon became obvious that Dale wasn't interested in trains and he was only playing along to humour me. My daughter Jamie took a bit of an interest, but not in the trains. She rented a small farm alongside the main line where she kept a few 1/72nd scale sheep and horses. She would wander in once a week or so to check on her livestock, but I'd be in the railway room every day, working from early in the morning until late at night, up to my knees in sawdust, plaster, papier-mâché, paint and wire. Every time I finished a section I'd start on a new extension. Gradually the railway grew and grew until eventually it did fill the entire room.

As well as time and space I also had a limitless amount of money to spend on my railway. I'd go back and forth to model shops almost on a daily basis. I'd kept all the train catalogues I'd drooled over in the 1970s and all of a sudden engines that I'd dreamed of owning were available again, through eBay online auctions. And for Christmas 1999 Dolores got me the one engine

I'd always wanted more than any other, an '00' gauge Clayton Type 1 Class 17 Bo-Bo diesel electric, No. 8592.

After almost a year of frantic work I had finally realized my dream. I had the *perfect* model railway and every engine I'd ever dreamed of owning. And it had all cost a mere fraction of what I spent on my full-scale railway station restaurant.

But, as with the restaurant, realizing the dream turned out to be a disappointment. I was beginning to notice a pattern here. Once you realize a dream – as someone blessed with more money than sense is often able to do – you discover that *dreaming* the dream was actually the whole point of the exercise. Once you've *realized* that dream, the fun is all over. It's like chasing a butterfly, I suppose. Once you've caught the bastard all you can do is stick a pin through it and bung it in a cabinet. Or, in the case of an enormous model railway, once you've built it all you can do is sit there in the middle of the room driving your little trains around in circles, and looking like a bit of a twat. A guard's hat and whistle are optional extras. And so my perfect model railway is now in pieces, taking up half of my garage. Only mice pass through the long-abandoned tunnel now, stopping perhaps to nibble a wire and have a shit on the platform of my once-busy station. Who knows? Maybe in another twenty years I'll get it all out again and try and foist it on my grandchildren.

I still do the odd bit of freelance writing, and very occasionally contribute to *Viz*, but my best customer is probably Richard Ingrams at *The Oldie* (the very same Richard Ingrams who, ten years ago, cited his dislike of *Viz* as one of the principal reasons for setting up his new magazine). But most of my time is spent working in a bookshop. I met Stuart and Mary Manley through a shared interest in books and former railway stations. They are the owners of Barter Books, a vast second-hand bookshop located in a magnificent Victorian station building in the market town of Alnwick. The money they pay me is pretty average – a fraction above the minimum wage – but the job itself is ideal. I do a bit of graphic design, bookshelf maintenance (at long last putting my Woodwork A-level to use) and of course a lot of librarianship (utilizing my anal retentiveness). And I also get to work behind the till.

We get some interesting customers in the shop. Only the other day I was kneeling down fitting a shelf beneath the counter when I heard a strangely familiar voice. 'Excuse me,' it said. I stood up and saw an ageing but unmistakable Pam Ayres waiting to be served. 'You're that poet, aren't you?' I said, struggling to think of her name. 'My mother-in-law is a big fan of yours.' Pam Ayres smiled politely. As I served her she pointed across to the poetry section. 'I see you've got a few of my books in over there,' she said with a hint of pride. We had indeed. And we had dozens more in the giant stockroom out the back of the shop. I didn't tell her, of course, but the reason we have so many of her books is that we can't give the bloody things away, let alone sell them.

I hope she'll forgive me for saying so, but for a brief spell in the 1970s Pam Ayres's career went into overdrive and she seemed to enjoy a level of success totally out of proportion to her modest talents as a comedy poet. I know the feeling. We have an awful lot of unsold *Viz* books out the back as well.

Appendix of Viz Cartoons

I tried compiling a proper index for this book but it ended up a bit on the long side and, to be honest, it was pretty boring. So instead I've included this, a list of every cartoon character that appeared in *Viz* during my 20-year tenure as editor. The person(s) originally responsible for the strip/character is in brackets, together with the year in which it first (and usually last) appeared in the comic.

The following abbreviations of artists are used:

AC – Alex Collier
CD – Chris Donald
DJ – Davey Jones
GD – Graham Dury
JB – Jim Brownlow
JF – John Fardell
MS – Martin Stevens

NS – Nicholas Schwab
RR – Roger Radio
SE – Simon Ecob (freelance
   illustrator)
SD – Simon Donald
ST – Simon Thorp

Acne Street Gang (ST 1985)
Adventures of Billy Connolly (DJ 1998)
Adventures of Human League in Outer Space (GD/CD/ST 1990)
Adventures of Ian Paisley (GD/CD/ST/SD/DJ 1999)
Adventures of Jimmy Hill (CD/GD/ST 1990)
Adventures of Joe Robertson-Crusoe (CD/SD 1994)
Adventures of Rolf Harris the Cat (ST 1991)
Adventures of Wet Wet Wet and their Pellow Submarine (DJ 1997)
Advertismint (Tony Husband 1986)
Afternoon Tea With Mr Kipplin (SD 1979)
Albert Gordon Traffic Warden (GD 1985)
Albert O'Balsam and his Magic Hat (CD 1983)
Alcan Foil Wrapped Pork Stock Warrior (CD 1991)
Aldridge Prior the Hopeless Liar (SD 1984)
Andy Crapp by Reg Shyte (GD/ST/SD/DJ 1998)
Ant Master (SD 1997)
Arse Farm (DJ 1997)
Arseache (ST 1994)
Arsehole Kate (GD 1994)
Arthur P. Clarke's Strange & Interesting World of Unusual Things (CD 1985)
Auntie Climax (SD 1986)
Baby Anderson (JB 1984)
Badly Drawn Man (JB 1983)
Bairn, The (CD 1979)
Balsa Boy (CD/GD/ST 1990)
Barbara Cartland's Farmyard Thrill (DJ 1995)
Barmy Bill (CD 1984)
Barney Brimstone's Biscuit Tin Circus (CD/ST/GD 1989)
Barney the Complete Bastard (NS 1987)
Barry the Cat (CD/GD/SD/ST 1989)
Bart Conrad Store Detective (CD 1982)
Baxter Basics (ST/GD 1994)
Bees of Barnton Hall (DJ 1993)
Ben and the Space Walrus (CD 1979)
Ben Turpin in Prime Suspect 6 (GD/ST 1996)
Benny's Hedges (DJ 1991)
Bereavement Beavers (DJ 1996)
Bernie Winter's Circus of Horrors (ST 1994)
Bert the Burglar (RR 1986)
Bertie Blunt 'His parrot's a cunt' (Sean Agnew 1988)
Biffa Bacon (CD 1981)
Big Vern (CD 1982)
Billy Bananahead (GD 1986)

Billy Bar and his Invisible Car (RR 1987)
Billy Bee's Nest (CD 1984)
Billy Bloater 'He's got a gob like a skip' (ST 1986)
Billy Boggles Kid Inventor (CD 1983)
Billy Bottom and his Zany Toilet Pranks (CD 1985)
Billy Bound 'It's always his round' (Guy Campbell 1987)
Billy Brat (SD 1982)
Billy Brisket 'He takes the biscuit' (RR 1987)
Billy Britain (CD 1981)
Billy Bumble-Beard (CD/GD/SD/ST 1991)
Billy Quizz (CD 1987)
Billy the Fish (CD 1983)
Billy's Bollocks (CD 1985)
Billy's Fridge (CD 1989)
Bippo Barrington of The Squadron (CD 1980)
Bird Shite (RR 1983)
Biscuits Alive (ST 1991)
Bishop Sandwich Band (DJ 1992)
Black Bag the Faithful Border Bin Liner (Dave Smith/Graham Murdoch 1988)
Blind Man (JB 1980)
Bob the Philosopher (JB 1980)
Bob-Faced Betty of the Biscuit Shop Ballet (DJ 1993)
Bodley Basin the Strict Freemason (ST 1987)
Boswell Boyce 'He throws his voice' (ST 1986)
Bottom Inspectors (SD 1985)
Box-Spoon Billy (DJ 1992)
Boxing Brain Surgeon (GD/ST/SD/DJ/SE 1999)
Boy Racer (GD/ST 1989)
Boys'R'Uz (GD/ST/SD/DJ/AC 1999)
Bram Stoker Practical Joker (ST 1994)
Brian Trousers (GD/CD/ST 1989)
Brian's Bannister (CD 1986)
Brown Bottle (CD 1982)
Brown Eye P.I. (GD/ST/SD/DJ 1997)
Bugger Me Bob (JB 1982)
Bully Beef and Yeoman Soft (GD/ST/SD/DJ 1997)
Burrowing Church (DJ 1991)
Buster Gonad and his Unfeasibly Large Testicles (GD 1986)
Canal Court (DJ 1995)
Captain Captured (Dave Smith 1986)
Captain Incontinent (CD 1984)
Captain Magnetic (GD 1987)
Captain Morgan and his Hammond Organ (CD/ST 1990)
Captain Muscle (SD 1980)
Captain Oats (ST/GD/SD/DJ 1998)
Captain Unreliable (NS 1987)

Careless McKenzie (ST 1988)
Case of the Missing Twat (DJ 1994)
Casualty Gang (ST 1992)
Charitable Chester (GD/ST 1990)
Charlie Cheddar's Deceased Comedian
Cheeseboard (Tony Harding 1993)
Cheat on the Track (GD/ST/SD/SE 1996)
Cheese Mice (GD/ST 1995)
Chester and The Man (JB 1979)
Chums of Samson's Circus (DJ 1991)
Cider Woman – *see* Brown Bottle
Ciggies and Beer (MS 1981)
Clamper Van Beethoven (GD/ST/DJ 1999)
Clarence Coxes 'He puts used matches
back in boxes' (DJ 1988)
Claws the Cat (JB 1979)
Cliff Richard's Path of Righteousness (DJ
1997)
Cockney Kenny (ST 1986)
Cockney Wanker (GD/ST/CD/SD 1994)
Colditz Kids (GD/ST 1993)
Colin the Amiable Crocodile (CD 1979)
Colin's Conker (GD/ST 1995)
Colin's Curtains (GD 1992)
Coming of the Executioner (SD 1982)
Community Shop (CD 1981)
Conference Kids (JF 1992)
Conman the Barbarian (NS 1987)
Cop of the Antarctic (DJ 1993)
Corky the Twat (ST 1995)
Coward of the County Ice Cream
(GD/ST/SD/DJ/SE 1988)
Cowboy Builder (GD/ST 1995)
Crawford Crayon (ST 1987)
Critics, The (JF 1991)
Curse of Devil's Rock (DJ 1996)
Cuthbert Stokes and his Tedious Jokes (DJ
1987)
Cyril Thompson, Absolutely Fascinating
Adventures of (CD 1983)
D.C. Thompson the Humourless Scottish
Git (ST/CD/GD/SD 1995)
Dai O'Rea (ST 1988)
Daley Starr (GD/ST/CD 1991)
Danish Plastic Toy Brick Boy (Tony
Harding 1993)
Danny's District Council (JF 1991)
Darren Dice (ST 1986)
David Bellamy (SD 1981)
David Cassidy's Time-Travel Bathroom
(DJ 1994)
Davy McGraw and his Magic Door (JB
1986)
Davy Stoat and his Gravy Boat (GD/ST
1993)
Denis Helium the Fatso Silly Billy (GD/ST
1993)
Department of Employment (CD 1982)
Derek Anorak (JF 1994)

Derek's Boots (CD 1986)
Desperately Unfunny Dan (CD 1988)
Diana Ross's Dogshit Museum (DJ 1998)
Dick Twitcher the 'Horny'thologist (ST
1995)
Dickie Beasley (GP/CD/ST 1991)
Disco Dancing Champion of the World
(CD 1979)
Doc, The (JB 1980)
Doctor Marten Boot Story (GD/ST/CD/SD
1997)
Dog, The (CD 1980)
Donald Sinden in 'There Goes My
Knighthood' (DJ 1997)
Door Matt the Spineless Twat (Teg/AC
1999)
Dr. Bolus (ST 1985)
Dr. Crapulence (SD 1985)
Dr. Death (SD 1984)
Dr. Dick (Rabbit/Ostrich 1981)
Dr. Kagoul and the Anarax (Dave Smith
1987)
Dr. Mental (JB 1981)
Dr. Poo (SD/ST/GD 1996)
Dr. Poolittle (SD/ST/GD 1996)
Dr. Theodore Gray and his Fantastic
Growth Spray (GD 1985)
Dr. Thrilldare (GD/ST/SD/DJ 1999)
Dracula (NS 1987)
Drum Miner (ST 1992)
Eddie Angelo (MS, 1982)
8 Ace (GD/SD/ST 1995)
Eight Ball Joe (CD 1981)
Electric Space-Copter Kid (GD/ST/CD 1991)
Enema At the Door (Trev Faull 1980)
Enemy Below (CD 1986)
Eric Daft (ST 1985)
Eskimo Mel (GD/ST 1990)
Esther Rantzen's Heart of Gold (DJ 1999)
Euro School (GD/ST 1992)
Everard Buys a Newspaper (SD 1980)
Farmer Palmer (GD/ST 1990)
Fatha Bacon – *see* Biffa Bacon
Fat Slags (GD/ST/CD/SD 1989)
Fat Sod (CD 1979)
Father Christmas (GD/ST 1993)
Fatty Balatty (SD/ST/GD 1996)
Feet and Two Reg (GD/ST/SD/DJ 1997)
Felix and his Amazing Underpants (CD
1984)
Fido (GD 1985)
Finbarr Saunders and his Double
Entendres (ST 1987)
Fint Snitt (Ed Lux 1980)
Fisherman Sam (DJ 1992)
Flash Harry (GD 1988)
Flying School (DJ 1991)
Folkie (Tony Harding 1988)
Fox in a Box (JB 1982)

Frank the Princess (SD 1982)
Frank Xerox Private Dick (Neil Kilpatrick 1986)
Frankenstein's Cock (CD/GD/SD/ST 1992)
Frankie Feel (SD 1984)
Fraser the Frank Fish (JB 1986)
Fred Dibnah's Pop Fables (DJ 1999)
Freddy Flee, Adventures of (SD 1981)
French Postman (CD 1980)
Fritz the Robot Cat (SD 1985)
Fru T. Bunn the Master Baker and his Gingerbread Sex Dolls (GD/SD/ST 1995)
Fry's Turkish Delight (GD 1993)
Garry and Barry the Identical Twins (DJ 1987)
Garry Bushell the Bear (DJ 1998)
General Jubblies (GD/ST/SD/DJ 1999)
Gilbert Cole and his Remote Control (Les Heywood 1986)
Gilbert Goul (ST 1987)
Gilbert O'Sullivan's Pirates of Ben's Pants (GD/SD/DJ/ST 1997)
Gilbert Ratchet (DJ 1990)
Godzilla vs. Dr. Robert Chartham and his Ring of Pubis (GD/ST/SD/DJ 1998)
Good Humoured Hamilton Winterbottom (CD 1984)
Gordon Zola and Cheddar George (GD/ST/SD 1989)
Gordon's Grandad (CD/GD/ST 1989)
Graffiti Art (ST 1996)
Graham's Grenade (Les Heywood 1986)
Grandfather Clock (GD/ST 1991)
Grange Park (CD 1982)
Granny Smith (MS 1982)
Grassy Knollington Conspiracy Theorist (GD/SD/ST/DJ 1998)
Greedy Sodd (GD/ST/SD/DJ 1997)
Grimage and Vomit (Nick Parker 1996)
Gumboils (RR 1982)
Hairdressers (RR & Jilly Jargon 1986)
Hambo (NS 1986)
Harry Hooter and his Computer (ST 1987)
Harry Quartz Para-Dental Hygienist (NS 1988)
Hawaiian Vice (NS 1986)
Heads (JB 1986)
Hector the Collector and his Metal Detector (CD 1983)
Hefty Holmes 'Heavyweight Chump of GMTV' (CD 1999)
Helpful Herbet (ST 1985)
Herman's Hermit (GD 1991)
Hippopotamus Man (CD/GD/ST 1993)
Hobby Horse (DJ 1996)
Holey Joe (GD/CD/ST 1990)
Hooray Henry (Tony Harding 1987)
House in Leafy Woods (DJ 1991)
HRH The Duke of Edinburgh and his

Wacky Capers (DJ 1999)
Hugh Phamism (SD 1987)
Hugo Hall 'He makes things small' (CD 1986)
Hurricane Heather (RR 1985)
Iceman Cometh (SD 1999)
Incontinent Boxing Tortoise Hero (CD/GD/SD/ST 1991)
Incredible Dr. Sex, The (CD 1985)
Independent Financial Adviser of the Lamp (CD/GD/SD/DJ/ST 1997)
Inspector Morse and his Glove Puppet Police Force (GD/ST 1993)
It's A Knockout Family (GD/SD/ST/Phil R 1996)
Ivan Jelical (SD/GD/ST 1991)
Ivor Better and Tony Worse (GD 1998)
Ivor the Skiver 'His dad's a bad driver' (CD 1988)
Jack Black and his dog Silver (CD 1985)
Jack in the Box (CD/GD/ST 1991)
Jack Spratt and his Dead Rat (RR 1986)
Jamie Bond 007 (GD/CD/ST 1992)
Janet Street-Porter Crusoe and her Researcher Friday (DJ 1999)
Jarvis Cocker's Quest for Knockers (Bear Hackenbush 1996)
Jelly Head (Charlie Higson 1988)
Jeremy Futcher 'His dad's a butcher' (CD/ST 1988)
Jimi Hendrix's Journey to the Centre of the Earth (SD/CD/ST/GD 1991)
Jimmy Nail's Crocodile Clips (CD/SD/GD/ST 1997)
Jimmy's Jamjar Grandpa (Lew Stringer 1994)
Johnny Condor (CD/GD/SD/ST/SE 1988)
Johnny Fartpants (SD/CD/JB/Andy Barnden 1984)
Johnny Jones the Pathetic Cartoon Character (CD 1980)
Jonathan Ringpiece (CD/GD/ST 1991)
Journey to the Centre of the Earth (CD 1980)
Judge Dudd (NS 1987)
JumpJet Fanny and her Hawker-Siddeley Twat (GD/ST 1992)
June & Terry Sitcom (GD/ST 1990)
Junior Cop (CD/GD/ST 1990)
Kappa Slappa (AC 1997)
Kenny Ball and his Jazzmags (GD/ST/SD/DJ 1998)
Kid Politician (GD/CD/ST 1990)
Kids, The (JB 1979)
Kilted Cowboy (CD/GD/ST/SD/Graham Murdoch 1994)
Kipling Kid and his Cake Trolley of Justice (GD/ST 1995)
Lager Lads (SD 1981)

Larry Lad and his Ambitious Dad (GD/ST 1992)
Lazy Disinterested 16-year-old Shop Girl (GD/ST/SD/DJ 1997)
Lenny Left (GD/ST/CD 1990)
Let's Go Huntin' (JB 1982)
Life of St. Ivel Patron Saint of Processed Cheese (GD/ST/SD/DJ 1997)
Liquidizer (ST 1987)
Little Old Man (GD/ST/SD 1992)
Little Plumber (GD/ST 1993)
Lonely Sidney Sidebottom (CD 1982)
Lord Shite and Nanny No-Dumps (DJ 1997)
Lucky Frank (CD 1983)
Luke O'Like (Tony Harding 1988)
Luvvie Darling (GD/ST 1993)
Lying Old Witch in the Wardrobe (GD 1995)
Major Misunderstanding (GD/ST/SD/DJ 1999)
Malcolm the Maladjusted Child (SD 1984)
Man..., The (JB 1980)
Mary Shitehouse (CD 1987)
Max Power (GD/SD/DJ/ST 1997)
Max's Plank (GD/ST 1992)
Maxwell Straker Record Breaker (GD/ST 1990)
McBroons (T. Bam/ST 1990)
Meddlesome Ratbag (DJ 1992)
Medieval Knievel (GD/ST/SD/DJ 1998)
Merlin and the Dragon (CD/JB 1981)
Michael Angelo and his Invisible Yo-Yo (RR 1985)
Michael Winner Gets his Dinner (ST 1999)
Mickey the Martian (SD 1980)
Mickey's Miniature Grandpa (DJ 1989)
Mickey's Monkey Spunk Moped (GD/ST/SD 1993)
Mighty Orgon (JB 1983)
Mike Smitt, He's a patronising git (DJ 1987)
Millie Tant (SD/ST/CD/GD 1989)
Miserable Sod (CD 1983)
Miss Demeanour and her Concertina (CD 1987)
Miss Marbles Who Dunnit (RR 1988)
Mission Fairly Awkward (NS 1987)
Modern Parents (JF 1991)
Morris Day Sexual Pervert (CD/ST 1989)
Morris Stokes Paranormal Grocer (GD/ST/SD/DJ 1997)
Most Perfectly Developed Man (CD 1980)
Moustache of the Mounties (DJ 1994)
Mr. Crazy Face and his Funny Monkey (JB 1984)
Mr. Eating Charlesworth (SD 1981)
Mr. Logic (SD/CD 1982)

Mr. Mediocre (JB 1980)
Mr. Nuggin (CD 1980)
Mr. Rudewords (CD 1985)
Mrs. Brady Old Lady (CD 1987)
Mrs. Mad Bastard (SD 1985)
Mrs. Maybee and her Crazy Baby (CD 1981)
Mrs. Neat (NS 1988)
Mungril (Ed Lux 1980)
Mutha Bacon - *see* Biffa Bacon
My Mother's a Whore (A. Hepworth/C. Hollingworth 1995)
My Old Man's a Dustman (GD/ST/SD/DJ 1999)
Nancy Boys (David James 1988)
Napoleon Bonaparte and his Nephews (GD/ST/SD/DJ 1997)
Ner ner, ner ner, ner ner (Tony Husband 1987)
Nice Honest Gypsies (GD/ST/CD 1990)
Nigel Smith Space Adventurer of the Future (ST 1987)
Noah's Ark of Soup (ST 1991)
Nobby's Piles (GD/Ann Hedley/ST 1990)
Noddy Holder (GD/ST 1991)
Noja Spig (Ed Lux 1981)
Norbert Colon (ST 1986)
Norman the Doorman (CD 1981)
Norman's Knob (SD 1986)
Nude Motorcycle Girl (GD/ST/CD/SD 1989)
Odd Job Bob-a-Job Bob (ST/GD/SD 1989)
On The Farm Type of Thing (CD 1980)
One Cut Wally (GD 1996)
Orson Cart 'He Comes Apart' (Steve Donald 1988)
Oswald 'Mind My Brolly' Mosley (DJ 1999)
Our Neighbours are Bastards (GD/ST 1995)
Our Teacher's a Microbe (AC 1999)
Our Teacher's a Wardrobe (GD 1994)
Our Wardrobe's a Teacher (ST 1995)
Owl Hospital (DJ 1994)
Page 3 School (CD/GD/ST 1992)
Parkie (SD 1981)
Pat-a-Cake Pete (DJ 1992)
Pathetic Sharks (CD 1980)
Paul Daniels' Jet-Ski Journey to the Centre of Elvis (SD/ST/GD/DJ 1997)
Paul Whicker the Tall Vicar (JB 1981)
P.C. Blouse (GD/ST 1990)
P.C. Copper Kettle (GD/ST 1994)
P.C. Hopper the Bent Copper (GD/ST/SD/DJ 1998)
"P.C." Plod (SD/ST 1995)
P.C. Rea the Cop that's Queer (CD 1986)
P.C. Victor Foxtrott (CD 1985)
Penny Arcade (GD/ST/Lew Stringer 1994)

Peter Brent and his Bucket of Cement (GD/ST 1991)
Peter Potter's Valley of the Dinosaurs (GD/CD/SD/ST 1990)
Peter Pretend (CD 1985)
Phantom of Fairpools (DJ 1991)
Phantom of the Bastard Opera (CD 1982)
Phil's Spectre (CD/GD/ST 1990)
Pierre le Petit Lapin Français (JB 1979)
Planet Bore (John Armstrong 1985)
Plankton Boy (DJ 1990)
Playtime Fontayne (ST 1992)
Pole-Vaulting P.C., The (DJ 1998)
Pop School (GD/ST 1994)
Pop Starr (ST 1992)
Porn Again Christian (GD/ST/SD/DJ 1998)
Posh Street Kids (GD/ST/SD/DJ 1998)
Postman Plod (CD 1988)
Preston Ironed (GD 1995)
Professor Piehead (CD 1979)
Psychonormal Bill (SD 1981)
Psychotic Sid (ST 1987)
Q-Shoes (CD/GD/ST 1990)
Quentin Taranteeny (Nick Parker 1995)
Raffles the Gentleman Thug (ST/GD 1996)
Rat Boy (AC 1999)
Ravy Davey Gravy (GD/ST 1996)
Raymond Porter and his Bucket of Water (CD 1987)
Raymond Scanty Vigilante (NS 1988)
Raymond the Large Caterpillar (CD 1980)
Rays from Space (JB 1980)
Real Lives (RR 1986)
Remarkable Mind of David Beerglass (CD 1986)
Renegade of Salvation (GD/ST/SD/DJ/SE 1999)
Reverend Milo's Lino Rhino (DJ 1994)
Reverend Ramsden's Ringpiece Cathedral (GD/ST/CD 1991)
Road Rushdie and Wile E. Assassin (DJ 1999)
Robbie on the Run (DJ 1992)
Robbie Rickerby (SD/ST/GD/DJ 1998)
Robot Nun (GD/ST 1991)
Rock'n'Roll Dogturds (Al Cartwright 1986)
Rod Stewart and the Island of Death (DJ 1996)
Rodney Rix 'He does tricks with bricks' (CD 1987)
Roger Irrelevant (DJ 1987)
Roger Mellie the Man on the Telly (CD 1981)
Roger the Lodger (ST 1992)
Roswell Stiles and his Intriguing 'X' Files (CD/ST/GD/SD 1996)

Rotating Chin Men (DJ 1994)
Roy of Crescent News (SE 1996)
Roy Schneider Joy Rider (GD/ST 1991)
Rubber Johnny (ST 1988)
Rude Kid (JB 1979)
Run For Your Life (Ray Fury/ST 1999)
Russell Grant's Fat World of the Unknown (DJ 1995)
Sammy and his Stammer (SD 1982)
Sammy Smalls 'He runs into walls' (RR 1985)
Sandra Burke – see Fat Slags
'Scoop' Thomson, Adventures of (DJ 1995)
Scooter-Dolphin Boy (CD 1987)
Scottie Trotter's Tottie Allotment (DJ 1993)
Scratch & Sniff (ST 1988)
Secret of Rattlesnake Creek (DJ 1991)
Segs Maniac (GD/ST/SD/DJ 1997)
Sergeant Death (CD 1985)
Shaven Capers with Barbara Cartland (DJ 1996)
Sheila Sherry 'She's got trifle tits' (GD 1994)
Sheridan Poorly (GD/ST 1990)
Sherlock Homo (GD/ST 1992)
Shipwrecked Craft Fair (GD/ST/SE 1996)
Shirker Bee (GD/SD/DJ/ST 1998)
Shitty Dick (GD/ST/SD/DJ 1998)
Sid the Sexist (SD 1982)
Simon Lotion Time and Motion Man (SD/ST/GD 1996)
Simon Salad Cream Story (CD/GD/ST/SD 1995)
Simon's Snowman (GD/ST 1990)
Skinheed (CD 1979)
Slouch (Mike, 1979)
Smiles the Clown (SD 1980)
Smiling Susie (DJ 1994)
Smutt, Sidney – see Sid the Sexist
Snake Charmer (JB 1980)
Snowman, The (GD/ST 1994)
Soft Mick in Vile Bodies (MS 1981)
S.O.S. We Have No Bananas (GD/ST/SD/DJ/SE)
Spawny Get (GD/ST 1990)
Specky Twat (SD/GD/ST 1990)
Spice: 1999 (DJ 1999)
Spider Person (NS 1988)
Spitfire McGuire and his home-made Mini-Plane (GD/ST 1991)
Spoilt Bastard (GD/ST/SD 1989)
Spot the Clue with Celebrity Botanist David Bellamy (DJ 1998)
– with Channel 4 Racing's John McCririck (DJ 1997)
– with Hugh Scully of BBC TV's Antiques Roadshow (DJ 1995)

– with The Body Shop's Anita Roddick (DJ 1997)
– with TV Celebrity Chef Delia Smith (DJ 1996)
Squaddie McDowell (GD/SD/DJ/ST 1999)
Stag Knight (DJ 1997)
Stan the Statistician (Chris Stanley 1990)
Steel Skull (MS 1979)
Steptoe's Son (A. Hepworth/C. Hollingsworth 1996)
Streetcorner Sid 'Three lighters a quid' (Lew Stringer 1994)
Student Grant (CD/GD/ST 1992)
Suicidal Syd (CD 1985)
SWANT (SD 1981)
Sweary Mary (ST/CD/GD/SD 1994)
Tara Palmer Banana Pajama Thompkinson (AC 1999)
Tarquin Hoylet 'He has to go to the toilet' (Kev Sutherland 1987)
Tarzan in my Pubes (GD/ST 1994)
Tasha Slappa – *see* Kappa Slappa
Ted Dempster (CD 1979)
Teevee Twins (GD/ST 1988)
Terry Addict (ST 1994)
Terry Fuckwitt (CD 1986)
Terry Tree 'He turns into a tree' (RR 1986)
Tex Wade Frontier Accountant (ST 1986)
Thieving Gypsy Bastards (GD/ST/CD 1990)
Thermos O'Flask (GD/ST 1995)
Thingy from the Swamp (MS 1980)
Three Chairs (GPD/CD 1988)
Three Shakespeares (GD/ST/SD/DJ 1999)
Thunderflash the Wonder Horse (DJ 1992)
Thursday's Adventures of Jacjac (GD/ST/SD/SE 1999)
Tim of the Texas Longfords (DJ 1998)
Timothy Potter Train Spotter (CD 1987)
Timothy Timpson – *see* Spoilt Bastard
Tina's Tits (CD 1986)
Tinribs (DJ 1987)
TNT Tommy (DJ 1988)
Toast Kid (GD/ST/SD 1990)
Toby and his Time Machine (JF 1992)
Toby's Jug (ST 1988)
Tom and Gerry (CD 1983)
Tommy 'Banana' Johnson (CD 1984)
Tommy and his Magic Arse (CD/GD/SD/ST 1989)
Tommy and his Magic Shoes (JB 1979)
Tommy and his Trifle (CD/GD/SD/ST 1989)
Tommy Salter's Chemical Capers (GD/CD/ST/SD 1989)
Tommy Toots and his Speedy Boots (SD/ST 1989)

Tommy's Birthday (CD 1979)
Tommy's Gun (CD 1986)
Topless Jan Fox and her Cornflakes Box (Lew Stringer 1994)
Topless Skateboard Nun (GD/ST/CD 1990)
Tracey Tunstall – *see* Fat Slags
Training Dogs the Snodhouse Way (SD 1980)
Tree Musketeers (GD/ST/SD/DJ 1997)
Tristram Banks, and his Jocular Pranks (GD 1985)
Tubby Johnson (GD 1986)
Tubby Round (MS 1980)
Tubby Tucker the Big Fat... Person (CD 1987)
Tunnel of Death (CD 1980)
Turd of Frankenstein Must Be Destroyed (SD/GD/ST/DJ 1998)
Two Ronnies and their Gang (GD/ST 1993)
Typhoon of the Trenches (GD/ST/SE 1996)
Undersink Cupboard of Jacques Cousteau (ST 1995)
V.D. O'Nasty (CD 1986)
Very Bloody Murder (JB 1980)
Vibrating Bum-Faced Goats (DJ 1992)
Vicki Drake (AC 1998)
Victor and his Boa Constrictor (GD 1984)
Victor Pratt the Stupid Twat (CD 1979)
Victorian Dad (GD/ST 1991)
Vince Valentino the Ladykiller (CD 1980)
Vincent Goes to the Pictures (SD 1980)
Violence 2000 (CD 1980)
Vlad the Impaler and his Cat Samson (DJ 1987)
Waggy Tail 'He loves a good shit' (DJ 1987)
Walter Weaver's Band of Beavers (CD/GD/ST 1990)
Wanker Watson (GD/ST 1995)
War Games (DJ 1998)
Wayne Son of Jane (Tim Quinn/Lew Stringer 1986)
We Love Those Old Movies (MS 1981)
We've Got A Puritan (GD/ST/SD/DJ 1997)
Wee Jock Poppycock (A Hepworth/C Hollingsworth 1999)
Wild West Brothers (GD/SD/ST 1989)
Willy Banks, and his Silly Pranks (JB 1982)
Woolly Wilfy Wichardson (CD 1981)
Yankee Dougal (GD/ST 1990)
Young Bailey (GD/ST 1991)
Young Stan Son of Man (Sean Agnew 1989)
Zip O'Lightning (DJ 1989)